WILL WE BE SMART ENOUGH?

WILL WE BE SMART ENOUGH?

A Cognitive Analysis of the Coming Workforce

Earl Hunt

RUSSELL SAGE FOUNDATION

NEW YORK

HD
5724
.H88
1995

The Russell Sage Foundation

The Russell Sage Foundation, one of the oldest of America's general purpose foundations, was established in 1907 by Mrs. Margaret Olivia Sage for "the improvement of social and living conditions in the United States." The Foundation seeks to fulfill this mandate by fostering the development and dissemination of knowledge about the country's political, social, and economic problems. While the Foundation endeavors to assure the accuracy and objectivity of each book it publishes, the conclusions and interpretations in Russell Sage Foundation publications are those of the authors and not of the Foundation, its Trustees, or its staff. Publication by Russell Sage, therefore, does not imply Foundation endorsement.

Library of Congress Cataloging-in-Publication Data

Hunt, Earl B.
    Will we be smart enough? : a cognitive analysis of the coming
workforce / Earl Hunt.
        p.   cm.
    Includes bibliographical references and index.
    ISBN 0-87154-392-3
    1. Labor supply—United States.   2. Labor supply—Effect of
education on—United States.   I. Title.
HD5724.H88   1995
331.11'42'0973—dc20   94-39625
                                                                   CIP

The paper used in this publication meets the minimum requirements of American National Standard for Information Sciences—Permanence of Paper for Printed Library Materials. ANSI Z39.48-1992.

Text design by John Johnston.

RUSSELL SAGE FOUNDATION
112 East 64th Street, New York, New York 10021

10 9 8 7 6 5 4 3 2 1

Contents

Preface and Acknowledgments

Throughout my professional life I have been interested in how well people think. I've also been discouraged when they do not think so well. I satisfied my curiosity by the usual academic routes—reading and research. In addition, though, I had the opportunity to work on research contracts with the United States Navy, through the Office of Naval Research (ONR) during the 1970s and 1980s. At that time the ONR took pains to ensure that its academicians met with people who had problems in the field. I am not sure that I ever helped any admirals or captains, but I certainly learned a lot from talking with commanders, lieutenants, and petty officers.

In the mid 1980s the National Research Council invited me to join the Board on Army Science and Technology, a group of industrialists and academicians who offered advice to the Office of the Secretary of the Army. As boards do, this board spawned a study: Strategic Technologies for the Army (STAR), and I was involved in it. Both the Board and the STAR study concentrated on "hard" science and engineering, but they also dealt with personnel and human factors issues. I tagged along as the personnel representative. (One of the presidents of a high firm referred to me as "the philosopher," a characterization that I am sure philosophers all over the country would resent.) The more I saw of the high technology the military was using, the more I realized how much more productive people were when they knew what was going on.

During this time I read numerous headlines about how the schools were failing, the workforce was not being prepared, and so forth. More usefully, I talked with business people, craftsmen, and entrepreneurs. From time to time an academic paper helped, as well. I came to realize that cognition really is important, and that psychology has something to say about how people can participate in a high technology society.

Not the weird type of psychology where someone asserts that they have found a grand new theory that will suddenly answer questions that have baffled everyone since Aristotle. I have little use for such ostentation. What I find useful is a psychology that blends engineering, experimental observations that are not individually exciting, but which do add up to something when taken together, and a philosophy that says, "If you want to understand what a human is doing, ask yourself how a robot would have to be programmed to do the same thing." Such reasoning will appear over and over again in this book.

I now come to my acknowledgments. There is nothing new under the sun, including my ideas. I have been influenced by two men with whom I have never worked directly: Professors Herbert Simon and the late Professor Allen Newell, both of Carnegie-Mellon University. While I do not always agree with their ideas, I have always tried to understand what they have said. It has been well worth the effort. Readers will find their influence throughout my writing.

The research and first draft of this book were completed while I held a Russell Sage Foundation fellowship. I thank the Foundation and its president Eric Wanner for their support. Dr. Wanner did more than act as a grant administrator. He arranged for contacts and for the sort of careful, constructive criticism that is essential for an effort such as this one. His own editorial comments were of great assistance throughout my work.

My students at the University of Washington have provided a sounding board for my ideas for years. I particularly thank those who were willing to tell me why they thought I was wrong, and then gave accurate explanations why.

Professor Tony Greenwald, a colleague at the University of Washington, wrote a superb critique of a first draft of this manuscript. So did Professor Howard Gardner of Harvard University and two anonymous reviewers. Professor Greenwald and one of the two reviewers really took my first effort apart. I hope that they will find the second effort much improved.

I also want to thank John Breur of the John S. McDonnell Foundation for providing me with many opportunities to get an insight into modern educational research. My research colleague, Jim Minstrell, pushed me into taking a realistic look at learning outside of the laboratory, and showed me what can and cannot be done in our schools. I also want to thank Professor Irwin Sarason, another University of Washington colleague, for his encouragement.

Many thanks to the business leaders, workers, professionals, and academics who were willing to take a few hours out of their busy days to tell me how the workplace works, from their point of view.

At various stages in preparing this manuscript Linda Lansing-Smith, Kevin Varden, Candace McKenna, and Holly Hinman saw that something actually happened to all these papers and diskettes. I thank them for their adminstrative support.

My wife Mary Lou has been supportive, tolerant, bemused, and amused throughout. She, herself, is a professional career consultant and, in addition to her personal support, she made as much of an intellectual contribution to my thinking as anyone.

Earl Hunt

1

Thinking and the Workforce

THE PROBLEMS WE FACE

This is a book about wheth er or not Americans are smart enough to make it in the twenty-first century. I would not write the book unless I was concerned. I am, and I am certainly not alone. The day I began writing it, in March 1991, a newscast reported a presidential commission's worry that the United States was losing leadership in the technologies that will dominate the twenty-first century. The news report reminded me of another commission that was worrying about the skills in the workplace of the future. That evening my university sponsored a talk by Ira Magaziner, who was subsequently to become a high-level policy advisor to President Clinton. Mr. Magaziner had chaired a third commission, worrying about the same thing!

As I busily gathered data and processed words, the concerns continued. President Clinton's successful 1992 presidential campaign made an issue of the need to retrain the American workforce to ready it for the demands of the high-technology workplace of the twenty-first century. In March 1994 the Clinton administration introduced legislation that the president described as changing unemployment programs from an emphasis on temporary assistance until the old job opened up again to permanent retraining for new jobs. In a sense, this book is an examination of the evidence behind President Clinton's concern. Is the American workforce ready for the next century? If not, what can be done about it?

The issue is usually stated competitively: "How can we stay number one?" It is not surprising that we think this way, because for most of the twentieth century leadership has meant military leadership. It makes sense to worry about being number one in a military confrontation.

This sort of thinking may not be appropriate in the future. Most serious thinkers believe that over the next 20 years the United States will face social and economic, rather than military, challenges (Halberstam, 1991). The historian Paul Kennedy (1987) has argued that the great empires before us—Rome, Spain, and Great Britain—lost their world dominance because they emphasized military power at the cost of economic and social dislocation. Kennedy, Halberstam, and others worry that America is repeating this error. While military might will not be irrelevant in the near future, it will not be as relevant as it was at the height of the cold war. One of the great strategic challenges we face is finding the proper mix between the military and domestic agendas.

Is being number one still relevant? Economic and social exchanges are more subtle than military confrontations. The element of competition is certainly present, as many of our corporations have found to their discomfiture. On the other hand, the "I win–you lose" aspect of military competition—in the jargon of academics, the zero sum game aspect—is muted. For example, the automobile industry competes with its Japanese counterpart, but the United States as a whole is not being threatened by Japan as a whole. And suppose that by some not unreasonable economic index, Swedes enjoy a "higher standard of living" than Americans. This is not a cause for national consternation. The real issue is whether or not the United States has enough wealth, distributed equitably enough, so that our citizens enjoy economically stable and socially productive lives.

Competitive indices, such as balance of payments accounts, and relative indices, such as children's proficiency in mathematics, are important. Indeed, this book contains more than enough of them for most readers. However, they are important as indicators of well-being rather than as points on a scorecard. Indices let us monitor potential problems in the creation and distribution of wealth. However, the indices are seldom crucial in themselves. We have to consider what they mean: Do we have problems and why? After we answer this question, we can explore answers to those problems.

Throughout the book, and especially in the first chapter, I am going to argue that we do have problems and that many of our problems and their solutions lie in the characteristics of our workforce.

A NATION'S WEALTH AND THE SKILLS OF ITS WORKFORCE

A country generates wealth internally, by production and prudent exploitation of natural resources. A country can also generate wealth externally, by advantageous dealings with other nations. The accumulated wealth can be spent, either internally or externally, to purchase goods and services that improve the well-being of the citizens. How much accumulated wealth a country has to spend is more important than where it came from. As a bookkeeping device, countries monitor their balance of payment accounts to be sure that they are not overspending (which the United States probably is at present), but a country can safely maintain a negative trade balance for long periods, providing that the internal economy can generate the surplus to afford it.

Since this is not a treatise in economics, and I am certainly not an economist, I must connect this to psychology. Here is my argument.

Wealth is generated in basically two ways. One is by the direct sale of both renewable and nonrenewable natural resources that are available because of a country's location, such as oil, minerals, wood, and fisheries. Some "inheritances from nature" can be sold only once. Other natural resources, chiefly agricultural products, can, with proper management, be a steady source of income for a nation. In this case, location is likely to provide some advantage but not enough to keep competitors out if economic conditions change. The pineapple industry is a case in point: Hawaii's climate gave it an advantage for years, but the industry has now disappeared because of the development of more cost-effective plantations in Central and South America.

The second way wealth is generated is by adding value to a product or service. For example, in my home state of Washington the Boeing Aircraft Company adds value to metals, plastics, and rubber by assembling airplanes. Similarly, banking and accounting services add value to bank accounts by providing the communications network necessary for international credit operations. The people involved exercise their skills as they add value, they charge for these skills, and thus they acquire wealth.

In the last analysis all wealth from value-added operations depends on the skills of the people adding the value. *The wealth of a nation is therefore inextricably tied to the skills of its workforce.* Japan and Germany, two of the healthiest economies in recent history, illustrate this point. In terms of natural resources, both countries are poor. Their wealth comes from the skills of the German and Japanese people. These skills range from the industry of the worker on a production line to the talents of engineers, scientists, and management.

The United States will prosper if we find domestic and international markets for the skills of our people.

This is the point at which competition becomes relevant. In itself, I do not worry about the overall trade balance with Japan. I do worry about the fact that two of the three best-selling cars in the American domestic market are made in Japan.[1] Why can't we compete in our own backyard?

In the short run, workforce skills are only one aspect of successful economic competition; local factors (e.g., government subsidies or trade barriers) have their influences. In the long run, though, workforce skills are a major factor. If country A and country B are competing over industry X, A will have an advantage if A's workforce offers better value for the dollar than does B's workforce.

To deal with these issues, we need to answer some questions about skills: First and foremost, what skills are going to be needed in the profitable economic sectors of the future? Second, at the absolute level, do we have these skills? Third, at the relative level, do we have these skills to the same extent, and at the same cost, as our likely competitors? Fourth, and finally, if the answers to the second and third questions do not leave us comfortable, what can we do about it?

The final question is the most important. In a world of rapid technological change, no workforce—ours, Japan's, Germany's, or anyone else's—has all the skills today that are going to be needed 20 years from now. Even more worrisome is that every workforce contains a substantial number of people whose skills may not be needed in 20 years. That is why there is so much talk about continuing education. When President Clinton and his advisers stress retraining, they are asserting three things; that there will be good jobs to be had, that many Americans are not now trained to fill them, and that those improperly skilled Americans can indeed be retrained for new and profitable work. To what extent is this optimistic view warranted?

These questions have been analyzed before, but usually from the viewpoint of the sociologist or economist. I am going to take a different view. Sociological and economical analyses are certainly useful to indicate what the problem is and what has to be fixed, but they do not tell us how the problem was created or what we can do to fix things. These questions are best answered by another branch of science, psychology.

This may sound surprising to those who think of psychology as primarily a therapeutic profession, designed to help people adjust to the world. In fact, the science of psychology ranges from studies of the neural mechanisms of learning in sea slugs to studies of the determinants of interpersonal attraction in young adults. Two subfields of psychology that will particularly concern us are *psychometrics* and *cognitive psychology*.

Psychometrics deals with the measurement of mental traits. This science developed the tests for intelligence, achievement, and personality that are now so widely used in schools, firms, and counseling offices. For instance, the well-known Scholastic Aptitude Test, which is taken by most high school students applying to college, is a psychometric test. Psychometric tests can be used to measure the overall cognitive capacity of a population and to relate these capacities, as measured, to performance in the workplace. Many articles have been written on these topics. I have combined the findings of the articles with demographic projections, to estimate the abilities of the future American workforce. Insofar as I know, such a combined analysis has never been reported before.

Cognitive psychology deals with the processes of thought. In the context of this book, cognitive psychology and psychometrics are complementary sciences. Consider the relationship between scores on an intelligence test and performance in school mathematics. The psychometrician is interested in knowing what these correlations are in order to predict math performance from an IQ test. Once the statistics have been determined the psychometrician stops. The cognitive psychologist wants to know, in considerable detail, what mental steps a person takes when performing well in mathematics, and which of these steps are most crucial for success.

Cognitive psychologists proceed by developing general theories of how the human mind works and then applying these theories to particular situations, ranging from learning mathematics to operating machinery. In an analysis of the workforce, cognitive psychology complements psychometrics by asking what specific cognitive demands a particular work situation places on a person, and by determining how successful workers meet those demands. In the closing chapters of this book I will use findings in cognitive psychology to explain how changes in technology are changing the demands that the workplace makes on the worker, and I will speculate about what this means for training the workforce. The operative word here is *speculate.* Economists and sociologists have not hesitated to speculate about how the future will appear from their points of view. Insofar as I know, my attempt is the first such speculation based on psychology.

The remainder of this chapter takes a statistical view of the issues. Since statistics are dreary, I have relied on graphs and charts to present a picture of our position internationally, the composition of our workforce, its current cognitive competence, and the extent to which it seems prepared to cope with the twenty-first century.

Some International Comparisons

It is interesting to look at yourself from another person's perspective. When I lived in Australia, in the early 1960s, I read a book to my chil-

Figure 1.1   Relative purchasing power in the United States and selected countries. Source: U.S. Bureau of the Census (1993).

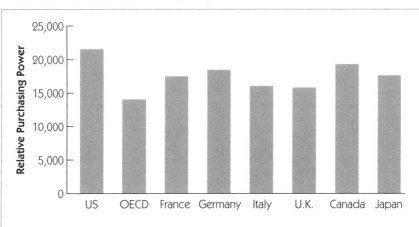

dren that told about how children lived all over the world. The chapter on the United States was entitled "The Richest Country in the World." While I was somewhat uncomfortable about having that aspect of my homeland stressed, I had no reasons to question the accuracy of the title.

Things have changed. It is not clear what country is the richest in the world, but one thing is clear: The United States is certainly one of the richest. In 1990 the gross national product (GNP) was about $5.5 *trillion* (one thousand billion) dollars. The Japanese GNP was $2.9 trillion, West Germany's $1.5, and $7.0 trillion for all of Western Europe (Bureau of the Census, 1993). Of course, the absolute comparison does not take into account the size of the countries involved. If you simply divide GNP by the population, Germany and Japan are the richest countries, closely followed by the United States. But this does not take into account the cost of living in each country. A better method is to consider the gross domestic product (GDP) per capita, and then adjust this figure to a comparable currency unit, which takes into account both exchange rates and the cost of goods within each country. The results of this calculation are shown in Figure 1.1. The United States is the leader, by a slight margin.

"Who is first?" is hardly the point. We are clearly one of the richest countries in the world. Perhaps most important, we are by far the largest country with a high level of wealth per person.

What is a bit more disconcerting is that changes in our wealth are not keeping pace with changes in other countries. Figure 1.2 shows

Figure 1.2 Purchasing power relative to U.S. purchasing power. Selected countries. Source: U.S. Bureau of the Census (1993).

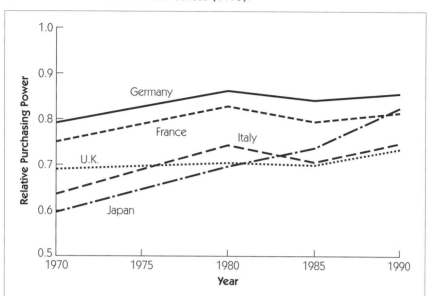

changes in income per capita during the 1980s in several leading countries, expressed as a fraction of U.S. income per capita. On this scale the figures for the United States form a straight, horizontal line. An upward tilting line indicates that a country is gaining in wealth per person, relative to the United States, while a downward tilting line indicates that the United States is gaining on the country. All the lines in the figure tilt upward. Average incomes are increasing faster in other countries than in ours—for both the economic giants, Germany and Japan, and for relatively weak economies, such as Italy and the United Kingdom.

Clearly, the United States lost ground during the 1980s. The recession and slow recovery of the early 1990s, coupled with political upheaval in Eastern Europe associated with the collapse of the Soviet Empire, have changed the picture somewhat. As of 1992 the GDP in the United States grew more rapidly than that of its major competitors (2.1 percent for the United States, compared to .8 for Germany and 1.5 for Japan). However, 1992 was the first time in years that the United States had gained the lead. Only time will tell how permanent the 1992 figures are.

Competitive figures are not important in themselves. There is no supernatural law that says that Americans have to be the richest people on earth. The concern is that the figures may be symptomatic of a deeper malaise. Why has the United States fallen from the preeminence that it enjoyed only 25 years ago? And, more to the point, what can we do about it?

Reduced American dominance on the international scene could simply reflect a return to "normalcy." Most of the statistics that have been cited as evidence of America's decline begin with a baseline in the 1960s—that is, only 15 years after the end of World War II. In 1945 the economies of all our major competitors had been devastated by the war, while the U.S. economy was unscathed. What we may be seeing is a return to "more normal" times.

While this argument has something to recommend it, there is no sense in accepting it fatalistically. Of course, no nation is going to hold all the world's wealth. Indeed, such a situation would not be healthy. On the other hand, it is not clear that economic laws hold the United States in a particular place in the economic world, in the sense that the law of gravity holds the earth in its orbit. Why should we not compete for as good a living as possible, consistent with our long-term, enlightened self-interest in a generally prosperous world? We should assume that our competitors will do the same.

Excessive military spending is another favorite explanation for our decline. The 1950–1990 arms race with the Soviet Union cost trillions of dollars. Furthermore, as of 1994 it is clearly the intention of the United States to remain the paramount military power in the world. Whether our past investments in military power were wise ones or not cannot be known, since we do not know the consequences if they had not been made. There is a clear-cut evidence that in the future there will be a much more careful weighing of the costs and benefits of military solutions. Witness the careful distinction made in 1992–94 between intervention in Bosnia, which was seen as a risk of great cost for possibly little gain, and intervention in Somalia, where, whatever the outcome, the risk was relatively small.

The United States has also been accused of following monetary and tax policies that encourage short-term profit taking rather than long-term investment. Most economists direct this argument at the Republican administrations of the 1980s and 1990s. However, the trends that seem to be most bothersome go back further than 1980. While one deplores bad government policies (especially with the advantage of hindsight), the problems we are facing seem to be more deeply rooted in society itself.

In assessing our problems, we must realize that the distinction between the domestic and export markets is rapidly breaking down. Economically, our borders leak. Reich (1991, p. 113) offers a succinct example. Suppose that an American purchased a Pontiac Le Mans from General Motors in 1990. The purchase price of $20,100 would be split the following ways:

South Korea: labor and assembly	$6,000
Japan: advanced components	3,500
Germany: styling, design	1,500
Southeast Asia and Japan: components	900
Great Britain: marketing	500
Ireland, Barbados, data processing	100
United States: residual	7,600

Almost two-thirds of the cost of the "American" car went out of the country. Indeed, as Reich notes, this figure is a minimum, since the $7,600 for the United States includes the profits sent to GM shareholders in foreign countries.

Reich's example illustrates an important point: Goods and services can be shipped all over the world quickly; people cannot. However, the workforce in one country, *if it is capable,* can quickly enter a competition with the workforce in another country. This idea is foreign to the thinking of only a few years ago.

The Movable Workplace

Throughout the nineteenth century and most of the twentieth century, people migrated to the places where the jobs were. The most notable example is probably the migration of Europeans to the factories and mills of North America in the late nineteenth century and early twentieth century. In a few cases, manufacturers sought out the workers and transported them. A century ago, at the same time that skilled workers were sailing from Europe to America, English manufacturers subsidized a "reverse immigration" of skilled workers from North America to England to introduce new technologies there (Rosenberg, 1982, pp. 19–20). Two hundred years earlier Peter the Great offered large inducements to Western craftsmen willing to settle in Russia. Today, offshore factories all over the world seek skilled workers.

Earlier migrations were relatively slow, not for transportation or technological reasons but for human reasons. People, especially people with families, do not lightly pick up and move from one land to another.

The means of production have no such emotional attachment to their birthplace. That is how technology has changed the game.

In the early days of the Industrial Revolution the location of a factory was determined by access to markets and raw materials, control by the ownership, and the availability of an appropriate workforce. The access and control factors dominated. Therefore, once a political entity acquired an industry the prize was seen as a more or less permanent one. In the 1950s Detroit thought of itself as the motor capital of the world—forever.

Modern technology has changed this. Decreased transportation costs make it easy to ship both raw materials and finished products around the globe. The rapid increase in worldwide communication facilities has similarly made it possible for the "central office" to be anywhere. We can fax a directive across a continent as easily as we can send it down the hall. As of 1994 it is technologically possible to have a conference in which the participants are thousands of miles apart. By the turn of the century, it will be economically feasible to do so.

Because of these technological changes, businesses can establish production facilities wherever they will be most profitable. Very much the same thing is true for services. As of 1994 British Air is a major shareholder in USAir. British Air has no concern about maintaining management control from London, any more than Ford USA is concerned about providing management services to its worldwide empire.

At one time company managers were reluctant to use their transport capability, because of implicit or explicit loyalties to the home country. Such loyalties are rapidly breaking down (Halberstam, 1991). Products that historically have been associated with particular nations are, in fact, often the result of an international assembly process.

The United States seems to be losing in the global exchange of goods and services. As has been widely publicized, we went from being a creditor nation in 1980 to being the world's largest debtor, a position that we have solidly held onto through the 1990s. In the short term, balance of payments accounts are influenced by international trading practices, tariff barriers, and a host of administrative reasons. In the long term, the prosperity of America rests on the skills of its people. We will look at these skills more deeply later in the book. First, we look at another indicator of economic health. Are we distributing our internal wealth in a way that leads to long-term social stability?

THE DISTRIBUTION OF PRODUCTION AND WEALTH

National wealth is not the only measure of a country's economic well-being. The majority of the citizens must share in both production and

Figure 1.3   Trends in the relative values of goods and services. Source: U.S. Bureau of the Census (1993).

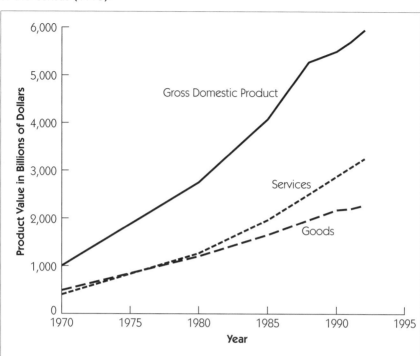

receipt of wealth. Otherwise the poor will resent the wealthy, and the workers will resent the shirkers—not a happy combination for a democracy. Let us look beyond the gross statistics to see how income and productivity are distributed within the country.

Productivity, measured in the value of output per worker per hour, has increased steadily since the end of World War II. However, there is a marked difference in productivity in the manufacturing and service industries. This is shown in Figures 1.3 and 1.4. Figure 1.3 shows the value of products of the goods and service industries since the 1970s. Goods and services contributed approximately equal value to the economy in the 1970s. The relative value of the service sector began to rise in the 1980s. In 1992 the value of services was about 1.4 times the value of goods. Figure 1.4 shows the employment figures, which tell a rather different story. The number of people involved in manufacturing has dropped slightly, while the number of people involved in services has almost doubled. These results are largely due to changes in technology, which permit us to do more things with fewer people. New tech-

Figure 1.4 Employment in manufacturing and services (2005 projected). Source: U.S. Bureau of the Census (1993).

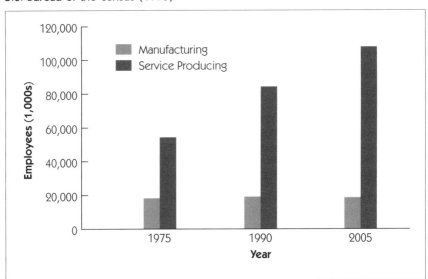

nologies have made their impact on both manufacturing and services, but the impact on manufacturing has been far greater.

Since manufacturing jobs generally pay better than service jobs, the result of this process has been that high-wage jobs are being lost, while low-wage jobs are being created. This trend is expected to increase. This is shown in Figure 1.5, which plots the expected growth in employment in selected occupations against the average 1990 income in each group. With some exceptions, the points drop as they move to the right. This indicates that high growth has been concentrated in low-paying jobs.

How did the end of the recession of 1990–1992 affect these trends? Although economic recovery began in late 1992, unemployment remained high. As of January 1994 the unemployment rate was estimated at 6.7%, a figure that would have been considered a recession 30 years earlier. The better-paying industrial jobs were particularly hard hit. Many jobs were permanently lost, either to competition or because employers had retooled so that they could make things with fewer people. In March 1994 the *New York Times* reported that in 1993, during a recovery from a recession, 615,000 jobs were eliminated. A *Times* quotation presents the reason in a nutshell: "Manufacturing employment is primarily governed by technology, and new technology requires half the number of people in product assembly every six years" (Laurence

Figure 1.5   The relation between annual compensation and projected changes in the number of jobholders in selected occupations. Source: U.S. Bureau of the Census (1993).

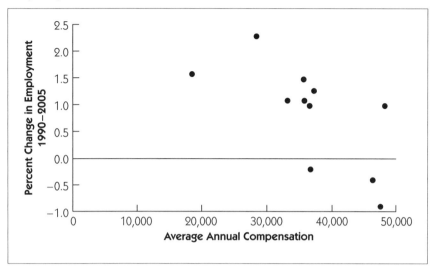

C. Siefert, AT&T VP for Manufacturing, *New York Times,* March 22, 1994).

Of course, new jobs were being created, but they were not good jobs. In 1989, 6 percent of the new jobs created were for temporary workers. In 1992, the first postrecession year, 26 percent of the new jobs were for temporaries. In 1993 that fell to "only" 15 percent. Skilled workers in manufacturing, laid off from $15 to $18 per hour jobs, were finding employment in the service industries at $6 to $8 per hour. The anecdotal reports and case studies are mirrored by statistics on earnings. The average weekly earnings in 1992, in constant dollars, were 7 percent below the figure for 1980 and 14 percent below the figure for 1970. This is not just a reflection of the 1990–1992 recession. Annual earnings for employees, again corrected for inflation, decreased in seven of the eight years from 1985 through 1992. We are dealing with a stable, long-term trend.

A small ray of light appeared by the end of 1994. Unemployment had fallen to below 6 percent, and there had been an increase in the number of new, high-paid jobs. Whether or not this represents a reversal of fortune or a minor blip in a long-term trend remains to be seen. Meanwhile, another, and perhaps more disturbing, trend has continued unabated.

Although the general trend has been loss of individual wealth the

Figure 1.6   Distribution of national income by quintiles. Source: U.S. Bureau of the Census (1993).

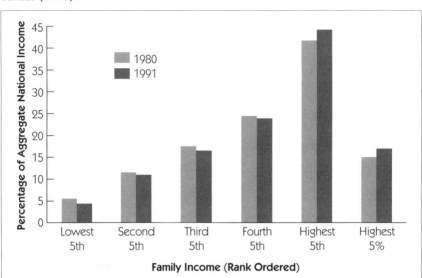

losses have hardly been distributed equally. Figure 1.6 shows the percentage of income received by the lowest 20 percent of the population, the next highest 20 percent, and so on. The figure also shows the percentage of the national income received by the top 5 percent. Figures are shown for 1980 and 1991. If the relative income distribution over the population had been unchanged, the black and gray bars would be of equal height. They are not. Every group lost in its share of the national income, except the top 20 percent. Within that group, about half of the increment was due to a rise in the share of the wealthiest 5 percent.

The absolute figures on income illustrate these disparities even more dramatically. In 1980 the median income of families in the bottom 40 percent of the income distribution was (in 1991 dollars) $17,023. In 1991 it was $17,000—virtually unchanged. To gain some feeling for this figure, in 1991 a family of four with an income of $17,405 or less were defined as "working poor" (income of less than 125 percent of the poverty rate); 18.9 percent of all Americans fell into this category. By contrast, the median figure for families in the top 10 percent was $89,465 in 1980 and $102,824 in 1991, an increase of 15 percent (Bureau of Census, 1993, Tables 722, 735). The rich got richer, while the lower middle class and below stayed the same. In absolute terms there has been virtually no movement in the percentage of peo-

Figure 1.7 Trends in median family income, by ethnic status. Source: U.S. Bureau of the Census (1993).

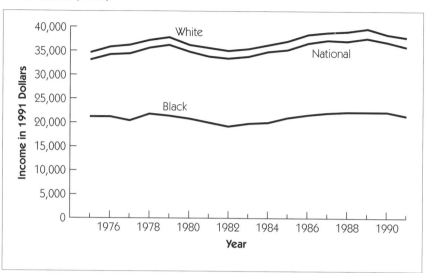

ple below the poverty level and below the working poor level since 1980. These figures have remained at the 13–15 and 17–19 percent levels.

The United States has been plagued by a persistent disparity in income across demographic groups. Figure 1.7 shows the median family income in constant dollars for the nation as a whole, and for black and white families for the period 1970–1989. In spite of major social efforts to improve the situation, the median family income of a black family was 61 percent that of a white family in 1970, 58 percent in 1980, and 58 percent in 1990. For Hispanics the relevant figures are 69 percent, 67 percent, and 63 percent. The poverty level figures reflect the same trends. In 1980, 32.5 percent of all blacks and 25.7 percent of all Hispanics were below the poverty level. In 1990 the figures were 31.9 percent and 28.1 percent.[2]

The increasing disparity in income extends to both blue-collar and white-collar jobs. Blue-collar workers have been particularly hard hit. In 1972 craft workers received, on the average, 98 percent of the wages of professional and technical employees. In 1987 the figure was 73 percent. Clerical wages dropped from 68 to 54 percent of the professional-technical earnings, and retail sales wages from 65 to 46 percent (Commission on the Skills of the American Workforce, 1990).

The disparities in earnings between workers and "top management"

Figure 1.8 Weekly earnings of selected occupations relative to the weekly earnings of machine operators. Source: U.S. Bureau of the Census (1993).

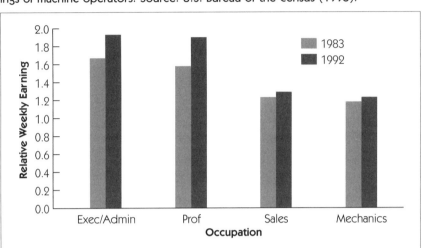

have widened dramatically. Figure 1.8 shows the relative salaries for four different occupations; executives and administrators, professionals (physicians, lawyers, accountants), sales personnel, and mechanics. Figures are shown from 1983 to 1992. If you wanted a raise in pay, it was clearly better to be an administrator than a mechanic. Some recent figures are even more dramatic. From 1989 to 1990 the average income of an American worker, not corrected for inflation, increased a little less than 5 percent. The average increase for corporate executives was 8 percent.[3] Preliminary figures for the years following the 1990–1991 recession suggest that the situation has gotten even worse. In some cases major industries have asked for wage concessions from employees while paying executives more than a million dollars a year.

Numerous commentators (e.g., Reich, 1991) have maintained that this degree of disparity in wealth is neither appropriate nor healthy for our society. The United States is not approaching the extremes of wealth and poverty seen in some third-world countries, such as India or the oil-producing Arab states. That comparison is not relevant. We are developing greater disparities of wealth than are seen in the industrial nations of Europe and Asia.

Technologies that sharpen the difference between the productivity of highly skilled and less skilled workers redistribute job opportunities in Germany and Japan in exactly the same way that they do in the United States. Advances in robotics offer equal unemployment opportunities! Several European countries are experiencing social problems because of selective rates of high unemployment. Even Japan has had to compromise its vaunted reputation for high employment by forced retirements. Clearly the difference between us and our competitors is not in the challenges we face.

We and our competitors do differ in our overall social response. The United States and, to a somewhat lesser extent, the United Kingdom, provides minimal social support for the unemployed. Therefore, when a relatively well-paid worker is laid off, he or she has a powerful incentive to accept a new job at lower wages. Several of the continental European countries offer superior welfare support systems. Predictably, these countries are experiencing higher levels of unemployment, ranging to nearly 20 percent in Spain. In effect, these countries place a larger cushion under the poor, at the expense of the rich and, for that matter, the moderately affluent. For instance, 1991 payroll tax rates for social security programs averaged 19.3 percent in the United States, 24.44 percent in Japan (which also has extensive retirement systems and company-financed benefit programs), 36 percent in Germany, and 55 percent in Italy. As is well known, income tax rates are also much more progressive in other industrialized countries than they are in the United States. This system of transfer of wealth does reduce the disparity between the poor and the affluent. However, it is not a perfect solution. There is increasing evidence that the cost of social support systems is becoming an increasing economic burden on the European countries. In any case, it is unlikely that the United States could politically adopt the European solution, because of strongly held beliefs that government social programs are inherently wasteful, and that government interventions in the distribution of wealth stifle individual inventiveness and productivity.

The statistics tell us something about who is or is not finding work. But who are these people, and how well are they prepared for work?

SOME DEMOGRAPHICS OF THE AMERICAN WORKFORCE

In 1990 the American civilian workforce contained 125 million people.[4] By the year 2000 it is expected to grow to slightly over 141 million workers (Johnston and Packer, 1987), but it will not just be an expansion of the same workforce.

The workforce is aging. The median age of the population of the United States was 26 in 1930 and 28 in 1970, not much of a change. By the year 2000 the median age will be 36 (Johnston and Packer, 1987).

The change in the workforce age distribution is shown in detail in Figure 1.9, which displays progressive changes in the composition of the workforce from 1960 to its projected state in 2000 and 2005. The

Figure 1.9 Age distribution of the U.S. workforce, 1960–2005. Source: U.S. Bureau of the Census (1993).

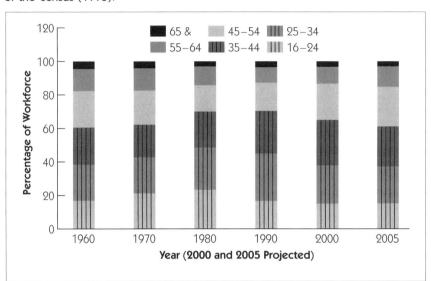

American workforce at the turn of the century will not be dominated by workers over 55. In fact, the percentage of workers in this group actually decreases. There will be a substantial increase in the percentage of workers in the 35–54 age range, at the expense of lowered percentages of workers under 35.

This trend is likely to have a major impact on the availability of psychological skills. Older workers are not simply more or less intelligent than younger workers. The old and the young have different cognitive skills. There is a predictable shift toward more knowledge about how things are done, coupled with a reduction in the speed with which new ideas are grasped (Salthouse, 1990). Thus, aging increases the value of a workforce when the workplace is static, but it may decrease the value of the same workforce if the methods and technology of the workplace are changing.

There has been a good deal of discussion about the increased feminization of the workforce. Statistically this will be a fairly small effect. The present workforce is about 45 percent female; this is expected to increase to 47 percent by 2000. What may change, but what is much harder to predict, is the sort of jobs that women hold.

The third trend is a change in ethnic constitution, away from the present dominance of whites. The changes are complex.

Figure 1.10 shows the ethnic distribution of the population in 1990

Figure 1.10 Percentage of workforce and percentage of increment of workforce in various ethnic groups, 1990 and 2005. Source: U.S. Bureau of the Census (1993).

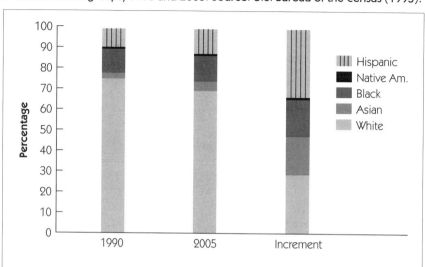

and the projected distribution in 2005. Clearly, there is little change in the overall distribution. The picture is quite different if one looks at the ethnic distribution of increments in subpopulation sizes. This is shown in the right-hand column of Figure 1.10. Although the population as a whole will still be predominantly white, the increment to the population will be split approximately evenly between Asians and non-Hispanic whites and then minority groups. Hispanics will be the most rapidly expanding group. This reflects both a high birthrate, relative to the rest of the population, and anticipated immigration from Central and South America.

Immigration is one of the "wild cards" in the projections. The Office of Technology Assessment (OTA) pointed out that immigration accounted for 22 percent of the growth in workers in the United States in the period 1980–1987 and projected that immigration would have an increased impact on workforce growth in the next 10 years.[5] Immigrants are a mixed group: Some immigrants to the United States contribute at the very top of the workforce, in sciences and the professions. Most immigrants, however, are poorly educated compared with the U.S. workforce, and about one in six does not speak English (Office of Technology Assessment, 1990). Even those who do speak English often have only marginal skills, especially with the written language (Kirsch, Jungeblut, Jenkins, and Kolstad, 1993). Thus, the immediate impact of increased immigration is on the lower-paid, less desirable jobs. The long-term impact is virtually impossible to assess.

Another trend is a change in mobility. By world standards, the American workforce is unusually mobile; Americans change jobs frequently compared with workers in other industrial nations. Job changing is closely related to age . Younger workers change jobs much more often than older workers. This is understandable. On the one hand, older workers are more likely to be occupying permanent, relatively well-paid positions, hence, have less incentive to change. On the other hand, older workers and their families tend to have firmer ties to their community and are therefore less able to change locations. As has been argued, accelerated technological changes are clearly decreasing job stability and accordingly increasing pressures on workers to be mobile. For instance, in early 1994 there was a fairly good market nationwide for machinists and electricians, but an excess of these skills in Los Angeles, Kansas City, and Seattle, due to reductions in employment associated with fluctuating demand and technological changes in the aerospace industry. Unfortunately, the increased pressure to be mobile is not accompanied by an increase in ability to move. Older workers are more likely than younger workers to have working spouses, school-age children, and economic ties to their communities.

COGNITIVE CHARACTERISTICS OF THE WORKFORCE

In the last economic report of his administration (1993), President Bush claimed that the American worker is the most productive in the world. Whether or not this is correct depends on how productivity is defined, but, as we have seen, the American worker, averaged over the entire economy, is certainly one of the most productive in the world. Productivity can be obtained in two ways: by the skills of the workforce or by capital investment in technologies that reduce the need for large numbers of workers, but increase the productivity of the individual worker on the job. Thus, the cognitive skills of the workforce depend upon the competence of the workforce in managing the machinery it has. The greater the skills of the workforce, the less incentive management has either to invest in new technologies or, more frighteningly, to seek a new workforce.

But how are we to assess workforce skills? Traditionally this has been done by determining the amount of education that workers have, on the not unreasonable assumption that the more educated people are, the more skilled they are. While this is a valid argument, it is not entirely correct. Marshall and Tucker (1992) offer an instructive analogy to the engineering distinction between *design standards* and *perfor-*

Table 1.1 Educational Levels Attained by the Present U.S. Workforce

	Not High School Graduate	High School Graduate	College (one year or more)
Total	18.2%	39.6%	42.1%
Whites	15.8	39.8	44.4
Blacks	22.7	42.4	34.4
Hispanics	39.0	33.5	27.4

Source: Office of Technology Assessment (1990), Table 1-3.

Note: Totals are extrapolations based on OTA estimates of ethnic groups in the workforce.

mance standards. A design standard specifies how a product is to be made, while a performance standard specifies what the product must be able to do when it is used. Marshall and Tucker argue that the same distinction applies to education. Requiring that all U.S. citizens attend school until age 16 is a design standard. Requiring that all high-school graduates be able to summarize the argument in a newspaper editorial is a performance standard. Following Marshall and Tucker, we must distinguish between the design standards used to prepare entrants in the workforce (and to maintain their skills once they are in the workforce) and the performance standards that educated workers are expected to meet.

Workforce capabilities are usually expressed in terms of education level. The United States does very well, relative to the rest of the world, in terms of percentages of its citizens who have graduated from high school or have attended college. However, there are major causes for concern because educational qualifications, like wealth, are not spread equally across our population.

Table 1.1 presents the statistics for education levels attained by the present workforce and for the three major ethnic groups (whites, blacks, and Hispanics). As the table shows, the workforce as a whole is relatively well educated. Although comparable figures are not available worldwide, I suggest that the percentages are quite high compared with other countries. However, there are obvious disparities between ethnic groups.

In order to estimate the future workforce, we need to look at present enrollment in the schools. Table 1.2 compares enrollment rates in high schools and postsecondary education in seven industrialized countries. The United States is one of the leaders insofar as high school enrollment is concerned, and the leader, by a considerable margin over Europe and Japan, in postsecondary (college and university) education.

Table 1.2 School Enrollees

	Canada	France	Germany (West)	Italy	Japan	United Kingdom	United States
High school	106	99	104	79	96	84	96
Beyond high school	70	40	33	31	31	25	72

Source: National Center for Education Statistics (1993), Table 385.

Note: 1990 Enrollment ratios in high school and post-high school programs in selected countries. The enrollment ratio is the number of enrolled students divided by the number of people in the appropriate age group in the population. For post-high school education, the age group used is the number of people in the 20–24 age range.

The latter figure is a bit misleading, however, because the U.S. figure includes enrollees in vocational training courses. In Germany and Japan comparable education is often provided by employers.

Table 1.2 shows enrollment in educational institutions, rather than completion. Figure 1.11 shows the high school dropout rates for the

Figure 1.11 Percentage of dropouts from high school in the population of 16–24-year-olds. Source: National Center for Educational Statistics (1993).

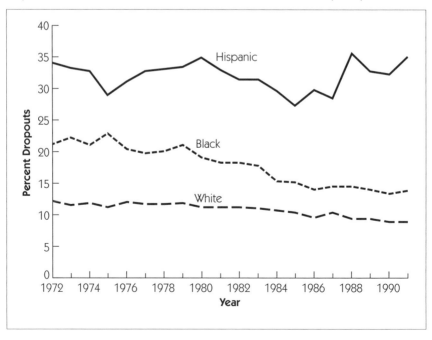

Table 1.3 Percentage of College and University Degrees Granted to Members of Various Ethnic Groups, as a Percentage of Total Degrees Granted

Degree	White	Black	Hispanic	Asian and Other	Alien
Bachelor's	83.6	6.0	3.4	4.2	2.7
Master's	77.7	4.9	2.6	3.7	11.1
Doctor's	65.7	3.1	1.9	4.1	25.2
M.D., D.D.S., LL.B., or similar	84.4	5.0	3.5	5.7	1.7

Source: National Center for Education Statistics (1993).

Note: Data from 1990–91.

United States from 1972 to 1991.[6] Overall the dropout rate has decreased from about 13 percent to just under 10 percent. As is well known, dropout rates are higher for the larger minority groups than they are for whites and Asian Americans. The dropout rate for black students is declining, but the dropout rate for Hispanics remains high. This is particularly discouraging because Hispanics are the most rapidly growing ethnic group in the United States.

Higher education figures also show a marked discrepancy between ethnic groups. Table 1.3 shows the distribution of degrees to members of different ethnic groups in 1989–1990. Among our largest minorities, blacks and Hispanics, half as many degrees were granted as would be expected on the basis of their percentage of the population. The discrepancy grows greater the higher the degree and the more technical the field. In 1990–1991, 4,164 Ph.D. degrees were granted in the physical sciences, 103 to blacks and Hispanics combined and 1,326 to nonresident aliens.

Direct Indicators of Competence

As educators frequently say, and students occasionally hear, the point of education is not to get a degree, it is to learn something. How cognitively proficient is our highly educated workforce? There are three ways to assess workers' cognitive capabilities. One is to ask employers whether they think that their workforce performs adequately. Another way to proceed is to determine whether employers pay higher wages to more highly educated employees. Finally, cognitive competence could be measured directly, by testing people in the educational or workforce systems. Each of these methods has its advantages and drawbacks. Interestingly, each produces a somewhat different picture.

Over the past 10 years there have been numerous surveys of employ-ers' attitudes about the entering worker. Indeed, the oldest of the sur-veys that I shall cite, the National Academy of Sciences report (1984), began by apologizing for yet another educational report. The NAS re-port, and three subsequent commission reports (Commission on the Skills of the American Workforce, 1990; U.S. Department of Labor, Ed-ucation & Commerce, 1988; Secretary's Commission on Achieving Necessary Skills, 1991) all reached the same three conclusions:

1. Members of the entering workforce are generally deficient in basic skills in language use (reading, writing, speaking) and in mathematics. A few large companies have instituted training programs to decrease these deficiencies.

2. Employees ought to have better "learning" or "problem-solv-ing" skills. These are rather vaguely defined as the ability to adjust to new situations, solve problems, and so on.

3. New entrants to the workforce lack a number of interpersonal skills, such as disciplining themselves to meet time commit-ments, being motivated to do a better than minimally neces-sary job, working with others, and presenting a good face to the public. These nonintellectual skills will be referred to col-lectively as a "work ethic."

Findings from these surveys have generated what might, at best, be described as a panic reaction. In 1989 the journal *Human Capital* put the "sky is falling in" argument neatly in a cover headline, which asked, "Is U.S. future held hostage by nation's poor schools?" The head-line introduced articles by various business executives and economists, who argued that (1) the nation's educational system is a mess, (2) the only hope is that business either intervene in the schools directly or assume responsibility for education in the workplace, and (3) U.S. working practices must be reorganized to take advantage of the cogni-tive skills of the workers. *Human Capital* is by no means alone in its concern. Similar articles appear regularly in the *Wall Street Journal, Fortune,* and many other business magazines.

Employers are clearly unhappy. It is not clear, though, whether they feel that the schools have deteriorated from previous good performance or whether work demands have changed. When pressed, few employers cited serious shortages of qualified workers, with the exception of the craft trades and a large number of fairly low-paid jobs that have tradi-tionally been performed by women (secretaries, nurses, nurse's aides, etc.). Most employers viewed the work ethic problem as more serious

Figure 1.12 Annual earnings as a function of educational attainment. Source: National Center for Educational Statistics (1993).

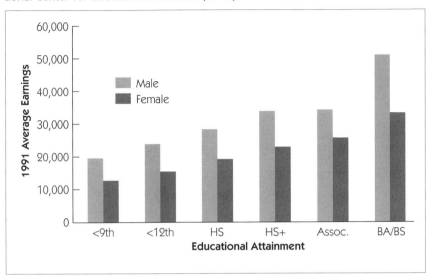

than cognitive skills problems. However, employers in high-technology industries such as IBM and Motorola dissented. These employers expressed more concern over cognitive qualifications (Commission on the Skills of the American Workforce 1990).

What are we to make of these reports? The work ethic problem is virtually impossible to evaluate on the basis of subjective reports. Employers have been complaining for generations that employees do not work hard enough. On the other hand, it would be possible to determine objective indices of workforce ethic, such as absenteeism. Zuboff (1989) has pointed out that this has been a problem since the nineteenth century. We simply do not have adequate data to make a comparison across time.

Although employers seem to denigrate education, and especially the high school diploma, the same employers do pay higher wages for higher education. Figure 1.12 shows the 1991 median income for male and female full-time workers, by educational level. Men and women are shown separately because women generally occupy lower-paid jobs than men do. Income and education are closely associated. The median income of a person without a high school diploma was about half of the median income of a person with a college degree. In spite of all the jokes, it pays to be educated.

Figure 1.12, together with some other statistics in this section, shows that some of the inequalities in rewards received by different ethnic groups are due to differential distributions of educational rewards. Society is paying relatively more to better-educated people, especially at the college level and beyond. The higher one goes up the educational ladder, the greater the disparity between the number of whites and Asians versus blacks and Hispanics. It is also true that, in general, blacks and Hispanics without college educations receive less than comparably educated whites and Asians.

The fact that education increases with income is not in itself a denial of employers' contentions that the educational system is failing, especially at the high school level. In the last few years the constant-dollar income of "lower-level" employees, without college experience, has decreased. Evidently employers are either exporting low-skill jobs, eliminating them with automation, or devaluing those jobs that require lower levels of skill (Wegmann, Chapman, and Johnson, 1989). What is startling is that "lower level of skill" now seems to mean lacking at least some college education.

The evidence suggests that the American higher education system produces a pretty good product. Foreigners appear to agree with this contention, since our colleges and universities import far more students than we export, especially at the graduate level. Insofar as student preparation is concerned, the problem does not seem to lie with the colleges and universities, but with the elementary and high school (K–12) system. In order to take a closer look at the problem, let us examine some results of the third way to assess cognitive capabilities, by directly testing what people can do.

In 1992 the Educational Testing Service (ETS) conducted an extensive survey of adult literacy (Kirsch et al., 1993). Over 13,000 U.S. residents were interviewed. The sample was carefully selected to make it possible to extrapolate the results to the population as a whole. The tests themselves were designed to reflect the ways in which language and cognitive skills are used in everyday life. Three types of skills were examined: reading newspapers and instruction-like material; using documents, such as a bus schedule or a government form; and using quantitative skills, varying from balancing a checkbook to determining the interest on loans.

For purposes of reporting, test scores were grouped into five levels. Level 1 tasks required test takers to locate a single clearly stated fact in a newspaper article or balance a checkbook. Level 5 tasks, by contrast, required them to draw inferences from information presented in articles, use documents in a sophisticated way, or solve reasonably complex arithmetical problems. *Almost half the population performed at Levels 1 and 2.* Performance at this level indicates an ability to understand things that are directly and clearly stated, but not to use information in any creative or integrative way.

Members of minority groups did particularly poorly. Depending only slightly on which test was examined (prose, documents, or quantitative skills), about 15 percent of all whites tested, 40 percent of blacks, over 50 percent of Hispanics, and about 30 percent of Asians and Pacific Islanders performed at Level 1.

As the ETS report points out, levels of quantitative and literacy skills are closely related to education. In general, minority group members are less well educated than whites. This is especially true for older adults and for immigrants. When educational level is taken into account, the difference in mean scores of whites versus blacks and Hispanics drops to about half its level, but is still substantial. (The white–Asian difference is unchanged.) Since minority group members are becoming a progressively larger percentage of the U.S. population, improvement of their cognitive skills must be a matter of national priority.

What is perhaps most discouraging was evidence of deterioration in skills of the groups containing younger entrants to the workforce. The 1992 results for workers aged 21–25 can be compared with results of a comparable survey taken in 1985. The 1985 examinees, on the average, outscored the 1992 examinees by 10 or more points on all three tests of skills.

What is the status of people who are still in school, but who will be in the workforce during the next 10 to 15 years? The National Assessment of Educational Progress (NAEP) program, which tests basic skills in large samples of schoolchildren at various ages, provided most of our data. Since we are concerned with the workforce of the near future, we are especially interested in high school students' performance in reading and mathematics.

NAEP reading test results are presented in terms of mean or median scores. Carroll (1987) has suggested the following interpretation of the numbers.

1. Basic. Can read stories in third grade readers and follow simple labels and instructions. (NAEP score 200)

2. Intermediate. Can read simple popular magazines. (NAEP score 250)

3. Adept. Can read most newspaper stories and popular novels. (NAEP score 300)

4. Advanced. Can read newspaper editorials at the *New York Times* level. Generally the level expected of graduating college students. (NAEP score 400)

Figure 1.13 Percentage of students reading at or above indicated reading levels. Source: National Center for Educational Statistics (1993).

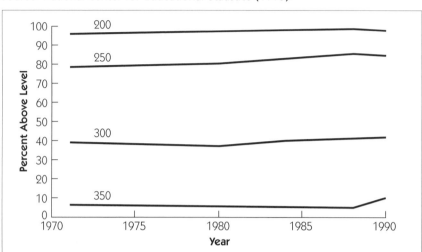

Figure 1.13 shows NAEP reading assessments for 17-year-old students between 1975 and 1990. In spite of great concern over "why Johnny can't read," there has obviously been little improvement overall. However, focusing on the overall picture masks some important details. Figure 1.14 shows the percentage of students reading at Carroll's intermediate level, which is probably the minimal level of competence needed in a job beyond entry level. The data are shown separately for whites, blacks, and Hispanics. Two trends are immediately apparent: while blacks and Hispanics still come out of the K–12 system less well prepared than whites, the gap has been reduced dramatically. About 50 percent of the black and Hispanic 17-year-olds were reading at the intermediate level in 1974–1975. Fifteen years later over 70 percent were at that level.

Unfortunately, there has been little change in the percentage of readers at the adept and advanced skill level. In fact, the percentage of readers at the advanced level has declined slightly. It is not clear whether or not this is a problem. As Carroll points out, we do not know what percentage of very good readers we need, because we do not have a good idea of how much essential reading (manuals, directions, legal instructions, and the like) is written at the adept level or above, nor do we know how many people need to understand this material.

Mathematical ability is generally considered a necessary cognitive

Figure 1.14   Percentage of students above NAEP intermediate reading level, by ethnic status. Source: National Center for Educational Statistics (1993).

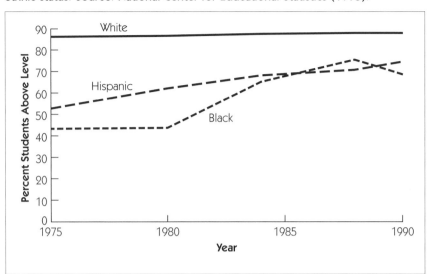

skill second only to reading. NAEP mathematics scores have been grouped as follows:

1. Basic. Can do arithmetic operations. (NAEP score 250)
2. Moderately complex. Can use fractions and percentages and understands simple geometric concepts. (NAEP score 300)
3. Advanced. Can use mathematical reasoning to solve multistep problems and can use algebra. (NAEP score 350)

Figure 1.15 shows the percentage of 17-year-old students scoring 300 or more on the 1990 NAEP test. The data are shown separately for males and females and for various ethnic groups.

A great deal has been written about male-female differences in mathematical ability. More extreme proponents of a difference sometimes seem to write as if women, generically, "can't do math." The low point in this debate may have been reached in 1992, when the Mattel Corporation marketed a talking Barbie doll that complained that "math class is hard." The facts are more complex. As Figure 1.15 shows, 17-year-old males do very slightly better than females. Some of this difference is because girls tend to take fewer high school mathematics classes than do boys, but that is not the whole story. On the average, males

Figure 1.15 Mathematics proficiency (percentage above NAEP 300 level), by gender and ethnic group, 1989–1990. Source: National Center for Education Statistics (1993).

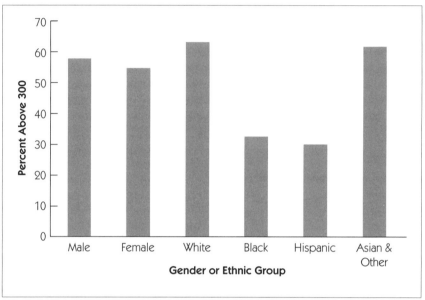

outscore females at every level of mathematics education. For instance, males who have taken precalculus or calculus courses averaged 347 on the NAEP mathematics test, compared to 341 for females with equivalent training.

The mathematics skills of black and Hispanic students lagged markedly behind those of whites and Asians. The difference is considerably larger than the male-female difference. Like the male-female difference, ethnic differences remain after taking the amount of mathematical training into account. This is consistent with the observation that black and Hispanic students are underrepresented in the more technical fields of higher education, which place a premium on mathematics skills.

The data presented so far have focused on all high school students. Figure 1.16 shows changes over time in the Scholastic Aptitude Test (SAT) scores achieved by college-bound high school seniors. Proficiency dropped from the 1960s until the late 1970s, rebounded slightly, and dropped again. The 1991 and 1992 mathematics scores were the lowest ever.

Figure 1.17 shows ethnic group differences in SAT scores in 1991. The picture is similar to the picture obtained from the NAEP tests.

Figure 1.16 SAT scores of college-bound high school seniors. Source: National Center for Education Statistics (1993).

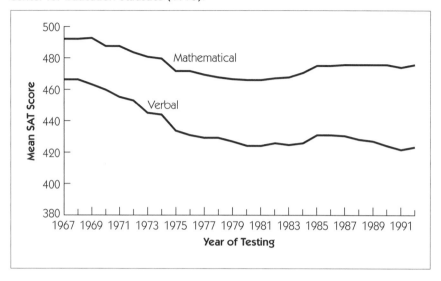

Figure 1.17 SAT scores, by ethnic groups, 1992. Source: National Center for Education Statistics (1993).

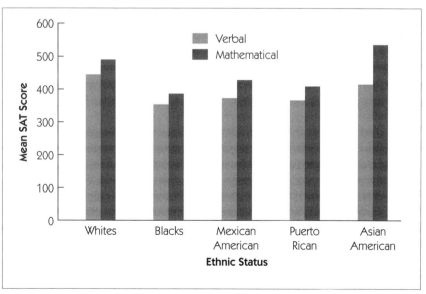

Figure 1.18 Performance of 13-year-olds on a standard mathematics test, 1992. Source: National Center for Education Statistics (1993).

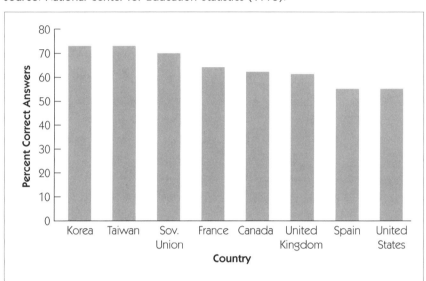

Blacks and Hispanics do markedly worse than whites and Asians. Asians show a marked superiority in mathematics but have lower verbal scores that are intermediate between the scores of whites and other ethnic groups.

Where do we stand internationally? Reading scores cannot be compared because students read different languages. Mathematics scores can be compared, and the United States does not do very well. In 1981 an international comparison of mathematics knowledge in both 13-year-olds and twelfth graders found that the United States ranked last compared with Japan, Canada, France, and the United Kingdom. In 1992 a larger survey of 13-year-olds found that the United States had moved up a bit. We were tied for last place with Spain (Figure 1.18).

Ideally, we should compare U.S. twelfth graders in 1992 with foreign twelfth graders, as was done in 1981. Unfortunately, the data are not available, but it is doubtful that things have changed. The U.S. internal statistics indicate that while we have made progress, we have made little progress in improving the work of our better students. There is no reason to believe that foreign countries have slipped backward.

CHANGES IN THE NATURE OF WORK

What skills will be in demand in the coming workplace? This is a difficult question to answer, because the forecast depends upon what assumptions are made, how much, and how rapidly, technological changes will impact upon the workforce. As a result, well-informed prognosticators have reached different conclusions.

Workforce 2000 (Johnson and Packer, 1987), a widely publicized forecast, concluded that the American workplace would have a need for highly skilled craft workers and technicians, that is, more highly skilled blue-color positions. The *Workforce 2000* report and several that followed it (Commission on the Skills of the American Workforce, 1990; Office of Technology Assessment, 1990; Secretary's Commission on Achieving Necessary Skills, 1991) argued for major expansions of education programs designed to prepare Americans for a highly automated, decentralized workplace. They argue that the jobs will be present and that it is up to the educational establishment, broadly conceived, to provide appropriate workers. The same spirit permeates President Clinton's 1994 proposals to shift unemployment relief from a support system designed to provide temporary relief to laid-off workers until their old jobs reopen to a training system to prepare the unemployed for new jobs that are supposedly waiting for them.

Other prognosticators, and many newspaper articles describing failures of employment recovery following the 1990–1991 recession, reached a much more pessimistic conclusion. They question whether or not the new jobs are there at all. These writers argue that jobs are becoming "deskilled," in the sense that tasks formerly done by people are being turned over to automated "smart" machines. The result is that there are a few good jobs designing the machines, and a large number of low-paid jobs, in which a person essentially works under the direction of a machine.

Retail clerking provides a good example. A few years ago retail clerks had to be able to do elementary arithmetic calculations, rapidly and accurately, in order to make change. Today the computer in the cash register handles the arithmetic. In many stores all the clerk has to be able to do is hold a barcode scanner over the goods being sold and to recognize the denomination of the bill offered in payment. If the customer chooses to pay by credit card, the clerk does not even have to do that (Hartman, 1987). To the extent that such scenarios are correct, people will not move from one good paying job to another, they will be laid off from a good paying one and have to accept a lower rate of pay.

There are some discouraging statistics indicating that the de-skillers may be correct. Referring back to Figure 1.5, we have already seen that job growth is slowest, and in some cases is actually negative, in those sectors of the economy with the highest hourly wages. Some larger-scale statistics support this conclusion. With some fluctuations, U.S.

unemployment rates generally went down from 1980 (9 percent) to 1993 (6.9 percent). Median income in constant dollars dropped by about 10 percent over the same period. As a matter of elementary economics, when a commodity decreases in supply its price goes up *unless some alternative commodity appears that fulfulls the same need* and thus decreases demand. That is what has happened to U.S. domestic labor. Over the past 15 years labor has faced increasing competition from foreign labor, due largely to changes in technology that make offshore manufacturing and service supply economic, and from increased productivity per worker, due to automation. Both of these trends are being driven by changes in technology rather than by governmental actions or tariff changes. It is unlikely that there is any way to slow the trends. If a useful device can be built, someone will build it.

Let us take a closer look at these trends, by examining a few cases. The first is a contrast between two companies that are widely considered dominant in their fields: Microsoft Corporation, the world's largest computer software firm, and the Boeing Corporation, the world's largest manufacturer of airplanes. While both companies operate worldwide, their major production facilities are located within a few miles of each other, in the Seattle region, so local factors are more or less constant. Both companies can be considered "high technology," but Microsoft is in a rapidly growing field in which the basic production workers, programmers, and system designers are highly educated. Boeing is a heavy manufacturing concern, and the basic production workers are well-paid blue-collar machinists and electricians.

In 1993 Microsoft expanded its worldwide employment to something over 13,000 people. Boeing laid off 20,000 workers in the Seattle region alone and appears to be stabilizing at a workforce of about 70,000 in its Seattle facilities. Even as it contracts, Boeing makes more new hires than Microsoft.

By generalizing this contrast, we gain some insight into why different projections come up with different pictures of the future. The optimists and the pessimists are looking at related but different trends. Should you look at where the largest number of jobs is going to be, or where the fastest growing professions are? The largest number of jobs will be in fields where there are already a large number of jobs. These, in general, are relatively unskilled jobs with fairly low educational requirements. (There are some striking exceptions.) The jobs with high growth rates, although perhaps also low in absolute numbers, are generally associated with expanding technologies and high skill requirements.

These remarks can be given some content by examining some statistics on the projected growth rates from 1985 to 2000 for the 225 occupations providing the most jobs, as of 1985 (Wegmann, Chapman, and Johnson, 1989). These occupations were sorted five times to determine (1) the occupations with the most jobholders; (2) the occupations showing the largest number of new jobs, based on a 1985–2000 projection; (3) the occupations with the highest growth rate over the same period; (4) the occupations with the most job losses; and (5) the occupations with the highest loss rates. Table 1.4 shows the top ten jobs after each of these sortings.

First let us look at the ten occupations that will provide the largest total number of jobs. These tend to be jobs with rather limited career development: food services, retail sales, chefs and cooks, janitors. The only exceptions are personnel jobs and executives, an occupation that contains a highly varied set of jobs. If we look at the ten occupations expected to provide the most number of new jobs, only three—general managers, registered nurses, and general engineers—require considerable formal education beyond high school. The message is clear. If we look at the largest total number of jobs that will be available, we find that they are concentrated in occupations where the requirements of job holding are either rather low or can be lowered by technology, as in the case of retail clerks. By the inevitable laws of supply and demand, salaries will be reduced.

The picture changes if we look at occupations that are showing the highest growth rates, albeit not the greatest absolute number of jobs. With one exception, security guards, these are jobs that either require high-level intellectual skills or that require skill in dealing with people. The most sought-after employees, system analysts and computer scientists, are the high priests of the new technology. Most people in these fields have at least a bachelor's degree, and advanced degrees are common. Registered nurses, another rapidly growing occupation, receive years of formal training in biological sciences and have to learn to manipulate the formidable technology of modern medicine.

Real estate agents and managers, two other rapidly growing occupations, provide an interesting case. Realtors and managers deal with people. Face-to-face interactions are perhaps the hardest information exchanges to automate. What is more, they provide an interesting example of a skill with an unusual distribution in the population. Everyone has this skill to some degree, but there seem to be very wide individual differences in the extent to which each of us can go beyond the basics. Virtually any two people who speak the same language can talk to each other and carry on a conversation that defines automation, but good salespeople and successful politicians are few and far between.

The last two columns in Table 1.4 show which jobs are being lost. With one exception, college and university faculty,[7] job losses, in both

Table 1.4 Projected Growth for U.S. Occupations

1 Occupations with Most Employees	2 Occupations with Most New Jobs	3 Occupations with Highest Growth Rates
Food service workers	Food service workers	Systems analysts
Retail sales clerks	Retail sales clerks	Computer programmers
Personnel related jobs	Chefs and cooks	Service sales representatives
Secretaries	Registered nurses	Health service workers
Chefs and cooks	Janitors	Security guards
Janitors	General managers and executives	Computer operators
Truckdrivers	Cashiers	Electrical/electronics
General managers and executives	Truckdrivers	repairs and service workers
General clerks	General clerks	Real estate agents
Cashiers	General engineers	Registered nurses
		Receptionists

4 Occupations with Most Job Losses	5 Occupations with Highest Loss Rate
Farmers	Textile machine operators
Typists and word processors	Farmers
Clothing workers	Data entry key operators
Moving equipment operators	Machinists
Textile machine operators	Typists and word processors
Data entry key operators	Moving equipment operators
Metalworkers	Clothing workers
Machinists	Metalworkers
College teachers	College faculty
Quality control inspectors	Quality control inspectors

absolute and relative terms, are concentrated in fields where automation has reduced the number of people needed to produce a product or provide a service. Consider typists, an occupation that was once a first step toward better-paid office jobs. They are being automated out of existence. The modern word-processing program is so simplified that even general managers and executives can use it.

I referred earlier to a series of articles in the *New York Times,* written in March 1994, about how the new technologies were selectively impacting upon the higher-paid blue-collar jobs. The *Times* articles made their case by anecdotes, describing how different families were coping with their new situations. A common trend ran through these articles: surprise. The people who lost their jobs had thought that it never would happen to them. In fact, this was naive. The problems of today were quite predictable. In fact, Table 1.4 is based on projections from statistics gathered by 1985. Highly paid blue-collar jobs are at risk for two simple reasons. First, the technology is there. Second, the higher paid the worker, the greater is the incentive to design a machine that can do the worker's job, either alone or when operated by a less-skilled worker.

The workplace is not just shrinking or contracting; it is changing. The change is partly a change from highly paid manufacturing to lower-paid services. It is also a change in the sort of services that are required. Robert Reich, President Clinton's Secretary of Labor, has referred to this trend as the "growth of the symbol analyst" (Reich, 1991). Within the service sector, the demand for physical services, such as barbering or lawn mowing, have roughly grown with the society. The explosive growth has come in information processing rather than physical services. This does not mean information processing, narrowly defined as something to do with computers and communication. Advertisers, stockbrokers, and newspaper reporters process symbols rather than people or things.

The increase in Reich's symbol analysts has been going on for a long time. In a perceptive book, Katz (1988) has documented a steady growth in information services, relative to the rest of the economy, since 1860, with a sharp acceleration from 1940 to 1980. The pace has not slowed since then. Table 1.5 shows the distribution of the workforce in some selected occupations in 1980 and 1992. The table also shows relative changes, such as the ratio of the number of workers in the occupation in 1992, compared to the number in 1980. Computer-related information processing and legal services, quintessential symbol manipulating industries, exhibited the highest growth rates. Service occupations that do not primarily involve symbol manipulation, such as the hotel industry, grew faster than the workforce as a whole, but did not grow as rapidly as Reich's symbol analyst occupations did.

Table 1.5   Growth Rates for the Workforce, Manufacturing, and Selected Service Occupations (1980–1992)

Occupation	Jobs, 1980 (thousands)	Jobs, 1992 (thousands)	Relative Change, 1980–1992
Workforce	90,406	108,437	1.20
Production of goods and services	20,285	18,190	.90
Financial and realty	5,160	6,672	1.29
Computer and data processing	304	817	2.69
Legal	498	906	1.82
Advertising	153	232	1.52
Education	1,138	1,716	1.51
Hotel industry	1,076	1,597	1.48
Personal services	818	1,107	1.35

Source: Bureau of Census (1993).

If anything, these figures understate the extent of the shift. Manufacturing itself has changed, so that the people counted as being in industrial plants may be symbol analysts themselves.

If anything, Table 1.5 understates the dominance of Reich's symbol analyst. Within the production industries, symbol processing has become increasingly important. The Industrial Revolution moved people away from providing the physical energy needed to transform objects, but they still had to provide the perceptions that guided the machinery. Now they provide abstract information that a smart machine uses to guide its own cutting and mixing tools. A single example, Toshiba, the Japanese electronics manufacturer, employs 4,000 in its plant at Ome, Japan; 500 are blue-collar workers, and 3,000 are engineers and scientists (Zuckerman, 1991). All 4,000 of these workers can be counted as being "in manufacturing," but very few of them are involved in the physical manipulation of products.

Customizing the Product

The Toshiba example provides a bridge to a final comment about changes in the nature of work.

When Henry Ford first began producing a production-line car, the Model T, he is supposed to have said, "The customer can have any color he wants, so long as it's black." This apocryphal quotation very much captures the spirit of the industrial age. Production and, to a lesser degree, services were oriented toward making high volumes of standardized products. Top management decided, on a one-shot basis, what most customers wanted, and that is what customers were offered.

As of 1993, the Ford Motor Company offered its customers more than 50 different colors, depending on the model. If a customer is willing to wait two or three weeks, a car can be customized in nearly any way one desires.

The computerization of manufacturing is a key element in the move toward customization. Computer-driven "smart machines" make it possible to design and implement relatively low-volume, tailor-made product runs. Flexibility in responding to the needs of the customer has become more important than delivering a standard product. Therefore, the task of deciding how a product should be made (or a service should be delivered) cannot be planned ahead, the way Henry Ford did. In fact, the task may be passed on to workers on the line, who design their own working procedures as they develop the product.

The shift from high-volume production to low-volume problem solving has created a demand for workers who understand how their job fits into the big picture. This is a great departure from the earlier role of the industrial production worker. Charlie Chaplin's 1930s classic film *Modern Times* begins with the Little Tramp hard at work in a factory, tightening bolts. Tightening bolts on what? We never learn, and the tramp never knows. His job is to keep up with the production line (he doesn't), tightening the bolts on unidentified pieces of metal. Chaplin's factory was rigidly hierarchical: The foreman told the Little Tramp what to do and he did it, more or less. In real life Henry Ford ran his operation in much the same way. Today, Japan, Europe, and, more slowly, the United States are all moving toward factories in which the workers are organized into work groups. (The Ford Motor Company has been an industry leader!) The work groups distribute jobs among themselves and monitor their own output. Quality control inspectors are on the loser's list in Table 1.4. The production line workers do not need them any more.

The change from an assembly line to a working team has profound implications for the psychological demands on the workers. Recall that when managers were asked what they wanted from the workforce, "problem-solving skills" and "work ethic" were high on their list of requirements. These are vaguely defined skills, but nevertheless real ones.

SKILLS FOR THE FUTURE

When we look at the current work situation more closely we find two contradictory trends. The psychological demands of work are changing.

"Smart machines"—the computer and all of its relatives—have decreased the demand for skilled blue-collar labor and increased the demand for symbol analysts who can talk to machines on their own terms. The move toward tightly interconnected service systems and toward a society of specialists has increased the need for people who can facilitate person-to-person and person-to-machine transactions. At the same time, the smart machines insist on low level services from human beings whom they, the machines, will direct just as a cashier is told now just how to make change. This demand creates jobs but not good jobs.

The future workforce can meet the demands of the smart machines, but perhaps not in a way that makes us comfortable. The people whom the machines direct will need some facility in reading and mathematics, if only to be able to respond to the machine's direction. For instance, a modern cashier must know how to fill out a credit slip! Our educational system has done a good job of training people for such tasks. Absolute illiteracy and incompetence in elementary mathematics, which were major problems as late as the 1960s, have largely disappeared.

Obviously we are not satisfied with an educational system that trains people to respond to machines. We want a system that trains people to control machines. Our educational system is failing to produce the sort of quality workers that we need, a problem that appears to be particularly acute with respect to blacks and Hispanics, who will be an increasingly larger part of the working population. Nor are we making effective use of the quality workers in the workforce already in jobs. When senior workers are displaced, they typically find jobs that are considerably less desirable than their old jobs (Podgorsky, 1988). Since senior workers are the breadwinners that future generations depend on, we must try to minimize costly dislocations.

All this has been said before. All I have tried to do is to leaven the statistics with some psychological remarks. The real question is, "What are we going to do about it?" Both the problem and the solution have political, economic, sociological, and psychological dimensions. I am going to concentrate on the psychological ones. Why?

One of the major advances in academics in the last 20 years has been the development of *cognitive science,* an interdisciplinary area of study that encompasses both the design of machines that, in a nontrivial sense, can think, and the study of how people act when they, in an equally nontrivial sense, have to think. The following chapters are an attempt to apply what we have learned in cognitive science to an analysis of the workforce. First I shall try to define the dimensions of the problem, by looking at how cognitive skills are distributed in the pres-

ent workforce and by predicting how those skills are going to be distributed in the workforce just after the turn of the century. Then I will
ask what sort of cognitive characteristics are going to be demanded, by
projecting trends about machines, rather than trends about people. The
results will be discomfiting, but we do not have to accept them.

My second step will be to consider what can be done to improve
things. Modern cognitive psychology, one of the branches of cognitive
science, has a great deal to say about how we can train the workforce
of the future, if we have the will to do so. In the closing chapter I will
outline what cognitive science has to say about how we might improve
education: in the K-12 system, in the universities and colleges, and
throughout lifelong professional education.

NOTES

1. The three best-selling automobiles in 1993 were, in order, the Ford Escort,
   the Honda Accord, and the Toyota Camry.
2. U.S. Bureau of the Census, 1992.
3. *New York Times,* March 22, 1991.
4. The Economic Report of the President, 1991.
5. The OTA prediction was developed prior to passage of the North American
   Free Trade Act. The impact of a virtually open border with Mexico is hard
   to assess. It could increase immigration by reducing attempts to regulate
   the flow of migrants, or it could decrease immigration, by creating greater
   economic opportunities in Mexico.
6. The percentages shown in Figure 1.11 conflict with the widely reported figure of a 25 percent dropout rate, nationwide (*New York Times,* July 27,
   1991). Paradoxically, the same agency provided both figures. The 25 percent
   rate appears to be based on the number of students who do not graduate
   with their high school class. Figure 1.16 counts students who return to graduate, or who obtain general education diplomas, as having completed high
   school.
7. Academics may be surprised to find their profession listed as losing jobholders, since several forecasts show that there will be many new openings in
   the next 10 years. The disparity is due to the unusual age distribution of
   the present faculty workforce. Faculty were recruited intensely in the 1960s.
   This cohort is now approaching retirement age. Job openings in higher education during the 1990s will be for replacements, not for new positions.

2

The Psychological Measurement of Workforce Productivity

PREDICTING HUMAN ABILITY

Measures of Thinking and Predictions about the Workforce

From an economic viewpoint, human labor is like any other commodity. It is a resource required by an industrial process to create a product. The value of the labor is determined by the value that the labor adds to the product. In the wood products industry a standing tree is worth a certain amount. The same tree, delivered to the sawmill, is worth more; the boards from the tree are worth still more, and a house made from the boards is worth even more. The skills of the logger, sawyer, and carpenter are required to make the improvements. These skills have to be evaluated, priced, and entered into the equations for the economics of woodworking.

Labor (or, as it is sometimes termed, "human capital") itself is the target of the industrial process. Human beings of certain types are fed into an industrial process called "schools." If schooling is successful the students come out with greater economic value. The statistics presented in Chapter 1 showed that this is indeed the case. On the average, the more educated a person, the more the economy will pay that person to participate in the workforce.

In order to monitor the development of human capital, we must have indices of quality. We distinguish between hardwoods and softwoods because they can be worked into different sorts of artifacts. Similarly, we need to distinguish between good and poor candidates for engineering, medicine, aviation, or forest ranger training. As with many other materials, the distinction between good and poor candidates is not absolute. People can be trained to do many things, but not without expense. The quality of the candidate will affect both the cost of the training and the quality of the final product.

In the last few years there has been a great deal of concern about the cost and quality of modern workers. These discussions often take a curiously one-sided view. They focus on the cost of modern workers with much less concern with the quality of their work. The 1993 debate over the North American Free Trade Agreement (NAFTA) was a good example. Most of the argument was about the wages paid to Mexican or American workers. The NAFTA debate would have been more enlightened if it had included some discussion of the skills that each workforce possessed. Why was this point generally ignored?

Newspaper reporters might try to justify their one-sided view on the grounds that we can measure wages but not skills or that we should concentrate on wages because workers' skills are more or less the same. Neither statement is true. Cognitive skills can be measured. When we do so we find substantial variations of skill, both between individuals within a group and, on the average, between identifiable social groups. Furthermore (and somewhat contrary to popular belief), measurements of cognitive skills are related to workplace performance. Such measurements are the domain of *psychometrics*, which is the topic of this chapter.

In the popular mind psychometrics is closely associated with intelligence testing. Americans are ambivalent about this practice. On the one hand, testing fits into our publicly proclaimed desire for objectivity in personnel decision making. Our ideal personnel manager tries to hire the best person for the job, ignoring the fact that one of the candidates is the vice president's spouse's cousin. In practice, the spouse's cousin and the friend of a friend are hired more often than we care to admit.[1] In principle, though, we claim that employment decisions should be based on objective, clearly enunciated determination of qualifications, productivity, and seniority.

On the other hand, when it comes to administering tests, we often become uneasy. Is it reasonable to believe that impersonal test makers can really evaluate a person whom they never met, by looking at so little a slice of the whole person's capabilities? Many people reject testing on these grounds. In fact, though, statistics are on the side of the test makers. Interviews and personal recommendations are, in general, less accurate predictors of job performance than appropriate psychometric test scores.

Another reason that people are uneasy about testing is their concern that tests somehow fail to capture an essential part of human capability. Frustratingly, this belief is partly true and partly false. Psychometric tests are not nearly as accurate as we would like. This is not surprising. Measuring a person's intelligence is much more complex than measuring a person's height. But unerring accuracy is hardly to be expected, nor is it required. The real issue is not whether the tests are perfect, but whether testing, properly used, will increase the chances of getting the right people for the right job, even though errors may still occur.

Understanding just how psychometric tests work is important because they play a key role in predictions about cognitive skills in the future workforce. Such a prediction rests on three facts. The first is that, in the past, statistical relationships have been shown between test scores, educational accomplishments, and workplace performance. The relations are far from perfect, but they are not negligible. The second fact is that for the past 20 or 30 years, there have been stable relationships between various demographic measures, such as aging and ethnic group membership, and test scores. The third fact is that we can predict the demographic constitution of the workforce in the 2000–2010 period with a good deal of accuracy.

Knowing the relation between educational-cognitive measures and demographic measures in the present workforce, we can estimate the educational and cognitive characteristics of the future workforce. Finally, knowing the present relationship between educational and cognitive characteristics, employment, and productivity, we can estimate the productivity of the future workforce.

The validity of this procedure depends on two assumptions. The first is that over the next 20 years there will be no great change in demographics—no massive influx of immigrants, no war with high civilian casualty rates, and no radical change in the rate of participation of various groups in the workforce. The second, more debatable assumption is that the relations between demographics, cognitive measures, and workplace activities will be the same in the future as they are today. In this chapter and the next two chapters, I assume that the workplace, and the cognitive skills required by that workplace, will remain pretty much the same as they are today. In Chapters 5 and 6 I speculate about what might happen if revolutionary changes occur.

Finally, a word about the presentation. People who think of psychology as a "talking science" are often surprised at the amount of mathematical modeling behind the design and use of psychological tests. There is no way to present a fair picture of psychometrics and its use without presenting some of the mathematical and statistical concepts involved. However, since many readers of this book will not be used to following formal mathematical arguments, I have tried to strike a compromise between presenting formal arguments and merely asserting that "it can be proven." The compromise relies on the use of graphs to represent mathematical concepts visually. Occasionally, notes will be provided either to elaborate on a mathematical point or to provide mathematically inclined readers with an entry point to the technical literature.

Cognitive Measurement

Since there has been a good deal of controversy about tests of "intelligence," "aptitude," and "achievement," we will begin with a broad view of the issues involved. Whether or not cognitive tests can be useful is an empirical issue. If there are reliable statistical relationships between test scores and workplace performance, then the scores can be used to predict performance. If there are no such reliable relationships, the tests cannot be used.

Of course, it is not quite that simple. "Reliable" to a statistician means "a larger relationship than one would expect to find by chance." If test-performance relationships are not reliable, then tests should not be used to predict performance. But if test-performance relationships are reliable, is the relationship large enough to be useful? This is a difficult question to answer, because an association that is large enough to be useful for one purpose may not be large enough to be useful for another purpose.

Tests are used in the workplace both as an aid to individual decision making and as a guide for personnel selection policy. The distinction between the two uses is necessary, because a statistical relationship can be too small to be useful as a guide to individual decision making, but large enough to be important as a guide to policy. Suppose that a high school student applies to a state university, which uses an entrance examination to estimate the time it will take the student to complete a bachelor's degree. Assume that the student's test scores are low enough so that the best statistical estimate is that he or she will take an extra year to graduate. The student could sensibly ask to be admitted, since the economic benefits of having a college degree, amortized over the student's working life, should more than offset the cost of an extra year in college.

From the point of view of the college, more caution is warranted. Since virtually all state universities recover only about half the cost of education in tuition, the state will be footing half the bill for the student's extra year, a subsidy (in 1994) of about $6,500. In the case of one student this amount may be trivial, but the state's policy decision to admit students with a particular minimum score applies to thousands of students. The aggregate costs of accepting students who take extra time may not be at all trivial.

There is another consideration. The university must be concerned with throughput—how many students it graduates each year. If four years of credits are required to graduate, then a policy decision to permit students to enter so long as they are *statistically* expected to complete four years of credits in five would, averaged over all students, decrease the number of graduating students by 20 percent each year. Individual students may argue that the extra costs are worth it. From society's point of view the costs may be exorbitant.

Now consider a slightly different case, in an industrial setting. Of necessity, more variables are involved than in the college example. Also, to avoid an excursion into mathematics certain statements about probabilities will be presented without proof. Readers familiar with mathematical models of personnel selection should have no trouble recognizing how the models have been applied. Our hypothetical situation is as follows:

1. There are a number of openings for a position that pays an average of $25,000 per year.
2. There are three applicants for every position.
3. Two-thirds of the applicants could do the job adequately.
4. The employer uses a screening test that correlates .30 with job performance.
5. The employer hires people in order of test scores. Therefore, the people whose test scores are in the top third will be hired.

All these assumptions represent a reasonable situation. The term *correlation* will be explained in more detail below. For the present, readers are asked to accept the fact that if the test were a perfect predictor of performance, the correlation would be 1.0. If the test had nothing to do with performance, the correlation would be 0. In the example the test is not irrelevant, but it is far from perfect.

Now consider two applicants, A and B. A is an "average" applicant, who obtains an average (mean) score on the screening test. A will not be hired because in order to be hired one must have a test score in the top one third. B just makes this criterion and so has the lowest test score of anyone hired.

Suppose that A had been hired. The probability that A would perform satisfactorily would be .67. B was hired. Under the conditions given, the probability of B's doing the job adequately would be .80. Understandably A would be annoyed on finding that he or she had not been hired for a job where there was a 2:1 chance for success.

The employer may look at things differently. Consider the attrition rate: the number of employees who have to be dismissed for unsatisfactory performance. Under a policy of random hiring, this will be 33 percent of all those hired. Under this policy both A and B have one chance in three of being hired. However, if the employer uses the screening policy to hire B *and all applicants with higher scores than B's*, the attrition rate will be about 13 percent. Attrition has been cut by more than half.

The disparity between the individual's and the employer's (or workforce's) view is even more pronounced if we consider productivity increases instead of attrition rates. Here the analysis becomes complicated, because the exact figure depends on the assumptions that are made about the relation between the predictor and productivity of labor. One method of analysis (Cascio, 1986, p. 149) predicts an expected gain of $8,600 per employee for this example.

These examples show that modest relationships between measures of cognitive capabilities and job performance can be used to make important predictions of future productivity. Clearly the topic is worth pursuing.

In the remaining parts of this chapter, I will discuss the mathematical and statistical details of how such predictions are made. Two responsible critics, Wigdor and Green (1991, p. 18) pointed out that test developers have rested their case on measurement and statistical issues and have been relatively unconcerned with the meaning behind their measurements. Both the usefulness and the weaknesses of this approach can be understood only by understanding the technical details behind it.

THE PSYCHOMETRIC MODEL OF COGNITION

Mental Space

Virtually all mental tests in use today are based on a representation of human cognition that has come to be called the *psychological measurement* or *psychometric* view. Sternberg (1990) characterizes it nicely as a geographic metaphor for human intelligence.

Psychometricians regard a person's performance on a problem as an integration of the person's general abilities and abilities that are specific to the task at hand. For example, suppose that several people were hired to assemble mail-order computers, using only the instructions that arrive with the package. This task requires skill in reading and understanding diagrams, and also assumes some general knowledge of computers. Suppose further that we score each person's performance as a computer assembler. According to the psychometric view, a person's score could be predicted from knowledge of his or her underlying mental abilities. The prediction would be

Success at putting computer together =   (2.1)
  A * (verbal ability) +
  B * (spatial-visual ability) +
  C * (reasoning ability) +
  D * (knowledge of computers) +
  (error due to unmeasured factors).

Verbal ability, spatial-visual ability, and *reasoning ability* refer to abilities that are required in a number of situations: respectively, the ability to comprehend language, the ability to reason about visual and spatial images (e.g., diagrams), and the ability to apply logical reasoning, apart from whether the problem is expressed verbally or visually. Such broad abilities cannot be measured by any one test, but they can be inferred from performance on several tests. The basic idea is that one averages over several tests, any one of which taps some aspect of the ability. For instance, verbal ability is determined by averaging scores on tests of vocabulary, grammatical usage, and text comprehension.

Knowledge of computers is clearly a more specialized mental property. However, if we wanted to predict a person's success in putting together mail-order computers, it would be a good idea to measure it.

Error due to unmeasured factors refers to the extent to which performance is influenced by other factors that were not measured. It is a correction term, required because prediction is never perfect.

The letter terms *A, B, C,* and *D* refer to numbers that are used to indicate how important a particular abstract ability is for performance in a particular situation. A large value indicates that the ability is important, while a near zero value indicates that it is almost irrelevant.

Figure 2.1 provides a graphic summary of this reasoning. The square on the left side of the figure is a *mental space* defined by verbal and spatial-visual ability. (To be completely true to the example, we should draw a four-dimensional figure that includes reasoning ability and knowledge of computers.) The black dot inside the square indicates the position of a person who has a verbal ability score of 100 and a spatial-visual ability score of 120. The white dot represents a second person, with scores of 80 and 65.

The vertical line on the right side of Figure 2.1 represents scores on

Figure 2.1   The psychometric view of selection.

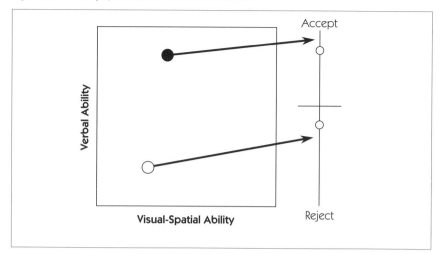

the task of assembling the computer. The arrows from the positions in the mental space to the line represent the equation used to map from positions in the space to positions on the line. The location that the arrow points to on the line is the *predicted* score for a person. The dots on the line represent the scores actually obtained. The difference between the predicted and the obtained scores represents the error term of Equation 2.1.

The horizontal line on the right represents a hypothetical "minimal level of predicted score." People whose arrows fell above the line would be considered qualified as assemblers, though their actual performance might fall below it. People whose arrows fell below the line would be considered unqualified, though their actual performance, if they had been hired, might have been above the line.

Prediction works to the extent that the predicted scores (the arrows) fall close to the actual scores (the dots on the vertical line). The extent of the agreement is indicated by the correlation coefficient (r) between predicted and obtained scores. This is called the *validity coefficient.*

Validity coefficients (like all correlation coefficients) vary between -1 and $+1$. Since a negative correlation can always be converted into a positive one by multiplying the predicted score by -1, we can consider only positive values. If the validity coefficient is one, the obtained scores will be equal to the predicted scores. In Figure 2.1 the arrows would point exactly to the dots on the right. If the validity coefficient is zero, the dots might be anywhere, no matter where the corresponding arrow is. Validity coefficients between zero and one indicate that the arrows are close to the dots, but not right on them. The larger the coefficient, the smaller is the average distance between dot and arrowhead.

The Psychometric Definition of Intelligence

In order to construct a mental space reflecting the cognitive abilities used in the workforce, psychometricians test people on a great many problems and analyze the results to see if a small set of relatively general abilities emerges. There is a good deal of debate over whether or not this has happened. Some psychometricians think that as many as 100 separate abilities are needed to define the mental space. At the other extreme are those who argue that all sorts of examples of thinking can be reduced to a single quantity: general intelligence. I think the truth lies in between. One ability will not do, but only a few are needed for most purposes.

Many definitions of mental ability reflect those skills taught in the schools. Psychologists construct tests that cover the academic subjects—arithmetic, text comprehension, geometry, history, and the like—and derive the mental space by analyzing data from those tests. Over and over again, psychometricians have found evidence for verbal comprehension ability, spatial-visual reasoning ability, and (somewhat less strongly) logical reasoning ability, apart from the content of a problem (Carroll, 1982). I will refer to this finding as the "standard model" of psychometrics.

A problem with the standard model is that since it begins with an analysis of academic thinking, it cannot capture any dimension of human thought that lies outside the academic field. Howard Gardner, a professor at Harvard University, made this point elegantly in *Frames of Mind: The Theory of Multiple Intelligences* (1983). He argued that in addition to the academic subjects, human activity encompasses such abilities as musical and artistic creativity, social sensitivity, and even physical movement. Gardner believed that these abilities must be considered part of intelligence and, therefore, we must extend our idea of a basic space of mental ability well beyond verbal, spatial-visual, and logical reasoning abilities.

Although a great deal has been made of Gardner's argument in terms of the philosophical definition of intelligence, logically he just expanded the standard model by adding more dimensions rather than changing it in a fundamental way. In fact, whether or not the expansion is required is an empirical issue rather than a logical one. Gardner is right to the extent that a person's abilities in music, art, social situations, and physical performances *cannot* be predicted by knowing their position in the mental space of the standard model.[2]

In the context of this book, we do not care whether the standard model or Gardner's expansion of it is "correct" in an ultimate sense. We are interested in what model works best on a case-by-case basis. Sometimes it will be possible to predict performance using a model of intelligence based on academic reasoning, and sometimes it will not. Hand-eye coordination, for instance, is probably essential for a watch repairer and irrelevant for a lawyer.

Gardner's viewpoint is diametrically opposed to the *general intelligence* theory of mental competence, which asserts that intelligence is almost a one-dimensional affair; people who are above or below average at one mental endeavor are likely to be above or below average at another. If this were true in all situations, then the three dimensions of the standard model, or the dozen or so intelligences of Gardner's model, could be collapsed into a single line representing *general intelligence*, usually denoted by *G*.

The general intelligence theory was first raised by the British psychometrician Charles Spearman (1904, 1923). His position has vigorous champions today, notably Arthur Jensen (professor of education at the University of California, Berkeley) and Hans Eysenck (professor emeritus at the University of London). Richard Herrnstein and Charles Murray (1994) have claimed that many of the social, educational, and economic inequalities in the United States today are driven by individual differences in general intelligence. As would be expected, this proposal has generated a great deal of controversy.

The evidence for general intelligence is based on a well-established fact. Virtually all studies of human intelligence find positive correlations between measures of verbal ability and reasoning ability, and even some (lower) correlations between these abilities and spatial-visual reasoning. To simplify, people who do well on verbal tests usually, but not always, do well on nonverbal tests. The same statement applies to many other test pairs. Spearman concluded that this was evidence for a general "mental fitness" variable, that is, general intelligence.

Jensen (1982) and Eysenck (1986), among others, believe that individual differences in general intelligence are closely tied to individual differences in brain functioning, which are mostly determined by genetics. Their position has stirred quite a bit of social controversy. Fortunately for our purposes, this controversy is virtually irrelevant to workforce projections. We are interested in what the implications of intelligence test scores are for the workforce, not in how the test takers came to have these scores.

What is important is the extent to which we have to be concerned with "special intelligences" compared with the extent that we should concentrate on measures of general intelligence. This issue is usually posed as being a general one, which applies to almost any workplace or educational situation. A finding by Detterman and Daniel (1989) suggests that this may be an oversimplification. They examined the extent to which different types of mental performances were correlated in high-ability groups (e.g., college students) and in low-intelligence groups (e.g., educable mental retardates). Substandard performances were highly correlated, but above-average performances were not.[3] The results indicate that poor verbal problem solving will be accompanied by poor spatial-visual reasoning, but that very good verbal performance might be accompanied by anywhere from good to below-average spatial-visual reasoning.

If Detterman and Daniel's findings are true over wide populations (and I believe they are), they have an important implication for predicting workforce performance. It appears easier to predict "low-end" performance than "high-end" performance. In other words, it may be more useful to regard test scores as a way of identifying potentially poor performers than as a way of identifying potentially superior performers.

Gardner's theory of multiple intelligences and the Spearman-Eysenck-Jensen theory of general intelligence are clearly endpoints on a continuum, with the standard view, that there are a small number of basic mental abilities, in an intermediate position. Raymond Cattell (1972) and his collaborator John Horn (1986) have proposed a somewhat different view of the mental space. As will be shown in subsequent chapters, it is a useful way of thinking about intelligence in the workforce.

Cattell and Horn identify three major dimensions for individual differences in cognition—spatial-visual reasoning and two types of more abstract abilities: *crystallized intelligence* and *fluid intelligence.* Crystallized intelligence (symbolized by *Gc*) is "the ability to apply culturally developed, acquired problem solving methods when they are appropriate." Fluid intelligence (*Gf*) is "the ability to develop new solutions to novel problems." The best way to appreciate the difference between *Gc* and *Gf* is to look at some examples of how they are measured.

Vocabulary tests are prototypical measures of *Gc*, since vocabulary is simply memorized.

Gf can be measured by observing how people react to new and unusual problems. An attempt is made to minimize the possibility that people will have learned "culturally approved solutions" (the definition of *Gc*) that work on the test problems. In order to do this, many tests of fluid intelligence consist of nonverbal problems, such as asking people to discover a pattern hidden in geometric designs. This will be illustrated in more detail in Chapter 3, where we look at some of the commonly used tests. For now, the thing to remember is that fluid intelligence is, by definition, the ability to reason about novel situations.

Horn and his colleagues point out that most real-world problems can be solved by applying either fluid or crystallized intelligence. Chess is a good example. Learning to play chess is an exercise in fluid intelligence, as one has to learn how to deal with an unfamiliar situation. Play at the master and grand master level seems to be much more an exercise in crystallized intelligence. When highly skilled players encounter chess problems, their solution methods rely a great deal on knowledge of previously used attacks and defenses. Novices seem to spend more time in original problem solving (Charness, 1989, 1991).

Which of these theories is *the correct* theory of intelligence? Much can be said for all of them. Some reviewers have concluded that the Horn-Cattell model is the best statistical summary of the available evidence on intelligence test performance (Carroll, 1992; Gustafsson, 1988; Snow, 1986). However, it is generally agreed that the fluid-crystallized theory and different variations on the standard model often lead to the same predictions. For the purposes of this book, the two theories can be thought of as alternative views of the same phenomenon. Three important generalizations are:

1. Verbal reasoning and spatial-visual reasoning are clearly separate dimensions of human thought. This is acknowledged by virtually every theorist.

2. Education, training, and communication in our society tend to be highly verbal. This fact has been deplored by some, who have argued for a "liberation" of spatial-visual reasoning (e.g., Fincher, 1976). However this may be, the ability to manipulate language is and will remain an important part of human mental capacity.

3. The different abilities respond differently to social, physical, and demographic changes. In general, verbal ability and crystallized intelligence measures are responsive to education, but are surprisingly unresponsive to biological insults, including old age.[4] Fluid intelligence (and general reasoning, which is much the same thing) and spatial-visual reasoning seem to be sensitive to aging and to other biological factors (Horn 1985).

Most personnel selection tests used in the United States today are based on a variation of the standard model. The mental space representation underlies the Armed Services Vocational Aptitude Battery (ASVAB), used by the Department of Defense; the Scholastic Aptitude

Test (SAT), used widely in education; and the General Aptitude Test Battery (GATB), used by the Department of Labor. These tests are discussed in some detail in Chapter 3, along with two widely used psychological tests, the Raven Progressive Matrix Test and the Wechsler Adult Intelligence Scale, which are better thought of in terms of either the *Gc-Gf* distinction or as indicators of general intelligence.

All this discussion has to do with predictors . . . the measures that we use to estimate performance. The other side of the equation is the criterion measure . . . how do we decide what performance actually is?

Measuring the Criterion

The idea behind psychometric prediction is that a worker's performance can be related statistically to test scores. This approach only makes sense if workplace performance itself can be evaluated. Doing so is called *criterion measurement.* It turns out to be a difficult task.

Wigdor and Green (1991) offer an interesting case: the selection of aviation cadets during World War II. In the early stages of the war, only about 30 percent of the volunteers for pilot training succeeded in winning their wings. The Army Air Force then developed a very successful paper and pencil cognitive test for pilot selection. Over 75 percent of the cadets in the two top categories of the selection test completed flight training. Less than 10 percent of the cadets in the bottom category did. But, as Wigdor and Green point out, getting one's wings is only the beginning of a career as an aviator. During 1944 and 1945 the navy conducted a series of interviews in which combat pilots were asked to rate each other. There was virtually no statistical relation between the cognitive tests and performance as a combat pilot. The army reached a similar conclusion (Wigdor and Green, 1991, pp. 23–25).

The World War II study epitomizes the problems and potentials of workforce prediction. Most strikingly, it illustrates the difference between training and performance. Both are legitimate aspects of a job, since people who cannot complete training never get to perform. Also, the costs of training may be a significant part of the costs of labor. Training is often relatively easy to evaluate and is reasonably well predicted by psychometric tests. Performance is quite another matter.[5] This study also illustrates the difference between clear-cut, objective criteria and rating data. Graduation from flight school is a recordable fact; it either happened or it did not. Ratings are subjective evaluations of how well other people think a person is doing his or her job. Performance and reputation are not the same things. Cognitive tests are consistently more accurate at predicting performance measures than predicting ratings.

Given these arguments, one might think that virtually all studies of personnel selection since World War II would have focused on the use of test scores to predict objective indices of on-the-job performance. In fact, studies that use test scores to predict peer or (more often) supervisor ratings are far more common than studies that try to predict objective performance measures. Why is this?

In many cases, the relevant data are simply not available. For instance, virtually every company records the number of sales it makes by store and by day, but many companies do not record the sales made by each salesperson. Indeed, in some cases labor agreements may prevent management from recording performance at the individual level.

There is also an intellectual objection to overreliance on objective but limited measurements of performance. Once a supervisor begins to record one aspect of performance, that limited aspect quickly comes to drive overall assessments. This can be unfortunate, since there are very few jobs in which any one measure adequately reflects a person's total job skills.

Many observers believe that occupations requiring a great deal of interaction with other people and the exercise of judgment are most difficult to evaluate. Scientists, medical and legal professionals, and educators have been particularly vocal in deriding objective evaluations of their performance. They argue that only knowledgeable individuals who are familiar with their on-the-job performance can evaluate them.

Let us return to the use of rating forms as criteria. In most cases this means a supervisor's rating of an employee. The argument for ratings by supervisors is that supervisors are able to integrate all aspects of job performance into an overall assessment. Indeed, a case can be made for the argument that a person is a good employee if the boss is happy! It is well known, however, that performance rating scales are affected by variables other than job performance. Social interactions between rater and ratee are clearly important and probably contribute to the notoriously low correlations that are found when two different raters rate the same people. Raters also have difficulty distinguishing between specific aspects of performance and the rater's overall impression of the ratee. This is the well-known "halo" effect, where people are seen as being uniformly good or bad.

More ominously, raters may react to variables other than legitimate criteria for job performance, such as physical attractiveness or social compatibility between rater and ratee. Racial issues are particularly touchy. In at least some situations black and white raters systematically give higher ratings to members of their own racial groups than to members of other groups (Ford, Kraiger, and Schectman, 1986).

This leaves us on the horns of a dilemma. Both productivity records and ratings have serious shortcomings. One solution is to conduct studies in which the researchers themselves choose measures that are appropriate for the sort of evaluation being performed. (Chapter 3 describes one such study, by the U.S. Army.) From a scientific point of view, such controlled studies are probably the best way to design a prediction experiment. Unfortunately, controlled measurement can be very expensive.

Researchers who have conducted studies using controlled or objective measures virtually all agree on one important point: Job performance is multidimensional. Therefore, whether or not psychometric tests can be designed to predict job performance often depends on precisely how job performance is measured. In the army study just referred to, enlisted soldiers were given written tests of job knowledge and were rated by their supervisors. The soldiers' job knowledge was substantially correlated with their scores on psychometric tests taken as much as two years earlier. There was a much lower relationship between the soldiers' job knowledge and the supervisors' rating of job performance.

Thus, Figure 2.1 is somewhat deceptive. The problem is not one of predicting from a space of mental abilities to a line representing job performance, but from a space of mental abilities to another, at least as complicated, space of job performance. Unfortunately, this fact is often not acknowledged.

Given these complexities, it is hardly surprising to find many studies showing that "intelligence tests do not predict this or that measure of real-world competence." But is the problem with the intelligence test or the criterion measure of competence? If the problem is with the criterion measure, as it often is, the statistics relating psychometric test scores to subsequent job or educational performance are virtually certain to underestimate the relation between the tests and some "true" measure of quality of work.

In spite of all these logical problems, in many situations the only feasible course is to act as if we had a single predictor of "ability" and a single measure of "productivity." What next? The following section describes the statistical issues involved in predicting employability.

STATISTICAL ISSUES IN PREDICTION

Correlation and Regression

This section deals with some important technical issues about the use of test scores to predict performance. Some parts of the argument will be familiar to those who have had an elementary course in statistics. Other material will be new.

The relation between test scores (x) and performance scores (y) is expressed by the Pearson or *product-moment* correlation coefficient, usually denoted by the letter r. This is a measure of association between two variables, x and y, with the following properties:

1. The value of r ranges from 1 to −1.
2. If r = 1, x and y are perfectly associated. That is, the value of x can be predicted exactly if the value of y is known and that of y if x is known.
3. If r = 0, there is no association between x and y.

Intermediate values of r indicate intermediate levels of associations. For instance, the correlation between the heights and weights of adult males is about .5, which indicates that tall people tend to be heavy, and vice versa, but there are exceptions.

Negative values of r indicate that high values of x are associated with low values of y. Since a negative value of r could always be changed into a positive value by multiplying one of the variables by −1, the degree of association between x and y is measured by the absolute value of r, not by its direction.

We expect that both test and predictor measures will vary across people. The *standard deviation* (written s(x) or s(y), for measures x and y) expresses the extent of the variation. If we can assume that the measure in question follows the normal distribution (the familiar "bell curve" found in many situations), two useful facts about the standard deviation are helpful:

1. In a normally distributed population two thirds of all scores will be within one standard deviation of the mean. To take an example from IQ testing, if the mean IQ of a group is 100 and the standard deviation is 15, two thirds of all people tested should have scores between 85 and 115.
2. In a normally distributed population, 95 percent of the scores will lie within approximately two standard deviations of mean. Continuing with the IQ example, we would expect 95 percent of the scores to fall between 70 and 130.

The *variance* is the square of the standard deviation. This will be written $s^2(x)$ or $s^2(y)$, as appropriate. There are mathematically interesting relationships between the variances of x and y and the correlation

$(r(x,y))$ between the two scores, but these are not very important for our purposes. See Edwards (1984) for a further discussion of this point.

Regression Analysis: Using Tests to Estimate On-the-Job Productivity

Suppose that we do a "perfect experiment," in which all applicants for a job are given a predictor test, such as the ASVAB or GATB, and then all are hired and their on-the-job performance is measured. We want to analyze the data in order to find out how well the test predicts performance.

To do this, psychometricians begin by assuming that there is a linear relationship between variables. This means that the performance score for individual i can be expressed as

$$Y_i^* = bX_i + A, \quad A, b \text{ constants,} \tag{2.2}$$

where X_i is person i's score on the predictor test, and Y_i^* is the predicted performance based on that test. In most cases actual performance, Y_i, is not identical to predicted performance. The difference between the two is the error in prediction for person i, E_i,

$$E_i = (Y_i^* - Y_i). \tag{2.3}$$

Figure 2.2 illustrates how this works. The figure shows some hypothetical data. The line slanting upward from left to right is the *regression line*. Mathematically, it is defined by Equation 2.2. A is the point at which the regression line intercepts the ordinate. This can be thought of as the predicted performance score for someone who received a score of zero on the predictor test, a situation that seldom actually occurs. The b term is the *regression coefficient*. It can be thought of as the increase in predicted performance for every unit increase on a person's test score.

To see how this applies to the individual case, consider a person who obtained a score of 120 on the predictor test. To predict this person's performance graphically, you would draw a vertical line from the 120 score on the test score axis up to the regression line, then draw a horizontal line from that point on the regression line across to the performance score axis, to obtain the predicted performance level. In this case the predicted performance would be about 106. To see how this is useful, suppose the test had not been used. Then we would have had to predict that every individual, including our example person, would be "average" and, thus, achieve a performance score of 100. By using the test information, we may adjust our performance. The adjustment

Figure 2.2   Hypothetical data generated from a population with test-performance correlation of .5; sample correlation .43.

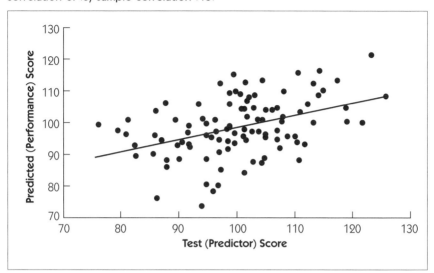

will not be perfect. If it were, all the points in Figure 2.2 would lie on the regression line, which they obviously do not. However, the predicted score would be more accurate, on the average, than a guess that everyone would achieve the mean performance score.

Extending the example, all points above the regression line represent individuals whose performance scores were higher than predicted from their test scores, while points below the regression line represent individuals whose scores were lower than predicted.

The next step is to explain how values were chosen for A and b in Equation 2.2, and how this relates to the correlation coefficient. If prediction were perfect ($r = 1$), the data points for all individuals would lie on the regression line. In this case E_i would be zero for every case, i. We want to choose values A and b that bring us as close to this situation as possible.

E_i is a value associated with an individual, just as X_i and Y_i are. Therefore, we can consider the error term, e, as a variable with its own standard deviation, $s(e)$ and variance, $s^2(e)$. In regression analysis values of A and b are chosen so that the expected value of e is zero ($E(e) = 0$) and the variance of e is minimized. If prediction were perfect, all points E_i would be zero, so both $E(e)$ and $s^2(e)$ would be zero. This ideal is seldom achieved. For instance, the regression line in Figure 2.2 was chosen to minimize $s^2(e)$, but there clearly are nonzero error terms.

Now consider the case in which there is no relationship between

Figure 2.3 Data from Figure 2.2 with added noise to reduce the correlation to .22.

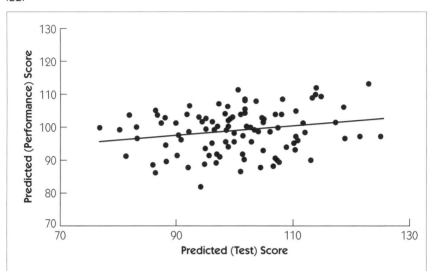

test and performance measures, that is, $r = 0$. The regression line will be flat, with $b = 0$ and A equal to the mean value of the performance score. (This amounts to predicting that everyone will have average performance, regardless of their test score.) The variance of the error term will be equal to the variance in the score being predicted, $s^2(e) = s^2(y)$.

In virtually all practical situations the correlation coefficient has a value intermediate between zero and one. Therefore, it is important to develop some intuitions about what different intermediate values mean. As one would expect, there is a precise algebraic definition. The square of the validity coefficient is the percentage of variance in the criterion (performance) score that is associated with the predictor score.[6] Unfortunately, the algebraic definition is not intuitive and can even be misleading. A better way of understanding the meaning of validity coefficients is to look at a concrete example.

Figure 2.2 shows some hypothetical data in which the correlation between the predictor and criterion score is .43. This is well within the range of the population validity coefficients obtained in industrial situations. Figure 2.3 shows a distortion of the same data, in which the validity coefficient is .22. In each case the regression line was calculated so that the average error in prediction is zero. However, the variance of the error term is smaller in Figure 2.2 than in Figure 2.3. More importantly, note how the regression lines have changed. In Figure 2.2.

the regression line is slanted. This means that we would predict substantially different performance scores for two individuals who had markedly different test scores. In Figure 2.3 the regression line is nearly flat, which means that there would be very little difference in the predicted scores for two individuals with different test scores.

A glance at Figures 2.2 and 2.3 shows that higher test scores are generally, but not invariably, associated with higher performance. Therefore, on the assumption that it is fair to the employer to hire better workers, and fair to two applicants if the apparently best qualified applicant is hired, it follows that the use of screening tests is good. This is what should be done:

1. Conduct a study to determine the validity coefficient and regression equation between test score and on-the-job performance. Be sure that the observed correlation is not the result of chance fluctuations.[7]
2. Define a minimum acceptable performance level.
3. Employ only those individuals whose predicted score is at or above this level.
4. If there are more qualified people than there are jobs, hire people in order of their predictor test scores until all jobs are filled.

The first step is to determine the validity coefficient, since everything hangs on its being reliably greater than zero. In theory, this is simple, but in practice there are two problems: *restriction in range* and *reduced validity due to unreliability of measurement.*

Restriction in Range

By definition, the validity coefficient is the correlation between job performance and test score, calculated over the entire applicant pool. In the ideal design the validity coefficient is determined by giving applicants a predictor test and then *hiring all of them, regardless of test score,* so that their performance scores can be observed. In practice this procedure could be expensive, because it requires the employer to hire unqualified applicants during the test development phase. So, the ideal design is seldom feasible. Two somewhat less satisfactory designs are substituted for it.

1. If the goal is to evaluate a new test, give the test to all current employees. By definition, all of these individuals will be per-

Figure 2.4 Relation between predictor and criterion scores.

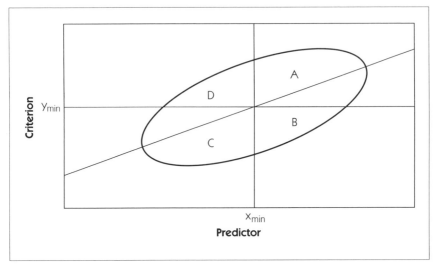

forming at or above the minimum acceptable level. A regression analysis is conducted on the reduced set of data.

2. If the goal is to evaluate a test that is already being used for hiring decisions, data will be available only for those individuals who had test scores above the preliminary cut score (since they had to be hired) and whose performance levels are satisfactory (since the employer has continued to employ them). The regression analysis is conducted on these employees.

Figure 2.4 illustrates what happens in each case. Suppose that we define minimum levels of acceptable performance (Y_{min}) and a minimum cut score (X_{min}). These scores divide the space of scores into four regions. Region A contains individuals whose test scores are above the cut level and whose performance level is satisfactory. Region B contains individuals whose test scores are adequate, but whose performance is not. Region C contains individuals whose test scores and performance levels are inadequate. Region D contains individuals whose test scores are below the cut point, but whose performance is adequate. In a case of perfect prediction $(r = 1)$, all scores would either be in region A (correct acceptances) or region C (appropriate rejections). Regions B and D fill up only to the extent that prediction is imperfect.

In the ideal design regression analysis is applied to data points in all four regions. In reduced design (1), where all current employees are given a new test, data are collected from regions A and D. In reduced design (2), where an existing test is to be validated, data are collected only from region A.

The statistics obtained from the ideal design and the reduced designs may differ substantially. This can be illustrated by continuing the example of Figure 2.2. Recall that the validity coefficient for this example, based on all data, is .43. Suppose that we establish minimum predictor scores (for being hired) of 100 and minimum performance scores (for staying employed) of 100. If design 1 is used, where all current employees (performance scores of 100 or above) are given the test the validity coefficient is .34. If design 2 is used, where we restrict our attention to employees who have both predictor and performance scores of 100 or more, the correlation is only .22.

These issues can be summarized by the following rule: If predictor and criterion measures are normally distributed in the applicant population, estimates of the validity coefficient based on measurements of current jobholders will underestimate the validity coefficient in the applicant population as a whole.

The problems introduced by restriction of range are statistical technicalities, in the sense that they are introduced solely by properties of the normal distribution. The next problem to be considered is more conceptual.

The Unreliability of Measurement

A supervisor's rating of an employee's worth to a company is an estimate of that worth, not the worth itself. By the same token, an intelligence or aptitude test is an estimate of the underlying psychological quality and should not be confused with the quality itself.

The distinction can be expressed mathematically. Let x be a measurement that purports to be an estimate of an underlying property, x_T. To be concrete, suppose that x is an intelligence test. Then for every individual, that individual's test score, X_i, should be considered an estimate of "true intelligence," X_{Ti}. It is important to realize that in this situation the true score, X_{Ti}, is a conceptual entity and cannot be measured directly. The same argument holds for criterion variables: for instance, if y were a rating of productivity and y_T were "true productivity."

Psychometricians assume that the observable measures, x, consist of a true score component and an error component, ∂, that varies randomly with the test and the individual. Therefore, if individual i were to take an aptitude test, yielding score X_i, and have his/her performance rated, producing score Y_i, the following relationships would hold:

$$X_i = X_{Ti} + \partial_{xi} \tag{2.4a}$$

$$Y_i = Y_{Ti} + \partial_{yi}. \tag{2.4b}$$

By the definition of random errors, the ∂ terms have an expected value of zero and do not correlate with any other variables.

This has an important implication. Suppose that we were to make two measurements of intelligence (or productivity) on the same individuals. For instance, we might give each individual two different intelligence tests and at the same time have their performance rated by two different judges. Call these measures x and x', and y and y', where the ' indicates the second test. Equations 2.4a and 2.4b would apply to the x' and y' measures (with X' substituted for X and Y' for Y). Furthermore, and most important, the correlations between the two equivalent tests, $r(x,x')$ and $r(y,y')$, would be less than one. (To see the reasonableness of this nonmathematically, suppose that we asked two judges to rate the performance of several workers. We would not expect them to agree perfectly, even if they were trying to judge the same qualities.)

In technical terms, $r(x,x')$ and $r(y,y')$ are called the *reliability coefficients* of tests x and y. Nonmathematically, the reliability coefficient specifies the relationship between two tests, each of which is an attempt to measure the same underlying variable using the same method.

Reliability coefficients set upper bounds on validity coefficients. Suppose, for instance, that we were interested in determining the relationship between the *abstract variables* of intelligence and worker productivity. In algebraic terms, this means that we would want to determine the correlation $r(x_T,y_T)$ between true scores underlying the observed measures of intelligence and productivity. The statistic cannot be computed directly, since true scores cannot be measured. On the other hand, we can compute the correlations between two observable measures, $r(x,y)$ and compute the reliabilities of each measure, $r(x,x')$ and $r(y,y')$. A well-known result in statistical theory relates these values to each other. The expected value of $r(x,y)$ is

$$E(r(x,y)) = r(x,x')r(x_T,y_T)r(y,y'). \tag{2.5}$$

This means that a best estimate of the correlation between underlying values, expressed in observables, is

$$r(x_T,y_T) = r(x,y)/[r(x,x')r(y,y')]. \tag{2.6}$$

To see how much difference this can make, let us return to the example provided earlier: If the ideal design is used, the correlation between *measured* aptitude and productivity is .43. Based on previous research, it would be reasonable to assume that the reliability of a measure of aptitude is about .90 and that the reliability of measurement of productivity ratings is .75. Therefore, the best estimate of the relation between *conceptual* productivity and aptitude is $r(x_T, y_T) = .43/(.9 \cdot .75) = .64$, which is 50 percent higher than the correlation between observable measures.

As the example illustrates, corrections for unreliability of measurement can be substantial. The problems are usually greatest because of criterion unreliability. Ratings are especially a problem. When the same people are rated by different judges, the correlations between ratings may be as low as .5. Reliabilities of objective measurements tend to be much higher. Most tests of aptitude and intelligence have reliability coefficients in the .8 to .95 range.

In addition, corrections for range restriction and for reliability are independent. This means that if it makes sense to apply each of them, on their own, it makes equal sense to apply both of them. In our example, one might reasonably observe a correlation between test scores and productivity of .22 (design 2), and then argue that the real correlation between intelligence and productivity is .64, practically three times the observed value. In fact, though, I think that most (not all) professional psychometricians would be concerned about this degree of extrapolation from "observed" to "true" results. When are the corrections appropriate?

The Debate about Corrected Validity Estimates

The algebraic manipulations needed to estimate the value of the actual correlation from the observed correlation are well known. Equation 2.6 can be used to correct for unreliability of measurement. While the mathematical derivations are more complicated than would be appropriate to discuss here, corrections for restriction in range are equally feasible (Dunbar and Linn, 1992). Nevertheless, well-qualified experts disagree vehemently about reporting corrected or observed coefficients. Probably the most common procedure is to report observed values, although some scientists routinely report corrected coefficients and present compelling arguments for doing so.

The debate is not confined to the scholarly journals. When the U.S. Department of Labor (1983b) reported validity coefficients for the GATB, they corrected for both unreliability and restriction in range. A National Research Council committee convened to review the same test concluded that neither correction should be used (Hartigan and Wigdor, 1989, p. 170). It is unlikely that we can resolve the debate here. However, some observations may be helpful.

The chief argument against correcting for reliability is that the observed reliability coefficients are themselves estimates of population values. Any error in the estimates of reliability will be magnified by the correction process. In some cases the magnification can be so great that the "corrected coefficient" exceeds one. Since this is a logical impossibility, it is understandable that many people distrust corrections for unreliability.[8]

Correcting for reliability is appropriate if our interest is in the conceptual variables underlying the observed measurements. Such corrections would be appropriate, for instance, in a study that tried to establish the relationship between "intelligence," as an abstract property, and "worker productivity," which is an equally abstract property. Since some of the discussions in this book are concerned with these relations, from time to time corrections for reliability will be used.

Correcting for reliability is not appropriate if the goal is to select a test for use in hiring. In such situations observable performance has to be predicted from actual test scores, not from a hypothetical variable that may underlie test scores. Therefore, the prediction has to be made in the face of any unreliability in the test and the criterion measures.

The issue of correcting for restriction in range is somewhat more complicated. The validity of the correction depends on three assumptions:

1. That the relationship between predictor and criterion scores is linear *throughout the entire population,* not just the population tested. The technical term for this is the assumption of *linearity.*

2. That the accuracy of the test as a predictor of performance is the same for all values of test scores; that is, low scores predict bad performance as accurately as high scores predict good performance. The technical term is *homoscedasticity of variance.*[9]

3. That the estimator knows the relation between the range of variation of test scores in the population tested and in the entire population. This will be called *identifiability of the referent population.*

Whenever our observations are confined to the performance of people already employed, assumptions (1) and (2) must be taken on faith. What happens if the assumptions are wrong depends on how they are violated. In some circumstances the corrected validity coefficients will overestimate the true validity; in other cases they will underestimate it (Dunbar and Linn, 1992). Rather than treat this issue statistically, it is more useful to consider the circumstances in which such violations might arise.

Nonlinearity will occur if the relationship between the performance and the predictor variable changes across performance levels. The Army Air Force study offers an example. The ability to learn to fly, a minimal level of combat pilot performance, was predicted by the test, while the ability to be a good combat pilot, a much higher level of performance, was not. Therefore, if one were to evaluate the validity of the predictor test, based only on the performance of combat pilots, a correction for restriction in range would underpredict validity in the applicant population.

More generally, virtually every study that has reviewed the field has found that the correlations between job performance and measures of cognitive ability decrease as people gain experience in their jobs (Ackerman and Humphreys, 1991). Indeed, there are excellent theoretical reasons why this should be so (Ackerman, 1987). In most situations inter-individual variability decreases as people learn a task, because everyone's performance approaches the best possible performance. This would have the effect of decreasing both the correlation and regression between job performance and predictor test scores.

Another widely observed finding is that the correlations between productivity measures and mental test scores are low in jobs requiring creativity or innovation (Simonton, 1988). As a result some people have argued that creativity and intelligence are different attributes. A closer look at the studies shows that this is not quite correct. Creative and innovative individuals seldom have low mental ability scores, but people with high mental ability scores are not always creative or innovative.

A more general conclusion may be that in virtually every job a certain level of mental ability is required in order to perform acceptably. Superior performance is achieved partly through ability, but also through motivation and personality factors. As the performance level increases *within the same job,* mental ability becomes relatively less important, while personality and motivation become relatively more important. Of course, if increased performance results in a change of job assignment, then the relation between performance and mental ability may go up or down, depending on the nature of the change.[10]

The gist of these arguments is that the relation between job performance and cognitive aptitude measures will normally be greater in the population of people considered not qualified for the job, and hence not measured, than in the population of jobholders, who were measured. If anything, correcting for restrictions in range will underestimate the population correlation between job productivity and test performance. Certainly it would be excessively conservative *not* to correct for range restriction. But assumption (3), identifiability of the referent population, complicates the issue.

Suppose we assume that the mathematical model for range restriction does hold. This means that *in the population* the predictor and criterion measures are distributed normally, with variances $S^2(x)$ and $S^2(y)$, respectively, and with a correlation r between them. However, all we can look at are those people who were tested and hired (region A) in Figure 2.4. The restricted set of scores will have variances $S_A^2(x)$ and $S_A^2(y)$, respectively, will be correlated with value r_A, where $r_A < r$, and will not be normally distributed. Also, by definition, if x percent of the applicant population is hired, the scores must represent the top x percent of scores on predictor test. This is called the *selection ratio.* For instance, if the "best 10 percent" are hired, the scores must represent the top tenth of predictor test scores.

Without going into the details of the model, it should be clear that there is a mathematical function relating $S^2(x)$, $S^2(y)$, and r to $S_A^2(x)$, $S_A^2(y)$, and r_A, and vice versa. Therefore, if we know one set of values, we can work out the second. This is true, providing that we know the relevant selection ratio. An estimate of r based on an observed r_A and a mistaken selection ratio may be a very bad estimate, indeed. In particular, if the selection ratio is underestimated (e.g., if we assume that the top 10 percent were hired, when in fact the top 20 percent were), correcting for range can substantially overestimate the value of the validity coefficient in the population.

This situation has arisen in practice, and the example is instructive. Recall that when the Department of Labor (1983b) based estimates of the validity coefficient of the GATB on correlations that were corrected for range restriction, a review panel objected to the correction. The objection was based on disagreement about the appropriate selection ratio. Simplifying somewhat, the Department of Labor estimate was based on a selection ratio calculated by taking the ratio (number of people qualified for a job)/(size of U.S. workforce). The review panel pointed out that job applicants are almost always a self-selected group, so the appropriate ratio should be (number of jobholders)/(number of people interested in the position). To take a specific example, should the selection ratio for medical school be (number of first-year students)/(number of graduating seniors) or (number of first-year students)/(number of applicants to medical school)? The review panel argued that the second ratio is much more likely to be appropriate and that it would always be much larger than the first ratio. Therefore, the Department of Labor must have overestimated the validity coefficients for the GATB. The review panel recommended not using the correction at all (Hartigan and Wigdor, 1989, pp. 166–167).[11]

Since the review panel's argument seems unassailable, why was an improper range restriction ever applied? There were probably two reasons. First, for the nonstatistical reasons given above, we believe that the corrected validity estimates will underestimate the population validity when the correct selection ratio is used. Therefore, doing nothing, as the panel recommended, can be attacked as being overly conservative. Second, obtaining the data required to compute "perfect" selection ratios would be a practical impossibility. One can find out what percentage of the U.S. workforce are, say, real estate agents, by consulting regularly published government statistics. Finding out what percentage wants to be real estate agents would be a much harder endeavor.

So, should we correct for restriction in range or not? A recent article advises

> To retain observed values gives an extremely misleading view of the relationship between predictor and criterion variables, but to correct observed values places one at the mercy of assumptions that will not be strictly satisfied in practice. . . . A balanced indication of the quality of a given predictor can be achieved by reporting both uncorrected and corrected validity coefficients, and by a careful documentation of the methods used to obtain the corrected estimates. (Dunbar and Linn, 1992, p. 154.)

Not all questions have simple answers. And in this case, we do need to have an accurate answer. To see why, we consider what happens when selection is, or is not, based on test use.

SELECTING INDIVIDUALS BASED ON TEST STATISTICS

Correlation and Selection

To what extent is personnel selection improved or distorted by using tests of varying degrees of accuracy? A naive but discouragingly common approach to this question is to focus solely on the validity correlation. The literature contains recommendations that certain ranges of validity be considered evidence of "low," "moderate," or "high" relationships between predictor and criterion variables. In fact, there are some situations in which a "low" correlation (r in the .2 range) can be quite useful and others in which a "high" correlation (r in the .8 range) hardly helps at all. To explain how this happens, we need to consider the effects of variation in the selection ratio.

The precise definition of the selection ratio is s = (number of positions to be filled)/(number of applicants). For example, if 100 applicants apply for 10 jobs, s = $10/100$ = .10.

The effectiveness of selection can be expressed by the efficiency ratio, which is $E(r,s)$ = (number of successes)/(number hired). If 9 of the 10 people hired had successful careers with a company, E would be .9. An alternative interpretation is that E is the probability that a person who is selected will perform satisfactorily. From an employer's view, a test is useful when it increases efficiency. *The extent to which a predictor increases efficiency depends on both the validity correlation, r, and the selection ratio, s.*

More precisely, $E(r,s)$ increases with r and decreases with s. This reflects two commonsense notions. The first is that efficiency will increase if we use better predictors. The second is that if we have a large number of applicants for a small number of jobs (s low), we can set standards high and have few failures. On the other hand, if we have only a few applicants for a large number of jobs (s high), we have to take what we can get and must expect failures.

These points hardly require mathematical proof. What is interesting is the relationship between them, that is, why having a high validity coefficient is of interest only at certain levels of selection. Some notation is needed to present the argument.

As before, we represent the ith applicant by a pair of scores (X_i, Y_i), where X_i is the applicant's score on the predictor test, and Y_i is the level of performance that he or she would demonstrate if given the job. In a perfect selection procedure, candidates should be selected in order of their criterion scores. But, of course, we cannot do this because criterion scores are not available until after applicants are given a job. Therefore, predictor scores are used to substitute for criterion scores in the following way.

Suppose that the selection ratio is s. Define Y_s to be the criterion score such that the fraction s of the applicant pool has a score equal to or higher than Y_s. For instance, if there are 100 applicants and 10 are to be hired, s = .1, as before, and Y_s is the tenth highest criterion score. Another way of thinking of Y_s is that it is the lowest performance that will be seen in the population of successful applicants, once they are on the job, assuming completely efficient selection ($E(r,s)$ = 1).

Since scores on the criterion are not available until after an applicant has been selected, the selector uses the predictor test as a surrogate for the criterion. Instead of ordering candidates by their Y scores (which is what the selector is really interested in), the selector orders candidates by their X scores and selects however many people are needed, in order of predictor scores. This is equivalent to setting a minimum value, X_c, on the predictor variable and accepting everyone with a predictor score higher than X_c. This is the cut score referred to previously. To maintain consistency of notation, assume that X_c is the predictor score that is exceeded by a fraction c of the applicants in the population.

To simplify the argument, I will assume that $c = s$, that is, that the employer hires exactly as many people as are needed to do the job.[12] Efficiency is defined as the percentage of initial employees who are retained after an initial probationary period.

$$E(r,c,s) = \text{probability that person } i \text{ has a criterion} \qquad (2.7)$$
$$\text{score equal to or higher than } Y_s \text{ given that person } i$$
$$\text{has a predictor score above the cutoff point}$$
$$= \text{probability } (Y_i \geq Y_s | X_i \geq X_c).$$

Equivalently, this is the probability that a person will perform successfully given that he or she has passed through the selection procedure with predictor-criterion correlation r, cut point X_c, and selection ratio s.

If the predictor perfectly predicts the criterion ($r = 1$), selection will be perfectly efficient, regardless of the value of the selection ratio. On the other hand, if there is no relation between the predictor and criterion measures, selection will be random. By definition, in a randomly sampled population the probability that a particular score will be equal or greater than Y_s is s. Therefore, we may write

$$E(1,c,s) = s/c \text{ for all } s \text{ and } c, \text{ where } c \geq s. \qquad (2.8)$$
$$E(0,c,s) = s \text{ for all } c \text{ and } s.$$

In the case we are considering, $c = s$, so $E(1,s,s) = 1$.

The benefit per person to be obtained by selecting the fraction c of those applicants with the highest test score is

$$B(r,c,s) = (E(r,c,s) - s). \qquad (2.9)$$

It follows that benefits can be substantial only if s and c are low. In the extreme, if $s = 1$, we take everyone who applies and do not use the test scores.

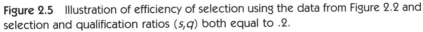

Figure 2.5   Illustration of efficiency of selection using the data from Figure 2.2 and selection and qualification ratios (s,q) both equal to .2.

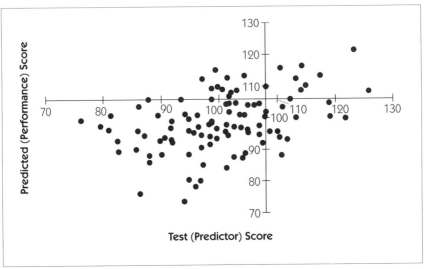

Figures 2.5, 2.6, and 2.7 present an example of the $s = c$ case. These figures were constructed by randomly sampling points for a hypothetical population in which the predictor-criterion correlation was .5. These points were then plotted. The vertical and horizontal lines in the panels correspond to the X_s and Y_s points for selection ratios of .2, .5, and .8. The efficiency of selection can be determined empirically, by comparing the ratio of the number of points above the horizontal line (qualified) and to the right of the vertical line (selected) to the number of points to the right of the vertical line (selected, regardless of qualification). The benefit of using the predictor can then be calculated using Equation 2.9. The results are shown in Table 2.1. Benefits increase as the selection ratio decreases, even though the correlation between the predictor and criterion measures is unchanged. Testing is most useful when there are many applicants for a small number of jobs.

Let us pause to consider what this means in the big picture. Virtually every analysis of economic recovery following the 1990–1991 recession has stressed the loss of permanent jobs. Many observers feel that, due to technological changes, this will be a permanent condition. If these analyses are correct, the future will be characterized by a higher ratio of applicants to jobs than the present is; selection ratios will be lower; and, therefore, employers will have more of an incentive to use screening tests than they do at present.

Figure 2.6 The example of Figure 2.5 repeated with selection and qualification ratios of .5.

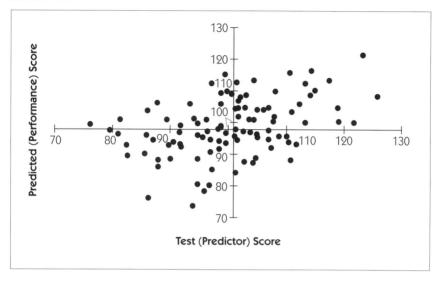

Figure 2.7 Efficiency of selection with $s = q = .8$.

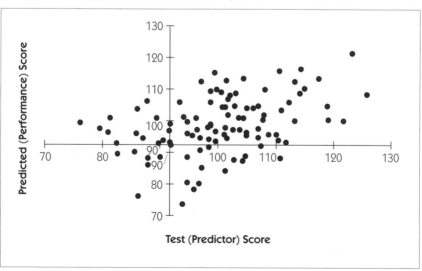

Table 2.1   Data Taken from the Simulated Data Shown in Figures 2.5–2.7

Selection Ratio	Efficiency Ratio $E(r,s)$	Benefit $B(r,s)$
.2	.50	.30
.5	.62	.12
.8	.84	.04

Note: Efficiency ratios and benefits were obtained from selection using the predictor test with a population validity coefficient of .42 and varying the selection ratio.

The figures and Table 2.1 are actually understatements of the normal benefits of selection, because they embody an overly rigid definition of "benefits." The selection case has been presented for the situation in which the selector tries to select exactly the best applicants: the top 10 for 10 positions, the top 20 for 20 positions, and so on. In most selection situations, the goal is to select qualified applicants, but not necessarily the best qualified. Also, in many cases the fraction of applicants who are qualified in the population is greater than the fraction who can be selected. An illustrative case was brought to my attention while I was writing this book: A major forest product company opened a sawmill that would employ about 100 people. Over 500 applied. It is likely that about half of them could have performed well had they been hired. The employer wanted to use tests to make sure that the majority of people hired would, in fact, be qualified. However, the employer did not feel a commitment to hiring exactly the best of the applicants.

This suggests an expansion of Equation 2.5, using an additional parameter. Let q be the fraction of applicants who are qualified in the applicant population, and for simplicity, consider only the $c = s$ case. Then

$$E^*(q,r,s) = \text{probability that a selected person will be qualified.}$$
(2.10)

In the case of perfect selection,

$$E^*(q,1,s) = 1 \text{ if } s \leq q,$$
$$= q/s \text{ otherwise.}$$
(2.11a)

This follows because the selector will first select the qualified, but will be forced to go to the unqualified if there are more positions to fill than there are qualified applicants. In the case of random selection,

Figure 2.8   Selection efficiency as a function of the validity coefficient (*r*) and selection ratio. A qualification coefficient of .3 is assumed.

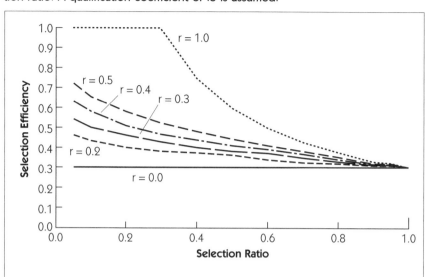

$$E^*(q,0,s) = q. \qquad (2.11b)$$

$E(q = s,r)$ can be thought of as a special case of Equation (2.10) in which $q = s$, which is equivalent to saying that the selector wants to select all available qualified applicants and no one else. Clearly, this is a rather unusual employment situation.

The mathematics for solving the necessary equations are well known (Taylor and Russell 1939). A typical case is shown in Figure 2.8. The figure shows the probability of selecting a qualified person for a job that 30 percent of the population can do, given selection tests with validities ranging from .2 to .5. These figures are well within the values typically found. The efficiency of random selection (validity of zero) and the efficiency of perfect selection (validity of one) are also shown. Actual selection efficiencies have to fall between these extremes. The figure makes it clear that at low selection ratios using tests with modest validity coefficients can make a major change in selection efficiency.

Accuracy of selection is not the only thing to be considered. In order to calculate the economic benefit of a selection program, we also have to consider how much it costs to hire (and then replace) a person who is not qualified.

Let C be the cost to the selector of making a mistake, such as hiring an employee who has to be replaced or admitting a student who cannot complete a course of study. The economic benefit of using a testing program based on a predictor with validity r is

$$EB(q,r,s) = N \times C \times (E^*(q,r,s) - E^*(q,0,s)) - N \times T, \quad (2.12)$$

where N is the number of people to be selected, C is the cost of an incorrect acceptance, T is the cost of testing, and q, r, and s describe the selection situation. The equation summarizes most of the major points. The economic benefits of testing will be highest when C and $E^*(q,r,s)$ are high. A high value of C is an indication that the cost of a mistake is high. For a fixed value of r, a high value of $E^*(q,r,s)$ implies that the selection ratio is low.

To translate these mathematical facts into words: Testing is likely to be most justified in a situation in which relatively few applicants are selected and the cost of failure is high. Two examples that spring to mind are the selection of medical students, where the cost of education exceeds $100,000, and selection programs in military aviation, where the training costs may exceed $1 million. In both cases the selection ratios are very low.

The benefits of testing also vary directly with the number of people to be tested (N in Equation 2.12). Therefore, a testing program for situations in which the selection ratio is high and the cost of a mistake is low can be justified, providing that the programs themselves are very large and that the predictor test is inexpensive.

The statistical and economic arguments can be summed up by these prototypical cases:

1. If you are selecting someone to cut your lawn, don't bother to test. Almost anyone can do the job, and the job can't be done too badly.

2. If you are selecting someone to drive a school bus, fly an airplane, or remove a kidney, a testing program is called for. Relatively few people can do the job (or you don't need very many people doing it) and the costs of a mistake are high.

3. If you are the head groundskeeper at the National Monuments in Washington, DC, you will have to hire many people to mow lawns. A testing program might be worth while.

Some Extensions of the Selection Situation

The argument for psychometric selection has been presented for a situation in which a fixed number of people are to be chosen, from a fixed number of applicants, and each applicant is either qualified or not qualified. In practice, the situation is usually more complicated. We look at how some of the complications can be handled.

In many cases selection is continued until all jobs are filled by qualified personnel. For instance, a city has to hire and train bus drivers until all positions are filled. Costs are incurred when a candidate drops out during training.

To formalize such situations, let N_j = number of positions to be filled; N_r = number of recruits needed to obtain N_j persons who complete training. In this case the purpose of psychometric screening is used to minimize the number of dropouts from training programs. The expected number of recruits needed to fill N_j positions is inversely proportional to $E^*(q,r,s)$:

$$N_r = N_j/E^*(q,r,s). \tag{2.13}$$

Fairly dramatic results can be obtained from modest increases in test validity, providing that the job is fairly difficult (q is low) and the selection ratio is also low. Imagine a situation in which 10 people are needed for a highly selective job, where $q = .05$ (only one person in 20 can do the job well) and $s = .05$ (only one applicant in 20 can be accepted for each training class). If random selection is used, it will be necessary to train an average of 200 people to fill 10 jobs. If the recruits are given a prescreening test with a validity coefficient of only .4, the expected number of trainees is reduced to 52.

A labor market is "favorable to the employer" whenever there are fewer jobs than there are people qualified to do them. In the formal model, this means that $q \geq s$. Not surprisingly, the higher the fraction of qualified applicants in the applicant population, the more chance an employer has of selecting qualified employees. However, variations in the fraction of qualified applicants in the labor market do not markedly change the argument for the use of screening tests. The utility of screening still depends on an interaction between the selection ratio and the validity coefficient. Figure 2.9 shows the relation between selection efficiency and the selection ratio for a test with a validity coefficient of .3, under two different situations. In one case selection is for a fairly easy job, which can be done by 70 percent of the workforce. In the other case selection is for a difficult job, which can be done by only 20 percent of the workforce. In both cases the utility of testing is greatest at low selection ratios.

Whenever the selection ratio exceeds the fraction of qualified workers in the workforce, some inefficiency is bound to result. Consider an idealized case, in which the workforce consists of 100 people, with only

Figure 2.9   Selection efficiency at various levels of qualification (q) and selection ratios. A predictor with validity coefficient .3 is assumed.

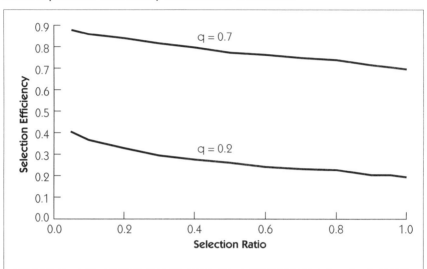

10 persons well qualified for a particular occupation. If industry has to fill 15 jobs, then 5 of the people hired are going to be "not well qualified," even if screening is perfect $(r = 1)$. This is shown by the $r = 1$ line in Figure 2.8.

The efficiency of selection can be greatly increased, regardless of the selection ratio or validity of the predictor, by increasing the fraction of qualified people in the population. Figure 2.9 makes this point dramatically. The figure can be looked at as a mathematical illustration of the arguments that governments make when they urge industry to relocate to their jurisdiction to take advantages of a well-educated workforce. We will return to this point in later chapters, when we consider the economic benefits of training and general education.

In many realistic situations people do not fall sharply into "qualified" and "not qualified" categories. Instead, we are concerned with the mean qualification of the individuals hired. Not surprisingly, this depends on how successful we are in identifying the best people among our applicants. Of course, this is what a predictor test is supposed to do.

The expected value of the performance of accepted candidates can be calculated if the predictor validity coefficient and selection ratio are known (Zeidner and Johnson, 1989, pp. 2–9; see also Cronbach and Gleser, 1965).[13] Figure 2.10 shows the expected performance level of

Figure 2.10 Expected performance of selected applicants as a function of selection ratio and validity coefficient (*r*). If no testing were used, the expected performance would be 100.

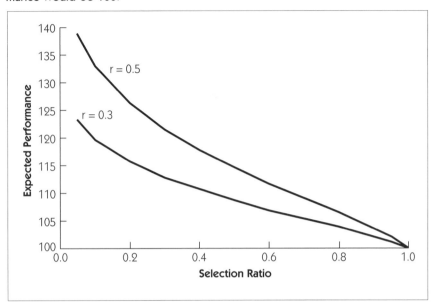

individuals selected using screening tests with validities of .3 or .5. The values shown in the figure should be compared to 100, the expected performance level using random selection (in arbitrary units). At low selection ratios marked improvement in performance can be obtained by using tests with validity coefficients in the .3 range.

Figure 2.10 describes a large number of realistic personnel selection situations. For instance, the figure can be thought of as the function that describes the relationship between the quality of work that would be done by college students who were either selected randomly or selected by psychometric tests of varying validity. Testing would be of most benefit for institutions that could afford to set low selection ratios, such as the prestigious private universities. Alternatively, Figure 2.10 can be thought of as the differences in productivity that could be expected from workers selected with or without a psychometric screening test. Testing would be of most benefit to employers who offered desirable jobs, as these employers could afford to set low selection ratios. Such employers could substantially increase productivity if they combined testing with inducements to apply. The testing would identify the better applicants, while the inducements would lower the selection ratio by increasing the number of applicants.

Selection from the Viewpoint of the Applicant

The argument presented here has taken the viewpoint of the selector. What about the selectee? Should an individual applicant encourage the use of testing? A well-publicized report criticizing testing refers to selection tests as gatekeepers (National Commission on Testing and Public Policy, 1990). This title illustrates the view that tests are a hurdle to be overcome rather than an opportunity to show one's stuff. From a statistical point of view, however, such a feeling is unwarranted because of a basic symmetry between the views of the applicant and the selector.

Applicants want to know how likely it is that they will obtain adequate scores on the screening test, given their qualifications. Selectors want to know how likely candidates are to be qualified, given their scores on the selector tests. The mathematical procedures discussed earlier treat the predictor and criterion tests interchangeably. (The reader might want to look at Figure 2.2 if there is any doubt on this point; the argument related to this figure would be unaffected by interchanging the figure's axes.) Thus, from the viewpoint of a qualified applicant, psychometric testing is always good, and it is especially good if the person is competing against many others for only a few jobs (i.e., there is a low selection ratio).

From the viewpoint of an unqualified applicant, testing is always bad. The mathematics are complex, but the reasoning is simple. The unqualified applicant essentially wants the selector to make a mistake, either by hiring someone who cannot perform adequately on the criterion measure or by hiring someone who is not as well qualified as someone who has been rejected. The more information the selector has, the less likely the selector is to make a mistake. Ergo, the unqualified applicant does not want the selector to use tests.

The applicant and the selector may differ in where the cut point (and hence the selection ratio) should be set. The first section of this chapter presented an economic argument for setting it at the point at which the person's expected contribution exceeds the expected value of training, including the possibility that the person will have to be replaced. If we let p be the probability that a selected candidate will prove to be acceptable, the selection ratio is set to achieve p such that $p \times$ (value of success) $\geq (1 - p) \times$ (cost of failure). A minor arrangement of this equation shows that p must satisfy the relationship $p/(1 - p) \geq$ (cost of failure)/(value of success).

The purpose of using a screening test is to get a better idea of what p is for a particular applicant. It is hard to see how the applicant can object, unless he or she wants to argue that the test is valid for people in general, but not valid for him or her. (In fact, some minority groups have made this claim; the evidence is examined in Chapter 4.) However, p is also determined by the rewards of success and costs of failure, and here the applicant and selector may have legitimate reasons to differ.

For instance, in deciding whether or not to go to medical school, a prospective student should weigh the costs (tuition, lost income during the school years, etc.) against the benefits (income, lifestyle, etc.) if the M.D. is received. The medical school dean should consider the estimated worth of the individual's contribution to society relative to the cost of training. These are different values and might lead the dean and the candidate to disagree, rationally, about where the cut point should be set.

SUMMARY

This chapter has dealt with two rather different themes, so a brief summary is in order.

First, the psychometric model of mental abilities was presented. This model is essentially a geographic metaphor for the mind. Cognitive abilities are thought of as the dimensions of an abstract mental space. An individual's capabilities can be thought of as a point in this space. There is some dispute over just what the basic dimensions represent. Probably the commonest model identifies three basic abilities: verbal comprehension, visual-spatial reasoning, and logical reasoning. An alternative model distinguishes between crystallized intelligence (Gc), fluid intelligence (Gf), and visual-spatial reasoning. Since tests of these different abilities are positively correlated, some psychometricians have argued that an underlying "general intelligence" (g) is involved in virtually all mental activities. Paradoxically, a few psychologists (most recently Howard Gardner) have argued that all these views are too restrictive and that we should expand our definition of intelligence to include such things as musical ability and control of movement.

I argued that in most workplace situations the best way to think of human abilities, from a psychometric viewpoint, is to accept either the three-dimensional model: verbal, visual-spatial, and logical reasoning, or to accept the crystallized intelligence–fluid intelligence distinction. These views are not either right or wrong: They are different views of the same situation. Which one is most useful depends upon the particular application. I view extensions of the standard view, such as Gardner's, to be less useful because they expand "intelligence" to include virtually every dimension of human variation. Such broad definitions do not seem to me to be sufficiently disciplined to deal with in any clearcut way. On the other hand, I believe that there is a massive amount of evidence for differentiating between verbal and visual-spatial reasoning and for differentiating between crystallized and fluid intelligence. Therefore, regarding "intelligence" as a unidimensional general factor is simply not accurate.

The chapter then moved to a discussion about how tests are used to make employment decisions in the abstract. Obviously, a predictor test is only useful if it has some nonzero correlation with criterion indices of worker productivity. How useful the test is, however, depends upon the specifics of the employment situation. Predictors that are highly correlated to criterion measures are always to be preferred to predictors with lower correlations. That is obvious. What is not obvious, though, is the extent to which less than perfect prediction can be useful. It was pointed out that substantial correlations between "true intelligence" and "true productivity," both unmeasurable quantities, can be masked by relatively low correlations between actual tests and performance measures. The extent of the masking depends upon a number of factors, not the least of which is our inability to obtain adequate measures of workplace performance. In addition, in some situations tests that correlate only modestly with criterion measures may still be used to make economically justifiable predictions. This is particularly true if the selection is for a job requiring a high degree of talent, where the differences between good and poor performance are substantial, and where there are many more applicants than there are positions to be filled.

What has been missing is a certain level of concreteness. Apart from occasional references, this chapter has not focused on specific tests, or upon the numbers for correlation, selection, and the like that are actually found in the U.S. workplace. Chapter 3 makes the discussion concrete by doing just that.

NOTES

1. About one-third of all job seekers get their jobs through social or familial contacts (Wegmann, Chapman, and Johnson, 1989, Chap. 2).
2. An adequate discussion of this issue would require a book in itself. The interested reader is referred to discussions by Brody (1992) and Sternberg (1990). I believe that Gardner is on firm ground with respect to artistic activities and physical movement, but that the case for a "social intelligence" apart from the standard model is weak.
3. This point had been made by numerous authors, on the basis of indirect evidence. The Detterman and Daniel study provided strong direct evidence of the contention.

4. Alzheimer's disease is a noticeable exception to this general rule. It appears to have a pervasive effect on both linguistic and nonlinguistic reasoning.

5. This does not mean that evaluating training is easy or even routine. In many industrial situations, the only training criterion is whether or not the student passed the course. This is obviously a gross measure. Within the educational establishment measures that look objective (e.g., grade point average) are readily obtainable. However, a closer examination shows that these are often suspect. Grades may not be comparable across institutions or across classes or training programs within an institution.

   From the standpoint of psychological theory, the finding that training is easier to predict than performance is not particularly surprising. During training a person may rely on general, across-situation abilities that can be assessed in a variety of ways, including testing. Asymptotic performance often depends on skills that have been acquired during training and, therefore, almost by definition, cannot be assessed beforehand. In addition, one of the results of training is often to reduce the range of individual differences in performance. Therefore, prediction is likely to be difficult on statistical grounds alone. See Ackerman (1986) or Fleishman (1972) for further discussions.

6. We can think of the variance of the criterion, y, as consisting of two components: the part of y that is identical to $y^\star$ (i.e., predictable from x) and the part that is not predictable (i.e., the error term, e). The square of the correlation coefficient is the ratio of the predictable variance to the total variance: $r^2 = (s^2(y) - s^2(e))/s^2(y) = 1 - (s^2(e)/s^2(y))$.

7. Even if two measures are not related, across the population of all possible test cases, spurious correlations will arise in a sample from that population because of random sampling fluctuations (Edwards, 1984). Courts have ruled that an employer may only use a screening test if the correlation between test performance and job performance is high enough so that there is only one chance in 20 that the association would have arisen by chance (Kaplan, 1985).

8. A possible solution is to consider the effect of variability in the estimates of both the observed validity and the observed reliability. These can be used to produce a "highest reasonable estimate" and "lowest reasonable estimate" of the true validity coefficient. The problem with this method is that it is difficult to explain to people who are not familiar with statistical techniques.

9. Recall that the criterion is assumed to be a linear function of the predictor score. The basic equation is $Y_i = bX_i + E_i + A$, where E_i is the error in prediction for case i. The linearity assumption is that the same constants A and b apply across all values of X_i. The homoscedasticity of variance assumption is that $s^2(E)$, the variance of the error term, is also identical across all values of X_i.

10. This is not an abstruse academic point; it actually happens. For instance, the correlation between cognitive ability tests and performance as a salesperson (including floor sales) is higher than the correlation between tests and performance as a sales clerk (Hunter and Hunter, 1984). On the other hand, it has frequently been observed that as scientists progress through

their careers they acquire more managerial responsibilities—larger laboratories, bigger grants, and so on. The job still requires intellectual skills, but interpersonal and management skills become increasingly important.

11. The reader may have noticed another problem. The model described here implies that everyone selected for a job will take it. In fact, of course, this does not happen. More sophisticated models are available, in which it is assumed that every individual takes the most demanding job for which he or she is qualified.

12. There are realistic cases in which $c > s$, that is, the employer hires more people than are needed and lets unsatisfactory performers go. This is especially likely to be the case if the initial period of employment requires completion of a course, such as police cadet school or pilot training. This would not invalidate the argument given in the text, but it would unnecessarily complicate the notation.

13. The equation is $Z_{exp}(r,s) = rf(s)/s$, where Z_{exp} is the expected performance of accepted applicants, expressed in terms of standard score units for the criterion, calculated for the population as a whole. On the right-hand side r is the validity coefficient, s is the selection ratio, and $f(s)$ is the value of the density function for the Gaussian distribution at the percentile point corresponding to s. The equation assumes that criterion scores are distributed normally in the population.

3

Psychometric Scores and Workplace Performance

KINDS OF TESTS

Do tests exist that would be useful predictors of workplace performance? To what extent does intelligence, as we measure it, have an impact on workforce performance? This chapter summarizes relevant data about three major scholastic and industrial testing programs—the Scholastic Aptitude Test (SAT), the Armed Services Vocational Aptitude Battery (ASVAB), and the General Aptitude Test Battery (GATB)—that have been developed as predictors of performance in three important workplaces. The chapter also examines two tests that are avowedly intelligence tests. These tests were developed for research purposes and as devices to aid in counseling individuals. They are the Wechsler Adult Intelligence Scale (WAIS) and the Raven Progressive Matrix Test. These two tests have been chosen because of their widespread use and because they have been prominently featured in scientific studies of intelligence. The WAIS is the most widely used intelligence test in the United States, but its use is confined to education and personal counseling. The test is administered individually by a specially trained technician or psychologist, and therefore is far too expensive to use in most industrial settings. The Raven test is widely considered to be an excellent indicator of fluid intelligence (Gf).

WORKPLACE AND EDUCATIONAL PERFORMANCE TESTS

The Scholastic Aptitude Test

The Scholastic Aptitude Test (SAT) is used to evaluate applicants for college and university education. The SAT was developed and is administered by the Educational Testing Service (ETS), a nonprofit corporation that specializes in test development and administration. The SAT is administered under the aegis of the College Board, a consortium of educational institutions, for whom ETS acts as a contractor. While it has competitors, the SAT clearly dominates its market.

The SAT is a paper-and-pencil, multiple-choice test that requires about two and a half hours to administer. (Actual times have fluctuated over the years, as the test forms have been changed slightly.) It is broken down into a number of subtests dealing with specific types of verbal comprehension or mathematical facility. Sample questions from different subtests are shown in Table 3.1.

Scores on the verbal and mathematical tests are summed to produce two composite scores: one for verbal aptitude (SAT-V) and one for mathematical aptitude (SAT-M). These scores are used on the quite reasonable assumption that different types of colleges (e.g., a liberal arts school and an engineering institute) place different emphases on language skills and mathematical skills. When a prediction is made based on "the SAT score," this usually refers to a prediction made using the combined SAT-V and SAT-M scores.

Although the SAT is based on less than three hours' behavior, it is a surprisingly accurate evaluation of educational potential. The estimated population correlation between SAT scores and first-year grade

Table 3.1   Sample SAT Subtest Questions

Verbal

Antonyms: Given a word choose the opposite in meaning.
Example: Good
　　　　　(a) sour
　　　　　(b) bad
　　　　　(c) red
　　　　　(d) hot
　　　　　(e) ugly

Analogies: Select the lettered pair that represents a relationship similar to the relationship between the word pair in capitals.
Example: YAWN: BOREDOM
　　　　　(a) dream:sleep
　　　　　(b) anger:madness
　　　　　(c) smile:amusement
　　　　　(d) face:expression
　　　　　(e) impatience:rebellion

Table 3.1   *(Continued)*

Sentence completion: Choose the word or set of words that best fills in the blanks in the sentence.
Example: Although its publicity has been ____, the film itself is intelligent, well acted, handsomely produced, and altogether ____.

    (a) tasteless . . . respectable
    (b) extensive . . . moderate
    (c) sophisticated . . . amateur
    (d) risqué . . . crude
    (e) perfect . . . spectacular

Reading comprehension: Examinees read a paragraph about a contemporary topic (e.g., use of National Parks) and answer multiple-choice questions about its meaning.

Mathematical

Regular mathematics: Simple algebraic and geometric problems are presented in multiple-choice form.
Example: If $2y = 3$, then $3(2y)^2 =$

    (a) 27/4
    (b) 18
    (c) 81/4
    (d) 27
    (e) 81

Data sufficiency: A mathematical relationship is presented, followed by two assertions about variables in the relationship. The examinee determines whether or not the relationship can be shown to be true on the basis of one, either, both, or neither of the assertions.
Example: Is $a + b = a$? Assertions: (1) $b = 0$ (2) $a = 10$.

Quantitative comparisons: Two quantities, A and B, are defined. The examinee indicates whether A is greater than B, B is greater than A, the two are equal, or a relation cannot be determined.
Example: A: The least positive integer divisible by 2, 3, and 4.
       B: 24.

Source: Descriptions and examples paraphrased from illustrations given in Marco et al. (1990).

point average has been between .50 and .57 since 1970 (Marco et al., 1990), in spite of substantial changes in the number and social characteristics of college students over the years.[1] As was shown in Chapter 2, this level of validity is quite high enough to be a useful economic predictor.[2]

The SAT was designed for the typical college entrant, a recent high school graduate in his or her late teens or early twenties. It can be argued that such tests, however useful in education, are not relevant to workforce issues. However, a particularly well-done study suggests that this is not the case, at least for high-level, white-collar performance.

In the 1960s the Bell Telephone Company, which at the time had a monopoly on telephone services in the United States, embarked on a longitudinal study of management potential. Several hundred recently hired junior-level managers were interviewed and tested extensively. The results were kept apart from the examinees' personnel records, to ensure that performance during the assessment would not influence the participants' subsequent careers. Over 200 of the managers remained with the Bell Telephone Company for at least 20 years. There was a correlation of .38 between their performance on cognitive tests much like the SAT and the management level that they reached 20 years after testing (Howard and Bray, 1988, Table 3.7). No other test did as well. But this is not to say that superior cognition was the only characteristic of the to-be-successful junior manager. Tests of motivation for professional advancement, although not as accurate as the cognitive tests alone, could be added to the cognitive tests to make a better prediction of future performance than either cognitive or motivational tests alone.

The Armed Services Vocational Aptitude Battery

The Armed Services Vocational Aptitude Battery (ASVAB) is taken by every applicant for enlistment into U.S. armed services.[3] During the 1980s from 300,000 to 400,000 people took the test each year. Slightly fewer than half of those tested actually enlisted in the armed services. In addition, the Department of Defense conducts a program in which the ASVAB is taken by a sample of high school students, in order to compare armed services recruits with the population of recent high school graduates.

The ASVAB is a paper-and-pencil, multiple-choice test with a format similar to the SAT. The test consists of the nine subtests listed in Table 3.2. A comparison of Tables 3.1 and 3.2 shows that the SAT and ASVAB cover similar ground, except that the ASVAB contains subtests that

Table 3.2 Armed Services Vocational Aptitude Battery
Subtests

General science	Paragraph comprehension
Arithmetic reasoning	Numerical operations
Coding speed	Word knowledge
Auto shop information	Mathematical knowledge
Electronics information	

evaluate knowledge about mechanics, automobiles, and electronics, which is required in a number of military positions. ASVAB questions are generally easier than comparable questions on the SAT because the SAT is intended to be maximally sensitive at identifying ability in, generally speaking, the "upper half" of the graduating high school population. The ASVAB is intended to evaluate abilities in the "middle half," that is, the 25th to 75th quartiles of ability, in that population.[4]

In addition to being a scre ning tool, the ASVAB is used in personnel assignment. Every armed services recruit begins his or her career in basic training ("boot camp" in the navy and marines), where the enlistee becomes generally familiar with the rules and customs of military life. Following basic training, an enlistee is assigned to an entry-level military occupational specialty (MOS). These specialties cover a wide range of occupations. During the 1980s the army alone had 276 entry-level MOSs. Some MOSs, such as infantryman, are specific to the military. Others, such as administrative specialist (clerk), are analogous to civilian occupations.

The subtests of the ASVAB are used to compute several composite scores, somewhat like the SAT-V and SAT-M scores. Each composite is based on a different weighted sum of subtest scores. The Armed Forces Qualification Test (AFQT), which stresses verbal skills and mathematical reasoning but does not count the different specialized knowledge tests or coding speed, is a summary composite used to decide whether or not to enlist a candidate. Other composites are used to predict performance in selected groups of MOSs. For instance, the electronics composite is the sum of scores on the arithmetic reasoning, mechanical knowledge, electrical information, and general science subtests (Johnson, Zeidner, and Scholarios 1990).

During the 1980s the armed services conducted an extensive study aimed at both evaluating the ASVAB and determining whether or not other predictors of the performance of enlisted personnel could be found (Wigdor & Green, 1991). The study was probably the largest industrial assessment study ever done. Its results are relevant to our interests.

Table 3.3 Military Occupational Specialties Selected for Intensive Study in U.S. Army Project A

Specifically military specialties
Infantryman
Cannon crewmember
Armor (tank) crewmember
Specialties with civilian analogs
Single channel radio operator
Motor transport operator
Medical specialist (technician)
Vehicle mechanic
Administrative specialist
Military policeman

Source: Campbell (1990), Table 1.
Note: Classification into military and military/civilian specialties is my own.

While all four armed services participated, the largest single study was the army's Project A (Campbell, 1990), which was continued into the 1990s. It involved testing and evaluation of the performance of over 10,000 soldiers and will be described in some detail. We will be concerned here with results bearing directly on the validity of the ASVAB.

Nine MOSs selected for intensive study are listed in Table 3.3. The sample in this portion of Project A consisted of slightly more than 4,000 soldiers, with from 300 to 600 in each MOS. All the soldiers had taken the ASVAB when they were enlisted. (As part of the study, the soldiers took a number of further tests that will not concern us, as they are not typical of widely used industrial personnel tests.)

Four different techniques were used to evaluate performance (Campbell, McHenry, and Wise, 1990). Written personnel records were examined. Supervisors and peers were asked to rate the soldiers' performance on a variety of tasks associated with either their technical MOS—that is, their job narrowly defined—or more generally their performance as soldiers. This distinction would apply to virtually any job. Conceptually, at least, one can distinguish between an individual's technical competence and his or her performance as a member of a working group. Soldiers were also given written tests to determine their knowledge of their specialty, as defined by army manuals. Finally, and perhaps most interestingly, soldiers were asked to perform certain hands-on tasks that had been selected as important for their MOS. Their performance was evaluated by trained raters from the Project A research group. For instance, a vehicle operator was evaluated for the

Table 3.4 Job Factors Identified in Project A

Core technical skill:	Job performance as defined by the MOS.
General soldiering:	Ability to perform tasks generally required of soldiers.
Effort and leadership:	Extent to which soldiers attempted to improve themselves and the extent to which they assumed leadership roles.
Personal discipline:	Interpersonal reliability in social and organizational settings.
Fitness and bearing:	Extent to which soldiers were physically fit and conformed to the army's expectation of a good soldier's appearance.

Note: The factors are further defined by Campbell, McHenry, and Wise (1990).

ability to drive without riding the clutch. Thus, Project A, and the other service studies, went well beyond the usual practice of relying on supervisor ratings and personnel records for criterion measurement.

The standard psychometric model (see Chapter 2), in which abilities are described in terms of underlying factors, was applied to job performance (Campbell, McHenry, and Wise, 1990). Five factors underlying job performance were evaluated. The factors, together with my own gloss of the authors' longer description, are shown in Table 3.4. Except for "fitness and bearing," which seems to be unique to the military, the job factors apply to both military and civilian jobs.

The five factors fall into three separate groups: the two technical proficiency factors, the personal discipline and fitness and bearing factors, and, between these two groups, the effort and leadership factor. The best indicators of the technical knowledge factors were the hands-on tests and the written tests of job knowledge. The best indicators of the personality and appearance aspects of job performance were leader and peer ratings.

The Project A findings show, quite clearly, that a person's performance on the job depends on technical skill and "personality" variables, including attitude and motivation. Are either (or both) of these dimensions of job performance predictable from psychometric measures of mental competence?

Figure 3.1 shows the ASVAB validity coefficients for each of the five job factors. Technical aspects of job performance were predicted quite well. The population validity correlation estimates between score and skill are in excess of .60, which is impressive, when one considers that

Figure 3.1   The correlation between the appropriate ASVAB composite and different components of performance as a soldier. Source: McHenry et al. (1990), Table 7. The correlations shown are estimates of the population correlation.

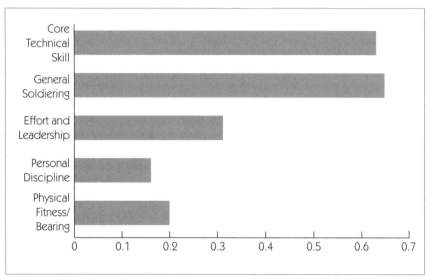

many of the soldiers took the ASVAB two years or more before their performance was evaluated. It is clearly a useful personnel screening device for jobs whose performance is primarily determined by cognitive variables.

On the other hand, the ASVAB did not do nearly as well in predicting the personality and motivational aspects of job performance.

One final statistic from Project A should be noted. Recall that three broad classes of measures were available: knowledge assessed by a written test, hands-on performance observations, and ratings by supervisors and peers. The correlation between cognitive abilities and the written scores was .64; the comparable correlation between cognitive abilities and ratings was .16 (McHenry et al. 1990, Table 9). This is a striking example of a widely held conjecture: Cognitive tests will predict objective measures of on-the-job performance better than they will predict ratings of that performance.[5]

It has been frequently found that cognitive tests are more accurate in predicting performance in training and education than they are in predicting workplace performance after training. This fact has sometimes been used to argue that, given training, differences due to initial cognitive ability are unimportant. The Project A findings challenge this view somewhat, since there were substantial correlations between test

Figure 3.2   The relationship between AFQT category and performance of enlisted soldiers. Source: Redrawn from Wigdor and Green (1991), Figure 8-1.

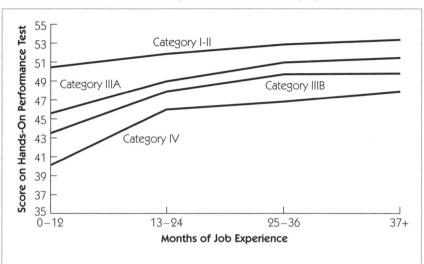

performance and objectively evaluated job performance. An overall summary of the total Department of Defense effort provided even more striking evidence that cognitive skills do continue to make a difference, even after years on the job.

Figure 3.2 shows a summary of the relation between tested performance, ASVAB scores (grouped into categories that are used in recruitment), and time on the job (Wigdor and Green, 1991). Three points are noteworthy: (1) People with higher level scores do better on the job. Years of experience do not eliminate this difference. On the average, enlisted men and women in ASVAB categories I and II did better during their first year on the job than those in category IV with more than three-years' experience. (2) On-the-job learning does take place; tested performance improves with experience within every ASVAB category. (3) The cognitive skills and experience variables interact. The greatest improvement over time was shown by category IV personnel during the first year on the job. Category I and II personnel reached their stable performance levels more quickly.

How generalizable are the results of these studies to the civilian workforce? There are two obvious drawbacks: They were restricted to military jobs, and they examined a workforce that is, on the average, substantially younger than the general civilian workforce.

The first drawback is probably not a major one. Of the more than 4,000 individuals studied in project A, slightly fewer than 2,000 were in specifically military jobs. Statistical evidence (not reviewed here) suggests that the variables that predicted performance in the combat arms jobs were, except for nuances concerning the technical skills required, generally the same predictors as those required to estimate performance in military occupations with civilian counterparts (Wise, McHenry, and Campbell, 1990).

There is also direct evidence that the ASVAB is a valid index of some important behaviors in the civilian workforce. In order to maintain its currency, the ASVAB is periodically updated with new civilian samples. In 1980 the Department of Defense gave their test to over 12,000 young adults who were participating in a Department of Labor longitudinal study of workforce experience. In 1990 the Department of Labor interviewed the examinees to determine their employment and social status. Herrnstein and Murray (1994) analyzed the data to predict 1990 social indicators from the 1980 test results. They concluded that the AFQT composite, which they referred to as an index of general intelligence, was a strong predictor of employment status (unemployed vs. employed), participation in relatively high levels of criminal activity (for men), and being on welfare (for women). The relations held up after a number of other predictors had been controlled, including schooling. Herrnstein and Murray used a different technique of analysis than the ones described here, and the details of their methods may be debated by specialists for some time. Also, Herrnstein and Murray dealt with extreme outcomes. In our terms, this corresponds to low selection ratios, and, as we have seen, situations with low selection ratios are particularly sensitive to prediction. However, the qualitative conclusion that the AFQT composite did reliably predict economically important outcomes is not in serious doubt.

The General Aptitude Test Battery

The General Aptitude Test Battery (GATB) was developed in the late 1940s by the U.S. Employment Service (USES), a branch of the Department of Labor (DOL) to assist in job referrals. From 1950 until 1990 the DOL both used and promoted the use of the test throughout the economy.

In the 1980s the GATB was attacked on the grounds that it did not accurately predict the performance of minority group members. The department responded to this charge in two ways: It adopted a policy of reporting scores by the relative standing of an examinee within his or her own ethnic group, instead of the usual practice of reporting a score relative to the scores of all other test takers, and it asked the National Academy of Sciences (NAS) to prepare a report evaluating

Table 3.5 General Aptitude Test Battery Subtests

Paper-and-Pencil Tests

(1) Name comparison. Compare names to see if they are identical.
(2) Computation: Simple arithmetic. The test is timed.
(3) Three-dimensional space: The examinee is shown a diagram of a flat "piece of metal" to be folded along marked lines and must decide what the object will look like when folded.
(4) Vocabulary: Identify words with the same or opposite meanings.
(5) Tool matching: The examinee is shown a "probe" picture of a common tool and four comparison pictures and must decide which of the four comparisons exactly matches the probe.
(6) Arithmetic reasoning; Simple arithmetic word problems.
(7) Form matching: The examinee must pick out two identical figures in a group of abstract geometric figures.
(8) Mark making: The examinee must make three pencil marks in a small box. The score is the number of boxes marked in a minute.

Manipulation-of-Objects Tests

(9) Place: Move pegs from one place to another in a peg board. The score is the number of pegs moved in 15 seconds. Three attempts are allowed.
(10) Turn: Turn over as many of the pegs as possible in 30 seconds.
(11) Assemble: Assemble rivet and washer units for 90 seconds.
(12) Disassemble: The examinee disassembles as many of the units assembled in test (11) as he/she can within 60 seconds.

both the GATB and various scoring methods for it. The NAS report contains an excellent review of the GATB studies and in addition makes a number of points about the use of tests in general (Hartigan & Wigdor, 1989).[6]

Although the NAS report generally endorsed the GATB, further attacks were made on the test, both by minority group advocates who argued for within-group scoring and by others who argued that within-group scoring amounted to an illegal quota system. In 1990 the DOL ceased using the test for employment referrals. This was essentially a political decision.

Even though the sponsor has ceased using the GATB, the large body of research done on the test is relevant for our purposes. A discussion of this research both furthers our understanding of test use in industry and illustrates some of the problems that arise in evaluating tests that are not targeted to a particular, easily identified group of individuals, such as college freshmen or military personnel.

The GATB consists of the 12 subtests shown in Table 3.5. The problems in subtests 1–8 are presented in the familiar paper-and-pencil, multiple-choice format seen on the SAT and ASVAB. Indeed, the principal difference between the ASVAB and the GATB is that the ASVAB contains subtests evaluating specific knowledge areas (e.g., general science, shop knowledge), which the GATB does not, and the GATB contains explicit tests of spatial-visual reasoning, which the ASVAB does not.[7] In subtests 9–12 examinees must assemble, move, or manipulate small objects with their hands. This is an attempt to evaluate psychomotor performance. While most psychologists do not consider psychomotor ability to be part of intelligence,[8] the ability is clearly important in some jobs.

As with the ASVAB, subtest scores are used to compute composite scores, supposedly representing different psychometric abilities. The GATB composites are:

Cognitive composite: computation, three-dimensional space, vocabulary, arithmetic reasoning.

(Visual) perceptual composite: name comparison, three-dimensional space, tool matching, form matching.

Psychomotor composite: mark making and the four tests requiring object manipulation.

The first two composites are substantially correlated ($r = .76$). The psychomotor composite has lower but nonnegligible correlations with the other two ($r = .35$ with the cognitive composite and $r = .51$ with the perceptual composite) (U.S. Department of Labor, 1983a). Because of these correlations, it has been argued that the test should be regarded as a single test of general ability. (The same remark has been made about the ASVAB; see Hunter, 1986.) In practice, though, the USES classifies jobs into five different job families, based on the extent to which job holders are involved in dealing with data, people, or things, and suggests that slightly different composite score weightings be used to predict performance in each job category (U.S. Department of Labor, 1983b). The NAS review board concluded that the case for using different predictors was slight, possibly because the job classes are not well defined (Hartigan and Wigdor, 1989, pp. 145 ff.).[9]

There have been more than 750 studies of the validity of the GATB. Most of them are relatively small, and the quality of the investigations varies greatly. As with virtually every other science, in psychometrics it is usually harder to derive results from many limited studies than from a single, well-done, comprehensive experiment.[10] Supervisors' ratings are the most commonly used criterion measures, although, as was pointed out earlier, there are good reasons to believe that ratings measure the social and personality aspects of job performance at least as much as they measure technical competence.[11]

Nevertheless, a reasonably consistent picture has emerged. Most of the GATB studies have been of performance in the USES's job classes IV and V, which include mechanics, technicians, machinery operators, counter attendants, and high school teachers. The jobs in classes IV and V can generally be described as blue-collar jobs at the skilled technician level and white-collar jobs below the professional and managerial levels. The USES estimated that the population validity coefficients for these jobs are about .50, which is comparable to the levels for the population level coefficients for the SAT and the GATB (U.S. Department of Labor, 1983b).

The NAS study group questioned the USES estimates because the corrections of the observed correlations were based on assumptions about criterion reliability and on extrapolations of relationships observed in current jobholders to assumptions about relationships in the applicant pool. (See Chapter 2 for a more detailed discussion of the issue.)[12] Using much more conservative estimates, the NAS group concluded that the population validity coefficients for supervisor ratings were in the .25–.40 range, depending on the particular job used (Hartigan and Wigdor, 1989, pp. 163–170).

I suggest that we take a middle ground. The USES corrections do seem too optimistic, but the NAS study group's decision to reject any correction is too pessimistic. It seems reasonable to conjecture that if objective measures of job performance were obtained, the validity coefficients would have increased to the .3 to .5 range.

As is the case with most psychometric measures, the GATB is consistently found to be a better predictor of performance during training than performance after training (Hartigan and Wigdor, 1989, p. 168).

The NAS report calls attention to a puzzling trend. Validity coefficients are lower—often substantially lower—for studies done since 1972 than for studies done before that date. Statistically, the decline is due to a decline in the predictive validity of the perceptual and psychomotor composites. The predictive validity of the cognitive composite has remained unchanged. The NAS committee, by its own admission, was unable to come up with a convincing explanation for the decline, although it did rule out a number of intuitively plausible explanations. The decline was not due to psychometric artifacts, such as restriction of range, change in the types of jobs evaluated, or changes in the identity of the employers cooperating with the Department of Labor research program.

Two nontechnical reasons have been suggested. One is based on the claim that the GATB and psychometric tests in general are not good measures of the skills of minority group members. After 1972 a number of studies were conducted with the avowed purpose of increasing the number of minority employees measured, solely to determine if the charge against the test was correct. If the validity coefficients were lower for minority groups (i.e., if the claim is true), and if there were more minority group members in the experiments conducted after 1972 than in the earlier work, then the validity coefficients would decrease. However, they should decrease in a way that could be predicted from the difference between white and minority group validity coefficients. This relation did *not* hold (Hartigan and Wigdor, 1989, p. 162).

Many claims that psychometric tests are "ethnically unfair" are based on the argument that the tests depend on a knowledge of cultural factors, such as vocabulary, and that minority group members are less familiar with this knowledge than are whites. This criticism could be levied against the GATB cognitive tests, because they do indeed assess cultural knowledge. On the other hand, if test validities declined because the test was an inaccurate measure of the abilities of minority members, whose participation in the workforce certainly increased, then the decreases should have been found in the cognitive composite while the perceptual and psychomotor composite validities remained the same. In fact, the data were just the other way around.

The NAS committee also acknowledged another explanation of the validity decline based on an ethnic argument of a rather different sort. I have often heard privately (I know of no public statement) that during the 1970s and 1980s there was so much pressure to validate the tests for minority group members that the resulting studies were hastily and poorly done. However, this explanation does not fit with the data. If it were true, validity coefficients should have declined uniformly across all composites, and they did not. There was a selective decline in the validity of the psychomotor component.

I suggest another possibility that, unfortunately, is virtually impossible to evaluate statistically. It may be that the nature of work has changed, not in the sense that job definitions have changed, but in the sense that tasks within a job have changed. A substantial number of class IV and V jobs have been heavily impacted by automation and computerization. Consider, for instance, how an automobile mechanic's job has changed as automated test equipment has been developed. I shall argue in Chapter 6 that the impact of these changes has been to reduce the need for human perceptual and psychomotor skills. The impact of technological changes on the use of cognitive skills has been much more variable. Therefore, it is reasonable to expect that cognitive predictors will remain as good as they ever were (with perhaps more variability in validity coefficients across jobs), while the predictability and utility of perceptual and psychomotor skills will decline.

INTELLIGENCE TESTS

The Wechsler Adult Intelligence Scale

We next consider two tests that are avowedly intelligence tests. The first test to be considered, the Wechsler Adult Intelligence Scale-Revised (WAIS-R), is the most widely used intelligence test in the United States today. A comparable test for children, the Wechsler Intelligence Scale for Children-Revised (WISC-R), is also marketed. Since it is not relevant here, it will not be further discussed.

The WAIS-R is essentially a structured interview in which a trained tester observes the examinee as he or she attempts to solve different types of problems. The problems themselves are classified into two broad groups: verbal and performance tests. Table 3.6 lists and briefly summarizes the subtests in each of these groups. The content of the WAIS-R, as a whole, is intentionally similar to the content of the AS-VAB and GATB. Historically, paper-and-pencil tests were developed to be economical substitutes for the WAIS and similar individually administered tests. The WAIS-R is chiefly used in counseling and clinical psychology, where there is need to assess individual patients (Brody, 1992). It is especially useful in establishing degrees of mental retardation. The test is also used as a validation scale for other instruments. For instance, new and much cheaper paper-and-pencil tests are often validated by showing that scores on the new test are highly correlated with scores on the WAIS-R or WISC.

In common with the SAT, GATB, and ASVAB, the WAIS-R contains a substantial number of tests of the examinee's knowledge about the world. This can be justified on two grounds. First, what a person knows is often a good predictor of how easy it will be to teach that person other things. Second, if two people have equal opportunity to learn something, it seems relevant to note which of the two learned the target information. On the other hand, tests of knowledge can be, and have been, challenged on the grounds that they systematically discriminate against people who have not had the appropriate cultural experiences.

The Raven Progressive Matrix Test

The Horn-Cattell "fluid and crystallized intelligence" model of intelligence distinguishes between fluid intelligence—the ability to develop

Table 3.6   Wechsler Adult Intelligence Scale-Revised Verbal and Performance Subtests

Verbal	
Information:	Test of general knowledge, such as names of presidents.
Comprehension:	Answer simple questions about daily life and about hypothetical problems.
Arithmetic:	Simple arithmetical word problems.
Similarities:	Identify similarity between concepts, e.g., between "horse" and "cow."
Digit span:	Examinee must repeat a sequence of spoken digits.
Vocabulary:	Define words.
Performance	
Digit-symbol test:	The examinee must copy symbols that are arbitrarily associated with numbers.
Picture-completion:	The examinee must complete a picture with a missing detail, such as a horse without a tail.
Block design:	The examinee must arrange colored, odd-shaped blocks into a specified pattern.
Picture arrangement:	The examinee is given a set of "mixed up" pictures, rather like a comic strip that has been cut into frames, and must rearrange the frames into a coherent story.
Object assembly:	The examinee must put together objects from their constituent parts.

problem-solving methods in an unfamiliar situation—and crystallized intelligence—the ability to utilize acquired knowledge in an appropriate way. The Raven Progressive Matrix Tests (Raven and Court, 1960) are intended to evaluate fluid intelligence. The Raven test is actually a sequence of tests of progressively greater difficulty. All the tests, however, use the same format, which has come to be called a matrix question. Figure 3.3 displays a fairly easy, made-up example to illustrate the principle. Actual items vary widely in difficulty. Many psychometricians regard the Raven Progressive Matrix Test as a gold

Figure 3.3   An illustration of a matrix problem. Which of the boxes below the line should be used to fill the box in the lower right, above the line?

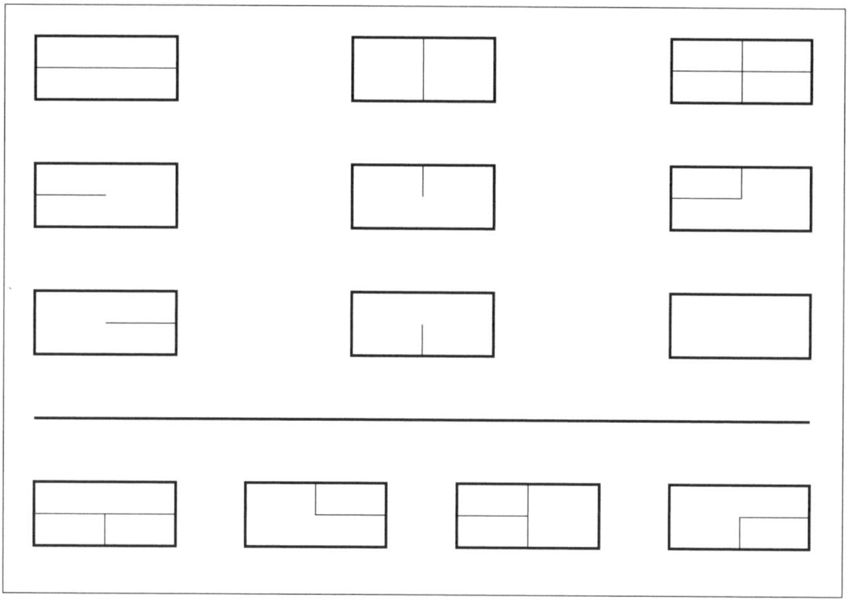

standard of tests to identify fluid intelligence, since it evaluates the examinee's ability to deal with what are almost certain to be novel problems.

There have been several analyses of the cognitive behaviors required to solve Raven matrix problems (Carpenter, Just, and Shell, 1990; Hunt, 1974). The gist of these analyses is that in order to solve matrix problems the examinee must be able to spot progressive changes in the patterns both across the rows and down the columns of the test figures and must be able to infer how these changes combine to produce the figure in the lower right. Thus, the test seems to evaluate the ability to notice regularities underlying change and the ability to combine different trends. Both tasks place a formidable information-processing burden on short-term memory.

In the United States Raven tests are primarily research instruments. In Europe they have been used for personnel evaluation, especially in the military. From 1950 through the 1980s several European countries routinely gave Raven tests to all military inductees. As a result we have a very good idea of the distribution of scores in different populations. Some of this information is relevant to projections of future workplace performance. I know of relatively little data on the utility of the Raven tests as a predictor of workplace performance.

Intelligence Tests and Workplace Productivity

Intelligence tests provide a link between scientific studies of factors that influence mental competence and industrial studies that relate measures of mental competence to measures of workforce performance. The link is through the relation between intelligence tests and industrial tests such as the SAT, ASVAB, and GATB. Since the nature of the linkage is somewhat different for the WAIS and the Raven tests, they will be considered separately.

Virtually all industrial tests are actually batteries of subtests of vocabulary, arithmetical reasoning, and the like, as is the WAIS. Indeed, the principal difference between the WAIS and the industrial tests is in the way that performance is measured—paper-and-pencil testing versus a personal interview—rather than in the content of the performances being measured.

The results of the SAT, ASVAB, GATB, and WAIS are, in the first instance, actually collections of numbers rather than a single number. In practice, prediction is made by taking a weighted sum of the scores on each of the subtests to get a single test score. In theory, different weighted sums could be computed to predict success in different types of occupations. For instance, arithmetical reasoning should count more than vocabulary if you are trying to predict success as a bookmaker, but vocabulary should count more than arithmetic if you are trying to predict success as a newspaper reporter. Weighting is done to some extent, as was noted in the discussion of the composite scores derived from the individual tests for the ASVAB and GATB. Several composites have also been proposed for the WAIS. Their primary use has been in clinical or educational, rather than industrial, settings.

In theory different composites might measure different abilities. In practice, though, it has been found that the composite scores of intelligence tests are fairly highly correlated. This suggests that a single "general score" can be computed to indicate overall mental competence. For example, the Armed Forces Qualification Test (AFQT) is a composite of ASVAB scores that is used in this fashion, as is the total of the SAT verbal and quantitative scores and the intelligent quotient (IQ) score computed for the WAIS.

The usual explanation for the correlation between composites is that it reflects the existence of "general intelligence" (g). More to the point here, since the composites are highly correlated, any external factor known to influence an intelligence test score, such as the WAIS IQ score, probably has a similar influence on the general composite of an industrial test. Exceptions to this statement could be imagined, but the burden of proof is on the person arguing that an exception exists.

As a result, it makes sense to consider composite measures on various industrial tests as measures of *g*. When this is done, two findings emerge. The first is that the mean general intelligence test score varies consistently across jobs. A World War II study found that holders of professional jobs had mean intelligence test scores around 125 (with a mean of 100 and a standard deviation of 15), while nontechnical blue-collar jobholders had mean intelligence test scores around 90.

The second finding is that there are correlations between "general intelligence" composites and performance within a job. Hunter and Hunter (1984) reviewed a large number of studies and found corrected (population) validity coefficients for performance within a job to range from .27 to .61. Hunter and Hunter estimate that the mean population validity coefficient is .53, using supervisor ratings as a criterion. In general, higher estimates are associated with more intellectually demanding jobs. For instance, Hunter and Hunter's estimate of the validity coefficient for "manager" is .53, while the estimate for "clerk" is .27.

Hunter and Hunter's estimates can be questioned on the grounds that they overcorrected for rating unreliability, and for a number of other reasons. Wigdor and Green (1991, Table 8-10) report a lower estimate of .38 for the AFQT (which is a "general component" for the ASVAB), based on an analysis of 23 MOSs examined in the Department of Defense's studies. If the composite is tailored to the MOS, the population validity estimate rises to .50.

These studies do not come up with precisely the same numbers, but the numbers are not based on precisely the same situations. I think it is wiser to focus on the common theme than to quibble over differences of .1 in a validity coefficient. General intelligence tests, based on a composite of different subtests, clearly do predict workplace performance.

The Raven Matrix Tests are of interest for slightly different reasons. The test is not a composite; all the items are nonverbal puzzles of the form illustrated in Figure 3.3. Suppose that test takers are asked to take a Raven test in addition to a standard test battery, such as the WAIS or SAT. Numerous studies (e.g., Snow, Kyllonen, and Marshalek, 1984) have shown that the Matrix test score is highly correlated *with the composite score.* In psychometric terms, this means that the Raven Matrix Test and similar tests are *markers* for the general factor. Therefore, in absence of a fairly strong argument to the contrary, it is reasonable to assume that any external factor that influences scores on a marker test, such as the Raven Matrix Test, will also influence the general factor score on an industrial test and, thus, adjust our prediction of an individual's performance.

The reasoning can be summarized by taking a hypothetical, though realistic, case. I do not know of any studies directly showing that alcoholism influences cognitive performance on the job.[13] However, I believe that there is such an effect. My reasoning follows:

1. There are studies showing that severe alcoholism affects performance on markers for general intelligence, such as the WAIS and the Raven Matrix Test.

2. I believe, for the reasons just stated, that these composites are markers for a "general (fluid) intelligence" trait, probably related to the ability to solve novel problems. Since the test scores deteriorate with alcoholism, I believe that the general intelligence trait is sensitive to alcohol abuse.

3. Since the marker tests are statistically related to the composites from the industrial tests, I believe that the general intelligence trait influences performance on the industrial personnel tests.

4. Since the industrial test composites predict job performance moderately well, I believe that job performance is influenced by, among other things, general intelligence.

5. Therefore, I conclude that alcohol abuse probably does cause a deterioration in the cognitive aspects of job performance. Whether or not this is the major cause of performance deterioration due to alcoholism is still an open question.

This argument is admittedly indirect. This does not make it invalid, only less strong than we would like it to be. In many cases we shall be forced to rely on such indirect approaches.

A SUMMARY OF EMPIRICAL RESULTS

By now readers may be adrift in a sea of statistics, but I felt that it was necessary to state the facts on which I base my conclusions about the value of psychometric tests. Our concern is what the testing movement means for the total economy. The following statements are sufficiently accurate to carry the discussion further.

1. *The tests work, but they don't work perfectly.* "On the average," population validity coefficients between psychometric tests and job or educational performance, objectively measured, are probably in the .4 to .6 range. (I will use a value of .5 in subsequent discussion.) For tech-

nical reasons, we expect observed correlations to be lower, generally in the .25 to .4 range. This means the tests are predictors that one would not want to disregard, but that they are far from perfect predictors. Accounts of low test scores who became Phi Beta Kappas or of high test scores who were incompetent workers are not germane to the issue at hand. The issue is how well the tests do on the average, not how well they perform in individual cases.

2. *The tests do better at predicting objective measures of performance than at predicting subjective measures, such as ratings.* This finding poses a substantial problem. Economists, quite naturally, prefer objective measures of performance because they can be tied to objective measures of value. However, objective ratings may give us only a limited view of performance. It is easy to calculate the correlation between a clothing clerk's salary and the value of his or her sales. It is harder to put a value on the probability that the clerk's manner will induce a customer to go to the shoe department in the same store.

3. *Is the relation between test scores and performance high enough to be of interest?* The only way to answer the question is to ask what our society regards as an important relationship. Salary provides a good example. Most Americans, and certainly most committed capitalists, would accept the statement that a person's salary ought to be related to the value of his or her work. It follows, therefore, that one ought to be able to predict a person's productivity from his or her salary.

Each year the business magazine *Fortune* prints an annual report relating the salaries of chief executive officers (CEOs) to company profits. Using this data, I found that in 1990 the correlation between the salaries of the CEOs in our major banks and the bank's return of investment to stockholders was .18. This is well below the validity of most psychometric predictions of job productivity. Nevertheless, boards of directors do not hesitate to argue that they must pay large salaries in order to get good executives.

Of course, the *Fortune* article was followed by angry letters from CEOs and their spokespersons explaining why "intangibles could not possibly be predicted." Perhaps, but the same argument applies to psychometric predictions. By definition, intangibles cannot be measured, and so they cannot be predicted.

Perhaps the best summary statistic to keep in mind is taken from the Bell Telephone Company's longitudinal study of managers (Howard and Bray, 1988), in which entering managers were extensively evaluated in the 1960s. The evaluations were compared with the management level that the study participants had reached in the 1980s. There was an uncorrected correlation of .38 between management level reached at a mature state in their career and their scores on a cognitive test battery taken *20 years earlier.* No other single predictor did as well. Psychometric tests do work.

NOTES

1. In 1970, 51.8 percent of high school graduates enrolled in college, 55.2 percent of the males and 48.6 percent of the females. In 1985, 57.7 percent of high school graduates enrolled, 58.6 percent of the males and 56.9 percent of the females. Minority group representation has gone up and down over the indicated period. Source: National Center for Educational Statistics (1992).

2. The SAT is sometimes criticized on the grounds that first-year grade point average can be predicted about as well from high school grades as from the SAT. Strictly speaking, this issue is irrelevant to our concerns, since we are interested in the absolute accuracy of the test rather than its relative accuracy compared with other predictors. Because of the general interest in the topic, though, two comments are in order. It is true that the SAT and high school grades are approximately equally good as predictors of college performance. Since high school grades are based on four-years' performance and the SAT is based on less than three-hours' performance, the equality alone is impressive evidence for the efficacy of psychometric testing. More important, high school grades and the SAT seem to predict different aspects of college performance. That is, the tests are not redundant. Statistically, since both predictor measures have a correlation of about .55 with the criterion measure, there is plenty of room for this to happen! Operationally, this means that the appropriate prediction strategy is to consider both high school grades and SAT scores when one is making an admission decision.

3. "Enlistment" here means recruitment as an enlisted person in the army, navy, air force, or marines. Officer recruitment is handled separately.

4. During the time for which statistics will be quoted, the U.S. military was composed entirely of recruits. Generally speaking, the recruits represented the middle range of general ability in the high school population, defined by the Armed Forces Qualification Test (AFQT) composite of the ASVAB. The top quartile was underrepresented, and, as a matter of policy, the military usually does not accept people with test scores in the bottom quartile.

5. The Project A ratings are somewhat lower than those found in other studies, which appear to hover in the .2 to .3 range. (See Ford, Kraiger, and Schectman, 1986, for further citations.) However, Project A was a much larger study than those generally cited in the literature, and its findings are within the range of variation one would expect to see from the earlier work.

6. Most of my material on the GATB is drawn from the NAS report or material cited by it.

7. The remark is true of the ASVAB as of 1994. Earlier versions of the ASVAB did test spatial-visual reasoning. Project A participants were given tests of

spatial-visual reasoning in addition to the ASVAB. The utility of these scores in job placement is currently under investigation. I would not be surprised to see spatial-visual reasoning reappear in a future form of the ASVAB.

8. See Gardner (1983) for a notable exception to this point of view.

9. A casual perusal of the jobs listed together in different job families gives one the impression that the classification is sensible on the whole. For instance, job family I includes machinists and cabinet makers; II includes agricultural machinery and cannery workers; III includes retail food managers and game wardens; IV includes automobile mechanics, radiological technicians, and (puzzling to me) high school teachers; and V includes various machine operators. One can always find "something wrong" with such schemes, and perhaps the NAS committee was correct in suggesting that a better scheme should be found. Actually constructing and validating a classification scheme is far from trivial.

10. These problems with the GATB do not reflect on the competence of its developers; they are a commentary on the way in which the GATB fits into the workforce. The ASVAB and the SAT are designed for identifiable customers who can collect statistics in a compatible manner from study to study. Because the GATB is used in a variety of settings, by many different customers, no one agency has either the authority or the finances to design studies similar to Project A, or even similar to the studies routinely conducted by the Educational Testing Service.

11. If personality and social attitude factors are important predictors of job performance, why not use personality and social attitude measures in personnel screening? In fact, such measures have been used for years. Project A, among other studies, found that noncognitive aspects of job performance could be predicted by personality and motivation measures better than by the ASVAB (McHenry et al., 1990, Table 7). On the other hand, a good deal of ambivalence has been expressed about the ethics of using "personality testing" to screen job applicants. Paradoxically, employers are willing to use personal interviews, which are notoriously unreliable and are certainly influenced by the personality and social attitudes of both the applicant and the interviewer!

12. Corrected correlations have also been reported for studies involving the ASVAB and the SAT. These corrections are generally based on observations of data beyond the data in the study in question, so there is more justification for accepting the correction.

13. While numerous studies show that alcoholism has a bad effect on overall job performance, the question here is about its effect on the cognitive aspects of job performance. Since alcoholism affects other aspects of performance (e.g., absenteeism), it is hard to separate these effects from job deterioration due to alcohol-induced cognitive loss.

4

A Psychometric View of the Future Workforce

DEMOGRAPHIC TRENDS IN COGNITIVE SKILLS

This chapter combines two different fields, psychometrics and demographics. It is an examination of how current demographic trends and social policies may alter the distribution of cognitive skills across the workforce in the next 10 to 15 years.

A workforce changes in three ways. People entering the workforce bring with them the cognitive skills established by their schools, family, and neighborhood. People leaving the workforce take their cognitive skills with them. Sometimes these skills have to be replaced; at other times the skills were already growing obsolescent. Finally, workers who stay on the job grow older each year. As they age they go through biological and social experiences that influence their cognitive capabilities.

The last trend, aging, will be the largest single influence on the American workforce in the next 20 years. Most of the people in the workforce today will be there in 2015, but they will certainly be older. In fact, during the early part of the twenty-first century, the proportion of the workforce over 35 will reach a historic high.

A great deal has been made of "workforce diversity," due to an increase in the proportion of women and minority group members. The coming workforce will contain a higher percentage of black, Hispanic, and Asian workers. As shown earlier, this change will be concentrated at the younger ages. Feminization of the workforce will be a smaller factor than aging and ethnic diversification, simply because women are already participating in the workforce at a historically high rate. There may well be a shift in the sorts of jobs that women occupy, but the details of this shift are very hard to predict.

The schools are by far the largest source of incoming labor for the U.S. workforce. Workforce projections must deal with changes in the quality of output of the educational system. The cry that "the schools are failing us" has been heard over and over again; Chapter 1 reviewed statistics showing that such a simplistic view is far from accurate. Over the last 20 years, American schools have done a good job of raising the cognitive skills of their poorest students. Most students go through at least the K–12 system and benefit from it. Even in one of the most persistently disadvantaged groups, black Americans, 80 percent of the young adults have high school diplomas or their equivalent (Jaynes and Williams, 1989, Chap. 7).[1] In the 1960s alarmists cried that "Johnny can't read." Today Johnny and Jane certainly can read, at least well enough to follow simple workday instructions.

Education begins to fail us as we increase our demands on the recent high school graduate. Reading and simple mathematics are one thing; understanding subtle arguments and using mathematics in problem solving are quite another. The schools are not doing as good a job for the average or above-average student; the SAT scores of high school seniors intending to enter college have been dropping steadily over the past 20 years. The percentage of students who achieve very high scores has also dropped. Such observations are cause for a good deal of concern, because they indicate that our schools may be weakest in preparing our most valuable workers.

What does all this mean? This chapter will offer a number of projections of workforce competency in the year 2000, as seen from the macroscopic views of the psychometrician, economist, and demographer.

COGNITIVE EFFECTS OF AGING IN THE WORKFORCE

The American workforce is aging dramatically. Figure 4.1 shows the changes in the percentage of the workforce over age 35, from 1970 through projected figures for 2000 and 2005. This trend is the highly predictable result of two facts: the "baby boom" in increased fertility from 1945 to 1965 and the "baby bust" of decreased fertility thereafter.

Figure 4.2 takes a somewhat more detailed look at the same data. This figure displays the proportion of the workforce in various age groups as of 1985, 1992, and as projected for 2005. By the turn of the century, the largest group of workers shifts from the under 35 categories to the 35–54 range. The fraction of workers beyond age 65 remains almost constant. The workforce is becoming middle-aged, but not old.

These trends do matter. Changes in cognitive competence with age have been extensively studied. The facts are relatively clear-cut. The conclusions that can be drawn from the facts are complex.

Figure 4.1 Changes over time in the fraction of the workforce over 35. Source: U.S. Bureau of the Census (1993).

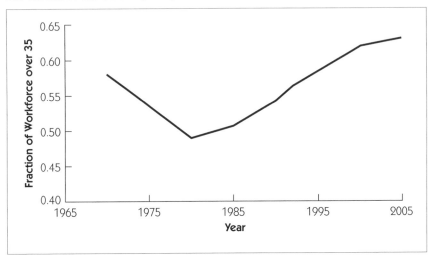

Figure 4.2 Age distribution of the workforce, 1985–2005. Source: U.S. Bureau of the Census (1993).

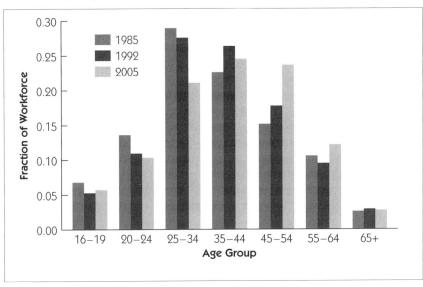

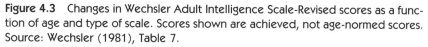

Figure 4.3 Changes in Wechsler Adult Intelligence Scale-Revised scores as a function of age and type of scale. Scores shown are achieved, not age-normed scores. Source: Wechsler (1981), Table 7.

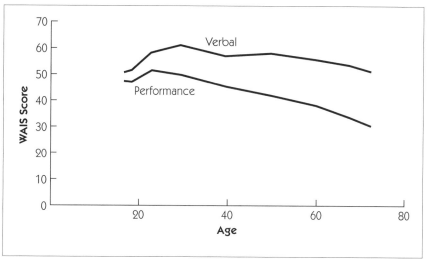

One of the most frequently repeated findings in the literature is that age affects verbal and nonverbal intelligence in different ways. A typical finding is shown in Figure 4.3, which displays the mean scores achieved on the WAIS-R by different age groups (Wechsler, 1981).[2] There are only small differences between 25–30-year-olds and 50–60-year-olds in verbal intelligence scores, but there are substantial differences in performance scores.

A number of psychologists prefer to distinguish between crystallized (*Gc*) and fluid (*Gf*) intelligence rather than verbal and nonverbal intelligence. (See Chapter 2.) They interpret the verbal-nonverbal distinction shown in Figure 4.3 as basically a *Gc-Gf* distinction (Horn, 1985).

These views can be amalgamated by distinguishing three different types of intelligence. The first type can be called either crystallized (*Gc*) or verbal intelligence. The reason for not distinguishing between the two is that, in practice, most tests that are used to predict success in the workplace require skills that fit the definition of either crystallized or verbal intelligence.[3] The second type, somewhat related to the first, is an ability to deal with abstract reasoning problems. This is probably the closest to what we mean by fluid intelligence. I shall use the terms "reasoning" and "fluid intelligence" more or less interchangeably. The third type is the ability to deal with visual-spatial reasoning. In the workplace visual-spatial reasoning seems to be important in certain rather specialized jobs, such as airplane pilots, architects, and surgeons. Furthermore, as Salthouse's review of aging effects (1990) shows, the relations between age and general reasoning tests almost exactly parallel the relations between age and visual-spatial reasoning tests. Therefore, for what follows here, we can treat fluid intelligence and visual-spatial ability equivalently.

Horn (1985) argues that crystallized abilities (*Gc*) increase throughout the working years, while reasoning and visual-spatial abilities decrease. He bases his argument on a good deal of data and some rather sophisticated analyses, which will not be repeated here. Salthouse (1990) is somewhat less optimistic about purely verbal abilities. He concludes that most of the data show some decline in verbal test scores and a marked decline in both general and visual-spatial reasoning scores.

When the National Research Council reviewed the GATB (Hartigan and Wigdor, 1989), it pointed out that test-performance (validity) correlations were almost uniformly lower for older workers than for younger workers. Less statistically, the tests do not predict the performance of older workers as well as they predict the performance of younger workers.

In the light of Horn's data, we can conclude that the fairly small declines in verbal performance test scores that are observed with age mask an increase in job-relevant knowledge that is not evaluated by a general intelligence test. Thus, the assumption that there is "crystallized intelligence," logically apart from verbal intelligence, is at least not counterindicated and is very probably supported by the data.

Extrapolating from Horn's summarization (1985), we can assume that crystallized intelligence (including job-relevant knowledge) increases by about .03 standard deviation units per year from age 20 through the working years (i.e., to age 65). The decline in reasoning and visual-spatial ability is somewhat more complex. After examining various figures and tables reported by Horn (1985) and Salthouse (1990), I have concluded that these abilities are constant from ages 16 through 30 and then decline at about .04 standard deviation units per year. No single study dictates these values, but I am willing to defend them as reasonably accurate summaries of many papers reported in the literature.

These figures can be used to estimate changes in workforce cognitive abilities that are associated with aging. A three-step calculation is needed:

1. Determine the mean *Gc* or *Gf* score expected for a particular age group.

2. Multiply the score by the percentage of the working population in the age group, separately for the 1985 workforce and the projected 2000 workforce.

3. Add the scores over all ages, separately for the past and future workforce.

This calculation shows that compared with the 1985 workforce the 2000 workforce will show an increase in crystallized intelligence skills of about .11 standard deviation units, due solely to an increase in aging. On the other hand, the same workforce will show a decrease of about .08 standard deviation units in fluid intelligence and visual-spatial skills, also solely because of aging. Numerically, these are small effects. However, they apply to the entire workforce, so very small differences could make large differences in terms of the number of individuals affected. I will postpone further discussion of this issue until other demographic changes have been discussed.

COGNITIVE EFFECTS OF RACIAL AND ETHNIC CHANGES IN THE WORKFORCE

Racial and Ethnic Differences

The discussion of racial and ethnic differences in cognition touches on one of the most explosive issues in American life. To make things worse, it is an issue on which any speaker is extremely likely to be misunderstood. Therefore, my presentation will be as precise as possible, at the expense of being somewhat pedantic. In turn, I hope that readers will take at face value what is said and will not attempt to draw inferences about what is not said.[4] Because the issues are so emotion laden, I shall first describe my view of the philosophical and political issues involved.

The historic fact of racial and ethnic group discrimination in the United States is well known, so there is no point in repeating the discussion here. Until the 1960s there were quite open legal and social barriers that denied minority group members an opportunity to compete for jobs commensurate with their abilities. Beginning in the 1960s the legal basis for discrimination changed, and, if anything, the present legal weight has shifted toward various forms of affirmative action. However, legal equality has not been accompanied by economic equality. Family income statistics show this clearly. In 1971 the median income for white families (in 1991 dollars) was $33,725. The figure for black families was $20,351. The figures for 1991 were $37,783 and $21,548, respectively.[5] This is only one of many statistics showing that our dominant minorities, blacks and Hispanics, do not begin to share equally in America's wealth. This is widely perceived as an undesirable social situation, a view that I personally share. The question is, "What can be done about it?"

It is important for us to consider this question because the way in which workforce diversification impacts upon cognitive skills depends on social policies about job assignment. This contrasts with the effects of aging, which are obviously uniform across the workforce and largely unamenable to social policies except retirement policies, which affect a relatively small proportion of the workforce. In the extreme, two policies for placing minority workers have been urged. Some people have maintained that, as a matter of justice for the group, the members of different ethnic groups should share equally in social rewards, such as good jobs. This will be called the Equality of Group Outcome (EGO) policy. The simplest way to ensure equality of outcome is to enforce a quota system in which a certain number of jobs are reserved for members of each ethnic group. Other people argue that our commitment to equal opportunity means a commitment to each individual to let that individual compete for whatever job he or she is qualified for, without regard to any favoritism one way or another because of ethnic status. This will be called the Equality of Individual Opportunity (EIO) policy. Proponents of EIO policy point out that if there are a finite number of jobs, reserving some of them for one ethnic group is in effect a discrimination against the other group.

A great many political and ethical arguments have been presented for or against each of these positions. Many of them have to do with appeals to moral principles, varying from retribution for past wrongs to the belief that the law should be "color blind" when it comes to judging the merits of individuals. Such issues, though real, are hardly suitable for analytical study. However, two of the arguments about EGO and EIO policies are amenable to analysis. The first has to do with efficiency. It seems unarguable that the ideal assignment policy should put people in jobs that are commensurate with their talents. The second is fairness. It seems equally unarguable that a good assignment policy should be perceived as fair by the people being assigned.

In practice, of course, both of these ideals are unachievable. Saying that the best people should have the best jobs carries with it a unidimensional notion of "best," which simply is not true. Lawyers, physicians, stockbrokers, and major league baseball players all make good incomes, but the people in these jobs are not interchangeable. Similarly, it would be wildly optimistic to assume that we could ever have an assignment policy that satisfied everyone, including those not assigned to particularly good jobs. On the subject of intelligence tests,

Kaplan (1985) remarked that many people think that a fair question is one that they can answer. The same remark applies, with even more force, to job assignment. We all know that good personnel decisions are made when *we* are hired, instead of *them*.

In spite of these remarks about reality, it is useful to analyze simplified, idealized cases of pure EIO and EGO policies. Such an analysis can highlight conflicts between them and, even more important, can point to situations where there is no conflict. Therefore, the analysis will now be offered. Then, knowing the results in the esoteric pure case, we may be better prepared to deal with the imperfect situations that actually do occur.

Of course, there would be no point to this analysis unless we had reason to suspect that workplace cognitive skills are not equally distributed across all ethnic groups. Unfortunately, we do. Most of the evidence is based on comparison of various cognitive achievement and intelligence tests. As we have seen, these tests do in fact predict workplace performance, and, therefore, they cannot be ignored. But more precisely, what is the evidence?

The Distribution of Cognitive Talents Across Ethnic Groups

Racial and ethnic differences in intelligence test scores were observed almost as soon as the tests began to be used. Blacks tended to score well below whites, urban dwellers scored above rural residents, and native-born Americans scored above immigrants. It is now believed that many of the initially observed differences were due to cultural biases in the tests. Early tests contained questions generally favoring native-born, well-educated Americans. Many differences between groups in test scores disappeared as various immigrant groups were assimilated into mainstream America. However, there were two notable exceptions: the difference between black and white scores and the difference between Hispanic and non-Hispanic, "Anglo" American scores remained.

Until about 1970 numerous research studies were carried out to investigate these differences. During the 1970s, though, political pressures mounted against research projects on racial and ethnic differences in intelligence. This pressure virtually stopped research in the field because good population studies tend to be expensive and, thus, cannot be carried out without federal sponsorship. I know of no carefully balanced racial or ethnic group comparisons that have been reported since about 1975.[6]

Loehlin, Lindzey, and Spuhler (1975) published an excellent summary of black-white comparisons, based on the data available at the

Figure 4.4   SAT Mathematics and Verbal scores of major ethnic groups, 1978–1992. Source: National Center for Educational Statistics (1993).

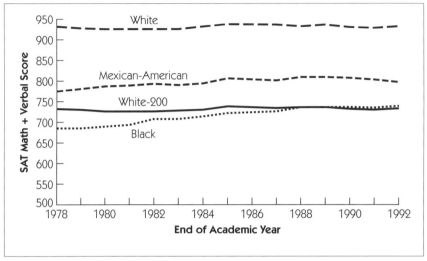

time. Their conclusions were carefully worded, and it does some injustice to the original authors to present a summary. Nevertheless, I shall try. The most accurate "one liner" describing their conclusions is that the black American population mean on general intelligence tests was, as of 1970, about one standard deviation below the white American mean. Jensen (1980) reached a similar conclusion. Subsequently, Humphreys (1988) reviewed a number of results on scholastic achievement tests, largely conducted in the 1970s and early 1980s. He agreed with Loehlin, Lindzey, and Spuhler and with Jensen, and noted that the Hispanic American mean score appears to be about .8 standard deviations below the white mean.

Figure 4.4 provides a concrete example. The figure shows SAT scores from 1978 to 1992. Scores are shown separately for whites, blacks, and Mexican Americans. The figure also shows the score 200 points below the white mean, which is the score that would be achieved by a group whose mean score on each subtest was approximately one standard deviation below the white group's score. The black score approximates the white 200 score, while the Mexican American score lies somewhat above it. The group differences are remarkably consistent, even though during this period considerable efforts were expended to improve educational opportunities for minority students.

Differences in SAT scores do not automatically generalize to differences in cognitive skills throughout the workforce. People who take the SAT are a self-selected group. In order to draw any general conclusions, we need to look at a variety of tests aimed at different portions of the workforce and, especially, the people in the latter high school years, who are about to become workforce entrants. Do these tests also show that our major ethnic groups trail white groups by about one standard deviation unit? Some illustrative results will now be offered, again relying heavily on graphic presentations. For those who wish more detail, Appendix 4.A presents the mathematical model behind the graphic demonstrations.

The basic idea is fairly simple. If we assume that test scores (i.e., achievement levels) are normally distributed, we can use well-known mathematical properties of the normal distribution to calculate what percentage of all scores falls between any two values. For instance, scores on the WAIS intelligence test (described in Chapter 2) are assumed to be normally distributed, with a mean of 100 and a standard deviation of 15. If this assumption is true, then two-thirds of all WAIS scores in a representative sample (*referent group*) of people should fall between 85 (100 − 15) and 115 (100 + 15). In fact, the scores in the WAIS referent group do fall very much in this way.

Suppose that we were told that some imaginary population had a mean score one standard deviation (i.e., 15 points) below the score of the referent group. Call this the "−15 group." To answer the question of what percentage of the −15 population would have test scores between 85 and 115 we have to ask the same question about the original sample, except that we add the difference to the scores. That is, instead of asking what percentage of the representative sample falls within the range 85–115 we ask what percentage falls within the range 100–130. (The answer is 48 percent.)

We could have begun with percentages of the referent group, instead of the absolute numbers. For instance, suppose that we begin with the observation that 30 percent of the referent group members have a WAIS IQ score above 108. What percentage of the −15 group would be expected to have scores above 108? This is equivalent to asking what percentage of the referent group would have scores above 123, and the answer is 7 percent.

I will now report some applications of this sort of analysis to the contrast between white-Asian and black-Hispanic scores on a variety of tests of cognitive skill as they have been revealed in survey studies.

The first study to be examined was performed by the National Center for the Assessment of Educational Progress and subsequently discussed in a National Academy of Science study panel report on the status of black Americans. A representative sample of young adults in the workforce, as of 1985, were tested on their understanding of the

Figure 4.5   Percentage of white and black young adults reaching various levels of competence on tests of workplaced-oriented document reading tasks. Also shown is the score predicted for the black group assuming that the mean black score is one standard deviation below the mean white score. Source: National Center for Educational Statistics (1993).

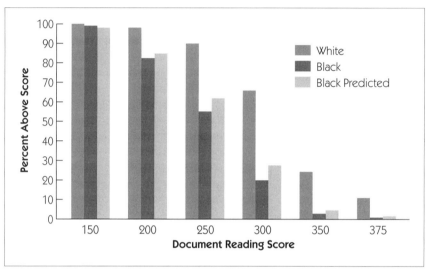

sorts of documents one has to deal with in the normal workday. The National Academy panel suggested the following nonstatistical points of reference (Jaynes and Williams, 1989, pp. 353–354):

Documents test:
    200 = ability to select and match store coupons.
    300 = ability to follow directions, using a map.

Quantitative test:
    200 = ability to add simple checkbook entries.
    300 = ability to enter and add accounting items.

The National Academy panel summarized the results by saying that the same percentages of blacks and whites could accomplish fairly simple reading and quantitative analysis tasks, but that whites showed a greater advantage as the tasks became harder.

It is possible to go a good bit beyond the National Academy's statement. Figure 4.5 shows the percentage of white and black young adults who achieved various levels of competence on a document reading test. Figure 4.6 is a similar figure for the evaluation of quantitative skills. Also shown is the percentage of blacks who would be predicted to

Figure 4.6 Percentage of white and black young adults reaching various levels of competence on tests of workplaced-oriented quantitative tasks. Also shown is the score predicted for the black group assuming that the mean black score is one standard deviation below the mean white score. Source: National Center for Educational Statistics (1993).

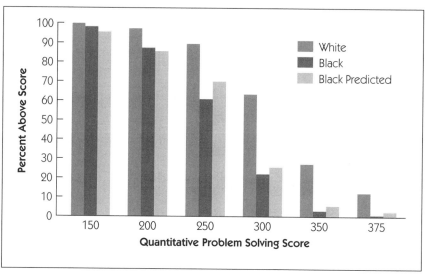

achieve each level of competence, on the assumption that (a) both black and white scores are distributed normally, with the same standard deviation, and (b) that the mean of the black population is one standard deviation unit below the white mean. (In the terms of the example computations, if the NAEP test had been scored as the WAIS is, the white scores would serve as the referent group and the black scores as the −15 group.) As can be seen, the match between data and prediction is quite close.

A similar picture applies to assessments of explicitly taught school topics. Knowledge of science is particularly important, because most observers believe that the possession of elementary knowledge about science will be a central skill in the coming workplace. Figure 4.7 shows how 17-year-olds fared in the 1989–1990 school year. The relevant levels are:

1. Understand simple scientific principles.
2. Apply basic scientific information to problems.
3. Analyze scientific procedures and data.
4. Integrate specialized scientific information in comprehension.

Figure 4.7   Percentage of 17-year-old students in major ethnic groups who achieve various levels of science understanding. (See text for description.) Also shown is the predicted percentages for a group whose mean score is one standard deviation below the mean for white students. Source: National Center for Educational Statistics (1993).

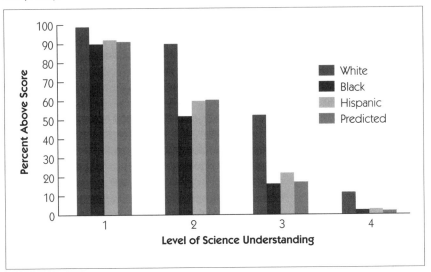

These scientific skills are quite different from document reading and elementary quantitative skills, but the relative picture across ethnic groups is very much the same. The distribution of black and Hispanic scores is approximately what would be expected if the skill level of the minority populations was about one standard deviation unit below the skill level of the white population.

These studies, and many others that there is not time to review (cf. Humphreys, 1988), strongly indicate that in most tests of cognitive competencies the black population mean is about one standard deviation level below the white population mean, and that the Hispanic population mean is slightly above the black mean. These intergroup differences seem to have been constant since 1975. There are some older data, which I have not cited, indicating that there were even greater differences in educational and cognitive achievement before 1970. The push for minority education has not been a failure, but progress toward intergroup equality seems to have stopped sometime in the 1970s. This conclusion is consistent with, although somewhat more detailed than, the conclusion of the National Academy panel on the status of black Americans (Jaynes and Williams, 1989). Furthermore, the result is definitely not confined to schoolchildren and young adults. In 1992 the Educational Testing Service, at the request of the Department of

Education, conducted extensive tests of cognitive skills in adults who had completed school (Kirsch et al., 1993). The ethnic group comparisons in this survey are generally consistent with the conclusions presented here.

The findings refer to test scores. Our interest, however, is in workplace performance. It has been claimed that test scores are not fair to minority group members, because the test scores do not predict their performance as accurately as they predict the performance of whites. To what extent is this claim warranted?

Whether or not test scores are "fair" to one or another group hinges on one's definition of fairness. This issue has been discussed extensively, because different definitions of fairness lead to different statistical conclusions. See Kaplan (1985) for a clear statement of the statistical issues involved. Hartigan and Wigdor (1989) provide a more abbreviated statement, with special attention to the GATB. The consensus seems to be as follows:

1. The tests predict that blacks and Hispanics will not perform as well as whites in a variety of criterion situations (college, workplace, military). This is not surprising, since there are systematic differences in test scores in the three populations.

2. In fact, blacks and Hispanics do not perform as well as whites in the criterion situations. However, the difference in performance is substantially less than the difference in test scores. Hartigan and Wigdor's analysis of the GATB suggests that the mean minority group performance is about .25 standard deviation units below white performance. This compares with the one standard deviation difference in test scores.

3. At the individual level, the accuracy with which a person's performance is predicted may be slightly less for minority group members than for whites, possibly because predictions of poor performance are not as accurate as predictors of good performance. This is clearly true for the prediction of college grades (Morgan, 1990) and may be true for other criteria. There would be a slight improvement in prediction if separate equations were used for whites and minority group members, but the improvement is not large enough to affect the sorts of arguments that will be made here.

Point 2 is most relevant here. Why do performance scores show smaller racial-ethnic scores than the tests do? It is not because the "tests are not accurate for minority group members"; if this were the case, prediction would fail at the individual level. Such failures, if they exist at all, are small (point 3). Some other causes could produce the effect.

We would not expect group differences in criterion performance scores (in standardized units) to be as large as differences in predictor scores unless the population validity coefficient was 1, that is, unless we had a perfect predictor. In fact, the size of the criterion difference, relative to the predictor difference, is proportional to the validity coefficient. Therefore, if a test had a population validity coefficient of .5, and there was a one standard unit difference in predictor scores, we should expect a .5 standard unit difference in criterion scores.

Second, Hartigan and Wigdor's estimate of .25 was not corrected for reliability or for restriction in range on the grounds that our interest is in the performance of people hired rather than people not hired, which is arguable. Also, it is not clear what the appropriate correction should be. Thus, all we know is that their estimate is probably a lower bound of the true value, but we do not know just how far it is from the best estimator.

Finally, there is a legitimate, but virtually unanswerable, question about differential validity of criterion ratings across groups. Both the objective measures of workplace performance and the ratings by peers and/or supervisors are subject to influences other than the abilities of the individual being evaluated. If assignments to workstations are affected by ethnic group status, objective measures of performance may not accurately reflect a person's ability. For example, there may be pressures either to assign minority salespersons to good territories or to do the opposite. Similarly, and once again depending on the situation, raters may be loath to assign high marks to a minority group member because of prejudice or may be afraid to assign low marks, even when deserved, for fear of charges of discrimination.

It is easy to imagine scenarios that would produce any one of these outcomes, and, in a workplace as large as the American workplace, no doubt all of them have some truth to them. There is no way to know which scenario is more prevalent. In all cases, though, the various scenarios represent noncognitive sources of variation in criterion scores that apply only to minority group members. Therefore, the effect of all of these social factors would be to reduce the validity coefficients for predictor tests within minority populations, not because the tests do not properly measure minority abilities, but because the criterion measures have been contaminated.

The Influence of Intergroup Differences in Cognition on the Distribution of Talent Across Job Classes

We now begin the first of several analytic studies of ideal cases, in which pure equality of individual opportunity (EIO) or equality of group outcome (EGO) policies are pursued. We start with an analysis of the effect of reasonable amounts of intergroup differences in cognitive skills, under the assumption that an EIO policy is in effect.

Under an EIO policy, jobs are ordered in terms of their cognitive demands, and assignment to jobs is made on the basis of estimated cognitive skill, regardless of ethnic status. The 10 percent most qualified people are assigned to the 10 percent most demanding (and presumably best paid) jobs, the next 10 percent of the most qualified to the next 10 percent most demanding jobs, and so on until all people are assigned. The lowest job class includes the unemployed, so assignment applies to everyone.

The alternative, the equality of group outcome (EGO) policy, is to determine the percentages of individuals in each group within the population and to use these percentages to reserve jobs for particular groups within each category. For instance, if this model were to be applied to the workforce in 2000, about 20 percent of the jobs at every level would be reserved for blacks and Hispanics. The EIO assignment policy would be followed within each subpopulation, so that the best-qualified people *within each subpopulation, but not necessarily within the population as a whole,* would be assigned to the best jobs, then the next best jobs, and so forth, down the line.

It is easy to make qualitative statements about these models. The predicted average performance level, across all jobs, will be identical under each assignment model—it will simply be the mean of the population as a whole. The models differ in their effect on the various job classes.

Under an EIO model, the most demanding jobs will have occupants whose job skills approximate those of the best-qualified population, as can be seen by doing some rough calculations based on the NAEP data presented in the last section. Imagine that we define the job class "entry-level professional and white-collar worker," for which document reading skills are the best predictor. Assume further that this job will take the best 20 percent of the available workforce. Looking at Figure 4.5, we see that in terms of document reading the top 20 percent consists, approximately, of the 25 percent of the whites (who are 80 percent of the workforce) who have scores of 350 or above and perhaps 3 percent of the blacks and Hispanics (20 percent of the workforce) who have equivalent skills. The professional–white-collar workforce would have a majority:minority ratio of better than 20:1, even though the population ratio is 4:1.

If we looked at the other end of the population, we would find an opposite effect. Minority group members would be disproportionately represented in the least demanding jobs, because most majority members would have been assigned by the time the bottom jobs were to be filled.

Under an EGO model, we require that the population majority : minority ratio be maintained in each skill group. In our example the professional–white-collar entrants would consist of the top 20 percent of the white group, all with scores ranging upward from 350, and the top 20 percent of the minority group, whose scores would range upward from 300. Clearly, the average skill level in the high-skill job category will have dropped from its value under the EIO model.

The point should be clear. There are two relevant outcome variables: the mean skill level of individuals in each job category and the majority : minority ratios. If we maximize the skill level, we let the ratio vary; if we hold the ratio fixed at the population level, we will drive down the skill level in the higher jobs and raise it in the lower jobs. This is usually considered undesirable, on the assumption that the most skilled jobs are most valuable to society. While one can carp about the extraordinary salaries paid to a few special individuals, such as entertainers and athletes, the assumption is generally reasonable.

How large would these effects be, given some reasonable assumptions about the percentage of minority group members in the workforce and the disparity in workplace skill that might exist across groups? I have worked out effect sizes for these variables, and for some others to be presented shortly, under a number of different assumptions. (The mathematical details have been relegated to Appendix 4.B.)

Consider an idealized workforce in which job classes are grouped into deciles, from the 10 percent most desirable jobs (job class 9) to the 10 percent least desirable jobs (job class 0). The following assumptions were made about the workforce and the population.

1. The workforce consists of two subpopulations, A and B, with 80 percent of the workforce in population A and 20 percent in population B.

2. Within each subpopulation cognitive abilities are distributed randomly, with means μ_A and μ_B and standard deviations ϕ_A and ϕ_B, respectively.

3. Scoring will be by standard units in the distribution of scores in subpopulation A. Therefore, $\mu_A = 0$ and $\phi_A = 1$ in all analyses.

4. Across different analyses the mean of the ability distribution in population B will vary between $\mu_B = -1$ and $\mu_B = 0$. The standard deviation will vary from $\phi_B = 1$ (identical variability in the two subpopulations) to $\phi_B = 2$ (twice as much within subpopulation variability in population B as in population A).

5. Two job assignment policies are considered: the EIO model, in which people are assigned to jobs in order of skill, without regard to group membership, or the EGO model, in which the top 10 percent of the individuals within each group are assigned to job class 0, the next 10 percent to job class 1, and so forth.

Assumption 1 is intended to make the analysis mirror the majority-minority distribution in the workforce, as projected for the year 2000. Assumptions 2 and 3 establish scoring conventions. Under these assumptions the "average" majority group performance is always zero. Negative scores represent below-average performance (with respect to the majority group); positive scores represent above-average performance. Two thirds of all performance scores in the majority group will lie between 1 and -1.

Assumption 4 establishes the abilities of the minority group with respect to the majority group. Since we are concerned with a situation in which B group has lower average skills, we consider only cases $\mu_B \leq 0$. To avoid dealing with negative numbers, it will be more useful to express an assumption about intergroup differences in terms of the size of the difference, d, where

$$d = \mu_A - \mu_B. \qquad (4.1)$$

In this notation $d = 1$ represents the difference in between-groups performance scores that would be expected if cognitive tests were perfect predictors (validity coefficient equal to one). This represents an upper bound on group differences in performance. The value $d = 0$ represents a situation in which there is no difference between groups or, equivalently, the situation if the cognitive tests did not predict workplace performance at all. The data reviewed show that this is not the case, so $d = 0$ is a lower bound on group differences. The value $d = .25$ corresponds to Hartigan and Wigdor's estimate (1989) for the GATB review. I argued earlier that this is a reasonable lower bound on the true value of d. The value $d = .5$ is the value that would be expected if the cognitive tests have a population validity coefficient of .5. I regard this as the most reasonable estimate, but others might disagree.

Assumptions about ϕ_B refer to relative variability within groups. Assigning $\phi_B = 1$ assumes equal within-group variability. However, some studies suggest that minority group test scores are more variable than majority group scores, particularly if different ethnic groups are lumped together. Therefore, it is of some interest to explore situations in which ϕ_B is greater than one.

The first thing to do is to dismiss a pernicious myth. Occasionally

Figure 4.8 The mean effectiveness within job classes, as a function of the decile level of the job class and the mean difference between population subgroups. The figure assumes that .8 of the population fall into the more effective subgroup (A) and .2 fall into the less effective subgroup (B).

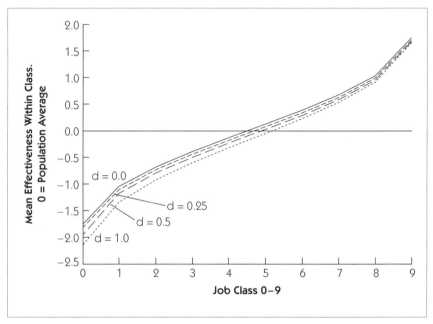

comments are made that the entire workforce is being dragged down by an "incapable" group of minority workers. Indeed, T. Nakasone, the prime minister of Japan in the late 1980s, caused something of a furor by a statement very much like this. (He later denied that he said it, but the press had a transcript of his remarks.) Such statements are simply not true.

Figure 4.8 shows the relevant data. This figure plots the mean effectiveness of the population, under the conditions described previously. Look at how close the lines are to each other. For the topmost job classes, effectiveness is virtually constant, regardless of the value of d, that is, regardless of the size of the between-groups differences. Intergroup differences do affect performance levels in the less desirable jobs, but they are sizable only for $d = 1$, the highest estimate we consider for the size of intergroup differences. Even if this estimate is correct, the effect may be of little economic importance, since there is relatively little difference in value between high and low performance in the less desirable job classes.

Virtually all discussions of the economic effects of intergroup differ-

Figure 4.9 Mean effectiveness within job classes as a function of the differences between mean effectiveness of subgroups (d) and the relative variation (SR) in effectiveness within the two subgroups (see text).

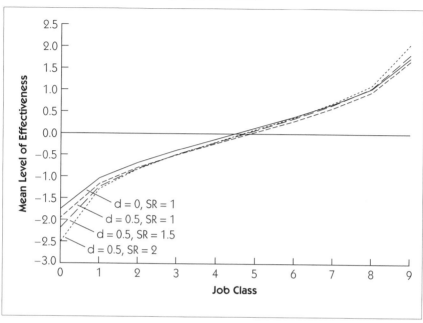

ences in talent focus on mean differences. Differences in the within-group variation in ability can be quite important. Figure 4.9 shows mean effectiveness levels for different job groups under the assumptions that $d = .5$, with the ratio (SR) of group B:group A standard deviations varying from 1.0 (equality) to 2. For comparison, the case of a uniform population ($d = 0$, ratio of standard deviations $= 1$) is also shown. Clearly, differences do appear as within-group variation increases. In fact, if we assume extreme variation (SR = 2), performance in the best jobs (9th decile) actually exceeds the effectiveness observed in the equality condition. On the other hand, as variation increases, the effectiveness level in the lowest job classes decreases, relative to the equality condition.

Arguments about the effects of within-group variation are more than mathematical/statistical niceties. The term "minority" lumps together a number of disparate groups. Blacks do not show the same test score distributions as Hispanics, and various Hispanic groups differ among themselves. Since the 1960s a substantial number of blacks have moved into the economic middle class, while, as is well known, the economic and social conditions of poorer blacks have not improved.

Figure 4.10 The effect of an EIO policy. Ratio of group A to group B members in different job classes as a function of the difference between group A and B members in mean effectiveness (*d*) and relative within group variation in effectiveness (SR). The case of equality (*d* = 0, SR = 1) is shown for comparison.

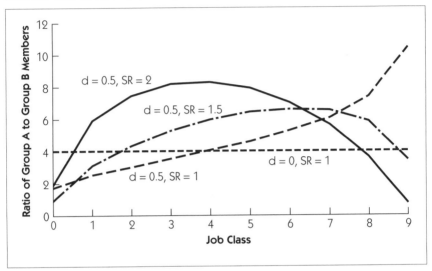

All these effects would produce greater within-group variation in group B, and, as Figure 4.9 shows, these effects are not small.

The reason for the effects shown in these two figures can be understood without a lengthy excursion into statistics. Under an EIO policy, reduced effectiveness in the smaller group does not influence the more desirable job classes (Figure 4.8) because very few group B members are assigned to those jobs. The reason that increases in within-group B variation influence effectiveness in the extreme job classes (Figure 4.9) is that as the variation increases some very talented B group members begin to occupy the top job classes, thus increasing effectiveness in those jobs, while some quite untalented group B members must be assigned to the least desirable jobs.

The upshot of these analyses is that under a pure EIO policy the effects of intergroup differences in mean performance are, on the average, quite small. Perhaps more important, these effects are negligible for the most desirable jobs. Under an EIO policy, effectiveness is not the problem. Perceived social justice is.

The EIO policy maintains effectiveness within job classes by permitting large discrepancies in the representation of group A and B members across classes. Group B members virtually disappear from the top job classes and are heavily overrepresented at the bottom. This is shown in Figure 4.10, which plots the ratio of group A:group B members for each job class, under the same assumptions used to construct Figure 4.9. Dramatic differences are immediately apparent. Group B members are generally disproportionately underrepresented in the top 70 percent of the jobs and overrepresented in the bottom 30 percent. The only exception to this situation is that if there is a great deal of variation in performance within group, B members of that group may capture a good many of the jobs at the very top.

Let us consider what these graphs imply. Imagine a simplified society consisting of an upper class, "movers and shakers" (the top 10 percent of the population); an upper middle class, white-collar and upper blue-collar workers (50th to 90th percentiles); a lower middle class, "blue-collar trades" (20th to 50th percentiles); and a lower class (the bottom 20 percent of the population). Assume the case of a mean difference between populations of .5 and a ratio of standard deviations of 1.25. Under the EIO model, the following statements would be true:

1. Within the upper class, there would be a slight excess of group A to group B members, 5.2:1 instead of the 4:1 in the population.

2. The performance of the group B members in the upper class would, on the average, exceed that of group A members; the values would be 1.73 to 1.82 in group A standard deviation units.

3. Within the upper middle class, there would be a larger disparity between group A and group B members, varying from 6.2:1 to 5.5:1, depending on where in that class one chose to look.

4. There would be no difference in performance levels of groups A and B within the upper middle class.

5. Within the lower middle class, the ratios of group A to group B members would be 4.4:1, approximating the 4:1 ratio in the population.

6. There would be no difference in performance levels of groups A and B within the lower middle class.

7. Within the lower class, group A members would be underrepresented, 1.9:1 instead of 4:1.

8. The performance of group A members in the lower class would exceed that of group B members, the opposite of the case in the upper class population.

This example shows how an EIO policy can present the perception of discrimination. The statistical effects presented here are solely due to selection on merit, without explicit consideration of group membership, but consider the perceptions of the individuals within each job class. Based on their personal experiences, the movers and shakers would not understand why group B members should be underrepresented in the upper middle-class jobs. This perception would be reinforced by studies that showed that, throughout the middle-class job range, jobholders from groups A and B performed equally well. Such observations could well lead to a conclusion that efforts should be instituted to recruit talent for the upper middle class from among the group B members in the lower-class jobs. Indeed, many affirmative action programs are justified on precisely this rationale. Such programs might well be resented by group A members holding lower-class jobs, because, based on their personal experience, they actually outperform group B members.

An analysis like this cannot prove that the present disparity of economic rewards in U.S. society is due solely to intergroup differences in performance. That question can be answered only by empirical studies that are hard to design and even harder to evaluate. The analysis does show that many of the characteristics of disparities in job assignment that might be seen as evidence of discrimination can be mimicked by a mathematical model of job assignment based on just two assumptions: that jobs are assigned on merit only and that intergroup differences in mean and variability of talent level do exist.

Economic and Social Effects of an EGO Policy

Under an EGO policy, jobs are assigned to group members in each job class in accordance with their group's share of the population. Within a group, though, jobs are assigned according to perceived merit.

Such policies are not unknown. In the late 1980s the Department of Labor applied an EGO policy to make job referrals based on the GATB. Employers were informed of an applicant's relative standing on the test within his or her ethnic group rather than in order of standing within the overall population. The Department of Labor's procedure (and other similar examples) was called a "quota system" by its attackers and "within-group norming" by its defenders. The policy was dropped in 1991, when the attorney general ruled that it amounted to a quota system, which was forbidden by law.[7]

Whatever the legal aspects of the situation, the attorney general was on impeccable mathematical grounds. A job assignment system that scores individuals relative to their own group's norms will inevitably lead to a referral system in which individuals from two subpopulations are referred for positions in each job class in the exact proportion of

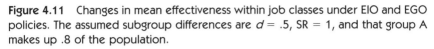

Figure 4.11 Changes in mean effectiveness within job classes under EIO and EGO policies. The assumed subgroup differences are $d = .5$, SR $= 1$, and that group A makes up .8 of the population.

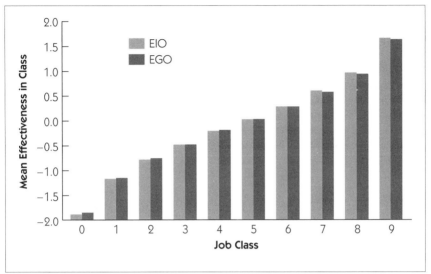

the two subpopulations in the overall population. If the employer uses the referrals, the EGO policy is complete.

The EGO policy does not necessarily force job qualifications upward or downward over the entire range of the workplace. In the top job classes group B members are offered positions over more qualified group A members, which reduces top-level effectiveness. On the other hand, effectiveness in the lower job classes should increase, as better qualified group A members are forced into them. Conceivably the two effects could balance each other out.

In practice such fortunate balancing is unlikely, because the relative worth of a highly skilled person compared with a barely qualified person is usually greater in the top job classes than in the bottom classes. The difference between an excellent and an adequate surgeon is greater than the difference between an excellent janitor and an adequate one.

In spite of our ability to generate such apocryphal examples, under the conditions of the total U.S. workforce, the differences in effectiveness under EGO and EIO policies are not large. Figure 4.11 displays the mean effectiveness within each job class under each policy. EIO performance is slightly higher in the top job classes, while EGO performance is slightly higher in the lower job classes.

A problem with this analysis is that it depends upon a rather esoteric

Figure 4.12   The fraction of the workforce that would be qualified for each job class under an EIO policy but would be assigned to a lower job class under an EGO policy.

measure, effectiveness measured relative to the variation in effectiveness in group A. Although this measure can be justified on statistical grounds, it does not have an intuitive interpretation. An alternative approach, which is more intuitive, is to calculate the extent to which implementation of an EGO policy forces people in the more skilled group to accept jobs below the level they would have obtained under an EIO system. One can argue that these individuals are being underutilized, since they are not allowed to contribute commensurate with their talent level. Thus, this analysis stresses suboptimal utilization of whatever cognitive talent is present in the workforce.

Figure 4.12 shows the extent of suboptimal utilization under an EGO policy. Two different cases are shown: the extremely pessimistic situation ($d = 1$, SR = 1) case and the more realistic $d = .5$, SR = 1.25 situation. The total fraction of the workforce suboptimally utilized is .41 in the pessimistic scenario and .19 in the realistic one. These two statistics should be disturbing to anyone who is concerned with workforce efficiency. Quite aside from any moral or legal considerations, underutilization of 20–40 percent of the workforce is a serious matter.

If we were to look only at effectiveness levels (Figure 4.11), we might be tempted to say that the difference between an EIO and an EGO policy is trivial. If we look at suboptimal utilization (Figure 4.12), it appears that the difference is substantial. The reason for this apparent paradox is that although a substantial number of people are underutilized by an EGO policy, they are not underutilized very much. In fact, by pushing talented group A members downward, the EGO policy upgrades or leaves unchanged the levels of effectiveness in all but the top job classes.

A major argument against an EIO policy is that it can lead to the perception of prejudice. An EGO policy can lead to a similar perception because of a ratio that I will call the jealousy quotient. It is not quite the same as underutilization, although the two are related. The jealousy quotient is intended to reflect the situation if a group A member has been denied access to a desirable job class, but knows that a group B member with equal or even lower job effectiveness has been accepted. The jealousy quotient, J_k, is defined as

J_k = fraction of group A members assigned to class $k - 1$
or lower, but with talent scores above that of the
lowest group B score assigned to job class k.

A person can be jealous without being underutilized because a person is in the "jealous" category if someone of lesser talent is assigned to a higher job class, while a person is underutilized only if he or she is sufficiently talented to be assigned to the higher class under an EIO policy. Anyone who is underutilized will always be jealous, but the converse is not true. A person will be jealous but not underutilized if he or she qualifies as jealous, but would be beaten out for the job by other group A members under an EIO policy.[8]

Figure 4.13 shows the jealousy quotients for the $d = 1$, SR = 1 and $d = .5$, SR = 1.25 cases. Clearly, there is a substantial amount of jealousy in each case. As was the case for the underutilization quotients, the jealousy quotients are highest for the intermediate groups and lower at the extremes. The jealousy quotient is low in the bottom ranks because these jobs are assigned only after a substantial portion of group A members have found jobs. At the top, even within a quota system relatively few group A members will be able to meet the standard set by the very best group B members, and hence will not be jealous.

Implications of the Analysis

A mathematical model is an abstraction of reality. Job assignment is seldom, if ever, made solely on the basis of test scores. However, it is useful to ask what would happen if this were the case. Under an EIO model, a group that is more talented, on the average, will be greatly

Figure 4.13 "Jealousy" under an EGO policy as a function of job classes. The jealousy quotient for a job class is the fraction of the group A workforce who have higher effectiveness scores than a group B member assigned to that job class, but who are themselves assigned to a lower job class.

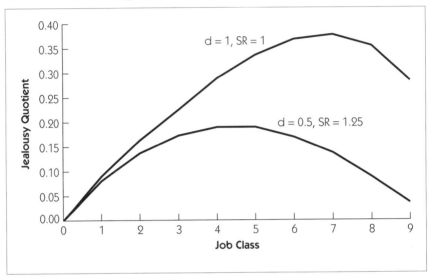

overrepresented in the more desirable job classes. Similarly, a group that is less talented, on the average, will be disproportionately represented in the less desirable job classes. Furthermore, the disparity in average ability does not have to be very great to produce a marked disparity in representation at the extremes.

There is a somewhat surprising codicil to this conclusion. If there is greater variance in the less talented group than in the more talented group, then under some circumstances the less talented group may actually have higher representation in the very best job classes than it does in the upper middle range of job classes.

The disparities in job assignment within an EIO model could easily lead to the perception that assignment has been made on the basis of group membership. Consider how the situation might look to a majority group member who is a committed EIO advocate and is in the upper job class—that is, one of the "movers and shakers" in our society. This person would look around his or her own job class and see a reasonable number of minority group members. Therefore, on the basis of personal experience, the society leader would be justified in concluding that there is no group difference in cognitive skills. The society leader then discovers that minority group members are hardly ever found in the jobs immediately below the top level. Clearly, someone is prejudiced, and a program is called for!

A minority group member in the lower job classes could well come to the same conclusion. This individual would see a disproportionate number of his own group at the bottom and would be aware of sharp disparities in representation in favor of the majority group just a few ranks above his or her own. The minority group member would be aware of a few fellow minority members at the very top, but this could be dismissed as tokenism.

I have intentionally chosen language to dramatize how a pure EIO model might produce a society that looked prejudiced. The perception could lead to demands for some form of quota system. The demands would probably be based on a sincere desire for equality of individual opportunity and a mistaken belief that such equality did not exist. Furthermore, there would be a rational argument for introducing a quota system, if only to stave off wasteful intergroup conflicts. So what would happen if the EGO model was used?

An EGO policy would have very little effect on mean group performance within most job classes, but the effects would be most severe in the top job classes. While the exact economic cost is hard to evaluate, it is disturbing to realize that the job classes most impacted by an EGO policy are, by definition, the jobs where performance is most valuable. It is also clear that an EGO policy underutilizes talent to a considerable degree.

In the cases investigated here, an EGO policy could place up to 70 percent of group A members in the jealous category. While this has no direct economic implication, it could produce undesirable intergroup tensions by convincing group A members that reverse discrimination was holding them down. It is of some interest to note that, on solely analytic grounds, the number of people who might feel discriminated against, on the grounds that they were more qualified than an individual who actually received a desirable position, is always greater than the number of individuals who are actually displaced due to an EGO policy.

The results have been presented as an analysis of a hypothetical case. They do seem tied to reality. The $d = .5$, SR = 1.25 model seems to be the most likely description of the projected U.S. workforce, with the white-Asian group playing the role of group A and the black-Hispanic group playing the role of group B. Furthermore, these conclusions do not seem to be terribly sensitive to the exact values assumed. Suppose that we were to accept the National Academy of Science panel's conclusions about ethnic differences in workforce effectiveness

(Hartigan and Wigdor, 1991). These are close to the $d = .25$, SR $= 1$ model, and would not change the conclusions in any material way.

The analysis has been conducted on a "what if" basis that assumes that all jobs in the workplace are assigned using either an EGO or EIO policy. In fact, no such sudden rearrangement of jobs would ever take place. What is much more likely is that employment policies would be applied to new entrants to the workforce. As we have seen in earlier chapters, the entering workforce in the 2000–2005 period will consist of about 60 percent whites and Asians and about 40 percent blacks and Hispanics, rather than the 80–20 contrast that applies to the workforce as a whole. If we apply the analysis to the entering workforce ($d = .5$, SR $= 1.25$, with group A containing 60 percent of the population), the trends seen in Figures 4.11–4.13 are somewhat amplified. The EGO and EIO policies produce only slight changes in mean effectiveness within job classes, but there is a 41 percent underutilization of talent using an EGO instead of an EIO policy. On the other hand, the EIO policy will produce marked disparity in group A:group B membership in the most desirable job classes.

There is no easy way out. An EIO model leads to an unacceptable degree of apparent discrimination, and an EGO model leads to an unacceptable amount of underutilization and jealousy.

This dilemma will remain with us as long as the U.S. workforce consists of groups who differ in their levels of cognitive competence. Therefore the constructive thing to do is to reduce that difference. Furthermore, the reduction must be real, not cosmetic. The issue is not one of placing members of varying ethnic groups into good jobs; it is of preparing the members of these groups to compete for these jobs, so that they win them on their own merits. We should also actively consider methods of altering jobs, so that they maximize the productivity of the individuals available to be assigned to them. Psychometric psychology has nothing to say about either issue, but cognitive psychology may. We will return to this point in Chapters 5 and 6.

Cognitive Effects of the Feminization of the Workforce

Since 1970 the percentage of women participating in the workforce has steadily increased. In 1970, 43.4 percent of all adult women worked, in 1989, 57.4 percent worked, and the projected figure for 2000 is 62.6 percent. The comparable figures for men are 79.7, 76.4, and 75.9 percent.[9] This is an important fact for social policy. Individual worker mobility will be reduced, and there will be a need for greatly increased child care (Johnston and Packer, 1987). There may well be a number of other changes in the social aspects of the workplace. Here, though, we are concerned solely with the implications of feminization in terms of cognitive power. These are small, because the cognitive differences between men and women are much more a matter of relative strengths in different areas, rather than any overall differences in general intelligence.

When dealing with cognitive differences between men and women, we must distinguish between verbal, visual-spatial, and problem-solving abilities. Within the normal range of language ability, there are virtually no differences between men and women in verbal ability.[10]

However, there are reliable and substantial differences between them in visual-spatial reasoning. Given comparable samples, the average male score on a visual reasoning test is usually about .5 standard deviation units above the female score, which means that about 31 percent of the women score above the male mean and about 69 percent of all men score above the female mean. This conclusion is based on a large number of studies, using many different tests (Halpern, 1992).

There is considerable debate about the cause of these differences: Most observers agree that male-female differences in spatial reasoning have both physiological and social causes, but there is disagreement about how much is biology and how much is sociology. Fortunately, for our purposes we do not need to go into the issue, since we are concerned about what the difference implies, rather than what produces the difference.

Male-female differences have also been reported in a variety of tests of "reasoning." The nature of this difference is hard to pinpoint, because in human beings logical reasoning is often content-specific. People reason well about familiar things and poorly about unfamiliar things, even though the same abstract reasoning methods can be applied to familiar and unfamiliar fields (Johnson-Laird & Byrne, 1991). Two areas of reasoning are worth special discussion because of their importance in the workplace.

Both scientific studies and popular wisdom hold that, on the average, men do much better than women in mathematics. The size of male-female differences depends on the level of mathematical reasoning required and the extent to which men and women have the same experience with mathematics. Male-female differences in grade-school mathematics are small. Males begin to score higher than females when the tests involve higher levels of mathematics, especially if they emphasize problem solving rather than procedure execution, and when those tested are adolescents or older. In the words of a review article:

> There is a slight female superiority in performance in the elementary and middle school years. A moderate male superiority emerged in the high

school years ($d = .29$) and continued in the college years ($d = .41$) as well as adulthood ($d = .59$). . . . It was in problem solving that the dramatic age trends emerged. (Hyde et al., 1990, p. 149)

Extreme cases best illustrate the truth of this statement. During the 1970s and early 1980s, Julian Stanley and his colleagues at Johns Hopkins University conducted an extensive study of junior high school students who had been identified as mathematically precocious. Roughly, the researchers tried to identify people in the top 1 to 5 percent of mathematical ability. Almost 50,000 12- and 13-year-olds were tested, using the SAT-M examination (which is intended for 17-year-olds). Among students who scored over 500 (the 17-year-old mean), the ratio was 2 boys to 1 girl. Among students who scored over 600, the ratio was 4 to 1; and over 700, 12 to 1 (Benbow, 1988).

It is clear that in the United States today high-level mathematical skills are more common among men than women. This is especially true for people of working age and for the highest skill levels. The cause of male-female differences in mathematical reasoning are irrelevant here; the important point is that unless we make some changes in education and society during the 1990s, the present male-female disparity in mathematical ability will continue, and an increase in feminization of the workforce will lead to a decline in the relative prevalence of high-level mathematical reasoning skills.

The data on a variety of mechanical reasoning tests are generally similar to the data for mathematical reasoning. On the average, men do better than women. In the case of mechanical reasoning, however, one has to be sure that the problem is not one of either familiarity with the content of the questions or a side effect of the well-established difference between men and women in visual-spatial reasoning. Visual-spatial ability may be a factor because many tests of mathematical reasoning present the examinee with a diagram of a device—for example, machinery with gears and levers—and ask questions that refer to the diagram.

As a rough approximation, I suggest that there is a .4 standard deviation unit difference between adult men and women (i.e., those in the workforce) in mathematical and abstract reasoning. This fact is not likely to have much effect on workforce skills in 2000, relative to 1985, for two reasons. First, when the .5 correlation between workforce skills and test performance is applied, it leaves only a .2 standard unit difference in job skills, a difference that applies only to specialized jobs. Second, the increased feminization from 1985 to 2000, although real, implies only about a 3 percent change in the male:female ratios in the workforce as a whole.

Hesitantly, because I regard the data here as perhaps the weakest of the data I have surveyed, I suggest the following estimates. Because of increased feminization, the following changes will apply to workforce 2000, relative to workforce 1985:

1. There will be no changes in average levels of verbal and/or crystallized intelligence.
2. Workforce 2000 will have a .01 to .02 standard deviation unit decrease in fluid intelligence and visual-spatial reasoning abilities. This is calculated on the basis of a 3 percent increase (from 44 to 47 percent) in the percentage of workers who are women and a .4 standard deviation unit difference between men and women on the relevant abilities. (Note that this difference is small compared with age effects.)

There are a few specialized tasks in which performance appears to be closely related to either visual-spatial or mathematical reasoning. For those jobs only, the male-female difference in psychometrically defined talent probably approximates the .5 deviation unit difference in general cognitive skills suggested for the white-Asian versus black-Hispanic ethnic groups. Therefore, the analysis of the effects of EIO and EGO policies discussed earlier applies to male-female differences within those occupations that strongly demand mathematical and/or spatial-visual reasoning skills.

A SUMMARIZING MODEL

Various reviews of the psychometric evidence indicate that the effects of age, ethnic status, and feminization are statistically independent. For instance, the age-related trends in fluid and crystallized intelligence appear to be about the same for men and women. Therefore, it is possible, in theory, to add them together. In practice the best we can do is make a rough approximation, because of deficiencies in both the psychometric data and in the economic statistics.[11] Rough as it is, this projection is informative.

Relative to the workforce in 1985, the workforce in 2000 will show an *increase* in verbal-crystallized intelligence skills of about .10 standard deviation units and a comparable *decrease* in fluid intelligence-reasoning and visual-spatial problem-solving skills of .10 standard deviation units. What does this mean in terms of the availability of adequately skilled workers?

In order to answer this question, I offer a somewhat idealized model. Let us assume that the workforces in 1985 and 2000 can be described as normal distributions of talent. Consider again the 10 deciles of job skills, ordered by desirability. The jobs in the 9th decile are those that required the skills held by the top 10 percent of workers in the 1985 workforce. The jobs in the 8th decile are those that required the skills held by the top 20 percent, and so forth, down to the first decile (90 percent of the 1985 workforce qualified). We then ask what percentage of workers in the projected 2000 workforce will qualify for each of the deciles.

This depends on precisely what we mean by skills. If we mean crystallized intelligence skills, then the percentage of available workers generally increases by about 2 to 3 percent in each decile. For instance, by definition, 10 percent of the 1985 workforce was qualified for the 9th decile of jobs emphasizing crystallized intelligence. About 12 percent of the 2000 workforce will be so qualified. On the other hand, if the job emphasizes fluid intelligence and problem-solving skills rather than skills acquired by experience, the opposite occurs. Only 8 percent of the projected workforce will be qualified for 9th decile jobs requiring fluid intelligence.

A useful way of looking at this problem is to ask how hard it will be to find a qualified person for each job class in 2000 compared with how hard it was to find such a person in 1985. To do this, consider an idealized employment market, in which an employer interviews applicants at random until a suitable applicant is found. How many interviews will this take, on the average, in 2000 compared with 1985? The statistic of interest is (number of interviews required in 2000)/(number of interviews required in 1985). If this ratio is above one, it means that more interviews will be needed in 2000 than in 1985; a ratio below one means the opposite.

Figure 4.14 shows how this statistic varies across different levels of job class, separately for jobs requiring crystallized or fluid intelligence skills.[12] To the extent that skill means experience, the workforce of 2000 will be better prepared than the workforce of 1985. If skill means problem solving, the workforce of 2000 will be, in a word, crystallized, and it will be harder to find people with appropriate levels of fluid intelligence. How strong these effects are depends very much on the general skill level involved: the higher the skill level, the greater the effect.

These results can be summarized by the following example: If the CEO of a manufacturing firm wants to hire a security guard, the job market in 2000 will be about what it was in 1985. If the firm has invented a product and needs to hire an experienced lawyer to protect patent rights (a job requiring a high level of crystallized intelligence), prospects will be better in 2000 than they were in 1985. But if the CEO wants to hire a creative scientist to invent a new product (a high-level fluid intelligence job), the CEO of 2000 will long for the good old days.

Figure 4.14   The effort (interviews per successful candidate) required to select a person with requisite *Gf* and *Gc* skills in various job classes: 2000 relative to 1985.

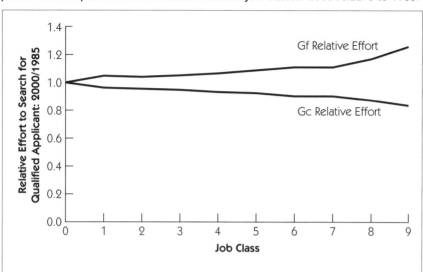

PROJECTIONS

Workforce skills associated with verbal intelligence and crystallized problem solving will increase during the next decade. The increase is almost entirely due to the aging of the workforce. Any absolute defects in the starting point, that is, the skill levels as they existed in 1985, will be retained. In particular, if we regard our workforce as competing against European and Japanese workforces, we must realize that those workforces are also aging and will gain the same benefits in crytallized intelligence as our own workforce.

A competitive advantage for our workforce could be obtained only if we either embarked on a retraining program for those in the workforce or if we markedly improved our school system and, through it, the qualifications of the entering workforce. The problems with the schools have already been discussed. Historically, the United States has been much less receptive to worker training than have the European and industrialized Asian countries. The analysis offered here does not provide room for complacency.

One fact emerges again and again. Any cognitive problems that are projected for the overall workforce are compounded at the top. The worst projections for Workforce 2000 are for those jobs that require a high degree of competence and emphasize problem solving rather than the application of previously learned solution methods. The issue of how we might teach problem solving in the schools and how much it might cost will be addressed in Chapter 7.

Finally, the discussion offered here assumes a workplace that makes cognitive demands on its workforce that are similar to those it made in 1985. The workplace of 2000 will, of course, be substantially like the workplace of 1985. Things do not change that fast. But there will be differences, and by 2010 there will be more differences. We cannot consider the workforce or the workplace alone; we have to consider how changes in one will interact with changes in the other.

In order to discuss these issues, we must move from a discussion of the standards of cognition that the workforce can meet to a discussion of how those standards are met. This moves us from a discussion of the measurement of thought to a discussion of the process by which thought takes place.

APPENDIX 4.A: Calculating Group Representation in Job Classes

This appendix describes how predictions can be made about the relative frequencies of different levels of performance of group members from two subpopulations, A and B, when the two subpopulations differ in size and in mean level of performance.

Consider a situation in which a population, P, is made up of two nonoverlapping subpopulations, A and B. Let subpopulation A contain some fraction, $q (0 \leq q \leq 1)$ of the total population and let subpopulation B contain the remaining fraction, $1 - q$. For instance, if the population is the U.S. workforce, as projected for 2000, and if A is the white-Asian group and B the black-Hispanic group, then q will be approximately .8, reflecting the fact that about 20 percent of the total workforce will be black or Hispanic.

Assume that the entire population takes a test and that the resulting scores are normally distributed, with equal variances within each subpopulation. The test is scored in terms of standard deviation units of subpopulation A. Therefore, the mean score of subpopulation A is 0 and the standard deviation for this subpopulation is 1. Positive scores represent above-average performance relative to the mean of subpopulation A, and negative scores represent below-average performance. If one assumes normality, two thirds of group A's scores will fall in the range -1 to $+1$, with one sixth of the scores below -1 and one sixth above ± 1.

Suppose further that group B's scores are, on the average, one standard deviation below group A's scores, so that group B's mean score is -1. We also assume that group B's scores are normally distributed with a standard deviation of 1.

The situation is shown graphically in Figure 4.A1, which displays

Figure 4.A1   The distribution of levels of achievement on a test in a population consisting of two groups, A and B. A is assumed to contain 80% of the total population. Group A has a mean test score of 0 and a standard deviation of 1, Group B has a mean test score of -1 and a standard deviation of 1. Above a score of 1.67, the population consists almost entirely of group A members. Below scores of -1.8 group B members predominate.

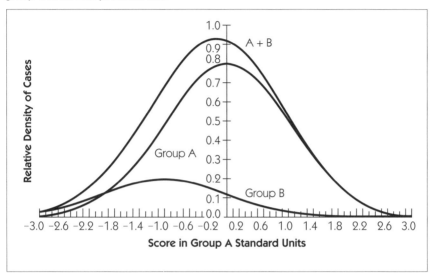

the distribution of scores for groups A, B, and the entire population.[13] The latter figure is obtained by adding the group A and group B population densities at each level of performance.

The positions and relative sizes of the two distributions follow from the assumptions. The group A distribution is larger than the group B distribution because group A is larger than group B. In Figure 4.A1, I assumed $q = .8$, which means that the area under the curve for group A must be four times as large as the area under the curve of group B. The group A distribution is centered on zero, and the group B distribution is centered on -1, reflecting the prior assumptions.

To find the fraction of group A and group B members that fall above or below some arbitrary score level, one calculates the relative area of each curve that lies beyond (to the right) of that score level. (These values can be obtained by consulting a table of density functions for the standard normal curve.) In Figure 4.A1, 5 percent of the area under group A's curve falls beyond (to the right) of $+1.67$. On the other hand, only four-tenths of 1 percent of the area under group B's curve falls to the right of 1.67.

To calculate the fraction of the population (A + B) with scores above an arbitrary value, Z, it is necessary to consider the fractions of groups

A and B with these scores, and the relative size of the groups. The equation is

> Population fraction
> above score Z = (group A fraction above score Z)*
>   (fraction of population in group A) +   (4A.1)
>   (group B fraction above score Z)*
>   (fraction of population in group B).

For $Z = +1.67$, this is

> Population fraction above $1.67 = .05 * .8 + .004 * .2 = .048$.

For many purposes we need to calculate the ratio

$$R(A, B, Z) = \frac{\text{(number of group A members above } Z)}{\text{(number of group B members above } Z)}. \quad (4A.2)$$

This is done by taking the first term on the right-hand side of Equation 4A.1 and dividing the second term into it. In the example case,

$$R(A, B, + 1.67) = (.05 * .8)/(.004 * .2) = 50,$$

so we would expect to find 50 times as many group A members as group B members in the $+1.67$ and above region, even though there are only four times as many group A members as group B members in the total population.

The situation changes dramatically if we go in the other direction. What would the relative frequencies of group A and group B members be at the bottom end of the scoring distribution, that is, below (to the left of) -1.67 in Figure 4A.1?

Assuming normality, 5 percent of the group A members fall in this region. Since -1.67 is only $-.67$ standard deviation units away from the group B mean, about 25 percent of the group B scores lie to the left of -1.67. If we apply Equation 4A.2,

$$R(A, B, - 1.67) = (.05 * .8)/(.25 * .2) = .8.$$

This means that there will actually be more group B members than group A members with performance scores below -1.67, even though group B members are only 20 percent of the population.

APPENDIX 4.B: A Mathematical Model
for Predicting the Distribution of Talent in a Workforce

Consider a society consisting of subgroups A and B, as in Appendix 4.A. Assume that the available jobs can be ordered by the cognitive demands that they make. This appendix describes mathematical models for calculating the effectiveness level of individuals within skill levels, as a function of the differences between the two subgroups and the assignment policy used to fill jobs.

The EIO Solution

Under an equality of individual opportunity (EIO) policy, individuals are assigned to job classes in order of their cognitive skills; that is, the most skilled individuals are assigned to the most demanding job class until all positions are taken, then positions in the next job class are filled, and so on. Group membership is never considered explicitly. The policy can be described by the following assumptions:

Assumption 1. The population of workers contains two subpopulations, A and B. Subpopulation A makes up some fraction, q, $(0 < q < 1)$ of the population, and subpopulation B makes up the complementary fraction, $1 - q$. Let A be the majority population, that is $q > .5$. Parameter q will be referred to as the *workforce mixture parameter.*

Assumption 2. Workforce talent is distributed normally in both populations. This will be written $N(d, s)$, where d is the population mean and s is the standard deviation. Talent will be scored in terms of standard deviation units in population A, that is, population A scores are distributed $N(0, 1)$. Talent in population B is distributed $N(d, S)$, where d is the mean score for population B, *in standardized units with reference to subpopulation A*, and S is the ratio (within-group standard deviation for group B)/(within-group standard deviation for group A). Parameters d and S will be referred to as the *workforce differential* parameters.

Assumption 3. Jobs are ordered into K job classes in terms of desirability. Job class 0 contains the most desirable jobs, class $K - 1$ contains the least desirable jobs (i.e., unemployment or marginal employment). Individuals are assigned to job classes in order of talent. Thus, if job class 0 contains some fraction, p_0 of the total number of jobs, the top p_0 fraction of talent will go into class 0. If class 1 contains the next most desirable fraction, p_1 of all jobs, this class will get the next most talented fraction p_1 of the $1 - p_0$ remaining individuals, and so forth, until all jobs are filled. By definition, the last fraction, p_{K-1} of jobs includes the unemployed.

The outcome variables to be studied are:

E_k = mean level of talent (in group A units) in job class k.   (4B.1)

R_k = ratio of group A to group B members in job class k.   (4B.2)

To make the argument concrete the following example will be used:

1. The workforce consists of 80 percent group A members and 20 percent group B members, approximately the mixture estimated for white-Asian and black-Hispanic workers in the U.S. workforce in 2000.
2. Jobs are divided into deciles. Class 0 consists of the 10 percent most desirable jobs, class 1 of the next 10 percent most desirable jobs, and so forth.

Let p_0 be the fraction of jobs in the "most desirable" category. These jobs should be assigned to the p_0th fraction of the most talented individuals in the entire population, without regard to group A or group B membership. Define the cutoff score, z_0 (in group A standard score units), for job class 0 as the score such that exactly p_0 of all individuals in the population have this score or higher. This can be thought of as the minimum score required for a person to qualify for jobs at level 0. Mathematically, z_0 is the unique score such that

$$p_0 = q(1 - F(z_0: 0, 1)) + (1 - q)(1 - F(z_0: d, S)),   (4B.3)$$

where $F(z:\mu, \phi)$ is the cumulative normal distribution function at point z for a distribution with mean μ and standard deviation ϕ. The first term on the left represents the contribution of group A to the pool of qualified individuals, and the second represents the contribution of group B to this pool.

The value of z_0 can be found by progressive iteration from an arbitrary starting value. All estimates calculated in the main text were determined this way.

Cutoff scores for subsequent job classes are defined recursively. Suppose that class $k = 1$, the second most desirable job class, contains p_1 of all jobs. The cutoff score for class 1 is the unique score z_1 satisfying

$$p_1 = q(F(z_0: 0, 1) - F(z_1: 0, 1)) + (1 - q)(F(z_0: d, S) - F(z_1: d, S)).$$
$$(4B.4)$$

Further cutoff scores for other job classes $1 \leq k < K$ are defined analogously,

$$p_k = q(F(z_{k-1}: 0, 1) - (F(z_k: 0, 1)) + (1 - q)(F(z_{k-1}: d, S) - (F(z_k: d, S)).$$
$$(4B.5)$$

An exception is the class $K - 1$, the leftover jobs, including unemployment. By definition $z_{K-1} = -\infty$, and

$$p_{k-1} = q(F(z_{K-2}: 0, 1)) + (1 - q)(F(z_{K-2}: d, S)).$$
$$(4B.6)$$

As in Equation 4B.3, the first term on the right-hand side of Equations 4B.4–4B.6 is the fraction of group A members in the relevant job class, and the second term is the fraction of group B members.

In order to measure the effectiveness of workers within each job class, we consider the expected level of performance of the individuals assigned to that class. Note that this is not the cutoff score, z_k, since the cutoff score is the minimum acceptable level of talent, not the average level of talent.

In a normally distributed population, the expected value of a randomly chosen score, x, lying above z is

$$E(x:z) = [(1/2\pi)^{1/2} \exp(-z^2/2)]/(1 - F(z: 0, 1)).[14]$$
$$(4B.7)$$

The term inside the squared brackets in Equation 4B.7 is the height of the normal density function at $\pm z$. Write this as

$$y(z) = [(1/2\pi)^{1/2} \exp(-z^2/2)].$$
$$(4B.8)$$

The expected value for performance of the group A population in job class 0 is

$$E_A(z_0) = y(z_0)/(1 - F(z_0: 0, 1)).$$
$$(4B.9)$$

Similarly, the expected value of performance of group A members in job class $K - 1$, the least desirable job class, can be determined by observing that this is simply a reflection of the $k = 0$ case, so

$$E_A(z_{K-2}) = -y(z_{K-2})/F(z_{K-2}: 0, 1), \qquad (4B.10)$$

where the negation is required because jobholders in this group are drawn from the bottom rather than the top tail of the normal distribution.[15] For intermediate job classes $(0 < k < K - 1)$ the expected value of performance is

$$E_A(z_k) = (y(z_k) - y(z_{k-1}))/(F(z_{k-1}: 0, 1) - F(z_k: 0, 1)). \qquad (4B.11)$$

Equations 4B.9–4B.11 refer only to jobholders drawn from group A, because the cutoff scores are defined in terms of group A standard score units. Analogous equations apply to group B, except that the cutoff scores must first be calculated in standard score units for group B.

Group B has a mean score d units below A, in A standard score units, and standard deviation S times as large as group A's. Therefore, a cutoff score of z_k in A units corresponds to a cutoff score of $(z_k + d)/S$ in group B standard score units. Algebraically, suppose that $z(A)$ and $z(B)$ represent equivalent levels of competence, scored respectively in group A and group B standard score units.

$$z(B) = (z(A) + d)/S. \qquad (4B.12)$$

The expression $z(A)$ can be substituted directly for z_k in Equations 4B.9–4B.11, since they are in the same units. The equivalent cutoff score for group B, expressed in group B standard score units, is given by Equation 4B.12. Therefore, the equations for expected performance of group B members in job class 0, expressed in group A units becomes

$$E_B((z_0 + d)/S) = y((z_0 + d)/S)/(1 - F((z_0 + d)/S: 0, 1)), \qquad (4B.13)$$

and if $k = K - 1$ (i.e., the lowest job class)

$$E_B((z_{K-2} + d)/S) = -y((z_{K-2} + d)/S)/F((z_{K-2} + d)/S: 0, 1). \qquad (4B.14)$$

For intermediate job classes

$$E_B((z_k + d)/S) = \frac{(y((z_{k-1} + d)/S) - y((z_k + d)/S - 1))}{(F((z_{k-1} + d)/S: 0, 1) - F((z_k + d)/S: 0,1)))}. \qquad (4B.15)$$

For simplicity, write $E_A(k)$ and $E_B(k)$ for the appropriate expectations. The expected value of talent within the kth job class, without regard to membership in subpopulations A and B, is

$$E_k = q_k E_A(k) + (1 - q_k)E_B(k). \qquad (4\text{B}.16)$$

where q_k refers to the fraction of individuals in job class k who are members of group A. Note that q_k will generally not equal the population workforce mixture parameter, q.

The EGO Solution

Under an equality of group outcome (EGO) policy, a certain percentage of the jobs within a class is reserved for group B members. The EIO model is then applied within each group.

For simplicity, assume that each group receives the jobs within a job class proportional to its relative size, q or $(1 - q)$, in the population. The mean level of talent within the kth job class is

$$E_k = qE_A(k) + (1 - q)E_B(k). \qquad (4\text{B}.17)$$

In this case, though, the definition of $E_B(k)$ has changed. Since the same within-group decile level applies for each job class, we may convert $E_B(k)$ to group A units by

$$E_B(k) = E_A(k) - d. \qquad (4\text{B}.18)$$

Substituting,

$$\begin{aligned} E_k &= qE_A(k) + (1 - q)(E_A(k) - d). \\ &= E_A(k) - (1 - q)d. \end{aligned} \qquad (4\text{B}.19)$$

An EGO policy will assign some members of group A to lower job classes than they would have been assigned to under an EIO policy, in order to provide spaces for the quota assigned to members of group B. The percentage of underutilized individuals can be calculated by determining, for each job class, the cutoff score that would apply to group A members under each of the policies, and then calculating the fraction of group A members who fall between the two scores. Exactly what this number is depends on the assumptions made about relative within-group variability. In fact, in a situation in which group B has high intragroup variability, the fraction can be negative, which indicates that group B members are being denied positions they would have held under an EIO policy in order to provide spaces for group A's quota. In this case the group B members are added into the pool of underutilized individuals.

NOTES

1. This figure may seem surprisingly high, in the light of reports of 25–50 percent high school dropout rates. These rates are calculated in different ways and may often simply reflect the number of students who fail to complete their courses in a particular year. Many of these students return or complete their high school work in various adult education courses only a few years after their "normal" graduation year. Also, dropout rates vary widely from place to place. High dropout rates are publicized; low ones are not.

2. Figure 4.3 displays scores for different age groups in the normalization sample for the WAIS-R. These are not intelligence quotient (IQ) scores. An individual's IQ score is calculated from these scores, after correcting for that individual's deviation from the mean of his or her age group. Therefore, IQ scores, as such, cannot show age differences because they are artificially equated to eliminate those differences.

3. I am not arguing that all verbal tests are necessarily tests of crystallized intelligence, or vice versa. The argument is simply that those tests that have been used to date to predict workplace performance have not distinguished between the two concepts.

4. I am not the first to make such a plea. I draw readers' attention to a similar request in the last chapter of Loehlin, Lindzey, and Spuhler's *Intelligence and Achievement in Black Americans* (1975).

5. Economic Report of the President (1993), Table B-28.

6. A number of genetic studies of racial and ethnic groups have been carried out since 1975 comparing the heritability of cognition across different populations. They were not designed to compare levels of performance across populations and, therefore, are not relevant to the discussion here.

7. "U.S. Forbids States to Score Job Tests According to Race." New York Times, Dec. 14, 1991 (p. 1).

8. To make this point less abstract, consider a professional tennis tournament, such as Wimbledon or the U.S. open. The tournament directors follow an EGO policy, since they award one championship cup for men and one for women. There is little doubt among tennis buffs that many of the top-ranked men could defeat the women's champion. (In the 1970s Billie Jean King, then the top-ranked woman player, said that "about 200" male professionals could defeat her.) By the definition given here, many male players would be jealous of the female champion. On the other hand, only the second best male player would be underutilized, in the sense of not receiving the championship cup (and several hundred thousand dollars) that he would receive in open competition.

9. U.S. Bureau of the Census (1991).

10. At one time the conventional wisdom was that women, on the average, had higher verbal abilities than men. The most recent studies indicate that this is not the case (Hyde & Linn, 1988). The fact that the difference disappeared over the relatively brief span of less than 50 years suggests that the earlier disparity in the normal range was due to social rather than biological factors. However, more men than women have severe language disabilities, such as dyslexia or stuttering.

11. The biggest problem with the psychometric data is that the vast majority of the reported studies are either of young adults in college or in the armed services or of senior citizens. Adults in the workforce are too busy to take psychometric tests. The biggest problem with workforce labor statistics is that reporting is not always by mutually exclusive categories. In particular, blacks and Hispanics are reported as separate groups, although it is possible to be both black and Hispanic.

12. If the fraction of people in the applicant pool who can fill a job is $p (0 \le p \le 1)$, an interviewer should have to interview $1/p$ randomly chosen applicants before finding a qualified one. Since the 1985 workforce has been taken as the standard, the probability of randomly choosing a person qualified for a job at the kth decile $(0 < k \le 9)$ is $p(k, 1985) = 1 - .1 k$. The value $p(k, 1985)$ defines a standard score $z(k, 1985)$ with reference to the 1985 population. This score can be converted to a standard score for the 2000 population by using the equation $z(k, 2000) = z(k, 1985) + .1$ for fluid intelligence and $z(k, 2000) = z(k, 1985) - .1$ for crystallized intelligence. If $z(k, 2000)$ is known $p(k, 2000)$ is defined. The statistic (plotted in Figure 4.14) is the ratio $R(k) = p(k, 1985)/p(k, 2000)$.

13. Technically, Figure 4.A1 shows a function proportional to the probability density function.

14. The expectation is determined by $E(x{:}z) = \int xf(x)/(1 - F(z{:} 0, 1)) dx$, where the integration is from z to $+\infty$, $f(x)$ is the normal (Gaussian) distribution function, and the division is required to normalize the probabilities, since x is constrained to lie above z. Substituting

$$
\begin{aligned}
E(x{:}z) &= \int_z x(1/2\pi)^{1/2} \exp(-x^2/2)/(1 - F(z{:} 0, 1)) dx \\
&= [(1/2\pi)^{1/2} \int_z x \exp(-x^2/2) dx]/(1 - F(z{:} 0, 1)) \\
&= [(1/2\pi)^{1/2} \exp(-z^2/2)]/(1 - F(z{:} 0, 1)).
\end{aligned}
$$

15. This argument applies exactly for the condition in which p_0 and p_K are both less than .5. This would be true in virtually all realistic cases. The mathematics is slightly more involved if this condition does not hold.

5

The Cognitive Psychology
View of Thinking

WHERE WE ARE AT

The evidence presented in the previous four chapters showed that the workforce of the early twenty-first century will be more experienced and socially stable than today's, but it will contain relatively fewer people with high levels of problem-solving and "learning to learn" skills. This is a matter for serious concern, since virtually every forecast of technology stresses the dynamic character of the coming workplace. In 1994 President Clinton stated that American workers must be prepared to change careers several times over their working lives. In the same spirit, in 1993 the Washington State legislature passed a law that mandated that school children must be taught creative thinking and problem-solving skills. Just how the legislators proposed to enforce this law was a bit unclear, since they did not define what "creative thinking and problem-solving skills" are, nor did they authorize any specific program to teach them. And the Washington State legislature was hardly alone. Virtually all political and far too many educational leaders seem satisfied to say that something must be done, but they do not say what is to be done, nor do they provide operational definitions that could be used to determine whether or not their goals have been met.

Such cries of woe, without clearly defined aims or proposals for action, are close to the leadership pose of Chicken Little. Consider the following analogy: Football coaches are often fired for not winning games. However, coaches cannot train players to win games. They can only train players to exercise specific skills: to pass the ball well, to run quickly, and to memorize plays, and so forth. The coach's job is possible because coaching combines knowledge of the capabilities of the human body with knowledge of the demands of the game.

If education is going to produce people who think the way they will have to think in the workplace, educators will have to take at least as sophisticated an approach to the mind and the workplace as coaches take to the body and the game. Instead of poring over correlations between test scores, workplace performance, and demographic trends, we need a detailed picture of how the mind works, how the workings of the mind apply to the workplace, and, most importantly, how mental capabilities can be improved.

The study of human mental processes lies within the domain of *cognitive psychology,* a branch of psychology quite different from psychometrics. Instead of representing the mind as a mental space, cognitive psychologists try to develop pictures of how the mind works, as an information-processing device. As a result, theories in cognitive psychology have the potential for explaining how superior thinking ability translates into workplace performance. This differs from psychometrics, which measures the extent to which workplace performance depends on mental ability, without making an attempt to explain why the dependency exists.

The cognitive psychology view of the mind is harder to grasp than the psychometric view, both because it is more complex and because the cognitive psychology–workplace linkage is not easily summarized in a few statistics. Instead, we have to rely on illustrative examples and occasional experimental studies. Nevertheless, understanding the cognitive view is likely to be worth the effort, because understanding the process of thought is a first step toward understanding how to improve that process.

THE PHILOSOPHY BEHIND COGNITIVE PSYCHOLOGY

Robert Sternberg, an eloquent writer on theories of intelligence, has said that in order to understand some isolated fact about cognition, one has to understand the metaphor for thought that the fact is supposed to amplify (Sternberg, 1990). In Sternberg's terms, psychometrics is rooted in a geographic metaphor. Psychometricians try to locate mental acts relative to each other in much the same way that geographers try to fit the earth's surface into a Euclidean space. Specific tasks have coordinates on verbal and spatial-visual dimensions (or crystallized and fluid intelligence dimensions) just the way that a city or a mountain range has latitude and longitude.

Cognitive psychology uses a different metaphor: computing machinery. Cognitive psychology arose as a subdiscipline of psychology about the same time that computer scientists were beginning to take seriously the concept of artificial intelligence.[1] Although the task of understanding the human mind is not the same as the task of designing an intelligent computer program, the two endeavors have borrowed each other's concepts, probably to the benefit of both fields. Therefore, cognitive psychologists' theories of "how the mind works" are often cast in terms of a hypothetical robotology. Cognitive psychologists ask, "How could I design a robot so that it would behave in the way that human beings do?"

Some philosophers have raised vehement objections to this approach, on the grounds that it ignores the subjective, intuitive nature of thought (Dreyfus and Dreyfus, 1986; Searle, 1992). The essence of their argument is that attempts to model human thought using an analogy to robots or computers will fail because the analogy has no place for the subjective consciousness of the thinker. This debate is certainly not resolved. Whatever its outcome, the computer analogy has considerable appeal as a device for explaining workplace cognition.[2] Our goal is not to understand all the thoughts of every person in the workforce, but to understand the capabilities of the typical worker. For this limited purpose, looking on workers as information processing devices is likely to be useful.

We will use cognitive psychology in two ways: to provide an explanation for the observed correlations between psychometric measures and workplace performance, and, more important, to design courses of action that might improve the cognitive power of the workforce.

THE PSYCHOMETRIC-COGNITIVE LINKAGE

We have seen that psychometric test scores do predict performance, not perfectly, but more accurately than any other prediction. Performance on psychometric tests is like any other type of performance. Since individual differences in psychometric test performance are far better documented than, say, performance in most workplace settings, psychometric performance is likely to be a rich source of data about what people can do and what variations in tasks make it easy or difficult for them to perform. Therefore, it is worth finding out what people do when they score well (or poorly) on a mental test.

This approach, called the *cognitive components* approach, was pioneered by Sternberg (1977), who analyzed the way that people solve problems requiring reasoning by analogy, a common form of intelligence test item. Since explaining Sternberg's work would require an extensive discussion of the particular intelligence tests he studied, I will offer a more general example, taken from work on verbal comprehension.

Verbal comprehension is central to workplace reasoning. People read a great deal in the workplace, even in situations that are not ostensibly verbal. For instance, mechanics read instructions and soldiers read the standing orders and the orders of the day (Sticht, 1975). Furthermore, research in psychometrics has shown that there are marked individual differences in the ability to comprehend verbal material (Carroll, 1993).

A robot that could understand natural language would have to have available a vast store of permanent knowledge. This knowledge falls into three general categories:

1. *lexical knowledge* of the surface form and meaning of all the words (technically, morphemes) in the robot's vocabulary;

2. *grammatical knowledge* of the rules for composing meaningful utterances from combinations of words; and

3. *subject matter knowledge* about the topic of the discourse, extending from facts, narrowly conceived, to linkages between facts, and including knowledge about how arguments in a particular field are usually presented. Such knowledge is needed because only a very few texts contain within themselves all the information required to understand them. For example, understanding virtually any article in the morning newspaper, including the sports pages, depends on having background knowledge of the topic at hand.

All this information must be stored in a permanent storage device, which cognitive psychologists refer to as *long-term memory*. If our robot is going to understand language, it must have the necessary knowledge in its long-term memory and must be able to access that knowledge in a timely fashion.

There is an important distinction between the information that a memory contains and the mechanisms that the robot (or human) being uses to store and access that knowledge. The fact that there are individual differences in knowledge is obvious. However, there are also substantial individual differences in the efficiency of the mechanisms that access knowledge. For instance, numerous studies have shown that people take anywhere from 60 to 100 milliseconds or more to access the meaning of a common word, such as "cat." This is known as *lexical access time.* It is a stable characteristic of the individual. People who have high scores on verbal comprehension tests tend to have short lexical access times. This does not mean that "speed of access to long-term memory" explains the psychometric concept of verbal comprehension, for the correlation between test scores and speed of lexical access is in the .3 to .4 range (Hunt, 1987). Access to long-term memory is part of our robot's verbal comprehension ability, but it is not all of it.

People use language to compose complex thoughts from simple ones. Because of the serial nature of language, in many situations the meaning of an utterance cannot be determined until the entire utterance has been received: for example, "The horse raced past the barn fell." Listeners are led to expect one syntactic structure and forced to rearrange their thoughts when they hear the final "fell." Somewhat less forced examples are given by the use of pronouns, as in "James Bond strode into the bar. When the villain saw him, he reached for his gun." Who saw whom, and who reached for whose gun?

In order to understand statements like this a language comprehender has to have some form of *working memory* that holds a representation (a *mental model*) of the current situation. People differ in the amount of information that they can hold in their working memory. This ability is statistically associated with high scores on verbal intelligence tests (Just and Carpenter, 1992).

While we cannot provide a robot with "verbal intelligence," we can provide

1. the capacities required to process language, as illustrated by the discussion of short-term and long-term memory; and

2. the information required to use these capacities to comprehend a particular language (e.g., if the task were to comprehend English, the robot's long-term memory would have to contain an English dictionary and an English grammar).

The distinction between the dictionary and the grammar highlights another important distinction about intelligent action, the distinction between "knowing what" and "knowing how." (Cognitive psychologists use the terms *declarative* and *procedural* knowledge.) Language comprehenders know explicitly what the words in their lexicon mean. They also know how to use the grammar of their language. However, very few speakers can provide an explicit definition of the grammar of their mother tongue. If a robot is to deal with language, it must know what words mean and know how sentences are analyzed. In the terms of conventional computing, the grammar is a program for understanding a natural language, while a lexicon is a file of information on which the program acts. We will meet similar distinctions between declarative and procedural knowledge in many other contexts.

Clearly, the "robot" is being used as a surrogate for human language users. This is the way that cognitive psychologists have proceeded for the past half century. Instead of trying to measure what human beings can do in a particular situation, they ask how human beings do what they do. This question is assumed to have three parts: what abstract

Figure 5.1   The relation between psychometric scores, performance evaluations, and productivity. The worker's ability and knowledge produce psychometric measurements. Performance evaluations and productivity are produced by the combination of the worker's ability and knowledge and the demands of the workplace. Correlational studies, indicated by the double-headed arrow, indicate that the two are related but do not explain why.

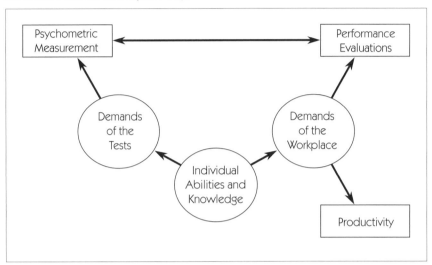

information processing machinery must a person have to solve a problem; what program, or, in more human terms, problem-solving strategy, does the person apply to use the machinery; and what explicit knowledge about the external world does the machinery operate upon?

The machinery question links us to our biological system. The efficiency of functioning of short-term and long-term memory, perception, and motor control are ultimately determined by anatomy and physiology. The knowledge question links us to our social system; we acquire only the information that the culture makes available to us. The programming question falls in between. Problem-solving strategies are limited by our information-processing machinery, but we can develop strategies that use that machinery in an efficient or inefficient way.

Figure 5.1 summarizes the argument. Psychometric tests present people with certain demands; how they use their knowledge and information-processing capacities determines what the resulting score is. Very much the same thing can be said of the workplace. People respond to workplace demands to produce performance that can be evaluated and that results in productivity. Psychometric research can establish a correlation between test scores and performance measures, but it cannot tell us why the correlation exists.

Cognitive psychology seeks to go beyond this, by determining just what knowledge and information-processing capabilities humans have, and how they are used both on the job and in the test situation. Cognitive psychologists look at the demands made by both the job and the test, and try to see how people respond to them. This is called a *cognitive task analysis* of both the test and the job. It is a job description of sorts, but the description is in terms of the psychological demand that the job (or test) makes upon a person, rather than a description of how the job (or test) fits into a larger social structure.

If we have a good cognitive analysis of the tasks associated with both a job and a test, we can determine how a person with a particular profile on the psychometric tests might best fit into different jobs. Unfortunately, though, we are seldom in this position. Doing cognitive task analyses is hard, expensive work. The psychometrician's job is finished when test–task correlations are found. This is all that is needed to predict *how well* a person is likely to do in a job. Cognitive task analyses, when available, can be used to plan training, to make the person more suitable for the job,[3] or as aids in job design, to make the job more suited for the person.

HOW THE MIND IS USED: SOME EXAMPLES OF MENTAL WORK

Cognitive task analyses rely on theories of human information processing that have been developed over the last 50 years. These theories are based upon an analysis of tasks that are intended to isolate specific information-processing abilities. This contrasts with the typical workplace situation, where multiple abilities are required at the same time. To appreciate how this is done, we now look at the cognitive demands imposed by a few selected situations. Some of the examples are taken from the psychologist's laboratory and are intended to isolate and measure a single ability. Others are taken from industrial situations and are intended to show how many different behaviors can be called "thought." The variety is enough to make one suspicious of proposals to "improve thinking" without saying precisely what sort of behavior is to be improved.

THE CHOICE REACTION TIME EXAMPLE

The first example illustrates what many psychologists consider to be a basic building block in mental processes, the ability to choose between different alternative responses.

Figure 5.2 is a cartoon depiction of a procedure frequently used in the experimental psychologist's laboratory. The examinee places his or her finger on a button marked "home" and then watches a computer display screen. When a number appears on the screen (either 1 or 2)

Figure 5.2 Schematic of a choice reaction time experiment. The observer places his or her hand on the "home" button. When a number appears on the screen, the observer presses the corresponding button as quickly as possible.

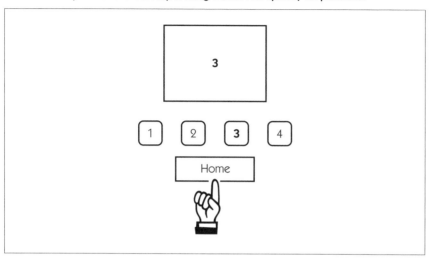

the examinee is supposed to move the finger from the home button to the button with the same number as that on the screen. The measurement of interest is the time between the instant at which the symbol appears on the screen and the time the person's finger moves off the home button toward the appropriate target button. This measure is called *choice reaction time* (CRT).

Mail sorting in the post office is a good example of an industrial counterpart to the CRT paradigm: Letters are moved past the sorter's station on a conveyor belt, and the sorter must read the postal code and punch it into a keypad as the mail goes by. The sorter's interpretation of the written code is used to route each piece of mail to the appropriate branch point off the conveyor belt and, hence, on to its destination. The sorter must be able to make a decision to punch one key in response to any of the symbols

9 9 9 9

and another key in response to any of the symbols

8 8 8 **8**.

In theory such decisions could be made by an optical scanner attached to a computer. In practice the U.S. postal service does not expect to

introduce automated scanning of handwritten addresses until sometime after the turn of the century. This apparently simple task turns
out to be quite hard to automate. But we can confidently predict that
sometime within the next 30 years automation will win out.

Intuitively we do not think of such jobs as "thinking" in the way
that, say, reading a *New York Times* editorial qualifies as thinking.
This may be a mistake. Reading an editorial can be broken down into
decisions, ranging from decisions about the editorial's intent to decisions about individual word meanings.

Psychologists study behavior in the CRT experiment to isolate the
discrimination process, which is a basic step in mental processing. This
argument is analogous to the one that computer engineers use when
they evaluate a computer's performance by asking how long it takes
to perform one multiplication or division or to fetch one number from
memory. If the analogy is correct, one would expect that people who
are "intelligent," as defined by psychometric tests, would have short
choice reaction times. And, generally speaking, they do.

A number of studies have shown that choice reaction time, measured
in the way just described, is modestly related (uncorrected correlations
in the .3 to .4 range) to the ability to perform tasks that demonstrably are
thinking, such as comprehending a paragraph or answering questions on
an intelligence test (Hunt, 1983; Palmer et al., 1985; Vernon, 1983).

More generally, psychologists argue that any act of thought can be
broken down into elementary information-processing actions, rather
the way that building a house requires a large number of elementary
acts of carpentry. Some examples of the information-processing abilities behind thinking are the ability to hold information in memory
briefly and the ability to recognize familiar words, sights, and sounds.
If you measured the quality of all the elementary mental processes in
a person's head, you might get a good idea of what he or she could do.
Analogously, if you examined all the tools in a carpenter's toolbox,
you would form an idea of the things the carpenter could build. This
approach is surprisingly successful. While no one measurement of a
basic mental operation correlates particularly highly with complex
mental performance, the combined measurement of several such operations can account for a large proportion of the individual variation in
tasks as complex as taking intelligence tests (Hunt, 1983).

The approach just described is usually called the *information-processing approach to thought.* It focuses on the characteristics of human
beings as abstract processors of "information," defined in terms of operations on symbols without regard for what that information means.
Emphasizing basic mental operations in thinking is like emphasizing
speed and body strength in football. Just as coaches look for strong,

Figure 5.3 A considerably simplified schematic of an air traffic control display.

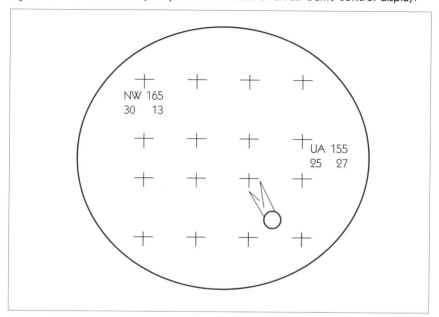

fast players and then have them go through conditioning workouts, we could try to develop selection and training methods to maximize jobholders' information-processing capacities. Alternatively, we could design the workplace to match the information-processing capacities that the workers have. To continue the athletic analogy, one of the reasons that athletes run faster today than they did in 1920 is because today's athletes have better shoes!

The Air Traffic Control Example

Air traffic controllers use radar displays to manage aircraft movement. Figure 5.3 is a simplified schematic of the display used for sector control, when aircraft are near major airports but are not actually landing. Each marker on the screen indicates an aircraft's location in two-dimensional space. Altitude, speed, and identification numbers are indicated in text beside the marker. In addition, the controller knows the schedule of aircraft that are expected to arrive but have not yet made radar contact. In order to manage the traffic flow, the controller has to work back and forth between verbal and visual information. The controller also has to have memorized information about aircraft capabilities, weather, and control procedures.

It is possible to break up the information-processing demands into finer and finer detail. For instance, one of the things the controller must do is project the screen forward in time, to imagine what the current position and motion of the markers implies for future displays. In fact, there are reliable individual differences in the ability to reason about moving objects, which can be evaluated in situations somewhat analogous to the CRT paradigm (Hunt et al., 1988).

Working memory is heavily involved in the controller's job. While controllers are attending to one aircraft, they must remain aware of the movements of others, including some that are not even on the screen. This is our first example of a very general finding. Working memory is involved in almost everything people do (Baddeley, 1986, 1992). In fact, tests of fluid intelligence, such as the Raven Matrix Test described earlier, make major demands on working memory. This is probably one of the reasons that they predict performance in so many different situations (Carpenter, Just, and Shell, 1990; Kyllonen and Christal, 1990).

Long-term memory is involved as well. Controllers must be able to recall aircraft characteristics and their implications. For example, they must know, without looking up the facts, that a Boeing 747 is a jumbo jet and that wide separations are required between such very heavy aircraft and other airplanes, because of the turbulence that the heavy aircraft create in their wake.

Finally, the air traffic controller has to combine information from multiple sources: visual displays, text, verbal messages, and long-term memory. Information-processing studies have shown that there are substantial individual differences in the ability to coordinate information from multiple sources (Yee, Hunt, and Pellegrino, 1991). To what extent can such an ability be trained?

The Pulley Example

The next example is intended to illustrate a common failing in problem solving. It has been chosen because this sort of failing, oversimplification of the situation, appears to limit problem solving in many practical situations.

Pulleys are devices that have been used for centuries as ways of redirecting forces in order to lift large weights. A simple pulley problem is shown in Figure 5.4. Suppose that a mechanic wants to haul a 100-kilogram weight off the floor, using the system shown. How much force must the mechanic apply to the rope to lift the weight? The successful problem solver does have to process visual information, but in addition the problem solver has to remember some principles from ele-

Figure 5.4   A simple pulley problem. How much force must be exerted on the rope to lift the weight?

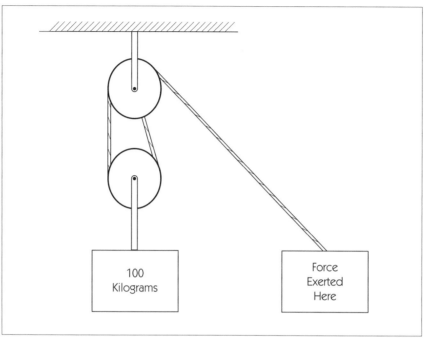

mentary physics, recall the necessary equations, and then use a knowl-edge of mathematics to solve them.

Let us contrast the air traffic control and pulley examples. The visual display facing the air traffic controller is much more complex than the one facing the mechanic. So is the amount of information required. The air traffic controller must be able to recall hundreds of facts. The mechanic who uses a pulley system need only know one principle—that the force on the rope must be the same throughout. However, the pulley problem is by no means trivial. In order to solve it, the problem solver must construct a mental model of the pulley situation and "run" it inside his or her head. Figure 5.4 shows a simple problem where this is easy to do. It is much harder to visualize what is happening when there are five or six pulleys in the system.

How complex a computing burden can an individual tolerate? Some problems so tax people's resources that they attempt shortcuts, such as counting the number of pulleys in the system and assuming that each pulley reduces the force required by a factor of two. This simplifi-cation ignores the fact that some pulleys simply change the direction of application of forces, without producing a mechanical advantage. Analogous oversimplifications have been observed in other situations in which people work with machinery (Hegarty, Just, & Morrison, 1988).

It is often useful to distinguish between obvious characteristics of a problem, such as the number of pulleys in a pulley system, and more abstract characteristics, such as the principle that the tension on the rope must be the same throughout the system. Psychologists use the terms *surface characteristics* and *deep structure* to distinguish between the two. Psychologically, it is easy to react to surface characteristics. All one needs to do is to react to perceptually salient objects. However, in many situations it is important *not* to react to the surface characteristics. Instead, as in the pulley problem, it is important to map the surface characteristics onto the deep structure, and then work with the deep structure. "Acquiring expertise" in fields ranging from mathematics to law seems to be very much a process of developing this ability (Ericsson and Smith, 1991; Glaser and Bassok, 1989).

The Travel Agent Example

The modern travel agent provides an interface between two different worlds: the world of business and recreational travelers, where individual idiosyncracies are paramount, and the highly computerized, formal world of the airline reservation system.

Most travel requests are initially phrased rather vaguely. The traveler will tell an agent, "I want to go to New York on Tuesday." The goal is almost always accompanied by a number of constraints. Sometimes these are explicit, as in requests for cheapest fare available, first-class tickets, or limits on departure or arrival times. Other constraints are implicit: for example, that overnight flights consisting of short legs and stopovers are to be avoided.

The travel agent has to rework the problem into a form acceptable to the airline's computerized reservation system. In most cases this is a simple operation: The travel agent translates the verbal request into the entry form required by the computer program. On occasion, though, considerable problem solving is required.

For example, in early 1992 I decided to attend a world's fair in Seville, Spain. The travel agent formulated the problem as one of getting me from the United States to Spain's main hub airport in Madrid. She located flights from New York to Madrid, and then tried to schedule the Seattle-New York and Madrid-Seville links, which was possible by following the route Seattle-Chicago-New York-Madrid-Seville (four links). The total travel time would be 26 hours, both tiring and expensive. After considerable discussion, the problem was reformulated as one of getting me to Europe, then to Madrid, and from there to Seville. The new problem had a Seattle-London-Madrid-Seville (three-link) solution, which took 20 hours and was considerably cheaper.

What cognitive skills did the travel agent have to have? The agent had to deal with two things: the traveler's linguistically expressed model of the world, and the computer program's model of a small part of that world, the airline reservation system. The agent first had to translate the traveler's problem, presented in a normal conversational manner, into a request comprehensible to a machine. In many cases the next step is simple: The agent translates the machine's solution back to normal language. But sometimes things are not so easy. When the machine returns a solution that is unacceptable to the traveler, the agent must know enough about how the machine works to be able to present the traveler's problem in alternative ways so that different solutions will be returned. In my own case, it is interesting to realize that at no time did the agent ever actually look up a flight schedule. That sort of detail was properly left to the machine. The agent's energies were focused on presenting the problem to the machine in a way that ensured it would search for appropriate solutions.

In principle, the airline reservation system could be programmed to contain a problem solver within itself.[4] This would not change the general principle. David Nagel, a senior executive at Apple Computers, put the importance of this to me in simple terms: "There will always be an interface." People at the interface have to know what real-world problem is being solved and know the strengths and limits of the computer part of the computer–human being problem-solving team.

Notice how the demands of the travel agent's job reflect a shift from the cognitive demands of the earlier examples. The travel agent is not limited by demands on his or her real-time computing capabilities. The travel agent needs knowledge, including knowledge about how his or her tools work, and a willingness to engage in problem solving rather than simply coding problems for a machine.

The City Attorney, the Landing Signal Officer, and the Wine Taster Examples

Table 5.1 is an excerpt from a job description for the city attorney of Fort Worth, Texas. There are two striking aspects of the cognitive demands of this job. One is the emphasis upon declarative knowledge: The city attorney is supposed to know a great deal in order to solve

Table 5.1 Job Description Excerpts for the City Attorney, Fort Worth, Texas

---

Distinguishing Features

This is administrative and legal work of a highly difficult and responsible professional nature in providing counsel for the general administrative offices of the city. . . .

Examples of Work

Directs activities of the legal department with responsibility for the proper and efficient handling of the legal affairs . . . in which the city is interested.

Provides legal advice to the city and all officers and departments.

Prosecutes and defends suits for and on behalf of the city in all courts.

Prepares all contracts, bonds, and other legal instruments for the city.

. . .

Required Knowledge, Abilities, Skills, and Other Attributes

Extensive knowledge of city codes and charter provisions and the general laws of the city and state. Extensive knowledge of the sources of legal reference. Extensive knowledge of court procedures and the rules of evidence. Ability to organize, interpret, and apply legal principles and knowledges [*sic*] to particular circumstances. . . .

Source: Wortman and Sperling (1975), p. 315.

problems and is supposed to be ready to justify his or her solutions explicitly, upon demand by judges and juries.

The second aspect of the job is its emphasis upon classification. The attorney is supposed to be able to fit actual cases into their appropriate legal pigeonholes. Case studies of judicial decision making have shown that this is one of the most important parts of an attorney's job. Experienced attorneys develop systems of "if → then rules" that guide them in the classification process. Sometimes these are codified into the law itself. For instance, the Washington State law covering driving under the influence of liquor can be rephrased as

1. If the defendant's blood alcohol reading was above .10, assume that the defendant was legally drunk.

2. If the blood alcohol reading was below .05, assume that the defendant was legally sober.

3. If the blood alcohol reading was between .05 and .10, inquire into the defendant's behavior at the time of the incident.

The first two rules describe how one moves from a surface characteristic of a problem to an abstract legal definition. The third rule tells the lawyer what to do if the first two rules cannot be applied.

While some rules are actually part of a legal code, experienced lawyers apply rules of inquiry that go beyond the narrow definition of legal procedure. For instance, early in the proceedings a sentencing magistrate will determine whether the primary goal of the sentence is to execute a general social policy (e.g., "get tough with drug dealers") or to channel the individual defendant into more acceptable behavior. The choice of a goal determines subsequent questions and legal decisions. Experienced magistrates seem to be much more efficient in this explicit categorization process than are novices (Lawrence, 1988).

Next we look at two jobs that depend on implicit rather than explicit knowledge: Landing Signal Officer and wine taster. Landing Signal Officers work on aircraft carriers. When an aircraft comes in for a landing, the Landing Signal Officer stands on the deck, in sight of the pilot, and determines whether or not the aircraft is lined up with the deck. The Landing Signal Officer himself is an experienced naval aviator who has spent months learning to recognize the visual characteristics of safe and unsafe approaches.

Professional wine tasters are employed by vintners to determine when a batch of fermenting wines has aged to the appropriate level for marketing and to estimate the quality of the mature wine. Wine tasters could be called quality control inspectors, but tradition demands a less commercial title.

Both the Landing Signal Officer and the wine taster need declarative knowledge. There are rules for what constitutes a good approach, and there are chemical formulae that describe generally acceptable wine. At the last moment, though, both the Landing Signal Officer and the wine taster make implicit judgments based on procedural knowledge. This requires a great deal of experience; it takes months or years of tutelage to become a master in each profession. The required knowledge is the implicit result of direct experience rather than the explicit result of book learning.

A THEORY OF THINKING

Levels of Thinking

There are three different ways of thinking about thinking. Thought can be explained at the *physiological* level, by describing brain actions; at the *functional* level, by showing how the mind acts as an abstract computing device; and at the *representational* level, by showing how internal processes reflect external realities. Their differences can be seen in the air traffic control example.

Physically, the controller must relate an incoming visual pattern to knowledge stored in the brain. Perceptual processing of visual displays appears to take place primarily in the occipital region, the area of the brain at the back of the skull. In order to interpret the perceptual display, the controller must relate it to verbal information received from pilots and other controllers. Linguistic processing occurs predominantly in the left temporal brain region, just above the left ear. Part of the controller's task involves planning, that is, projecting information to consider what might occur. Planning depends partly on structures in the prefrontal cortex, just behind the forehead (Ellis & Young, 1988).

This physiological explanation focuses on *where* in the brain certain things happen. Alternatively, a physiological explanation could focus on how brain events occur. For instance, we might have asked how the light waves from the display pass through the air traffic controller's eyeball, to produce chemical changes in the retina, which in turn produce electrical activity in the optic nerve, and then further chemical and electrical activity in the brain.

Physiological explanations deal with the brain, and infer the mind from brain action. An alternative approach, called functionalism, describes mental actions in terms of mental events (Bechtel, 1988; Pylyshyn, 1989). It emphasizes information-processing limits on human performance, without concerning itself with the meaning of the information being processed or the physical nature of the brain mechanisms doing the processing. A functionalist would explain the air traffic controller's action by saying that a mental buffer holds visually coded information about the stimulus. A recognition process, otherwise undefined, associates some of the visual information with highly overlearned information about letters and words. By using these associations, the controller can place all relevant information about a flight into a working-memory buffer.

The functional view focuses on how quickly visual symbols can be recognized as denoting a flight, the likelihood that the identification will be in error, and how many flights the air traffic controller can keep in mind ("keep in working memory") without confusing or forgetting any of them. The functional approach is similar to the one taken by most computer users. The typical user is interested in how much information a computer can hold and how quickly it can manipulate information, not whether the machine's internal circuits are based on silicon or gallium arsenide technology.

Functional and physiological explanations are not independent of each other, for every information-processing function has to have a physiological basis. Consider the distinction between working memory and long-term memory. Psychologists made up this distinction in order to explain some observed differences between our memories for events that happened in the past few moments and events that happened weeks or years ago (Baddeley, 1986, 1992). The distinction is supported by findings that show that short-term memory deficits are associated with damage to certain anatomical or physiological systems, while long-term memory deficits are associated with damage to other systems (Shallice, 1988; Squire, 1987).

Although both functional and physiological descriptions provide important ways of talking about mental capacities, they are not the way we usually talk about the mind. Instead of talking about how they are thinking, people are more likely to talk about what they are thinking about. Suppose you were to ask an air traffic controller what he or she was doing. The controller would not be likely to give a functional or physiological explanation. Instead, they might say something like this: "I'm clearing United Aircraft Flight 155 for landing. I cannot let American Flight 17 follow too closely behind, because United 155 is a jumbo jet, and there will be air turbulence behind it when it lands."

Such explanations are called *epistemological* (Sternberg, 1990) or *representational* (Pylyshyn, 1989). They refer to thinking in terms of the way that a person's internal processes reflect external realities. Epistemological explanations of thinking may be expressed as rules about what a person does in various situations. Individual rules are stated by describing a situation and the action to be taken when it is encountered. Two examples are the rudimentary rules for driving:

> If you see a red light → stop.
> If you see a green light → go.

Each rule is stated in the form, "Situation leads to action." Such rules are called *productions,* and a set of rules sufficient to perform a particular task is called a *production system.* Here is a rudimentary production system for automobile driving:

> If you see a red light → stop.
> If you see a green light → go.
> If you see a yellow light and you are close to the intersection → go.
> If you see a yellow light and you are far from the intersection → slow down.

You can construct a psychological theory this way. Indeed, some psychologists have argued that the only correct way to explain how someone solves a problem at the representational level is to write down the production system required to solve it (Newell & Simon, 1972; Simon & Kaplan, 1989). The production system can then be executed on a computer to see if the rules do mimic human behavior. This theoretical approach to cognition has been applied to many examples of thinking, ranging from algebraic problem solving to chess and checkers playing (Klahr, Langley, and Neches, 1987; Klahr and Kotovsky, 1989). For brevity, we will refer to it as the *computer simulation* approach.

According to the computer simulation approach, the only way to understand the demands that a job places on a person is to consider very carefully what sort of a computer program (production system) a robot would have to contain to do the same job. At the epistemological level, computer simulation forces us to build an explicit model of the cognitive task facing the jobholder. Since what a person is doing is defined in terms of how the person interprets the world, the resulting theory is clearly at the representational level.

Representational explanations implicitly presuppose functional capacities, just as a functional capacity presumes some sort of physiological mechanism. This point is more than an academic nicety. In industrial and social situations, we often want to "install" a particular representation in a person's mind. For instance, we want air traffic controllers to use their equipment in the manner set down by the rules of the Federal Aviation Administration (FAA). Those rules are themselves an epistemology, that is, they imply a certain representation. The representational demands cannot be met unless the person has the information-processing capacity that the representational demands require. Air traffic controllers are not asked to direct four dozen planes at a time, an epistemological goal, because this would overwhelm their working-memory capacities. But "working-memory capacity" is a functional concept.

Integrating Functional and Epistemological Approaches

From the psychologist's point of view, it often makes sense to study the functional and representational aspects of thought separately, though in the workplace they are inextricably linked together. Patrick Kyllonen and Ray Christal, two cognitive psychologists who have been concerned with applications of cognitive theory to selection and training in the U.S. Air Force, developed the graphic overview in Figure 5.5, showing the relation between functional and representational aspects of thought. They defined successful problem solving as the process of

Figure 5.5   The relation between external problems, memorized procedural rules, memorized declarative information, working memory, and responses. Source: Drawing based on a model proposed by Kyllonen and Christal (1988).

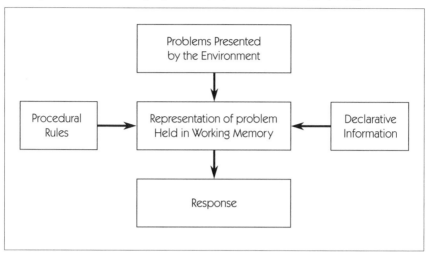

choosing an appropriate response (at the bottom of the figure) when presented with a problem-solving situation (at the top of the figure). In order to do this, the problem solver must develop an internal representation of the problem in working memory (the middle section of the box). Colloquially, the internal representation depicts how the problem solver sees the problem. What is the person's interpretation of what is going on?

Interpretation depends on an interaction between what is "out there" in the world and what we think is relevant "in here" in our long-term memory. This is shown by the middle and right-hand boxes of the figure. Think of the way a physician diagnoses a patient, by combining observations of patient's symptoms with knowledge about similar patients and diseases.

Building an internal representation is only a first step. The purpose of problem solving is to build an interpretation that can be recognized as a guide to action. This is depicted in the left-hand box of Figure 5.5, which shows that the internal representation triggers problem-solving rules (*procedural knowledge* in the argot of cognitive psychology) telling the problem solver what to do when he or she creates a particular interpretation of a situation. Some simple rules for driving in traffic were shown above. Procedural rules for medical and legal problem solving are far more complicated than those for driving, but the principles of execution are the same.

The internal representation resides in working memory and, therefore, is limited by the capacity of that memory. This is a rather clumsy, but appropriately scientific, way of saying that human beings can handle only so much complexity at any one time. Representations that are too complex simply will not fit.

Representation development is also limited by declarative knowledge. We use what we know to interpret what is before us. Physicians today code the problem of "person faint, white faced, and giddy" differently from the way they did in Roman times. One of the most important aspects of problem solving is our ability to recognize that certain facts are relevant and to fit them into our development of a problem representation. This lets us make efficient use of our limited working-memory capacity and, thus, in some ways, transcend functional limits on problem solving, so long as we are dealing with the familiar.

Problem-solving knowledge can be either very general knowledge about "rational ways to solve a problem" or highly specific knowledge about how to solve certain types of problems. In general, problem-solving procedures that work in highly specific situations depend heavily on prior knowledge, modified slightly by current facts. Therefore, they make little demand on working memory. By contrast, general problem-solving procedures tend to be slower, use fewer stored facts, and require more elaborate working-memory representations. Problem solving is often a trade-off between slow, flexible procedures that work in many situations and narrow, rigid ones that work very well on a limited class of problems, as illustrated by the following example.

The Carpenter's Problem

A carpenter wishes to place a right-angle brace against a wall, as shown in Figure 5.6. The brace is to consist of three pieces of wood, A, B, and C. Piece A is to lie flat on the ground and is to be anchored at point X. Piece B is to lie flat against the wall and rise to point Y. Piece C completes the triangle. Clearly, the length of pieces A and B are fixed by the problem. How long must piece C be?

Suppose that we take a geometric approach to solving this problem. Since both boards A and B are of fixed length, and since the angle between them is fixed at 90°, there is only one possible length for board C. The length can be found by geometry, but the solution requires that you rederive the Pythagorean theorem $(A^2 + B^2 = C^2)$. This involves a substantial bit of reasoning, and the chance for a mistake is high.

A trigonometric approach to the problem requires recall of some facts many of us have not used since high school mathematics class.[5] The solution involves recall of the rules of trigonometry, which are

Figure 5.6 A carpenter's problem. A brace is a triangle formed from three pieces of wood, A, B, and C. Board A lies flat on the floor, extending from the block at X to the wall at Z. Board B extends to point Y on the wall. How long does board C have to be?

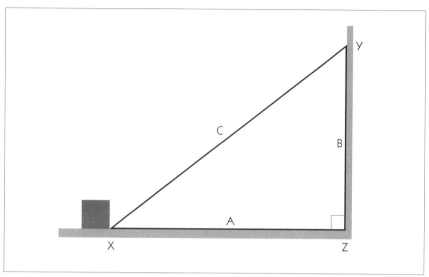

more specialized than the axioms of geometry, followed by a bit of arithmetic. Mistakes are certainly possible.

A third way to solve this problem is simply to remember the Pythagorean theorem and apply it. The task of constructing the internal representation is much simplified but the method is less general than the trigonometric or geometric method, because it works only with right triangles.

Or you could simply whip out a tape measure and measure the distance from X to Y. If the boards are too long to do this physically, draw a scale diagram and measure line C. This method provides only an approximation to the answer, because you will be limited by the accuracy of your measurements. Therefore, it works only in situations in which extreme accuracy is not required. Fortunately, though, most of the world seems to be that way. Hands-on methods of thinking can often reduce the strain on the brain.

Clearly, each method has its advantages and disadvantages. In almost every situation problem solving involves a trade-off between using general solutions that place heavy demands on working memory and using limited, remembered solutions that shift the burden from manipulations in working memory to retrievals from long-term memory or, in the extreme, to responding to perceivables in the world, without involving memory at all.

The distinction between fluid and crystallized intelligence closely parallels the distinction between relying on general, working-memory-intensive methods of problem solving and relying on situation-specific, long-term-memory-intensive methods. In fact, Kyllonen and Christal (1990) provide evidence showing that fluid intelligence is closely related to the ability to manipulate information in working memory. We will return to this point later. First, though, let us elaborate on the problem-solving model itself.

Measurement, Flexibility, and Efficiency in Problem Solving: The Sentence Verification Task

People can (sometimes) adapt their thinking to suit the circumstances. A cognitive theory that is to be applied to the workplace must be able to deal with flexibility of thought. To show how cognitive psychology deals with the different ways in which people approach the same problem, we will look at some detailed analyses of a simple laboratory task and at a workplace situation that illustrates virtually the same principles.

Figure 5.7 shows an experimental paradigm known as the *sentence verification task* (Clark and Chase, 1972). A participant is shown a simple sentence, such as "The plus is above the star," which is followed by a picture: either a plus above a star or a star above a plus. The task is to decide whether or not the sentence accurately described the picture. The time required to do this task is interpreted as a measure of the time the observer takes to compare a description of something to a view of the thing being observed. This is one of the basic uses of language.

Since the ability to deal with language is an important part of many jobs, it has been suggested that sentence verification tests could be used as rapid personnel screening devices. In fact, the British psychologist Alan Baddeley (1968) has shown that you can gain almost as good an idea of a young adult's verbal comprehension skills from his or her performance in a five-minute sentence verification task as you can from an hour's testing on more complex verbal tasks, such as paragraph comprehension. Apparently, performance in the simple task can provide a measure of a person's ability to process verbal information in working memory (Just and Carpenter, 1992; Hunt, 1983).

Verbal comprehension is not the only place where measures of working memory performance predict important real-world capacities. For instance, tests of working-memory capacity, using totally abstract ma-

Figure 5.7 The sentence verification paradigm. An observer sees screen 1, and then screen 2. The task is to indicate whether the sentence on screen 1 is a true or false description of the picture on screen 2. Since the two screens are not seen at the same time, the comparison must be made from memory.

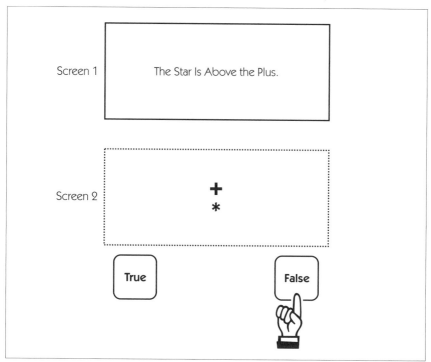

terial, are good predictors of air force recruits' ability to understand electrical circuits (Kyllonen and Christal, 1990).

Should personnel psychologists follow Baddeley's suggestion and include sentence verification in tests like the ASVAB or GATB? Let us consider how this task looks to psychometricians and to cognitive psychologists.

Psychometricians represent the performance of person i on task j, X_{ij} as

$$X_{ij} = \Sigma_k \, w_{jk}f_{ik} + e_{ij}, \qquad (5.1)$$

where k is the kth of $1..K$ factors (basic abilities) underlying performance, w_{jk} is the importance of the kth factor to performance on task j, f_{ik} is the level of person i's ability on factor k, and e_{ij} is a residual (error) term. While this equation can be used to *predict* people's performance, it does not say anything about *how* performance is achieved.

In order to complete a sentence verification task, a person (or a robot) has to have enough verbal ability to understand the sentence and enough perceptual ability to analyze the picture. The psychometrician regards this as a special case of the equation above,

Person's performance in sentence verification
$$= \text{(importance of verbal ability in task)}$$
$$\times \text{(person's verbal ability)} \quad\quad (5.2)$$
$$+ \text{(importance of perceptual ability in task)}$$
$$\times \text{(person's perceptual ability)}.$$

The mathematical machinery of psychometrics can then be used to find numbers for the importance values, which are assumed to be the same over people, and the ability values, which are assumed to be the same for a person over different tasks.

The cognitive psychologist wants to look at the process in more detail. A picture can be described in multiple ways. All of the following statements are true descriptions of the plus-star arrangement in Figure 5.7:

> The star is above the plus.
> The plus is below the star.
> The plus is not above the star.
> The star is not below the plus.

These sentences vary in linguistic complexity. Suppose that a person does the sentence verification task in the following way:

1. reads and memorizes the sentence,
2. looks at the picture and describes it using the simplest possible sentence structure, and
3. compares the description with the sentence being held in memory.

To illustrate, suppose that the sentence to be verified is

> The star is not below the plus,

followed by a picture of a plus above a star. The person must compare

The star is not below the plus.

The plus is above the star.

This can be done only by breaking down the meaning of the complicated sentence. In the example, the person must realize that "below" is the complement of "above," and that "not below" is the negation of the complement, and, therefore, it is equivalent to "above." The complicated sentence reduces to

The star is above the plus,

which, clearly, is not the same as "The plus is above the star."

As would be expected, the time required to verify sentences increases as linguistic complexity increases. To the psychometrician this simply means that difficulty increases. The cognitive psychologist goes one step further. By conducting systematic analyses of how sentence verification increases as linguistic complexity increases, the cognitive psychologist can estimate the time people require to do individual components of a task, such as dealing with negations or dealing with contrasts between complements like "above" and "below" (Carpenter and Just, 1975; Clark and Chase, 1972).

Such a demonstration by itself shows only that cognitive psychologists can make a finer-grained analysis of a task than psychometricians can. It is hard to imagine industrial situations in which such an analysis would be useful.

A second way of doing the task is to

1. read the sentence and analyze it,
2. form a visual image of the picture that the sentence describes, and
3. compare the picture with the visual image.

This strategy changes the task from verbal reasoning to spatial-visual reasoning. In terms of the psychometric analysis, for some people the weight for verbal ability is high, and for others the weight for perceptual ability is high. Psychometrics has no way of handling this situation, because the basic psychometric equation assumes that weights are invariant over people.

Cognitive psychologists are on firmer ground. By analyzing the relative times that people spend in the sentence analysis and picture examination phases, they can tell who is using which strategy, and they can then relate the effectiveness of a person's performance to his or her abilities, as they are required by the strategy the person is using (MacLeod, Hunt, and Mathews, 1978; Mathews, Hunt, and MacLeod, 1980). The analysis is more time-consuming than the psychometrician's, but it does allow for individual differences in the way that people approach the task.

Let us come up for air. Why is such a detailed analysis of the sentence verification task important?

In the introductory section of this chapter, I referred to a "cognitive task analysis" of how people (or people-mimicking robots) might do a particular task. What has just been illustrated is a cognitive task analysis, albeit of a laboratory situation. Perhaps the most important illustration was that there are often alternative analyses, suggesting that different people may approach a task in different ways. The choice of strategy can have important consequences for behavior.

Flexibility and Trade-offs in Cognitive Abilities

The Dairy Worker Example

Sylvia Scribner (1984) studied workplace performance in a "dairy" (actually a milk distribution plant). She observed a variation in strategies similar to that in the sentence verification task.

Scribner was interested in how workers dealt with the task of moving milk containers from the plant to retail delivery trucks. Milk was delivered to the loading dock in crates. Each crate contained milk in cartons of varying sizes and shapes (pints, half gallons, etc.). Delivery truck drivers were given lists of orders to be filled stated in units of less than a crate: for example, "one gallon of milk, one half gallon of lowfat milk, and two half pints of cream." The task was to load the truck quickly and to position milk in the truck in such a way that it would be easy to unload individual orders.

The task can be solved by arithmetic. Given so many half pints to a crate and so many half pints in the list of orders, calculate how many half-pint boxes are needed. However, this solution has two problems. First, since different drivers were loading from the same set of crates, there would always be a number of open crates, which should be loaded first. Second, the solution requires arithmetic, and most people are not very good at arithmetic.

Experienced loaders used visual-spatial reasoning. Because they had done the task many times they could imagine what "x gallons of milk" looked like. On reading an order they would visually scan crates that had already been opened to find the cartons they needed. Similar visual-spatial schemes were used to solve more complicated problems, including the problem of loading so that the truck could be unloaded easily.

Inexperienced loaders were slower and more mistake prone. Why? Because they used arithmetic.

Scribner's analysis of workplace performance and our own laboratory studies of sentence verification tell the same story. In order to understand how a task is done, one must carefully observe the people who are doing it. Not all people do the same task in the same way. Early studies of sentence verification assumed that it was a verbal task. One might also assume that a good dairy loader has to know arithmetic. Both analyses fail to consider the flexibility of human thinking.

Many, if not most, workplace problems are not solved by abstract reasoning. Workers develop faster, situation-specific ways to do their jobs. In the extreme, "problem solving" does not occur at all. Instead, people remember what to do. Here is a truism: The fastest way to solve a problem is to realize that you have solved it before and that you already know the answer.

The Master Chess Player Example

Formally, chess is an exercise in deductive logic. The perfect player should choose his or her next move by applying the rules of chess to the problem presented by the current board position. Therefore, one might assume that chess experts have superior information-processing functions, because they can keep many things in mind as they explore board possibilities. This is true only in a very specialized sense.

Chess masters and grand masters have memorized many standard chess situations and have learned how to code a chessboard in a way that is easily memorized, for instance, by coding "pieces attacking the rook" as a single unit. The chess master's memory for chess positions is much greater than the average person's, because the chess master uses his or her knowledge of the game to code the board, just as dairy workers code milk orders. Chess masters do not demonstrate unusually good memories, except in the context of chess (Charness, 1989, 1991).

This illustrates an important principle. People are, by and large, specialized thinkers. Good general-purpose problem solvers are relatively rare, but very many people are skilled thinkers within the domains that they know well. This is not just true for chess. The same point has been illustrated in medicine, physics, music, economics, and even warehouse stock management.

We are faced with a paradox. On the one hand, functional and physiological explanations of cognition have to be right. There is a sense in which people are general-purpose problem-solving machines. On the other hand, if we want to estimate what people can do in everyday situations, we will badly underestimate their performance if we focus on their physiological state and information-processing capacities. The way people look at a problem is important, and people are very good at finding an effective way to represent problems that they encounter in their everyday life. In order to reconcile these contrasting views of the importance of mental machinery and the importance of knowledge, we need a general theory of how the mind works.

The Blackboard Model of Thought

A functional theory of thought has to specify the elementary information-processing characteristics that the mind has and then specify how they interact with each other, and with knowledge, to produce cognition.

In order to see what this implies, suppose that we wanted to explain the "thinking" that is exhibited by a social system, for example, a university library. A possible description of a library might be: "In order to determine whether or not a book is in the university library a user can either search the electronic catalog, search the microfilm catalog, or search the card catalog. Given the title and the author, the user can retrieve the reference number from one of these catalogs and consult a map of the library to determine where books with this number and similar numbers are stored. The user then proceeds to this location. . . ."

This is a functional description, but it is not only a list of functions. The description explains how the functions are interrelated. Following computer science usage, I will call a description that relates functions to each other a *system architecture.* What we seek is a system architecture description of the mind.

The *blackboard model* is a system architecture that has been widely used in both cognitive psychology, as a model of how people might think, and in artificial intelligence, as a model of how computers might be made to think like people. The argument for using the model has been presented in great detail elsewhere (Jagannathan, Dodhiawara, and Baum, 1989; Klahr, Langley, and Neches, 1987; Newell, 1990; Newell and Simon, 1972), so all I will do is describe the idea.

The blackboard model is an amplification of the notion presented earlier that thought is based on an interaction between a working-memory representation of what is going on at the moment and a long-term memory representation of knowledge and strategies for problem solving. The interplay between the two is shown in Figure 5.8. The working-memory system can be thought of as a "blackboard" on which the mind writes messages. The messages come from two sources: the

Figure 5.8 A highly abstracted version of the blackboard model of mental action.

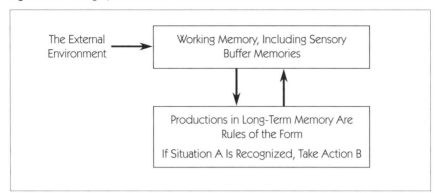

outside world and memory itself. Long-term memory contains rules governing how messages will be written on the blackboard.

The rules are stated in the production system notation, as pattern → action rules. These rules should be thought of as active agents who continually examine the contents of the blackboard rather than as passive lists of directions. Each production examines the contents of the blackboard independently of the actions of any other production. When a production matches some part of the blackboard, the action associated with that production is taken. (This is referred to as the production's *firing*.) If more than one production can be matched to the contents of working memory, a *conflict resolution rule* is invoked to determine which production is fired. Different versions of the model use different conflict resolution rules. But we need not be concerned with this level of detail.

When a production fires, its action usually changes the contents of the blackboard. You can think of productions as posting notes for each other in order to direct complicated sequences of actions. Since the notes establish a record of what is going on externally, the interpretation of a piece of information currently on the blackboard may be guided by the context of past actions.

The automobile driving example can be extended to illustrate these principles. Here is an initial production system for driving:

1. If the goal is to move → depress the accelerator.
2. If the goal is to stop → remove foot from the accelerator and depress the brake.
3. If the light is red → set a goal to stop.
4. If the light is green → set a goal to move.

These rules assume that working memory contains two types of information: information about the environment (here the color of the traffic lights) and information about goals. Since goals are posted on the blackboard, a production system model can guide its actions by intended results, as well as by the feature of the external stimuli.[6] For instance, an approximately context-sensitive way of dealing with yellow lights can be created by extending rules 1–4 as follows:

5. If the light is yellow and the goal is to hurry → place a goal to move on the blackboard.

6. If the light is yellow and the goal is to be cautious → place a goal to stop on the blackboard.

7. If you have recently had a traffic ticket → set a goal to be cautious on the blackboard.

8. If you are driving to a hospital with a woman who is about to give birth → set a goal to hurry on the blackboard.

9. If you hear a police siren → set a goal to stop.

Most cognitive psychologists believe that the blackboard should be thought of as having three separate areas: an auditory buffer area that can hold sound images, a visual scratchpad area that can hold visual percepts and images, and a more abstract working memory area that is not tied directly to a sensory modality (Baddeley, 1986, 1992). If we were to develop a complete production system for driving, different productions would read and post notes on different parts of the blackboard.

The reader is invited to try to invent rules for other everyday activities, such as cooking breakfast. Let us place this discussion in the context of the analysis of workplace performance.

The blackboard model–production system model should not be thought of as a scientific theory, in the sense that Newtonian mechanics is a scientific theory of the interaction between physical bodies.[7] These ideas provide a language in which a cognitive task analysis can be stated. The cognitive psychologist imagines a robot that literally contains a blackboard model as part of its control circuitry. The robot's actions are determined by the knowledge contained in its production rules and the efficiency with which the blackboard system can execute the rules. The last qualification is important. The execution of production rules is constrained by system architecture, which is what establishes the link between functional and representational explanations of action.

The analysis works if people are constrained by the same sorts of limits as the robot. The most obvious constraint is the size of working memory. If only so much information can be on the blackboard at any one time, then the pattern parts of the productions are similarly limited. When we interpret the blackboard model as a model of human action, "being on the blackboard" is roughly equivalent to "being information that a person is paying attention to right now." Every reasonable psychological theory sees this as a strong constraint on human action. We are not very good at paying attention to several things at once. A similar constraint applies to holding information on the blackboard over time. On a physical blackboard, or in a computer's memory, when information is put in place, it stays there until it is removed. No one thinks that human memory operates this way. Information will drop from our attention unless it is actively rehearsed.

These two constraints begin to let us respond to a complaint voiced at the start of the book. Recall that business leaders complained that American students "did not know how to solve problems," but were not very specific about what, precisely, the students did not know how to do. The blackboard model suggests that we ought to teach people problem-solving rules that fit together in such a way that the necessary information is in place when it is needed, and not placed in working memory long before it is needed.

In principle, the problem-solving abilities of a robot could be constrained by the size of long-term memory. The robot would be limited by the sheer number of rules that could be placed in its memory banks. People do not seem limited by the number of facts that they can learn. They are limited in their ability to organize these facts into coherent problem-solving schemes. Therefore, it behooves us to have memorized problem-solving techniques that solve the problems of daily life without overloading working memory.

The dairy worker's solution to loading milk cartons can be thought of in this way. The experienced workers had learned rules that were triggered by the sight of configurations of milk cartons: They knew complex rules, using visual stimuli, that let them solve a loading problem in a few steps. The inexperienced workers, who relied on arithmetic, used many more steps.

KNOWLEDGE-BASED PROBLEM SOLVING

Schematic Reasoning

While cognitive psychology theories are stated in terms of functional architectures, teachers, trainers, and job designers want cognitive task analyses to be stated in terms of the problem itself. For instance, a high school physics teacher wants to explain students' thinking in terms of what they know about physics. The statement "Your students confuse a force relationship with the expenditure of energy" makes sense to the physics teacher. The statement "Your students have not internalized appropriate pattern recognition rules for the concepts of force and energy" is psychobabble. Similar examples could be offered in fields ranging from chess to automobile repair.

I will call such analyses *domain-specific models of thought*. They amount to instructions for how to solve problems in a particular field, stated in such a way that they fit within the constraints of the blackboard model of the mind itself.

Many cognitive psychologists use the concept of a *schema* to describe domain-specific problem solving. Unfortunately, in spite of the ubiquity of the term, there is no agreed-upon definition of a schema. I shall use the term to mean the mental equivalent of a form used to compute a solution to a problem. What this means is best shown by an example.

Internal Revenue Service (IRS) form 1040, which is used to compute personal income taxes in the United States, is, in effect, a problem-solving schema for the Income Tax Code. It tells the taxpayer to retrieve certain facts from records (gross income, medical expenses, etc.) and then specifies the operations that are to be performed on these figures in order to calculate one's taxes. Studies in cognitive psychology that compare the problem-solving abilities of experts and novices in fields as disparate as chess and physics have shown that experts use memorized problem-solving schemata in very much the way that a taxpayer uses form 1040 (Chi, Glaser, and Farr, 1988; Ericsson and Smith, 1991). A study of expert problem solving in physics (Larkin et al., 1980) offers a good example of how detailed this can be.[8]

Consider the problem shown in Figure 5.9. A bobsled is placed on the starting block of a racecourse. If a man pushes the bobsled with fixed force F along a racecourse of angle A with respect to the horizontal, how fast will the sled be going after *t* seconds?

Experienced physicists will see this as a *balance of force* problem. As soon as this identification is made, the physicist knows what to do: Identify and write down the forces acting on the sled in all directions of motion. In order to determine the speed of the sled after *t* seconds, apply the equation

$$s = (1/2)ft^2, \tag{5.3}$$

where *s* is speed, *f* is the force in the direction of motion, and *t* is the time that the force is applied. Note the analogy to Form 1040, or for

Figure 5.9   The bobsled problem. A man applies a force F to a stationary bobsled resting on a course inclined at angle A to the horizontal. How fast will the bobsled be going after *t* seconds? Disregard friction.

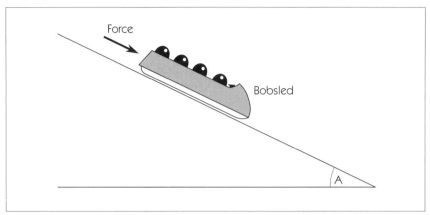

that matter, to the carpenter's 3:4:5 rule. The equation plus the definitions tell the problem solver what data to retrieve and how to manipulate the data. In the case of experts, the steps have been incorporated into a memorized schema. In the case of novices, the steps have to be worked out one at a time.

The dairy worker example can also be seen as a case of schematic reasoning. However, there is an important difference between the dairy worker's schema for visualizing milk cartons and the physicist's schema for solving balance of force problems. The dairy worker's schema was defined in terms of the manipulation of concrete objects—crates of milk cartons. Cues for its application are perceivable in the external world. The balance of force schema is defined in terms of abstractions. Therefore, we expect the balance of force schema to be more difficult to apply than the dairy worker schema, because the physicist has no external cue to indicate when the schema can be applied. The physicist must be able to make the leap beyond the perceivable, *surface* aspects of a problem to see it in its abstract form. (The abstract form is sometimes called the *deep structure* of the problem.) Learning to do this appears to be an important part of acquiring expertise in physics (Chi, Feltovitch, and Glaser, 1981) and in most other fields.

There is an important trade-off between deep and surface structures. Schemata based on surface characteristics are easy to apply and provide quick solutions to problems. However, they are generally limited in their applicability. The experienced dairy workers' visual schema, for instance, would be defeated if the dairy shifted to metric units, or even simply changed the shape of the containers. On the other hand, the inexperienced dairy workers' arithmetic schema would still work, albeit slowly.

The same principle applies to avowedly intellectual pursuits. An interesting example is an artificial intelligence program design that was offered by experienced physics teachers and cognitive scientists as a model of physics problem solving (Larkin, Reif, Carbonell, and Gugliotta, 1988). The program, called FERMI[9] by its designers, was organized around a hierarchy of progressively more general problem-solving schemata. At its lowest level it contained procedures for solving very specific problems, such as calculating the voltage, current flow, and resistance in a direct current circuit consisting of one battery and one resistor, attached in series, or for calculating pressure drops between two points, one directly above the other, in a medium of uniform density. At a higher level it contained rules for combining local solutions and for decomposing complex problems into simple ones, to which simple schemata could be applied. The program always tried to solve problems at the simplest, most concrete, level first. When this could not be done, it retreated to the use of more abstract schemata.

While not presented in these terms, the FERMI design was clearly the result of a cognitive task analysis of physics problem solving, conducted in a cooperative study between physicists and cognitive scientists. The same interplay between localized and general schematic reasoning has been observed in studies of dairy workers, chess players, and computer programmers. Mastering this interplay is clearly one of the chief skills we must acquire when we "learn how to think."

Problem Solving as Mental Manipulation

Thinking about problem solving as schematic reasoning is not an alternative to believing in the blackboard model: The two views are complementary. Problem-solving schemata can be stated in the production system notation. This fact, alone, is sufficient to show complementarity of the two approaches. Our interests are not in the logical fact of complementarity so much as they are in its psychological implications.

A person who is faced with a problem must first represent it in a way that will connect the problem to an appropriate problem-solving schema. At midcentury the famous mathematician and mathematics teacher G. Polya (1954) pointed out that how a problem is represented makes all the difference. A good representation should make the problem solution obvious. In the terms used here, a schema and its associated problem representation are good if they lead to a mental model that does not overburden working memory. Alternatively, the schema can include some mechanical aid, such as the physical Form 1040, that provides the problem solver with an extension of working memory. Let us look at a few examples of this point.

Old-fashioned (precomputer) accountants kept orderly records because they used them to augment working memory. The records were organized so that the necessary information was available to the accountant when it was needed. In theoretical terms the accountant's schema for solving problems included using an external device, working notes, to go beyond the limits imposed by working memory.

A similar schema can be seen in a very different field: piloting high-performance military aircraft. The cockpits of these aircraft contain a bewildering array of instruments. Pilots are trained to scan the instruments in a way that directs their attention to the most crucial instruments first, then the next most crucial, and so forth. Like the accountants, the pilots have developed a schema that extends their model of the world outside of working memory.

The good problem solver has developed efficient schemata for the problems he or she is likely to encounter. Efficiency is determined by a pattern recognition system that tells the problem solver when a particular schema is applicable and by a schema for manipulating a model of the problem in a way that does not exceed the problem solver's information-processing characteristics. In practice, this usually means some way of managing information so that working memory limits are not exceeded.

This casts the argument over the use of abstract or concrete schemata in a somewhat different light. Recall the truism that the best way to solve a problem is to remember the solution. When automobile drivers see a red light, they do not run the motor vehicle code through their heads, *they know what to do.* A schema that associates an external signal with an invariant action depends on so few mental steps that it is hard to see what could go wrong.

If we lived in a completely orderly world, simple schemata are all that we would need. We could simply memorize rules for all possible situations. But, since we do not live in such a world, we need more abstract schemata. The working-memory representations of variables in a perceptual schema, such as the red-light schema or the dairy worker schema, are supported by the sensory system. Abstract schemata, such as "linear system of equations" or "balance of force," depend on internally generated models of the world. Misrecognition and errors become more likely as memory moves away from environmental support.

Humanity in general is not well designed for abstract thinking, although some of us are better at dealing with reasoning problems than are others. The analysis offered here suggests that this is so for two rather different reasons. One is that the good reasoner must know the schemata that are appropriate for a given situation. This is usually the result of learning. The other is that the good reasoner must have a capacity for manipulating the mental models that a problem-solving schema constructs. Because of this requirement, we would expect that people with larger working memories, measured without respect to the content of those memories, would be better problem solvers. In fact, they are (Kyllonen and Christal, 1990).

Clearly, people are not born with prewired schemata for loading milk trucks or doing physics problems. We learn to do most of the things we do. Let us next look at learning from the cognitive psychologist's view.

PERFORMANCE AND LEARNING

Distinguishing Between Performance and Learning

In discussing human capabilities, it is useful to distinguish between *performance* and *learning*. Performance refers to using knowledge and/or skills to do some task. Learning refers to the acquisition of knowledge and skills. Performance can be observed directly, while learning is inferred from changes in performance over time.

Learning may call on different cognitive abilities than performance. Language learning is possibly the most extreme illustration. Everyone learns to talk well before he or she is an adult. In fact, children learn languages much more easily than adults do. It appears that at adolescence there is a loss in the ability to acquire languages (Johnson and Newport, 1989). On the other hand, the ability to perform well in a language that has already been learned is not only retained but is surprisingly resistant to the normal ravages of age (Salthouse, 1982).

Neuropsychology, the study of the relation between brain and behavior, provides additional striking examples of the distinction between information acquisition and information use. Korsakoff's syndrome, a concomitant of advanced alcoholism, leaves people unable to learn new information even though they can retain old information. A Korsakoff's syndrome patient may be quite capable of recalling what happened to him years ago, yet be unable to recall what happened the previous day. Similar behaviors are also sometimes associated with advanced age and certain other types of brain injury (Ellis and Young, 1988; Squire, 1987).

The distinction between learning and performance has major implications for the way that people are used in the workplace. Almost by

Figure 5.10 A schematic of the Nissen and Bullemer automatic learning task. The observer presses a button when the light above it is lit.

definition, workers who are on the job can perform the tasks that the job requires. But suppose new tasks are added to the job description? Will the worker be able to learn to perform them? This often depends upon how the worker has learned the original task.

Two quite different types of learning are possible, *procedural* and *declarative* learning. Roughly, the distinction between the two is the distinction between learning to do something (especially, make motor movements) and learning to know something, so you can examine your own knowledge. This distinction will be important in discussing the coming workforce, so it will pay to look at a laboratory task that highlights the difference between procedural and declarative learning.

Procedural and Declarative Learning

A learner is aware of declarative learning and often uses overt strategies to control what is learned. No student ever learned Shakespeare's plays without being aware that he or she was learning them! On the other hand, procedural learning can take place without conscious awareness. Some elegant work by Mary Jo Nissen and her colleagues at the University of Minnesota illustrates the distinction.

Figure 5.10 shows the experimental apparatus they used (Nissen and Bullemer, 1987). College students sat in front of a bank of lights. There was a numbered button below each light. The lights blinked on and off one at a time. The task was to push the button under each light as the light came on.

In fact the lights were turned on in a regular cycle—for example, 1-5-10-9-8-4-3-6-7. As this cycle was repeated, students began to punch the buttons more and more quickly.

This is hardly surprising. What is surprising is that some people learned to respond quickly without realizing that the sequence existed. In one of their studies Nissen and Bullemer had students perform the button-pressing task while simultaneously listening to tones that were sounded as the buttons were pressed. The students had to keep track of the number of high and low tones, which had nothing to do with the button-pressing task. Once again, they learned to do the button-pressing task rapidly. However, they were unable to describe the cycle that the lights had followed. In theoretical terms, the students had learned a procedure for responding to lights without noticing the regularities in the light sequence that the procedure implied. Procedural learning succeeded where declarative learning failed.

This does not mean that when you are learning something, it does not matter whether or not you can articulate your solution, so long as you can display appropriate improvements in performance. Having declarative knowledge of the principles behind learned procedures becomes crucial if you are asked to transfer the experience to a new situation.

Nissen and Bullemer showed this by changing the task slightly. Instead of asking their student participants to push a button under a light *after* the light was lit, they asked them to press a button under the light that was *about to* come on. This makes a major difference in the logic of the task. Instead of letting their fingers "do the walking," participants had to anticipate consciously what was going to happen. Those who had noticed the cycle (declarative learners) could perform the new task. Those who had had to count tones, and as a result had not noticed the cycle (procedural learners), could not.

Nissen and Bullemer's research illustrates a pure distinction between procedural and declarative learning. The two types of learning depend on different physiological mechanisms. Korsakoff's syndrome patients appear able to learn via the automatic mechanism but not via the controlled mechanism. An even more striking demonstration is the finding that a drug, scopolamine, can temporarily disrupt declarative learning while leaving procedural learning unaffected (Nissen, Knopman, and Schacter, 1987).

A great deal of research has supported the distinction between learning *how* to do something well, and learning *why* the thing one does works well (Schacter, 1987). So long as one's job is to do the thing that one has practiced doing, knowing how is important. If the job is to transfer skills to a new situation, knowing why becomes important.

The Importance of Understanding in Learning

To illustrate the important distinction between having experiences and acquiring wisdom from them, we shall examine a series of experiments conducted at the University of Michigan by Mary Gick and Keith Holy-oak, who asked students to solve puzzle problems that were superficially different, but had the same underlying deep structure. Gick and Holyoak were interested in how often and under what circumstances the students would extract general principles of problem solution from experience with apparently different problems. Here are two of the problems that Gick and Holyoak used.

1. *The radiation problem:* A physician wants to use x-rays to destroy a dangerous tumor. The tumor is completely surrounded by vital tissue, so an x-ray beam sufficiently strong to destroy the tumor would also pass through the vital tissue, thus killing the patient. How should the physician proceed?

2. *The general's problem:* A general has assembled a large army to attack an enemy fortress. He then learns that all the roads leading to the fortress have been mined. In order to avoid disrupting all traffic, the enemy has set the mines so that small groups of men can move over them, but they will be ignited if a large army marches over them. How should the general proceed?

Both of these problems can be solved by what Gick and Holyoak called the "concentration of force" principle. The solution to the radiation problem is to aim weak beams at the tumor from different points outside the body. Thus, each beam passes through a different part of the vital tissue around the tumor, but is too weak to damage it. An intense field of energy is produced at the tumor location, by the intersection of several weak beams.

The general's problem is solved by splitting the army into small units. Each unit approaches the fortress from a different direction, without setting off the mines on the road that the unit takes. The army is concentrated only at the fortress itself.

Although such problems seem simple when you know the answer, in fact they are rather hard. Fewer than 10 percent of college students solve the radiation problem when they first see it (Gick and Holyoak, 1980). What happens if the students first solve the general's problem (or something like it), and then attempt to solve the radiation problem, depends on how the problem solver conceptualizes the initial experience.

Gick and Holyoak (1983, experiment 4) asked students to solve two concentration of forces problems similar to the general problem, describe the principles involved, and then try to solve the radiation problem. Performance on the last problem depended dramatically on how well the students could articulate the principles underlying the first two problems. Fifty-one students participated in the experiment; 11 of them were able to give good summaries of their initial experiences, in which they clearly explained the concentration of forces principle; 10 of these 11 students solved the radiation problem, a success rate of about 90 percent. Of the 40 students who could not present good summaries, only 13 solved the radiation problem, a success rate of 30 percent.

Gick and Holyoak's experimental data have been mimicked in the classroom. Physics and mathematics students who can describe the principles behind an example can transfer those principles to new problems. Students who regard the example problems as "drill," and work through the details of computations without thinking about them, have trouble attacking new problems using the principles illustrated in the examples.

These points are certainly not surprising. Nevertheless, they illustrate an important and too often neglected point. Drill, alone, will work if your purpose is to teach people to respond rapidly, in a very narrowly defined situation. This is what happened to the participants in Nissen and Bullemer's serial reaction task; they learned to make a sequence of motor movements in response to a sequence of lights. However, such learning is task specific. If the purpose of learning is to teach people problem-solving methods that can be applied to new situations, then learning with understanding is a must.

A Brief Return to Psychological Theory

Allen Newell (1990) and John Anderson (1983, 1987; Singley and Anderson, 1989) have proposed blackboard models that provide a theoretical account of both automated and controlled learning. Although their models differ in ways that are important in terms of psychological theory, for our purposes the two analyses are essentially equivalent.

Newell and Anderson argue, in somewhat different terms, that "declarative learning," or "learning with understanding," is actually a form of problem solving. In Newell's terms, learning occurs when a problem solver is presented with an impasse; he or she cannot solve a problem using the problem-solving rules (i.e., schemata) currently available. Therefore, the problem solver sets a new goal: to develop a schema that will solve the problem. The result may be a sophisticated schema that deals with abstract, widely applicable principles or one that deals only with surface characteristics of the problem at hand. The solutions produced by Gick and Holyoak's good and poor problem solvers can be looked on in this way.

The quality of the schema is not very important for solving the original problem, since the problem solver will work at the problem until a solution is reached. Schema quality becomes important when a second, related problem is encountered. If the schema developed to resolve the impasse is general, it can be used to solve the new problem. But if it is specific, tied to the characteristics of the original problem, it is not available to attack superficially different problems that can be solved using the same general problem-solving methods.

How, then, do we account for procedural learning? Theoretically, automated learning occurs when the act of applying one production becomes a statistically reliable cue for the application of a second production. In Nissen and Bullemer's button-pressing task, suppose that a person is actually learning the example cycle, 1-5-10-9-8-4-3-6-7. The act of *pressing* button 1 under light 1 will become a cue for initiating the response of pressing button 5. Thus, an "automatic learning robot" should tie the two productions together; on seeing light 1, initiate a press to button 1 and then button 5.

Anderson (1987) calls this *compiling* two sequentially executed productions into a single production. Experienced typists, for example, can type commonly encountered strings of letters, such as "t i o n," almost as if they were a single unit. As a result, it is hard for an experienced typist to suppress doing this when the automated response is inappropriate. Typing "ratio" as "ration" is a common mistake.

Anderson argues that whenever people repeat the same sequence of actions over and over, they move from controlled to automated responding. Ackerman (1987) extended the argument to point out its importance for industrial work, by asking, "What sorts of people are easy to train?" His answer was that it depends on the stage of training. At first, during the controlled stage, learning appears to be an intellectual operation. The learner is trying to develop a schema for dealing with the situation. This ability seems to be close to what we think of as fluid intelligence, that is, the ability to articulate one's own thoughts as the schema unfolds. As learning progresses, the task shifts from one of assembling appropriate productions to merging them in an efficient manner. Ackerman pointed out that this is essentially an information-processing task: how quickly and how reliably a person can shift information from one location to another. Therefore, learning in the later stages of skill acquisition is likely to be more closely tied to performance on basic information-processing tasks, such as the CRT task described early in this chapter, than to the ability to articulate how a task ought to be done.

Ultimately, performance will be limited by perceptual-motor capacities: how quickly the individual can sense the outside world and respond, given that deciding how to respond has been automated.

Consider a learned and socially important task: automobile driving. In your first attempts to drive, you had to learn schemata for what the brakes are, how the steering wheel is used, what the motor vehicle rules are, and so forth. This is a confusing but largely conceptual exercise. The information-processing stage followed, where you knew what to do and the problem was to learn how to do it smoothly. At the same time you had to develop schemata for analyzing driving situations, learning to scan the instruments periodically and to scan the highway continuously. Once these schemata are acquired, their execution is limited by perceptual-motor capacities.

These different stages are mirrored by differences in automobile accident rates. Most Americans learn to drive when they are teenagers. They have notoriously high accident rates until they are 25 or so. Many of the accidents are associated with errors in higher-order judgment, that is, failures of controlled responding. For the next 20 to 40 years, most people drive relatively safely. The schemata for driving are in place, and many of the predictable tasks are automated. When drivers approach their mid-60s, accident rates begin to climb again. However, these accidents are often attributed to failures in information-processing capacity rather than failures in knowing how to drive.

SUMMARY: SOME PRINCIPLES OF HUMAN THOUGHT

The human mind is organized to think in a particular way. We have large long-term memories, so that we can store a great number of experiences, but we do not have large, fast, or reliable working memories. Therefore, it is generally safer to memorize a solution and recall it than to recompute a solution on the spot. We cannot solve problems using methods that unreasonably tax our working memories.

Because human thinking is best driven by memory, people are at their best when they are dealing with concrete situations that can be related unambiguously to previously learned activities. A car driver "knows what to do" at a red light because the driver has a schema for dealing with this specific, externally defined situation. The actions are clear and, equally important, it is clear when the schema is relevant.

Unfortunately, most of the world is not that simple. We have to have schemata that classify external situations into internal abstractions. In driving, "yellow light and a very expectant mother in the back seat" and "yellow light and only a few minutes left to catch the train" are different situations, but they both translate into "situation in which it is appropriate to speed," while "yellow light, two tickets in the last three months, and a police car behind me" has a different interpretation.

Similar analyses apply to our thinking about more complicated problems, ranging from machine operation to solving problems in physics. Thinking is the manipulation of an internal model of the external world. Because of the internal limits on our information-processing capacity, we must arrange for an orderly manipulation of the internal model. One of the ways we do this is by memorizing problem-solving schemata. Instead of solving all the new problems the world can present to us, we try to fit the present problem into some problem-solving schema that we have already acquired. Then we know what to do.

This mode of problem solving works if we have useful schemata and if we have good rules for recognizing when a particular schema is applicable. Education, training, and learning can be thought of as a process of schemata acquisition. Schemata that are cued by concrete external stimuli, such as the "red light" schema for driving, are perhaps the easiest to use. In the extreme, no abstraction is required. Once we perceive the stimulus, we react without further analysis. Of course, this is possible only in highly stereotyped situations, but such situations do occur. When we have acquired these primitive schemata, we say that the response is *automated*. When a response is automated, it can be emitted directly on perception of a stimulus, without an extensive use of working memory.

By contrast, actions are *controlled* when the response is determined by analyzing the external situation as one of a class of abstract situations, and then reacting to the abstraction. This is what a physicist does when he or she classifies a problem as, say, a balance of force problem. The analysis needed to classify a problem can be extensive and will typically place heavy demands on working memory.

The automated responses to red lights and the highly controlled responses that occur in physics and mathematics problem solving are different ends of a continuum. In practice, most of our problem solving contains elements of both automated and controlled responding. In the dairy worker example, the experienced dairy loaders had acquired visual schemata for breaking down cases into milk orders. Their actions tended to rely on automated perception, but did not do so entirely. The inexperienced dairy loaders solved the break-down problem using abstract mathematics. Their schemata were heavily weighted toward controlled responding. If one assumes that the workers were at all well educated, the elementary facts of addition and multiplication were probably well automated.

Education, in its broadest sense, is the acquisition of the schemata that we need to have in the world in which we live. If the goal of an education program is to establish automated responding, the appropriate thing to do is to practice specific responses to specific stimuli.

If the goal of the program is to develop more abstract schemata, the problem is harder. Learning becomes a by-product of problem solving, which means that the student's response to the educational experience will depend on the schemata that the student already has. The educator must engage the student in problem-solving activities that modify those schemata.

In order to do this, the educator must motivate the student to take the trouble to solve the problem. First, the educator and the student must agree on what problem is to be solved. After all, the student is going to resolve impasses in order to reach the student's goal, not the educator's. If the student perceives "achieving understanding of the material" as a reasonable goal, all is well. But what if it is not? In my high school Latin class, there was an ancient student tradition—cheat. Cheating did not solve the problem of "learning Latin," which most students were not motivated to do, but it did solve the problem of "getting out of Latin class without failing." I fear, though, that too many students acquired a schema in Latin class that could be applied in, say, physics class, in a way that satisfied their short-term goals but ultimately left them poorly prepared to become engineers and scientists.

The purpose of this example is not to deplore student morality. It is to make a point about learning. People will develop schemata to solve the problems *that they perceive to be problems,* that is, to satisfy their own motivations. If education and training programs are to be effective, the educators must deal with the learners' motivations.

NOTES

1. Two of the major figures in the artificial intelligence field, Allen Newell and Herbert Simon, worked in both psychology and computer science.
2. In fact, I reject the Searle-Dreyfus argument in its entirety. I believe that thinking should be studied within the framework of materialism, although occasionally we may have to resort to what philosophers call property dualism. Searle claims that this attitude has produced an intellectually sterile discipline. See Hunt (in press) for a considerable expansion on this point.
3. Cognitive analysis can also be used to alter a person physiologically. This is unlikely to occur in most workplaces, but it is possible. For instance, a person whose job required prolonged periods of wakefulness can be given drugs, including coffee!
4. The travel agent's problem-solving strategy very closely matched the strategy built into one of the first artificial intelligence programs, Newell and Simon's General Problem Solver (1972).
5. Let ϕ be the angle YXZ, that is, the angle between boards A and C. From the definition of the tangent function, $\tan(\phi) = B/A$. Therefore, ϕ can be

found from a table of trigonometric functions. From the definition of the cosine, $\cos(\phi) = A/C$. Therefore, $C = A/\cos(\phi)$.

6. In more complicated production system models, the strategy of activating productions by posting notes is not limited to posting goal information.

7. I have defended this position elsewhere (Hunt, in press; Hunt and Luce, 1992). I should acknowledge, though, that some psychologists do speak as if the blackboard model and related concepts constituted a theory. See especially Klahr, Neches, and Langley (1987), Newell (1990), and Simon and Kaplan (1989).

8. My example is a modification of one considered by Larkin et al. (1980).

9. Ostensibly for "Flexible, Expert Reasoner for Multidomain Inferencing," but actually to honor the famous physicist Enrico Fermi, who is said to have been exceptionally good at moving between special and general problem-solving methods.

6

Cognitive Demands
of the Coming Workplace

THE FUTURE SEEN THROUGH A MACROSCOPE

Having gained some idea of how psychologists think the mind works, let us now take a look at how the mind is going to be used in the coming workplace. This chapter is a forecast of the cognitive demands that the early twenty-first century workplace is going to present to its workers.

There is an important difference between this sort of forecast and the sorts of psychometric and demographic forecasts presented in Chapter 4. Psychometricians and demographers use a common language, applied mathematics. Therefore, in Chapter 4, I was able to use straightforward mathematical methods to combine psychometric and demographic statistics into a single forecast. People may argue about the appropriateness of the assumptions made, but the methods by which the forecast was made from the assumptions were clear.

It is not nearly so clear how one ought to make a forecast relating technological developments to psychological theories. The blackboard model presented in Chapter 5 does not lend itself to a simple summarization. Technologists cannot appeal to numerical tables in the *Statistical Abstract of the United States* to summarize how technology is changing the nature of work. We have to rely on anecdotes and the guesses of presumed experts.

A recent failure of prediction shows how fallible these guesses can be. In 1988 the Department of Labor (DOL) published its forecast of the nature of work, a volume entitled *Opportunity 2000*. Its authors focused on ways in which employers might cope with an anticipated *shortage* of skilled labor in the 1990–2000 period. They concluded that it made good short-term economic sense for individual employers to provide, among other things, basic skills training for minority group members and special work arrangements for women with families, older workers, and disabled workers.

Opportunity 2000's conclusions are desirable social goals in themselves, but the impending labor shortage does not seem to have happened. The early 1990s have been characterized by an excess of labor, unemployment rates hovering around 7 percent, with no sign of abatement, and a steady replacement of permanent, high-wage jobs with temporary, part-time, and low-wage jobs.

What went wrong with the *Opportunity 2000* estimate (and several others like it)? One possibility, which cannot be gainsaid, is that the authors were basically correct and that there will indeed be a labor shortage by 2000. The dislocations of the early 1990s may be temporary, caused in part by a downswing in the business cycle and in part by economic dislocations associated with the end of the cold war. If this is true, things will sort themselves out in a few years, and normal times will return again. The drop in unemployment in 1995 is encouraging. The continued reliance on temporary and contract workers is not.

A grimmer possibility is that the way in which work is done may be at a point of change. If this is so, the very methods of statistical forecasting are suspect, because past trends will not be good predictors of future facts. I, and many other observers, believe that the unemployment problems of the early 1990s were not cyclic adjustments. Instead, they were the economic analog of the first snowflakes to fall on a dinosaur's snout after the comet hit. While some of the argument for this pessimistic view has to be by rhetoric, there are some statistical trends that show what is happening.

If the nineteenth century was the age of industry, the twentieth has been the age of service. Over 70 percent of the workforce is involved in service delivery rather than manufacturing. Service occupations can be split into the delivery of physical services (e.g., laundry, heating) and the delivery of information services (e.g., banking and communications). In 1940 the information and services category was split almost evenly between the physical service sector (22.5 percent of the workforce) and the information service sector (24.9 percent). What we have seen over the years is clearly a decrease in the relative percentage of the workforce involved in manufacturing, which is characterized by a relatively high hourly wage, considering the educational characteristics of the individual worker, and an increase in the number of people who deal in information transmission—the people whom Secretary of Labor Robert Reich (1991) has called the symbol analysts. Some of the symbol analysts, notably managers and professionals, are both well paid and well educated. Others, secretaries, record keepers, and many people in sales, are reasonably but not exceptionally well paid. Even the lower-level symbol analyst positions, not surprisingly, do require language and other symbol-manipulating skills.

What has happened is that changes in computing and communication technologies have had a major impact both on manufacturing, a point which Reich and others have documented extensively, and also in the nature of the symbol analyst's work. Manufacturing methods have shifted from the use of production machines controlled by humans to the use of machines controlled by computers. This trend applies to the electronics field itself, where automated machinery is used heavily. Electronic devices are obviously proliferating throughout our society, but the production of these devices is not creating jobs. The Bureau of Labor Statistics has listed electronic and electrical assemblers as the fastest *declining* occupation for the 1990–2005 period, with a projected percent change in the workforce of −46 percent!

Instead, what is happening is that the new technologies are increasing productivity per worker, while decreasing the number of workers required, especially in the higher-paid technical and manufacturing job categories. Indeed, new jobs are being created by expansion as our economy recovers from the 1990–1991 recession, but they are in the lower pay categories. As a result, early 1994 saw a spate of articles about "the working poor," people who are employed, but employed in low-pay and often temporary positions.

Two Case Studies

The Boeing Corporation is the world's largest airframe manufacturer. During 1992–1993 the company experienced hard times, due to cyclic factors in the airlines industry, and reduced its Seattle area workforce by about 25,000. The company was not seriously concerned about its long-term prospects, because the slowdown was due to airlines' delaying purchases that they eventually will have to make. However, Boeing executives made it clear to the public that when good times returned for the company, good times might not return for the employees. The laid-off workers would have been replaced by advanced methods of automated assembly, which use robotics and computer-controlled manufacturing.

Just a few miles north of Boeing's headquarters lie the headquarters of Microsoft Corporation, the world's largest computer software developer. Microsoft is hardly a small operation. As of May, 1993, its capitalization (value of stock outstanding) exceeded the capitalization of Eastman Kodak! And as of the same date, Microsoft employed a worldwide total of 13,800 people—just slightly more than half the number of jobs that its larger neighbor had cut. A more extreme example is Genentech, the world's largest biotechnology company, which employs 2,100 people (Keichel, 1993).

Of course, this comparison is not entirely fair. The things that Microsoft, Boeing, and Genentech make are so different that one would not expect the workforces to be comparable. So let us take a within-industry example.

In the early 1970s the symbol IBM was virtually synonymous with computers. The computers of that day were devices to be put in large, specially prepared rooms. By the early 1980s there had been an evolutionary change in the technology, and IBM had lost a substantial part of the university-scientific market to Digital Equipment Corporation (DEC). IBM, however, retained its dominant position in business computing. By this time computers were only as big as refrigerators and did not need special environments. In the late 1980s IBM employed over 400,000 people, while DEC employed somewhat more than 100,000. By the early 1990s IBM was a wounded giant. Its employment was about 300,000 in 1993, and its share of the now vibrant PC market had dropped dramatically. DEC was not doing well, either. While a number of large companies make computers, usually through subsidiaries or subdivision (e.g., Toshiba, Hewlett Packard), the market has been dominated by much smaller companies, such as Apple, Compaq, and Dell.

An interesting and largely unanticipated side effect of changes in the manufacturing process has been the proliferation of very small companies that develop custom computer applications. Seattle lists over 70 such companies, many employing fewer than a dozen people. These are certainly manufacturing companies. Customers indicate specialized needs, and the company assembles the appropriate configuration almost on the spot. The specialist companies listen carefully to the individual customer's needs; the distinction between manufacturing and service has become somewhat confused.

What this means is that the good jobs will go to the workers who have the skills required to understand and even construct new applications for other people. To what extent is the American workforce likely to measure up? Arnold Packer (1989) has published a discouraging forecast. He compared estimates of the percentage of jobs that would be created between 1985 and 2000 that would require certain levels of reading skills to estimates of the percentage of the entering workforce who are expected to have these skills. The results are shown in

Table 6.1 Estimate of the Percentage of Jobs Created Between 1985 and 2000 Requiring Certain Reading Skills with Entering Workforce Expected to Have These Skills

Reading Skill Level	Percentage of Entering Workers at This Skill Level	Percentage of New Jobs Requiring Skill Level
1	7.0	2
2	71.0	38
3	17.0	21
4	3.0	31
5	1.5	7
6	.5	1

Source: Packer (1989).

Notes: Skill level 1 = 2,500-word vocabulary, reads 95–125 words/min, writes simple sentences; 2 = 5,000–6,000-word vocabulary, reads 190–215 words/min, writes compound sentences; 3 = reads safety rules and equipment operating manuals, writes simple reports; 4 = reads journals and manuals, writes business letters and reports; 5 = reads scientific/technical journals and financial reports, writes journal articles and speeches; 6 = same skills as 5, at advanced levels.

Table 6.1. Clearly, the new jobs are biased toward a requirement for high skills, while the new workforce is biased toward a prevalence of low skills.[1]

Statistical summaries such as Packer's are useful, but they do not communicate a psychological intuition about what has happened. To do this, I have constructed a small fable.

ALEXANDER THE GREAT, KING HENRY V, AND JOHN HENRY, A STEEL-DRIVIN' MAN

A sad fact of human history is that military technology has often outpaced civilian technology. The rate of progression of military technology dramatizes the changing nature of jobs through history.

Alexander the Great (356–323 B.C.) and King Henry V (1387–1422) had brief lives, even for their times, but their military accomplishments influenced world events for hundreds of years after they died. Would they have understood each other's worlds? Suppose that Alexander had been plunked down in fifteenth century England. Would he have been able to lead Henry's army?

Alexander would have had to learn about some new technologies. Englishmen in the fifteenth century used saddles with stirrups, levers, and gears, none of which were known in Macedonian Greece. Alexander would have probably grasped their use quickly, since they are all basically devices for multiplying and redirecting the energy generated from human and animal sources. The Macedonians had such artifacts, so the engineering of Henry's army would not have presented any new concepts to Alexander.[2]

The same reasoning applies to Alexander's soldiers. While they would not have been familiar with the details of the arms carried by Henry V's soldiers, probably they would have understood them when they saw a demonstration. Both the Macedonian and the English commanders relied on their soldiers' physical strength and on the discipline with which they fought, shoulder to shoulder, at the shouted orders of their commanders.

Suppose that we move Alexander and Henry forward another 500 years, to the end of the nineteenth century. There would have been a major change in the technology of warfare. Instead of shooting arrows and stabbing with spears, soldiers fought by firing cannons and rifles. Operating these weapons required perceptual-motor skills rather than brute force. The sharpshooter who could hit his target from 400 yards and the artilleryman who could estimate range were now far more deadly than the powerful swordsman. The skills demanded of both commanders and soldiers changed much more between 1400 and 1900 than between 300 B.C. and 1400 A.D.

Next we move our warrior kings forward 100 years to the Persian Gulf War of 1991. In that war killing was done by people who never saw their enemies. Aircrews programmed machinery to drop bombs, while artillerymen calculated trajectories for indirect fire weapons. Tank crews, the tactical analog of Henry's knights and Alexander's mounted Companions, went through a deadly choreography based on infrared detection devices, laser ranging, and computer-stabilized cannon. The troops still had to know their weapons. Indeed, if anything, they had to know them better than Alexander and Henry's troops did, for twentieth century weapons are far more complicated than a crossbow or a chariot. Skills shifted from muscle to hand-eye coordination to the mind. The change in military technology from 1890 to 1990 was far greater than the change from 300 B.C. to 1400 A.D.

The same principles apply to civilian technology. The psychological demands of work were very much the same in the days of Alexander as they were in the days of Henry V, and even in the early American colonial times. Workers transported goods using their bodies or, if they were lucky, horses and oxen.

The Industrial Revolution of the early nineteenth century changed this. In retrospect, the most important change was probably power generation. Instead of being limited by the energy provided by human beings and animals, industry could rely on the far greater sources of power available through destruction of fossil fuels. When portable engines were not feasible, power was transmitted from the place of generation to the point of application via electricity.

Access to superhuman power made the factory a feasible production device, which had profound social consequences.[3] Obviously, urban populations soared. Less obviously, at least to us today, factories forced the working classes to keep regular hours, at a regular job. The factory worker had to work within a rigid social system rather than within the loosely organized system that had been in place in medieval times (Schorr, 1991; Zuboff, 1989). Factories led to specialization, and specialization led to hierarchical control.

Perhaps most important, the workplace changed in the way it used people. Before the Industrial Revolution, work was hard because the worker was an important energy source. After the Industrial Revolution, workers still expended energy, since some factory jobs can be exhausting. However, the worker as an energy source had largely been replaced by the machine. These machines were "dumb oxen"; they generated power but needed human beings to control them. People still directed the application of machine-generated forces onto whatever material was to be altered.

We come to the last part of our fable, John Henry. John Henry was a miner, an occupation that would have been familiar to Alexander and Henry V. As the song goes, John Henry was a steel-drivin' man. He used a sledgehammer to drive a steel spike into coal chunks in the face of a mine wall. John Henry could swing a hammer harder and drive a spike further than any man who lived.

A modern human factors engineer would say that John Henry was responsible for two perceptual-motor actions, placing the steel spike and directing the hammer head onto the spike, and one power-generating action, swinging the hammer hard enough to drive the spike into the wall. And that is what killed John Henry. He died of a heart attack, after a competition against a newly invented power drill. The power drill operator performed John Henry's perceptual-motor actions; he placed the drill bit on the mine wall and controlled its direction. The difference between the drill operator and John Henry was solely in energy generation.

Let us move forward to 1994, and the construction of the "Chunnel," the tunnel that has been built under the English Channel, linking England to France. The Chunnel wall was not drilled by John Henry or a power-drill operator. A computer program read x-ray and magnetic assessments of the soil at the tunnel face. The drill bit was then positioned and rotated under computer control.

Before the Industrial Revolution, we threw our bodies into our work. After the revolution we threw selected parts of our bodies—our hands, eyes, and ears—into our work. An individual who had the muscles for preindustrial work might or might not have the hand-eye coordination needed for industrial work. In the twenty-first century those will not be enough. What is needed are mental skills, and these skills are acquired in a very different way than the way in which we acquire strength and perceptual-motor abilities.

The Key Technologies

The cognitive and social changes that are altering the workplace are driven by a few major technological changes. By far the most important, and best publicized, of these is the development of digital computers. But computers are not the only technological innovation involved. Communication technologies have changed as much as computers have. The two technologies are similar in many ways, but they are not identical. For instance, we could have computing without having communications satellites, but we could not have satellites without computers. Both technologies have made impressive changes on their own, and, in addition, they are synergistic.

Locally, computers give organizations vastly increased information-processing capacities. Globally, one unit in an organization can be almost instantly linked to another, virtually any place in the planet. Consider the stock market. There are some legal restrictions on this now, but there is no technological reason why we should not have a worldwide, 24-hour-a-day securities market. At a more prosaic level, automatic teller machines (ATMs) already offer minor banking services on a 24-hour-a-day basis, throughout Europe and North America.

Another technological development, which has been much less publicized than the computer and communications revolutions, is the development of sensor-effector technologies. One of the reasons that we have relied so long on human perceptual and motor capabilities is that people have superb vision, sensitive noses, adequate ears, and surprisingly agile hands. Designing a robot that can pick up a styrofoam cup of coffee without spilling or crushing it is no easy task. This particular advantage of humans over machines is rapidly coming to an end. Thanks to a variety of developments ranging from lasers to biotechnology, we can build machines with perceptual-motor capabilities that reach or exceed human capacities, albeit often realized in very different ways.

Another technological development is miniaturization. We can build things smaller, lighter, and stronger than ever before. In part the miniaturization technology has affected our lives by enabling computer technologies; the only way to build faster computers is to build smaller ones.[4] In addition, lightweight, cheap fabrication reduces the need to locate a production facility physically close to its market, since the transportation costs for the product are decreased. Moving the production facility itself becomes less of a problem than it once was, because the machine tools themselves are more easily transportable (or reconstructible). These and related changes in technology will make major changes in the way that work is done. Let us look at some case studies to see just what these changes may be.

Process Control: Making Paper

One of the key concepts behind the Industrial Revolution was the idea of *process control*, in which a product is developed gradually as it moves from station to station. The classic automobile assembly line can be thought of as a process control operation. Another example is papermaking, in which wood pulp is turned into a variety of paper and cardboard products. Papermaking has been the target of intensive automation in the past 10 years, which makes it a useful case study.[5]

Old-time papermaking resembled cooking in many ways. Wood pulp was placed in tanks, mixed with chemicals, heated, and stirred until the pulp was ready to be rolled out, dried, and cut into paper sheets. The process was both labor-intensive and physically demanding. Workers used paddles to mix and check the consistency of the pulp and chemical soup. In some cases the workers literally smelled the mixture to determine when it was ready to pour.

In the modern plant all that has changed. The mixing process is controlled by computers. Papermakers spend a substantial part of their time in a control room, reading instruments that tell them how the process is going and when the product is ready to be rolled out. The worker's job is to set the dials to tell the computer what sort of product is needed and to monitor the process to make sure that nothing goes wrong.

The same principles can be illustrated in commercial aviation. Piloting an aircraft has traditionally been pointed to as the example *par excellence* of perceptual and motor control. In the latest generation of aircraft, such as the Boeing 747-400 and Aerobus 300, computers can take the aircraft through all its maneuvers, including landing. In fact, it is more efficient to have the computer fly the aircraft than to have a pilot fly it, because the computer makes more economical use of fuel than a pilot does. As of 1994, human pilots can still manipulate controls, but they do so much less often than they used to. Much of their

Figure 6.1   The older method of making cardboard boxes. The operator received information about quality of output only after a production run had been completed.

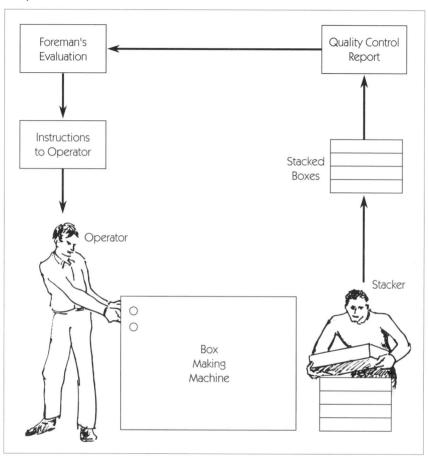

job consists in telling the computer what sort of flight is desired and monitoring it to be sure that everything is going well. The word "monitoring" is important. An executive in a forest products company gave me a good example of why.

Figure 6.1 shows how paper companies used to make cardboard boxes. Paper, glue, and various chemicals went into one end of a machine, and a box came out the other end. The machine operator set controls causing the machine to cut different lengths or to heat the product to different temperatures during the gluing step. This allowed the machine to produce different products and to compensate for varia-

Figure 6.2   The new methods for making cardboard boxes. The operator and assistant monitor quality control throughout production.

tion in the quality of the input, such as might occur when paper varied in water content. When the boxes came out of the machine, they were stacked by a fairly low-paid assistant.

The box-manufacturing process, like any other industrial process, was embedded in a system. Periodically, boxes would be inspected by a quality control inspector. Hours, days, or more could elapse between inspections. If the product from a particular machine was unsatisfactory, the line foreman would be told. The foreman would then direct the machine operator to reset the machine so that the error would not recur. This could be done effectively only if the foreman and the operator could reconstruct the situation at the time the error occurred.

Figure 6.2 shows how the manufacturing process has been changed.

First, the controls have been shifted from the front of the machine to the back. The operator and the assistant can now see the product as it is produced. Second, the operator and assistant have been trained in quality control procedures. As a result, they can take action as soon as poor products are noticed. This minimizes the probability of producing a large batch of unsatisfactory boxes. These small changes have made a major change in the social structure of the production system. The operator and assistant operator have had their jobs upgraded slightly, the quality control inspector has become a trainer, and the foreman has almost disappeared.

Why do we need people at all? Why not just set the machines and let them roll? The answer is simple: The system does not always work. That is why the paper-box operators have to be trained in quality control. And their role here is by no means unique. Let us consider another example: keeping control of inventories in factories and sales operations.

In theory, inventory control should be an ideal task for computerization. In practice, computerized inventory control almost works. One study found that stockroom personnel spend a substantial part of their time trying to reconcile differences between what's written on an inventory sheet and what they see on the shelves. In order to do this, they have to have a fairly sophisticated idea of how the computer-based inventory system works, so that they can understand the sorts of errors that the system is likely to make. They do not have to "understand" the inventory control program in the sense that a computer programmer might understand it. They have to understand how the inventory control program fits into a larger system, one that includes human clerks who sometimes write down the wrong order. The operators must have a working idea of a specific case of general system theory, even though they probably never heard the term (Scribner and Sachs, 1989).

This simple discussion of process control has highlighted several changes in the nature of work. There has been a steady movement away from using workers as sensors and controllers: People no longer feel, smell, and push; they read dials and set digital meters. Workers have to know their jobs intellectually but no longer need to know them perceptually. People oriented toward white-collar jobs might view this change as an advance, but not everyone agrees. Zuboff (1988) reported that experienced workers in a pulp mill complained that they no longer knew what was going on. One of them said, "In the old way you had control over the job. . . . I like to smell and feel the pulp sometime . . . these are artistic aspects of making pulp that the computer doesn't know about" (p. 66). Compare this with the remarks of an engineer employed to run a more modern paper-making plant, "Computer analysis lets us see the effects of many variables and their interactions. . . . You might say that truth replaces knowledge. People who have this analytic power do not need to have been around to know what is going on" (p. 67).

The first of these quotations seems a nostalgic plea for a gentler and less technological time. The second makes the speaker sound like a rather unpleasant technocrat making snide remarks about the old-timers. Pleasant or not, the technocrat may be right, providing that everything works the way that it is supposed to.

There has also been a steady movement away from using people as processors to using them as monitors and interveners in machine-controlled processes. Schaafstal (1991) observed that the "real" task of a worker in a modern pulp and paper factory isn't to do anything to the product; it is to watch the machine make the product and to figure out what has happened when something goes wrong. This change in work is not confined to process control. In the aircraft industry, one of the major challenges facing aviation psychologists is arranging systems so that the pilot notices when something goes wrong and then correctly diagnoses the cause of the malfunction. Virtually all electrical and mechanical systems today are easier to fix than their predecessors, once the operator has established what is wrong. On the other hand, the systems are much more complex, so diagnosis has become more challenging.

In manufacturing there has been a steady movement away from long production runs to rapid setups for short runs. This has occurred largely because of changes in technology. The most celebrated cases occur in plants where fabrication is done by general purpose robots. Here, "setting up for a short run" means reprogramming the robots, not rebuilding the factory. Similar flexibility can be achieved with less general equipment. In food-processing plants, for instance, the product typically flows through a complicated system of lines and cooking vats. At one time, whenever the plant began to produce a new product a person had to reconfigure the production line by resetting valves and flushing the system. In computer-controlled food-processing plants, the reconfiguration process, although logically as complex as ever, is physically much easier to carry out.

In other situations fabrication technologies have changed enough so that setting up a specialized plant is not a large capital investment. The very small companies that construct specialized computer systems build very little. They purchase parts and assemble machines.

These technological changes have changed the relative value of different sorts of labor. The perceptual-motor skills required to operate machinery have decreased in value, because so many operations are being carried out under computer control. This is a major blow to the experienced worker, since perceptual-motor skills can take years to acquire and are likely to be highly specialized once they are acquired. (See the discussion of procedural learning in Chapter 5.) On the other hand, abstract knowledge of how particular pieces of machinery might be configured to solve a problem becomes more valuable than before, because reconfiguration is occurring more and more often. The engineer that Zuboff quoted had a point. In many process control situations, truth has replaced knowledge, and contingency plans have replaced intuition. The days of the seat-of-the-pants operation are not over yet, but they are coming to an end. The skills that tomorrow's process control workers will need are the skills required to understand a plan rather than to take an action.

Changes in the Front Office

White-collar work has changed as much as blue-collar work has. Electronic databases, word processors, fax machines, and networked computers have made the modern office far more of a machinery operation affair than it was in the days of quill, pen, ink, and the typewriter.

In order to understand the changes that technology has brought to the white-collar workplace, we need to distinguish between three broad classes of white-collar workers: the professional-management class, people whose daily work demands continual and somewhat unpredictable contacts with people outside the organization, such as salesperson-customer contacts, and people who are involved in managing the flow of information within the organization. This latter group, which can be lumped under the umbrella title of "administrative worker," will be dealt with first.

Administrative Workers

Administrative workers themselves fall into two classes: support personnel and product processors. Support personnel do any of a variety of jobs for specified professionals or managers. The secretary is a prototypical support person. Product processors perform more routinized tasks, typically serving many people and often an anonymous public. The old-time typing pool was the prototype of a product-processing activity.

Insurance and banking are good examples of industries that rely on white-collar product processing. In traditional insurance and banking firms, paper moved along from office to office, very much in the way that material moves in a process control industry. As a result, the product processor's task is surprisingly like that of a process control worker. Different steps are executed by different people, so the paper flow comes to look much like the flow of a production line. The product processor's job has been greatly impacted by automation. The typing pool itself is well on the way to disappearing, a casualty of the word-processing age. The general-purpose typing pool has increasingly been replaced by specialized centers to perform routine functions, such as printing, duplicating, binding, and mailing. These centers are characterized by high volumes of repetitive work, usually done for some anonymous "customer" within the firm. The skill levels required have dropped as the work has shifted from doing something yourself to feeding paper into a machine.

Communications technology has had its impact. As the cost of telecommunications has dropped, it has become feasible to locate white-collar product processing at the most economical site, rather than at a site that is physically close to the user of the services. For instance, large bank and credit card operations are often decentralized in order to take advantage of a low-cost workforce or low-cost physical facilities. One of the largest insurance companies in North America balances its daily books in Ireland.

In general, what this has produced is an increasingly anonymous "paperless office" in which different specialists consult central data files, rather than working together, consciously, to form a document. The system is efficient, in the sense that low-level "keypunch" personnel can enter more information, in a shorter period of time, than was the case when one person was fully responsible for completing a document. As a result, fewer low-level personnel are needed. People can be key punch operators, or hold similar jobs, with only minimal reading and motor skills. The Bureau of Labor statistics has estimated that there will be an 11 percent reduction in such jobs from 1990 to 2005. This does not mean that forms and information processing will decrease! It means that by combining computer technology, direct sensing of information from documents themselves, and communications capabilities, industry will be able to reduce the number of people who have to process those forms.

Perhaps even more discouraging, the jobs that do remain tend to be less demanding of skills but apparently more stressful than the jobs held by earlier document processors. Because people have to keep up with machines, their time is much more closely monitored, reducing their control over breaks and their opportunities for social interactions between coworkers. In industries where unions have not fought the practice, employees can literally be monitored on a keystroke-by-keystroke basis.[6] At the individual level, low-level workers in the "paper factory" perceive more stress and feel more socially isolated than they did in earlier years (Zuboff, 1989, pp. 138–139). At the social level, white-collar workers with relatively low skills are at continual risk of permanent job loss due to changes in the technology of office work. This has meant that the very groups who were beginning to enter the white-collar workforce, minority group members, have been most vulnerable to layoffs (Balan, 1987).

The situation is quite different for support personnel. While word processors, fax machines, and electronic mail are faster and less cumbersome than their predecessors, this has not translated itself into an increase in productivity of office support workers much beyond the productivity of 20 years ago (Hartman, Kraut, and Tilly, 1986). What has changed is the way in which support workers work.

Prior to the 1980s, personal secretaries spent a great deal of time preparing and delivering "smooth" copies from handwritten documents and dictation. This part of the support job has been greatly reduced. Many of today's managers and professionals prepare their own original copy of documents, using word processors. This tendency will certainly accelerate as older executives are replaced by younger ones, who will have been using word-processing technology since their teens. Electronic mail systems are not quite so ubiquitous, but they are common in larger companies and in scientific and technical work. The secretary seldom runs down the hall to deliver a message from the big boss. E-mail is faster and more reliable.

The personal secretary is still a busy person, but in a very different way. Office support personnel function as gatekeepers and schedulers, maintaining an orderly flow of individuals and documents through their bosses' offices. They also serve as interfaces between the supervisor and the increasingly complex systems in which an individual office is embedded. Part of this job is interfacing in a literal sense; the secretary may be the first to use a new word processor or spreadsheet because the supervisor does not have time to learn how. Other interfacing is primarily social. As more and more information has to be exchanged between more and more people, the task of finding who knows what, or who wants to know what, falls increasingly upon the secretary. All things considered, the job seems to have become more complex and substantially less routinized. Simple psychomotor skills, such as typing or taking shorthand, have become less important. Problem solving has become more important (Hartman, Kraut, and Tilly, 1986). Indeed, the increasing use of the term "administrative associate" rather than secretary accurately reflects how the job has changed.

The changes in the nature of administrative support work have produced an unexpected change in the social structure of the office. As the routine jobs have become severed from the higher-level, increasingly managerial tasks of the secretary, the avenues of promotion have closed down for those who choose to enter the office system through the classic entry-level positions. In at least some reasonably well documented situations, this has had a special impact on minority workers, who tend to have lower basic reading and arithmetic skills. On entry, many of them cannot compete for the support positions. Therefore, they are more likely to be assigned to product processing than to administrative support positions. As the two lines of employment diverge, the entry-level workers do not have the opportunity to acquire the explicit and implicit skills required for advancement to the more prestigious, better-paid support positions.

Sales

In 1992 twelve million people were employed in sales-related occupations, just over 10 percent of the workforce.[7] The retail salesperson is a particularly interesting case, because salespeople are the interfaces between unpredictable human customers and a supply and inventory system that the customer does not—and does not want to—understand.

In theory the ideal salesperson should determine a customer's needs, locate the items in inventory that best satisfy those needs, arrange for their delivery to the customer, collect payments, and inform the inventory system of the changes in stock. The amount of effort that individual salespeople devote to each of these phases of a sale varies a great deal from job to job. People who sell cars and high-fashion clothing spend most of their time assessing needs and matching needs to inventory. Servers in fast-food restaurants and self-service stores concentrate on delivery, payment, and inventory updating.

Computerization has generally moved sales away from the car/boutique model and toward the fast-food model (Hartman, Kraut, & Tilly, 1986). Bar code labels, automated credit referencing, and automated inventorying have combined the payment collection and inventory control functions. These technological advances (and the possibility of electronic monitoring for pilferage) make open-shelf merchandising possible. Open-shelf stores where customers fill their own shopping carts and rush through a checkout line were almost unknown in the 1960s. People used to go to the greengrocer's and the butcher's, and *actually talk* with the sales force. That does not happen at K-Mart today.

I am not nostalgic for the good old days of more personalized service. Under the old system, salespeople were less productive in a strict economic sense. As a result, consumer prices were higher in constant dollars. In many areas of sales, we have replaced jobs requiring varied skills with one-dimensional jobs, such as checkout clerks who do not need to know how to make change because a machine does it for them.

Nordstrom clothing stores are a striking example of a company that has prospered by intentionally fighting the trend toward mass-volume sales. During the 1980s Nordstrom expanded from a regional store to a national firm that relied on the "personal touch" of well-paid, personal-service-oriented salespeople.[8] Of course, Nordstrom is far from unique. Boutique stores that emphasize service exist in virtually every industry, including retail food services. Some of the public will clearly pay for the personalized sales service.

On the other hand, the much larger volume done by large discount stores using computerized, open-shelf methods indicates that the greater part of the market is oriented toward low cost, at the expense of service, particularly when consumers feel pinched, as they did during the recession and slow recovery of the early 1990s. During that period most of the high-end, personal touch stores, such as Nordstrom, experienced major losses; some went out of business. Low-end retailers, such as K-Mart and Wal-Mart stores, prospered.

Management and Professional Work

Most American business organizations are strongly hierarchic and become more so as the business grows larger. Historically, hierarchical organizations arose as a way of ensuring that subordinate units acted in concert and in agreement with the wishes of top management. For example, in the automobile industry the supply department has to deliver the proper materials to manufacturing, and the advertising department has to be prepared to sell the products that manufacturing makes. If there are several different manufacturing facilities, someone has to ensure that each product is aimed at a different market, so that the company does not compete with itself.

In order to achieve these goals, most companies adopt a treelike command hierarchy, as shown in Figure 6.3. Policies are set at central offices, then amplified for local operations. Reports from the field are summarized at midlevels, and the summaries are sent upward to central management. Formal communications between operating units flow upward from the originating unit to a common manager and then downward to the destination unit.

Of course, no company works in exactly this manner. Organizations all develop informal channels of communication. Nevertheless, the hierarchic chain of command is enforced for important messages, for an excellent reason. Hierarchical systems reduce the information management problem at the individual nodes. Information flowing upward is

Figure 6.3 The traditional hierarchical organization of large business and government enterprises.

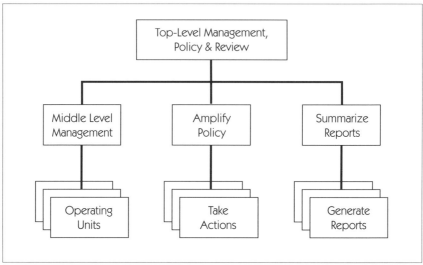

stripped of detail, so that top management can concentrate on the essentials. Information flowing downward is expanded to suit local circumstances within the general framework set by top management.

Modern communications and computer technologies have reduced the argument for hierarchical control, because they have increased the amount of information that can be handled at each node. The result has been a tendency toward "flattened hierarchies," where the number of nodes reporting to the central node is decreased. In the extreme, the middle management level simply disappears. The effects of this tendency can be seen by examining two very different institutions: universities and banks.

University Organization and the Computer

In most universities day-to-day teaching and research take place in the department headed by a senior professor who serves as department chair. Because the chairholder is a specialist in the department's discipline, he or she is usually conversant with the work of individual professors, who do most of the teaching and research. In fact, department chairs are usually expected to maintain some teaching and research programs while they are serving as administrators. This means that at the first line of management chemists coordinate the activities of chemists and psychologists supervise psychologists. The supervisor can understand what the supervisee is doing.

Intellectual continuity breaks down at the next level. Deans of colleges cannot possibly be familiar with all the disciplines under their charge. Furthermore, as universities have become very large, there has been an increasing tendency to draw still more senior central administrators, such as provosts, chancellors, and presidents, from the ranks of people who have spent most of their professional lives in administrative positions. Many of today's university presidents would not be considered attractive professorial appointments to the department that nominally serves as their home base.

Historically, the position of department chair was powerful because, in some sense, the chair was the only administrator who had local knowledge of the department. Decisions on class loads, space assignment, and promotion were effectively made by the chair, with some informal monitoring at the college and university level.

This is no longer true. Universities of the 1990s make the same decisions only after elaborate central review, based on "countable" criteria, such as number of publications, grant sizes, and student credit hours. With some local exceptions, the department chairs' ("middle management") administrative record-keeping function has increased, and their executive leadership function has decreased. The chair no longer has the power to facilitate or inhibit a professor's career based upon a personal judgment of the quality of the professor's work. Instead, personnel decisions are made on the basis of the sort of information that can fit into the university's computerized data management system.

The Effect of Computerization on the Banking Industry

Bankers and university professors think of themselves as very different people, but their response to automated management seems to have been the same. Zuboff's (1989, Chap. 3) observations of the banking industry look remarkably like my observations of the university.

Prior to computerization bankers spent a great deal of time getting to know their major customers personally. Golf games and business lunches were an important part of working life. Banking decisions were made by combining an objective evaluation of a customer's assets and liabilities with a personal evaluation of the customer's financial acumen. Most decision making was done at the local level, because doing otherwise would have exceeded the information-processing capacity of the central office.

Today the central office has the information-processing capacity needed to handle huge flows of objective evaluations, based on those indices that can be computerized. Centralized authority can, and does, make decisions that were formerly the province of local officials.

The common theme running through these examples is that in education, banking, and many other fields, centralizing the decision function has changed the nature of the decision-making process. In theory, managerial decision making is based on identifying alternatives and weighing risks and benefits. In practice, managers are usually more impulsive; they act as pattern recognizers. Managers see a situation that appears to call for a particular action, and they take it, without an exhaustive consideration of costs, benefits, and the viability of other alternatives (Wagner, 1991). Therefore, managers' personal experiences play a crucial role in the development of the pattern → action rules that actually represent how a decision is made.

Of course, managers are both rational, analytic problem solvers and pattern recognizers. What the computer revolution has done is to shift the balance between these roles. The analyzers have been given a powerful new tool, and it is being used.

For example, the number of accountants increased by 30 percent from 1978 to 1985. Why? Certainly not because computers are slower than human accountants examining the same records. What the computerization of accounting has made possible is more frequent interrogation of accounts and the invention of new forms of accounting (e.g., daily inventory control, management information systems). The change in management style was not quantitative. Managers were able to centralize decisions that had been decentralized, *providing that they made their decisions based on the sort of information that can be processed by a computer.* Information that cannot be quantified appears to play less of a role today than it did in the past.

I do not want to argue for or against intuitive decision making. While there are advantages to acting on one's gut feelings, there are also advantages to formal decision making. Indeed, there is a substantial literature showing that people grossly overvalue their ability to make good intuitive decisions and undervalue the wisdom of relying on statistical and analytic rules (Dawes, Faust, and Meehl, 1989). One effect of the information-processing revolution on business has been to increase the relative value of the manager who can understand computer analysis, including a realistic understanding of its limitations. Inevitably, this has meant a drop in the relative value of a manager whose primary talent is the ability to make intuitive decisions.

Using Flattened Hierarchies to Reduce the Reins

Although the new technologies can be used to increase centralized control, they can also be used to do the opposite. Instead of using increased information-processing capability to centralize decision making at the top, the increased capability can be used to decentralize decision making while enough central control is retained to ensure that the organization's various units are not operating at cross purposes. The history of industrial robots provides a good example.

During the 1980s there was a great increase in the use of robots (programmable, multipurpose machines) in manufacturing. This movement is generally seen as having succeeded in Japan but not having gone well in the United States and Britain. This is somewhat surprising, because in terms of engineering criteria, Japanese robots tend to be less sophisticated than British and American robots. The difference seems to have been in the way that the new automated machinery was introduced into the factory management system.

Japanese management regarded robots as devices to aid the worker on the factory floor, but acknowledged that the factory worker was still an important autonomous agent. Japanese workers were shown how to operate relatively simple robot devices, and then told to develop ways of using them on the production line. British and American practices were more oriented toward using programmable machinery to extend management's control over what was happening on the production line. British and American managers tried to determine how the new machines should be used and then told the workers what had been decided upon. This meant that the central managers and their technical aides had to anticipate almost everything that could happen on the factory floor, and then they had to build the appropriate responses into the robots (Cole, 1992).

The British and American management teams set themselves a harder task than their Japanese counterparts did, and they had more trouble completing it. The Japanese solution was simpler and easier to implement, providing that management was able to rely on their field agents to do just one thing—think.

Another way of responding to the computer-communications revolution is to replace the hierarchical organization itself. The extreme retreat from a hierarchy would be a fully connected network in which there is no central node. This is virtually never encountered in business organizations, but a variant of it is. The variant is shown in Figure 6.4. In this network any node can communicate with any other node, while a privileged node (top management) monitors all communications.

Network organizations, unlike hierarchical organizations, encourage a great deal of lateral communications between adjacent units. Keichel (1993) has pointed out that the network encourages the development of specialty centers within the organization itself. Individual units provide intracompany services, such as machine repair, to the other units in the system after a request is routed through the appro-

Figure 6.4 A network organization for a business or government enterprise.

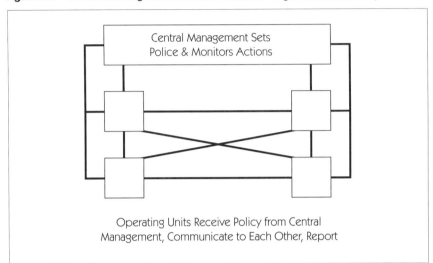

priate authorities rather than on command. At times several different nodes may "spontaneously" organize themselves into a unit to deal with a particular problem. The people within the system have to be flexible enough to understand each other's capabilities, and to appreciate what their role is, not in general, but in the task at hand.

There is no substitute for thinking. But what does thinking mean in the face of computer technology?

DEALING WITH COMPUTERS

Shoshana Zuboff (1989) called her analysis of the workplace *In the Age of the Smart Machine.* The phrase was well chosen. The greatest change between the workplace that was, in 1950, and the workplace that will be, by 2050 everywhere, and in some places much sooner, will be the extent to which people interact with smart machines. What roles are people going to play in this workplace, and what will the psychological demands of those roles be? To answer these questions, we have to consider what a computer is and how it fits into other changes in the workplace.

The phrase "the computer thinks" has come into our language, but it does not mean the same thing as "I think" or "You think." Computers do not deal with the world; computers deal with mathematical models of the world. Formally, a mathematical model of the world is an abstract *system* of variables. The value of each variable is determined by the value of the other variables in the system. The relationship between the variables is supposed to mirror the relationship between entities in the world. When we say "the computer thinks," we are actually saying that the computer is computing some transformation of the variables in its abstract system, under the assumption that this transformation reflects something going on in the external world.

These principles can be illustrated by a simplified discussion of modern financial transactions. Banks keep relatively small amounts of cash on hand. In order to manage the flow of wealth, they rely on up-to-date records of people's assets and obligations, including their own. Since the vast majority of these records are machine-readable, we can think of the check cashing/accounting function of the bank as a computerized control system that permits us to do business without having to handle money.

Suppose that you received a good or service from person X, for which you paid by check. In precomputer days your bank would not have been informed of the transaction until the check was presented. A teller would verify that the check was properly authenticated and would use the canceled check as an authorization to reduce the bank's record of your funds and increase the record of person X. If the check's amount exceeded the bank's obligation to you, as reflected by your checking account, the transaction would be terminated. X would be informed (probably by mail) and could then seek redress. Order would be maintained in the financial world.

For this system to work, the bank's records must be an accurate and timely model of what is actually happening in the financial world itself. There has to be some linkage between the physical transactions and the bank's record. To achieve this the teller acts as the bank's sensor. If the sensor fails the bank's model will not be accurate, and the bank's program cannot maintain order in the financial world. Consider three cases:

(1) The unscrupulous Y steals the check from X, appears at the teller's desk, and demands cash. It is up to the teller, acting as sensor, to establish an identity between the payee named on the check and the individual demanding payment. This is especially important if the individual wants to be paid in a medium—cash—that is outside the bank's model. If the check is made out to X, and the request is that the record of obligation be transferred to X's account, then anyone can present the check.

(2) You are unscrupulous and have issued many checks to many X's, far beyond the amount in your account. You intend to abscond before you are caught. You can get away with this only if the bank's records lag behind the real-time transactions. In the terms we have been using,

the teller, acting this time as an effector for the system rather than a sensor, must inform X of the problem in time for you to be caught. How tight this linkage has to be depends on the sort of transaction that is occurring outside the bank. It is easier to abscond with a car than with a house. It is hard to overdraw your account using an automated teller machine.

(3) If a Value-Added Tax (V.A.T.) is in effect, a percentage of the check should go from your account into the government account rather than X's account. To ensure that this happens, the government can require that the bank transfer taxes automatically when the check is presented. The government will receive what it is due only if the bank transactions accurately reflect the financial exchange in the real world. More crassly, if you pay X in cash or by barter, the government cannot rely on the bank records to collect the V.A.T. This sort of slippage between the world and the computer model occasionally (?) occurs in countries where a V.A.T. is in effect.

The remarks I have just made could have been applied to banking in the days of the quill pen. In fact, they did. The computer has changed things.

Banks today can handle many more customers and accounts than the old quill and ink bank could. That is, they can deal with larger, more complicated models of the world. In fact, thanks to our ability to make electronic transfers of information between banks, it (almost) makes sense to regard all the banks in the world as a single bank.[9] In a few years more, better communications will make the "(almost)" go away.

It is quite likely that instead of paying by check, you will pay X by an electronically readable credit card. Insofar as the bank is concerned, this serves as an instant, safe identification by the payer and payee, authorizing the transfer. What is more, the bank instantly verifies the availability of funds, thus lessening the chance for fraud.[10]

Where is the psychology in all this? People sell their skills in the workplace. In earlier years banks relied heavily on the arithmetical skills of bookkeepers and on tellers' ability to match pairs of signatures, and to recognize faces from pictures. The first skill is one that some of us have, and that is easy to duplicate in a computer. The second is a skill that all of us have and is quite hard to duplicate by machine. In an all-electronic banking system, there are fewer uses for these skills, so the price employers will pay for them is reduced. Supply and demand determine price for skills just as much as for materials.

My account of banking is certainly an oversimplified sketch, both of banking and of how computers are used. Nonetheless, it illustrates all the basic principles of a smart machine. The computing machine operates on a mathematical model of the world. In order to connect this model to reality, the computer must be connected to the real world by sensors that provide information about physical reality outside the machine and by effectors that let the smart machine transmit its conclusions to the outside world. The machine (or, more precisely, the machine's program) reasons by transforming its model from one state to another. From time to time, the program issues signals that are intended to correct the external world, so that it maintains an appropriate relationship to the world inside the computer.

In the banking example the model of the world is a set of account balances, which the machine's program tries to keep in financial harmony. Human and automated tellers and credit card readers serve as sensors. The same principle applies to an airplane's automatic pilot, where a computer analyzes a model of how the aircraft is passing through physical space and connects the model to the world by receiving signals from instruments and sending signals to control the aircraft's guidance and propulsion systems.

Obviously, the computer-controlled workplace replaces people with machines. Fewer tellers and bookkeepers are needed for banks with smart machines, fewer factory workers are needed in automated process control plants, and smaller aircrews are needed for smart aircraft. But humans are never eliminated. They occupy three crucial roles.

Someone has to design the system in the first place. Unless we are very trusting of the designer, someone has to monitor the system to make sure that it is working properly. Both these functions involve relatively small numbers of people. Many more people function in the third role, acting as sensors and effectors for the machines themselves. The following sections consider the skills required for each of these three roles.

The System Designer: Defining the Problem

Suppose that the decision has been made to install a computer-controlled system to run something. Just what "something" is can vary widely. At one extreme, we use computers to control purely physical processes, such as chemical mixing in food-processing and paper-production plants or setting aircraft flight controls. At the other extreme, computers manipulate information to be communicated to human beings in applications ranging from monitoring bankbooks to monitoring student progress in a large university.

In spite of the disparity of applications, the psychological demands on system designers are much the same in all cases. Figure 6.5 shows, in cartoon form, the three steps in the design process.

Figure 6.5 The steps in moving to automated control of jobs in the workplace.

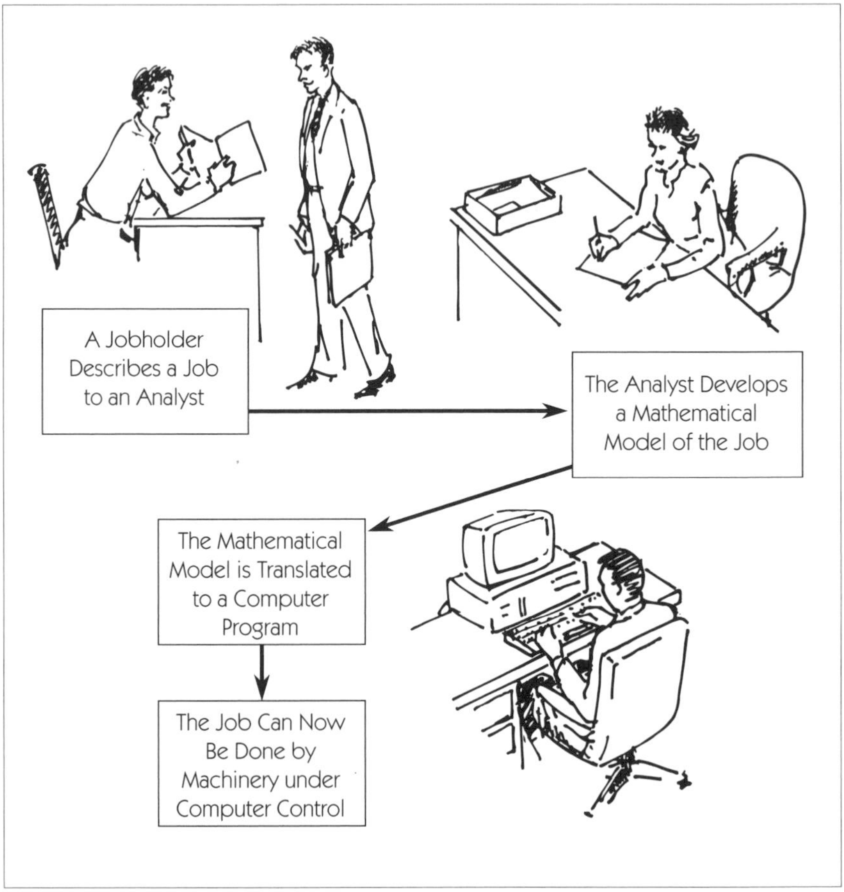

The first step is to determine precisely what real-world operations are to be placed under computer control. They can vary from the cut and paste operations in a word-processing program to sending out signals to control the thrust in an aircraft's jet engine.

Once the real-world system is defined, it has to be translated into a mathematical formulation. Physical operations on physical things, like erasing words in a typescript or moving the concave surfaces on an aircraft, must be redescribed as mathematical operations on variables.

Finally, the mathematical operations themselves are translated into a computer program. The computer program is not what we normally think of as a mathematical object. Instead, it is a list of physical operations, such as "fetch two numbers from locations x and y, add them, and put the result in location z," that can be executed by a physical device: the digital computer.

Different psychological demands are placed on the people who are involved at each step.

The designer must identify an appropriate model of the real world. Sometimes this is easy. A computer-controlled banking system should let us know where the money is. More often, though, the situation is murky. Should a computer-controlled banking system decide whether or not a loan should be granted? Should the only thing to be considered be, say, the debt-equity ratio of a small business? To take a stickier issue, should special provisions be made for loans to women or to minority group members? If so, what provisions should be made?

The answers to these questions depend on how one views a bank. Is a bank a device for maximizing the returns to its owners? In that case the bank ought to make only those loans that offer the best prospects of return. Or is a bank a device embedded in a more general social system that should respond to the nebulous goal of maximizing social goals? When we design computer systems, we have to make our answers to such questions explicit. You cannot say "Like, uh, y'know . . ." to a machine.

There is an amusing example. One way to look at a university computer program for monitoring student progress is to say that it should keep track of grades and courses, and graduate or flunk students when certain boundary conditions are met. What happens when a computer deals with a college athlete this way? In at least one case a dean came to grief because she acted as the unquestioning effector of the computer's explicit model of how the university should work. More concretely, she declared a key football player ineligible. Naturally, she was dismissed (Sperber, 1988, pp. 291–292). Reflecting on her experience, Marianne Jennings, former associate dean of business at Arizona State University, said, "There are certain truths in life. You don't spit into the wind, you don't tug on Superman's cape, and you don't mess around with star football players." The designer forgot to build this rule into the program.

The same thing can happen in dealing with physical systems. In the late 1980s a new commercial aircraft being unveiled at an airshow crashed while flying slowly by the viewing stands. While the cause was never completely determined, one of the possible causes is particularly illustrative.

The aircraft was one of the newer "fly by wire" machines, in which pilots do not control the aircraft directly. Instead, they issue commands to a computer, and the computer makes the necessary adjustments to the engines and control surfaces. The plan of the airshow required that the aircraft fly very low without preparing to land, a flight path that it would never take in normal operation. Because normal preparations, such as lowering the landing gear, were not being made, the computer program may have intervened in order to correct what appeared to be a pilot error. Since the pilot did not intend to land, the intervention may have caused the aircraft to stall and crash.

What do these diverse examples have in common? When computers are used to control a real-world system, what they are actually controlling is a mathematical model of the system. In order to create the model someone has to analyze the real-world system and decide exactly how it is to be described, what the permissible actions are, how they affect the system state, and what goals the system is supposed to be maximizing. The result is always a description of an idealized world of banking, student records, aircraft flights, or what have you. *Nothing outside this description counts.*

In the real world, systems are not so tightly encapsulated from the rest of the world. Banks operate inside a world of social goals, the university is an educational system whose football team plays an unclearly defined but very real role, and commercial aircraft sometimes do fly in air shows. The relevant computer programs do not know about these things unless they are told about them.

The problem is that in many cases system designers will be able to anticipate how system control should normally be exercised but will not be able to anticipate all possible abnormal situations. This means that the system designer has to define an idealized system that works well enough most of the time and that has clearly defined points at which the system user can intervene to put the system back on track. But when the designer does this, he or she is betting that the system user will know enough both about the computer control system and the real-world situation so that the intervention will be timely and effective. Alternatively, the designer has to develop a model of the user, so that the designer can anticipate how users will (and should) intervene.

These requirements pose a formidable challenge to human cognition. The first step in designing a computer-controlled system is to ask people to define precisely and abstractly exactly what they do. But this is precisely what people *do not* do very well. Instead of having prestated rules for dealing with every conceivable situation, they are aware of general goals, personal goals, and ways to solve local problems. Indeed, the more that people become expert in a field, the more they are likely to rely on using local and perhaps tacit knowledge to deal with a problem instead of falling back on algorithmic solutions. This seems to be true for as varied situations as truck loaders in a dairy (Scribner, 1986) to judicial decision making on the bench (Lawrence, 1988). Why?

We are far better at pattern recognition than abstract reasoning because that is the way our minds are built. Over tens of thousands of years of human existence, it has been more useful to get a reasonably adequate, concrete answer to a problem that is here and now than to get an abstract answer to all the problems that might come up. That may have been fine for past evolution, but it will not work for future system design. We need people who can reason abstractly about complicated situations. Both psychometrics and cognitive psychology tell us that these skills are not in great supply.

Building the System

After one finds a subject matter expert who has declarative knowledge of his or her field, the next step is to find a mathematical formalism that can capture this knowledge. The step is far from trivial; the person who takes it must solve a complicated mathematical word problem. Keep this analogy in mind as we go through an example much simpler than computer models that are developed every day.

Suppose that we want a computer model of the world's population from the present until the year 2050. Such projections actually exist (Olshansky, Carnes, and Cassel, 1993), and it seems to be the sort of project in which a computer model would be useful.

In words the problem is simple. We begin with a population containing men and women of varying ages, from 0 to 100 years old. (The subject matter expert advises us to disregard any individuals over 100, because there are so few of them.) Every year some fraction of the individuals in each age group die, and the survivors age a year. The fraction dying is called the mortality rate. It varies across ages and is different for men and women. In addition, every year babies enter as the age 0 contingent of the next year. The number of babies can be calculated by determining what fraction of women in each age group will have babies in a given year and then adding up the number of babies.

Mathematically, the state of the world population can be represented by an arrangement of numbers into rows and columns, that is, a *matrix*, in which the number in the ith row and kth column represents the number of individuals who will be i years old in year k. We need two such matrices, one for men and one for women. Let M be the matrix for men, and W the matrix for women. That is,

$$M_{i,k} = \text{number of men of age } i \text{ in year } k, \qquad (6.1a)$$

$$W_{i,k} = \text{number of women of age } i \text{ in year } k, \qquad (6.1b)$$

with i varying from 0 to 100 and k varying from the present to 2050. The total population over time is represented by the matrix T, where

$$T_{i,k} = M_{i,k} + W_{i,k}. \tag{6.2}$$

In order to represent mortality and birthrates mathematically we require three vectors (ordered sets of numbers). One is for the birthrate. Let $b = (b_1 \ldots b_{100})$ be an ordered set of numbers, $b = (b_i)$ $(i = 1 \ldots 100)$, where $b_i = $ (children born to women of age i)/(number of women of age i). Of course, the b_i values for preadolescent girls and older women will be zero.

We also know that male births exceed female births by about .52 to .48. Therefore,

$$M_{0,k} = .52\ \Sigma_i b_i W_{i,k-1}, \tag{6.3a}$$

$$W_{0,k} = .48\ \Sigma_i b_i W_{i,k-1}, \tag{6.3b}$$

where "Σ_i" stands for summation across all values of i.

Finally, we must consider the mortality rates, which differ across ages and men and women. Let $d_{m,i}$ and $d_{w,i}$ be the mortality rates for men and women, respectively, of age i. The number of survivors to the next year can then be counted. For $i = 1 \ldots 100$, we have for males

$$M_{i,k} = M_{(i-1),(k-1)}(1 - d_{m,i-1}), \tag{6.4a}$$

and for females

$$W_{i,k} = W_{(i-1),(k-1)}(1 - d_{w,i-1}). \tag{6.4b}$$

This provides an initial model. However, a subject matter expert might object that this is far too simple. The mathematical model assumes that birthrates and mortality rates will remain the same from now until 2050, which is questionable. For instance, contraceptive practices might spread in the third world. This suggests that the simple birthrate figure for age group i should be replaced by a term that varies over the years,

$$b_{i,k} = f(i,k), \tag{6.5}$$

where $f(i,k)$ is a function of the woman's age and the calendar year of the calculation.

To make things more complex, it can be argued that human behavior will be reactive. Thus, for young women the birthrate will decrease as contraceptives become acceptable, while for older women the birthrate will be a complex function of the base birthrate, age effects, and the fraction of women of that age who have already had a child. Mortality rates can be equally complex. As a crude approximation, the mortality rate is produced by three factors: deaths due to external agents (automobile accidents, war casualties), deaths due to infectious diseases (tuberculosis, measles, etc.), and deaths due to deteriorational diseases (cancers, heart failures, etc.). Over the years these will change, and a mathematical expression must be found for these changes.

The system designer cannot just say "a function has to be found." A specific function has to be programmed. Sometimes the system designer will receive a great deal of help from the subject matter expert. Sometimes the expert will not know what to say. The result is that the system designer's model of the world is only a model. It represents guesses about what will happen and intentional or unintentional decisions to ignore some aspects of the world.

This point applies to all computer programs used to predict or control real-world systems. The computer program that assigns airline passengers to seats assumes that any two passengers are physically capable of sitting next to each other. This is not so: Extremely obese or disabled individuals may physically restrict the seat next to them. When airlines use a computerized seat assignment system, they are betting that it will be accurate enough the vast majority of the time and that when it fails, human cabin attendants will be able to make on-the-spot adjustments. Translating from the real-world situation to a mathematical representation of that situation is a nontrivial task.

After the mathematical representation has been developed, it must be translated into a program, a machine-executable set of instructions that implement the mathematical expressions representing the real world. To understand the psychological problems that this represents, one has to understand something about computers as logical machines. In spite of the term "smart machine," a computer *without its program* is a dumb machine. All it can do is fetch numbers or strings of characters from precisely defined locations in a storage area, perform elementary operations on these characters, and store the results in other locations.

To continue the population projection example, let us see how the simple addition expressed in Equation 6.2 (the number of people of a given age is equal to the number of males plus the number of females) looks to a computer. Remember that the computer deals with locations, so variables A (age), M and W (men and women), and T (total) become the addresses of locations, like the numbers in a post office box. In fact, a good way to think about a computer's memory is that it is like a post office box, except that each box can hold only one number or string of characters.

Here are the machine operations for Equation 6.2:

> Copy the number in location A into temporary register 1.
>
> Copy the number in location (M + whatever is in temporary register 1) into temporary register 2.
>
> Add the number in location (W + whatever is in temporary register 1) into the number in temporary register 2.
>
> Store the contents of temporary register 2 in location (T + whatever is in register 1), writing over the current contents.

Clearly, this is a complicated way of expressing a simple idea. However, this level of detail is necessary if one wants to instruct a machine. At its most elemental level, a computer never knows about men, women, weather systems, or anything else external to itself. Internally, the machine is nothing more than a collection of numbers stored at locations, plus a few circuits capable of arithmetical operations on numbers.

Computer programmers seldom deal with computers at this level of detail. Instead, they write programs in a *programming language,* which is then translated into elementary machine language instructions. Statements in the programming language can be thought of as statements that are intermediate between a system analyst's mathematical description and program instructions. For instance, the sequence of computations just given could be expressed in the programming language Pascal as

$$T[i,k] := M[i,k] + W[i,k], \tag{6.6}$$

which is closer to conventional algebra than it is to machine language.

Programming languages greatly simplify a programmer's task, but they do not make it trivial. If the real-world problem is complex, the system designer's mathematical statement may of necessity also be complex. This can make the programming step difficult. A number of real-world problems require over a million lines of computer code, where each line is at least as complex as the equation above. Furthermore, *every line must be exactly correct,* in the sense that the computer instructions generated by the line must correspond precisely to the system analyst's mathematical representation of the real world. There is no allowance for stupid typos, let alone subtle errors. In our population example, suppose that the programmer writing the code to calculate the number of expected births types "M" instead of "W" in the right-hand expression of

$$M[0,k] := .52 * [b[i] * W[i,k - 1], \qquad (6.7a)$$

changing it to

$$M[0,k] := .52 * [b[i] * M[i,k - 1]. \qquad (6.7b)$$

The number of boy babies calculated for year k would be a function of the number of males alive in year $k - 1$, not the number of females. Unlike a human calculating assistant, the computer would not see that the typographical error had produced a senseless calculation. A person using the program might or might not notice the error.

Sometimes compromises are made. An unrealistic but "not too bad" model may be accepted, simply because a truly accurate model would be too difficult to program. Other times a very accurate, complex model is used, at the risk of making a programming error that can come back to haunt us. Computing errors involving financial transactions have literally cost billions of dollars.

On the other hand, computer programs to supervise financial transactions have saved billions of dollars. One cannot say, in general, that real-world systems should be represented in a way that is "accurate" or "computable." An inaccurate program, with known inaccuracies, is often far more useful than a program with unknown bugs (See Ford, Kraiger, and Schectman, 1986, for an interesting technical discussion.)

The limit on using computing machines is often psychological rather than mechanical. The new technology asks people to retrieve detailed, explicit information from declarative memory. We are not very good at this. Next, we are asked to find solutions to new and unfamiliar problems, the very definition of fluid intelligence. Finally, we are asked to do a task, programming, that, by its very nature, overloads working memory, arguably our weakest link with the outside world.

Virtually everyone has agreed that the early twenty-first century will be the age of information processing. The aristocracy of this age will be the people who can solve new problems using the new technology. The technological aristocracy may have difficulty recruiting from an aging workforce that is being replenished by workers who have demonstrably low problem-solving skills.

Using Computer Systems

What about the user? This section considers the real-time use of smart machines, that is, any situation in which a person-machine system is linked to a changing environment and must respond to it, such as the computer-controlled drill used to dig the Chunnel and the computer systems in "fly by wire" commercial aircraft. A less dramatic, but more ubiquitous, example is a word processor. The operator has an idea, external to the computer, of what a finished document should look like. The human and the computer work together to produce it.

A real-time system has to be able to sense the state of the world, decide what actions are needed to move the world from its present state to a desired state, and act on the world so that this movement happens. In a process control application, a robot might sense that a bolt is not firmly in place and tighten it. In word processing an operator might sense that the word "ratio" has been misspelled "ration" and make the appropriate key strokes to correct the error. In spite of the variety of computer-controlled real-time applications, the psychological issues involved at each functional stage are much the same from one system to another. Modern technology has dramatically reduced the role of human beings as sensors and effectors. The effects of technology on the human role as decision maker are more variable.

The Neurosurgery Example

Neurological surgery is an extremely demanding medical procedure. The structures involved are tiny but vital to life. They are so closely packed together that it is extremely difficult to remove damaged tissue without damaging collateral tissue. The twentieth century surgeon must have a keen eye and a steady hand, as well as knowledge of neuro-anatomy. In the twenty-first century the neurosurgeon's job will still be demanding, but perhaps in a different way.

The following high-technology, computer-controlled system has been suggested for removing brain tumors. First, the tumor would be located using in vivo imaging techniques, such as magnetic resonance imaging, that are themselves only possible with computers. Next, a tiny piece of metal would be introduced into the brain region, using surgical procedures that do not require direct exposure of the brain surface. The patient's head would then be placed inside the magnetic field generated by a bank of magnets. The magnetic field itself is harmless to brain tissue. The surgeon would combine on-line imaging of the metal's location with on-line computer control of the magnetic field strength to move the metal next to the tumor, detouring around any vital brain structures. Once the metal was next to the tumor, microwaves could be directed toward it. Since metal will concentrate heat in a microwave field (which is why metals are not used in microwave cooking), the metal could be made hot enough to destroy the tumor without destroying any healthy tissue not in direct contact with the metal. After the tumor was destroyed, the microwave generator would be turned off, allowing the metal to cool. The magnetic field would then be manipulated to withdraw the metal.

Something like this technique may be available within 10 to 25 years. Neurosurgeons will still have to know brain physiology and anatomy, but they will have far less need for a steady hand. Instead, like the airplane pilot of the very near future, the physicians of a more distant future will be decision makers who decide how the surgery is to progress. The actual manipulating of physical devices will be up to a computer.

Now let us look at quite a different task, which illustrates an important additional issue.

The F-15 and the Sherlock Program

The U.S. Air Force's F-15 (Eagle) fighter was, as of 1994, one of the most advanced military aircraft in the world. The plane is a marvel of on-board computers for flying, navigation, and weapon control. When an F-15 requires repairs a special electronic test station is plugged into the aircraft's systems. The station tests each electronic component, automatically, to determine where part replacement or repair is needed. The computers and sensors in the test station replace the human mechanic's perceptual and motor systems. The same thing can be seen (in a less expensive way) in the ubiquitous computer programs that monitor system components to tell computer owners when a printer, battery, or disk drive is nonfunctional.

There is no hope that we will entirely do away with human repair specialists, because someone has to be able to fix the testing apparatus when it breaks. (The Air Force has a special computer delivered training program, SHERLOCK, that prepares mechanics to repair the F-15 test station.) Of course, one could conceivably design a test station for the test station, but this would only move the problem to a higher level. *There is always an interface between human beings and the machine.* People on one side of that interface have to be able to understand what is going on on the other side.

The San José Airport Example

While I was writing this book I witnessed an exchange between two airline employees, a computer, and some of the traveling public at the San José airport. The exchanges took place near a boarding gate, where passenger agents 1 and 2 were greeting travelers. A woman asked agent 1 when the next flight was due in from Palm Springs. The agent consulted the airline company's computer and informed her that the flight was due in 10 minutes.

About 5 minutes later a second traveler asked agent 2 the same question. Agent 2 consulted the company computer and then looked out the window. She pointed to a jetliner that was being towed off the runway by trucks and suggested that although the computer *said* that the flight from Palm Springs was due in 10 minutes, she did not think any plane was going to land in San José until the runway was clear. Agent 2 was right. She realized that she knew something about the real world that was not part of the model, which enabled her to make use of both the model and real-world knowledge to do her job better.

The distinction between agents 1 and 2 is vital. Productive workers at the interface have to understand the difference between the world and the computer's model of the world. Too many workers at the interface simply pass on the computer's commands to their helpless customers. These people are candidates for replacement by robots, just as soon as the robot becomes cheaper than they are. Agent 2 has a brighter future ahead of her.

Making Decisions with Computers

Executives and managers have a unique position vis-à-vis new technologies: They can decide whether or not they personally wish to participate. This remark reflects more than an acknowledgment of the boss's arrogance. In fact, upper-level executives are people whose time is extremely valuable. One of the major limitations on executives' use of technology is the time they have available to be trained. As a result, many executives tend to confine their personal work with computers to straightforward examinations of databases and relatively simple communication functions (Bikson and Eveland, 1990). On the other hand, the advent of computers makes it reasonable for executives to ask that trained support personnel prepare detailed reports on fairly short notice.

To the extent that such reports are used, they change the nature of the executive function. Traditionally, most executives have thought of themselves as people managers, who spend a fairly large amount of time gaining information about their organization through personal contacts, especially with their immediate subordinates. As noted earlier, one of the reasons for the multitiered hierarchical organization was the limit on the number of people who can report to a single person, simply because of the time required for interpersonal communications. In addition, executives have always done a certain amount of "examining the books," that is, management of databases rather than people.

The increased power of computers and communication technology has greatly reduced the cost of database management. Furthermore, it is now possible to centralize the database management function to a much greater degree than in the past. This has resulted in a not-so-subtle change in management and executive practices. A training officer in a telecommunications company remarked to me that the younger sales personnel and executives picked up the business potential of the new technologies much more quickly than the older ones did. The older officers, however, were often superb performers because they emphasized selling (or managing) as a personal exchange. Both personal and database management will continue to be used as executive tools for a long time. We will see a shift toward a relatively greater reliance on database management but not an absolute adoption of decision making by report analysis.

Virtually all executives and managers that I have talked to regard this as, on the whole, a good thing. They have also expressed reservations. The telecommunication training officer worried that technology-oriented salespeople would lose touch with ineffable (and hence, uncomputable) aspects of their customers' businesses. Virtually the same worry was expressed by a vice president of a wood and paper products firm. We had been discussing the introduction of computer-controlled processing into pulp mills, as described earlier. I asked whether he was concerned that the operators would learn how to operate the computer's model of the pulp mill, at the expense of learning how to operate the mill itself. He replied that he was far more worried that management would learn how to operate the database program's model of the company, but would lose touch with what was happening in the field.

Neither the trainer, nor the vice president, nor any other knowledgable person I have met wants to conduct Luddite warfare against information technology. They believe that, on the whole, computers and telecommunications improve management. In their minds the ideal executive is one who uses the new technology and who understands its limitations. People who are going to make extremely important decisions have to know enough about their decision-making tools to know what sort of things those tools cannot tell them. Executives must know when to trust the computer's output and when to trust more nebulous signals. Either error can occur. The only cure that I can think of for this is to be sure that managers either are computer literate themselves or that they have people around them who are, and who are willing to describe both the strengths and weaknesses of the technology they espouse.

Telecommunications

In the past, computers and telecommunications were distinct, albeit related, technologies. Computers processed discrete digital signals, whereas until a few years ago telecommunications relied on the transmission of continuous analog radio or electric signals. Modern communications technology has shifted toward reliance on digital signals. The result is that most modern communications networks can be thought of as computing systems with widely separated input-output stations.

On the positive side, enhanced communications capabilities allow people to work together without being together physically. By using electronic mail and fax transmission, corporate headquarters can monitor the activities of subsidiaries located across the globe. The same thing is true of cooperative work. Two people working on the same project can exchange notes on a daily or hourly basis, no matter where they are. Computer and communication technology can be used to convene work groups linked only by electronic communication and let them pass information back and forth as freely as they would in a face-to-face meeting. In some fields the constraints on cooperative work due to distance are almost disappearing.

Communications technologies also reduce constraints introduced by time. Electronic mail and its relatives provide an option for transmitting messages between people who cannot be available at the same time. Thus, the tyranny of the schedule, which is a major factor in professional and managerial life, loses much of its force.[11] Finally, electronic conferencing reduces the cost of recording the arguments presented at these meetings, since, at least for electronic mail, the recording occurs as a by-product of the communication process.

The result is likely to be a major impact on the physical and temporal distribution of work. One prosaic but potentially important effect is that the electronic mail systems will facilitate communications between work shifts. Bikson and Eveland (1990) offer the example of a police officer assigned to a night shift, who was able to use electronic mail to participate in labor-management negotiations concerning working conditions. The cost of using consultants (including retirees) is greatly decreased. At-home work also becomes more feasible, an option that can be looked at either as a way of reducing the time demands on workers, because it removes the need for commuting, or, more darkly, as a way to lower wages by forcing in-plant workers to compete with workers who will accept a lower wage in return for being freed from the strict time demands of office or factory.[12]

While electronic work groups are possible, they are not the exact economic and psychological equivalents of the traditional committee meeting. The participants in electronic work groups behave differently than the participants in face-to-face groups (Sproull and Kiesler, 1990). Probably the most notable effect, to a participant, is that many of the social conventions modulating interpersonal interactions break down. More problem-solving ideas are presented per group member in electronic discussions than in face-to-face groups. Probably as a result, the members of electronically linked problem-solving groups report more satisfaction with the problem-solving process than do participants in physically present groups.

Other results are problematical. Electronic conversations are less inhibited than physical meetings. Participants are notoriously less deferent to rank and tend to express more extreme opinions than they would in a face-to-face conversation. A closely related effect is that group leaders exert less control over group members. It can be argued that this is good, if you do not like hierarchical discussions, or it can be argued that it is bad, especially if you are at the top of the hierarchy.

What is clear is that it is time-consuming. One of Sproull and Kiesler's findings was that decisions that were made in 10 minutes in a face-to-face meeting might take up to 30 minutes in an electronic meeting. And this assumes that the electronic meeting includes all people participating at the same time, which already yields up the major advantage of permitting meetings that are distributed over each individual's schedule.

Similar criticisms have been made of video conferencing, which seems to be more expensive than the personnel effort it saves (Egido, 1990). In part this may be because the current (but temporary) technology is fairly intrusive. A communications guru must be present to facilitate the meeting. The guru's presence and activity alter the flow of communications. This problem will lessen as the equipment improves. Other problems may be harder to solve.

Possibly the hardest of these will be finding a substitute for nonverbal communications during a group meeting. People have elaborate conventions for nonverbal signaling in social settings. These conventions are obviously irrelevant in an electronic mail conference. The video conference supports some of our nonverbal conventions but not all of them. For instance, people do not expect to be stared at in conferences except when they are speaking. In a video conference all conferees look at the camera on their own site, and, therefore, they appear to be looking directly at everyone in every other site. That can be a bit disconcerting. Perhaps we will develop social etiquette for video conferencing just as we have learned social etiquette for business meetings. It is also possible that we won't, because the role of nonverbal communications may be deeply ingrained in our species. The development of effective telecommunications techniques will depend on our being able to develop an abstract model of an individual whom we have never met. This means that businesses that rely on telecommunications will place a greater burden on their employees' explicit communication skills than businesses that rely on face-to-face meetings. Both employer surveys and objective assessments have shown that skills in dealing with language in even a mildly sophisticated way are in short supply throughout the workforce. What is worse, the shortage seems to be greatest among minority groups, the fastest growing segments of our population. The most recent surveys of adult literacy (Kirsch et al, 1993) are particularly discouraging.

The problem is made worse by a second aspect of communications technology: the "global village." In a sense, everyone who makes a living processing information competes with everyone else on the globe who provides the same service. I live in Seattle, but a major part of my personal banking is done through a company in Tennessee. In 1993 consumers in Washington State and in British Columbia discovered that they were receiving services from a major home appliance repair company that was located in southern California. Local calls from customers in Seattle and Vancouver were call-forwarded to a home office in San Diego, which then dispatched technicians by telephone in the two northwest cities a thousand miles away.

This means that an efficient information processor and telecommunications service provider can outcompete inefficient providers on a worldwide basis. Privileged islands cease to exist, and wages stabilize at a level determined on a worldwide basis. It does not necessarily mean that the lowest wage for a service always prevails, because the quality of the service must be considered. It does mean that people in the information-processing industry must be cost-effective on a global rather than a local basis.

A PSYCHOLOGICAL VIEW OF THE NEW WORKPLACE

Whose Job Is on the Line?

Computer aficionados offer a simple rule for deciding when human beings can be replaced. If a jobholder can provide a precise written description of his or her job, the job can be done by a machine. To the extent that the job description contains such vague terms as "determines customer needs" or "exercises judgment," humanity is needed.

In the past, there were certain important qualifications to this rule. People often regard certain pattern recognition tasks, such as recognizing that a piece of paper is a dollar bill, as too trivial to mention. Automating this particular task was not commercially feasible until the late 1980s. In spite of the jokes we make about our clumsiness, humans are very good manipulators of physical objects. Moravec (1988), an unabashed enthusiast for automation, reported that by the late 1980s there existed an advanced prototype robot that could pick up an egg. This is impressive, but it is hardly a demonstration of a superhuman ability *as of this moment.* Nevertheless, the camel's nose is clearly under the tent. While no foreseeable robot is going to do dentistry, most jobs make much more modest demands on human pattern recognition and motor control.

Let us revisit the checkout clerk at a grocery, certainly an unsophisticated job. Checkout clerks have to recognize items that customers place on the checkout counter, regardless of how they place the product relative to the clerk's line of vision. This would be hard for a machine to do, but not impossible. If the customer pays by credit card, the clerk, likely as not, will have the card recognized by a machine. If the customer pays by cash, the clerk will recognize either crisp or crumpled currency, a task that is hard for a machine but again not impossible. Finally, the clerk handles the customer's goods, firmly enough so as not to drop anything, but gently enough to avoid crushing fragile items, such as eggs. Taken altogether, there is no robot presently available that could do the clerk's job *as cheaply as the clerk does it.*

Getting the machine's cost down is simply a matter of time and technological development. At any one time those people whose jobs are on the line are those people whose jobs can be described precisely and whose pay is high enough so that someone will consider a mechanized alternative. As computer technology gets cheaper, and as workers ask for higher wages and fringe benefits, the mechanical wolf gets a little closer to the door.

With a few exceptions, human performance skills that are based on sensory pattern recognition, followed by subsequent, specifiable motor actions, are no longer safe from automation. It's just a matter of economics and time.

Jobs that depend on a person's being able to recognize unconstrained speech—for example, a food server in a restaurant or a salesperson whose job is largely to advise customers about products—are hard to automate. Perhaps the most advanced machine system designed so far is an experimental speech recognition system that can recognize and answer fairly simple questions about location (Zue et al., 1990):

Person: Where is the nearest library?
Computer: Where are you?
Person: Harvard Square.
Computer: The nearest library is . . . .

By the year 2000 systems like this should be able to carry on somewhat wooden conversations in situations where the conversation is predict-able: simple airline ticketing requests, requests for location, and the like. General-purpose speech comprehension by robots, at a level even approaching normal human conversation, is at least 10 or 20 years away, perhaps longer. The problem is not building the computers needed to comprehend speech; it is writing the programs for them. The linguists and psychologists cannot tell us what these programs should be.

There is one other "low-level" psychomotor function that humans do well but is extremely difficult to reproduce by machine. People can walk around on uneven terrain, but machines cannot. While mechanical walkers do exist (Moravec, 1988), they are generally more limited than a human toddler. The robot forest ranger is many years away.

Jobs That Are Not on the Line

What sorts of jobs are safe from the smart machines? The answer is simple, jobs are safe if the jobholder's task cannot be programmed. Cognitive scientists call such situations "ill-defined problem solving." A problem is ill-defined if the resources available and the criteria for success become clear only as problem solving progresses. Medicine is a good example. Although some aspects of the physician's job will be (and have been) profoundly changed by technology, physicians themselves are unlikely to be replaced, because the nature of a problem may only become clear as diagnoses and treatments unfold over time. Similarly, business executives typically solve problems by approaching them from various angles, offering tentative solutions, and reevaluating these solutions as they learn more about the true situation (Wagner, 1991). Indeed, the problem of designing an industrial information processing system is itself ill-defined. New problems and potentials become apparent only as the design task unfolds.

Ill-defined problems present some of the most interesting challenges in our society. People who work on them do have a place for computers, as tools. However, you cannot program a computer to replace the solver of ill-defined problems. All you can do is to ensure that the problem solver understands the capabilities of the available technology and then leave it to the problem solver to decide how those capabilities should be used.

Some ill-defined problem-solving tasks, such as medicine, business planning, and computer design, are the glamour jobs of our society. They are highly valued and highly paid. There is another huge class of jobs that involve ill-defined problem solving, but where the pay for jobholders varies widely. These are the jobs that depend primarily upon unconstrained interactions with people. I defy anyone to design a computerized system to operate an acceptable day-care facility.

Although people-oriented jobs vary greatly, they all rely on two important and subtle psychological abilities. One is best described as sensitivity to communication. In part, this means being able to understand free-form speech, which is itself a major technological challenge. Sensitivity to communication means more than this. Jobholders whose primary task is to deal with people in any but the most stereotyped ways must also be sensitive to the context in which something is said. They have to react to nonverbal communication and even to notice the importance of what the person they are talking to does not say. They must be able to understand the model of the world that is contained *in the mind of the person to whom they are talking.*

Of course, no one can literally get inside another person's mind. A sensitive jobholder must have a schema that specifies the types of mental models another person might have. These models can be altered.

This all sounds very abstract. Here are two examples.

A district prosecutor interrogating a witness to a violent crime finds that the witness is reluctant to testify. Is it because the witness fears that the criminal may retaliate, or is it because the witness has been engaged in nefarious activities? The prosecutor must have a schema for different types of reluctant witnesses and the means available to induce them to talk.

A salesperson in a fashionable clothing store encounters a customer who claims to be "just browsing." Has the customer indeed just wandered in out of the rain, or is the customer shy, but would really like to spend a bundle on clothes? The salesperson must recognize the difference and employ the appropriate schema.

The terminology of information processing has intentionally been introduced into these examples. If we examine the jobs that are safe from computerization, they are just those jobs where people have to understand what is going on, in the context of the total situation. Schemata and mental models let people reason inductively, so that they can use facts that are implied by the evidence, rather than the evidence alone. Specialty salespeople, lawyers, psychiatrists, and day-care operators all do these things. People deal with people all the time. Linguists and psychologists talk about broad principles that guide these communications, but these sciences have not advanced to the point of specifying the step-by-step rules to be followed to construct schemata for all but the most limited social situations. Until this goal is reached, we do not know what program to write, so the calculating power of the machine is quite beside the point.

My point was put very nicely by Stephen Wolf, the former CEO of United Airlines, one of the largest users of the highest technology in the world. He wrote, "As mankind continues to push . . . the development of technology, we must not lose our ability to communicate with one another" (Wolf, 1991).

The Need for Flexibility

In the traditional factory, workers often stayed at the same job for years. The longer they stayed, the better they got, because many traditional jobs required perceptual-motor skills that take years to acquire. Professional musicians, for instance, may practice from 10 to 20 hours a week over most of their working lives (Sloboda, 1991), and it may take 30,000 hours of practice to become a chess master (Simon and Chase, 1973). It has been argued that the most important thing that distinguishes the expert from the gifted amateur in a wide variety of fields is not skill, but the willingness to devote countless hours to practice (Ericsson, Krampe, and Tesch-Romer, 1993).

Such heroic striving for perfection in a single task is a reasonable economic strategy when the working environment is stable. In a stable workplace the more experienced worker will generally be a more productive worker, and the employer should be willing to pay for that experience, especially if the cost of establishing a new workplace is high. But in the age of computer control, the cost of reconfiguring the workplace is decreasing. Buildings can be constructed in a fraction of the time it used to take. Machinery can be retooled cheaply, and robots can be reprogrammed.

What happens to the workers? Their finely honed motor and perceptual skills are unlikely to be of much use in the new work environment, since such skills are usually specialized to the particular situation in which they were learned. Employers value two things, relevant experience and trainability. In an age when retooling is cheap, the value of experience drops, and the value of trainability increases.

When people are learning new tasks, their initial performance is best predicted by measures of general intellectual skill, fluid intelligence, because in the initial stages of learning a new task a good deal of problem solving is involved. Therefore, performance will be determined by those things that influence problem solving: efficient working memories and the possession of general problem-solving heuristics. Only after people have learned what has to be done do special pattern recognition capacities become relevant (Ackerman, 1988).

Experienced workers will still have an advantage if a substantial part of their experience can be transferred to a new work setting. But what is likely to transfer? If a production line shifts from making one kind of car to making another, or (to take a very likely scenario in the next few years) from building tanks for the army to building construction equipment for the building trade, in a sense the workers are performing the same tasks. The particular perceptual-motor actions may have changed, but the schema for assembling wheel casings, gear systems, and so forth, remains the same. The experienced worker will be more valuable than the inexperienced one to the extent that the experienced one can transfer knowledge from the original task to the new one. The ability to recognize specific sensory patterns, or to take certain motor actions, that were required in the old task may have very little to do with the ability to perform the new task.

An émployer who introduces a new technology must make a decision: to retain and retrain the old workforce or to look for a new one. It is clearly in everyone's interest to keep the retraining cost low! One way to do this is to be sure that present employees are doing their present job with a sense of how their actions fit into a big picture that will be retained even though the new technology may change specific jobs.

The Changing Values of Psychological Skills

During 1992 and 1993 TV advertisements for sneakers and for beer urged people to "Just do it" and "Why ask why?" The advertisements would not have been effective if we, as a society, did not view intuitive action as somehow more natural than coldblooded analysis. Our social structure similarly reflects our value for experience. Older, more experienced workers are paid more because their intangible experiences are supposed to be worth something. And that has been the way society worked for the last 5,000 years.

Computing and communications technology are changing the rules. Instead of valuing the ability to recognize patterns in the real world, we will value the ability to understand abstract models of that world. In Reich's terms (1991) we have moved from a world of doers to a world of symbol analysts. This term does not just apply to programming computers. The computer user and the person who serves as a complex interface between a computer system and human customers must fit reality to the computer's schema. They must understand how both human beings and machines work. Economically, the new technologies devalue experience and increase the value of the ability to learn.

At any point in time, there will also be a number of jobs whose job-holders are, in essence, simple input-output devices for a machine. People can be trained to do these jobs quickly, because the jobs are so limited. Of course, this does not mean that the performance of the total person-machine system is reduced. A smart machine serviced by an unsophisticated person often outperforms a system consisting of an unsophisticated machine controlled by a smart person. You just do not have to pay the unsophisticated person very much.

A CONCLUDING COMMENT

Somewhere in prehistory a protohominid got the other apes in the band to attack antelope herds all at once, from different sides. Ever since then system designers have been designing systems for other people to actuate. As an extreme example, a 50-person system has one person with an idea, 3 others to flesh it out, 9 to add details, and 37 do the work.

Computing and information technologies act as smart-people multipliers. The designer's ideas are instantly transmitted to the workers. If the design is successful, instead of 50 people, all we need is one designer and three workers. Of course, if the system designer has forgotten something, we may have a disaster on our hands, because there will be no people to adjust the system, but eventually things work out. We may go through several generations of systems, but eventually 4 people will be doing the work of 50.

The numbers are fanciful, but the idea is true. As computerized systems are perfected, they reduce the need for brain power, just as the steamship reduced the need for the brawny sailor.

Such a scenario is grim. It suggests that our society will evolve into a world of haves and have-nots, a few overworked system designers and a large number of underemployed or unemployed machine servers. Today we seem to be experiencing a curious sort of economic schizophrenia. The employed are working very hard indeed. The U.S. work week for all employed males is up to 44 hours, which is about 10 hours more than the work week for Europeans, although substantially lower than the same figure for the Japanese (Schorr, 1991; Munnell, 1992). At the same time unemployment hovers around 7 percent, which most of us find unacceptably high, and a substantial part of our population has become permanently workless, and even homeless. By a perversity of the labor statistics, these people do not count as unemployed—not because they have employment but because they have given up trying to get it. The desperateness of these individuals was shown dramatically in the Los Angeles riots of 1992.

It is more puzzling that some very talented people are finding it difficult to obtain appropriate employment. On the one hand, scientists in our research universities and industrial plants routinely put in 50- to 60-hour weeks. At the same time new Ph.D.s are making 30, 40, or even 100 applications for a position. Some are unemployed and even more are underemployed, eking out lives on a postdoctoral appointment at about $25,000 after 5 or more years of intensive training beyond the bachelor's degree.

Two forces appear to be driving this curious blend of overwork and underemployment. One is the structure of fringe benefits, which makes it more economical for an employer to offer one worker overtime than to employ a second or third worker. The second factor is technology. Computer control, rapid shifts in the manufacturing process, and cheap communications multiply the effectiveness of a few smart people. They devalue the prosaic.

What should we do about this? One alternative is to simply let things happen. In a book that the *New York Times* called the most controversial of the year, Herrnstein and Murray (1994) argued that there is inevitably going to be a cognitive elite who will run the technologies, that there will not be many of them, and that there is little we can do about it. Their recommendation for avoiding a bifurcation of society into the rich and the poor was to decentralize planning, because they did not think system designers would ever be that good, and to use modern information technology so that the cognitively non-elite could get by in a world whose complexities were hidden from them. One can hardly argue with part of this recommendation; the new technologies should be used to make it easier for all of us to go about our daily business. However, I disagree with Herrnstein and Murray's conclusion that demographic trends and technology developments inevitably leave us with a cognitively non-elite, who cannot fully participate in society. I prefer another solution. The demographic trends presented earlier do indeed raise the possibility that if we do nothing cognitive skills will be in shorter supply and greater demand. So let us do something to increase the cognitive skills of all of us. The next chapter considers some of the things that can be done.

It would be naive to think that all our problems can be solved by psychology or education. There is no guarantee that increasing the cognitive skills of the American workforce will ensure prosperity. The guarantee goes the other way—not increasing these skills guarantees a lowering of our place in the economic global village. We must make a conscious investment in the development of human resources.

NOTES

1. Since Packer's statistics are dramatic, it is important not to overinterpret them. The statistics make the point that new jobs tend to be high-skill jobs and that current educational trends indicate that entering workers are low-skilled. However, we would not expect the two to match perfectly. In general, new jobs requiring high skills will be filled by people already in the workforce. Most entering workers will find their first job in an existing occupation. The table should be seen as illustrating a trend, not making a prediction about job scarcities directly.
2. Other aspects of the fifteenth century, such as the medieval commitment to one universal God and Church, would probably have baffled Alexander.
3. There were certainly other factors, such as the development of transportation networks. These, too, depended on power. Distant markets became far more important in local economies when goods were moved by rail and steamship than when they were moved by horse and sailing ship.
4. A major limitation on electronic computing is the time that it takes to transmit electrical pulses along wires. The closer the computing elements are to each other, the less time is lost in transmission.
5. My remarks on paper production are based largely on excellent treatments by Schaafstal (1991) and Zuboff (1989) and on interviews with industry managers.
6. In Europe, where unions are generally more powerful than they are in the United States, such practices are often forbidden by law.
7. U.S. Bureau of the Census (1993).
8. Nordstrom's sales personnel earn most of their income on commission. Incomes in excess of $80,000 per year (1990 dollars) have been reported.
9. This is accurate regarding the bank's function in supervising transfers of wealth, which is what we are discussing. The bank's role as a lender is more complicated and not germane to our discussion.
10. Strictly speaking, all the bank knows is that a transaction is taking place between X and your credit card. This is one reason for a receipt; X can be challenged to prove that you had authorized him to record the transaction. From X's perspective, he also needs to make sure that you are who the credit card says you are. This is usually done by asking for further identification or by comparing your signature with the signature on the credit card. However, it is possible to develop systems in which the payer is responsible for identification. In fact, this is done at automated teller machines, where the bank assumes the role of X. You (the payer) have to demonstrate that you both have the credit card and know a personal identification number not on the card. It is easy to imagine more complicated

systems in which both payer and payee simultaneously provide electronic identification to the computing system.

11. Studies of electronic mail use have shown that most mail exchanges are between people whose offices are in easy walking distance of each other (Sproull and Kiesler, 1990). I frequently send messages to a faculty colleague next door. This is sensible, because it lets us communicate rapidly without having to coordinate our daily schedules. While I was preparing this chapter I arranged a financial support plan covering 20 graduate students. The planning process involved 10 faculty members and took about a week. Every member of the group had an opportunity to comment on all major decisions, and most of them did. We had only one 30-minute meeting, at which only 6 of us were present.

12. My wording implies that management would be exploiting the worker if it paid less, per unit of labor, for work done in the home than work done in the factory. But who is poorer, a worker who receives $8 per hour for 8 hours of home work, done at least somewhat at the worker's discretion, or a worker who receives $10 per hour for 8 hours of time-clocked factory work, plus a 2 hour unpaid commuting trip? More generally, our society's economic accounting generally fails to consider the value of personally controlled leisure time (Schorr, 1991).

7

Anticipating the Future

WHAT A CONSTRUCTIVE CRITIC NEEDS TO DO

The many forecasters of the economy seem to agree that the future workplace will need people who are capable of reasoning about what they and their machines are doing, and who are ready to meet new challenges as the nature of work changes. The social organization of work is likely to change from the present predominance of large, tightly controlled organizations toward an emphasis on small plants, ad hoc work groups, and networks of specialized suppliers of tailor-made products. Many of the social organizations of the workplace will be short-lived, changing from task to task. This means that workers will have to be flexible in both the cognitive and social aspects of their lives. The value of an employee who can adapt will increase, while the value of the employee who "knows how we do things around here" will decrease. And as for the employee who does not develop the cognitive and communication skills needed to work in ever-changing environments? There will always be dead-end, low-paid jobs, either working under the direction of machines or providing low-level human services.

Obviously, we want an educational system that prepares people for the good jobs rather than the dead-end ones. It is fairly easy to say what the schools ought to do; they should produce flexible thinkers, with good communication and problem-solving skills, and an adequate knowledge of the traditions and technologies that are important in our culture. The constructive critic has to attempt a harder task, by suggesting how the schools are going to do these things.

In this chapter I attempt to be constructive, first by asking whether it is possible to teach people to "learn" and "think" in the abstract, and then by suggesting the sorts of educational reforms that might achieve these ends.

248

The Prospects for Learning to Think and Learning to Learn

How people learn has been the subject of careful scientific scrutiny for over a century. A great deal of this work has focused on "pure" learning, in which an attempt is made to study the development of associations between ideas, in situations where previously learned information is essentially irrelevant. A good example is the *paired associates learning* paradigm, a widely used laboratory task in which people are asked to memorize arbitrary associations, such as this list of nouns and numbers:

21-frog

39-goose

17-fox

46-pig

Tasks like this have been used to build extensive theories of learning and memory. By seeing how performance on such tasks changes as the result of brain injury, or more recently by taking images of the brains of normal people as they do such tasks, psychologists have forged connections between cognitive behavior and the actions of the brain. No one who is conversant with the literature seriously questions the substantial contribution that such work has made to the scientific study of human thinking.

There is somewhat more controversy about the extent to which the findings from such research apply to learning in schools, or to naturalistic situations like the workplace. Psychologists have certainly argued that the laboratory studies should guide educational policies. One of the strongest such advocates of the use of laboratory principles in applied settings was B.F. Skinner (1953), whose development of general laws of learning, based largely on laboratory studies of pigeons, rats, and, on occasion, people, had a profound influence on both education and clinical psychology. However, Skinner's views are by no means unique. Many other laboratory-based psychologists have proclaimed the relevance of their own theories to life outside of the laboratory. And there clearly have been successful applications. Laboratory techniques have been shown to be good guides to learning rote skills, such as foreign language vocabulary acquisition, and for designing programs to teach very young or cognitively disadvantaged students. What is less clear is whether or not educational practices tied directly to laboratory learning ought to be applied to the training of older students, or to the training of more nebulous cognitive skills.

Some psychologists and anthropologists claim that cognition is so bound to the situation in which it occurs that training in thinking is inevitably bound to local circumstances. This position is known as the *situated action* view of thought (Norman, 1993). Its advocates argue that there is little utility in trying to predict everyday cognition from any general theory of thinking, learning, or problem solving because general theories cannot provide an understanding of crucial local circumstances (Greeno, 1989; Lave, 1988; Suchman, 1987). The advocates of situated action are suspicious of the utility of teaching general thinking methods, such as mathematical reasoning or abstract problem solving, because this approach fails to consider how people take advantage of local tricks to solve everyday problems.

Greeno (1989) provides a good example. A member of a weight watcher's club was given a one-ounce package of cottage cheese and asked, "If a recipe for cottage cheese is three quarters of an ounce, and you want to reduce this by a third, how much cottage cheese do you need?" This is a simple arithmetic problem: $3/4 \times 2/3 = 6/12 = 1/2$, but the woman did not use arithmetic. Instead, she opened the package of cheese, formed it into a circle, cut the circle into quarters, removed one quarter, and then removed the other. In Greeno's terms, she changed the problem from one of operating on an abstract mental model of arithmetic into one of operating on a mental model tied to visible objects.

Proponents of situated action argue that the weight watcher example shows that people prefer to work out situation-specific techniques for solving everyday problems, rather than relying on general problem-solving techniques. Carried to its extreme, the situated cognition approach implies that people cannot be taught to "think" or to "learn to learn," they can only be taught how to behave in specific situations. It follows that if we want our educational system to prepare people for the workplace, we should ensure that the system gets the students into that workplace so that they can learn how to act in it.

This view is accepted, at least implicitly, by our two most formidable international competitors. In the Federal Republic of Germany, just prior to German reunification, over half the workers had received formal apprenticeships. In Japan individual company-school programs are commonplace. By contrast, fewer than 1 percent of employed U.S. workers have participated in formal school-workplace apprentice programs (Office of Technology Assessment, 1990).

The debate between people who believe in general mechanisms of learning and cognition and those who advocate situated cognition underlies two very different models of education: the occupational-professional view that education should train a skilled worker and the liberal education view that students should learn to think about things, in general. There is no doubt that the values of a "liberal education" have, historically, been oversold. On the other hand, we ought to consider very carefully what a wholesale adoption of the situated cognition approach would mean to a nation faced with an aging workforce.

Suppose we combine the argument that learning to learn is inherently difficult, if not impossible, with the well-established fact that memorization and learning abilities decrease with age (Salthouse, 1982). This decline is not confined to the retirement years. Age-related drops in cognition become apparent in the 40s. These drops are too small, and vary too widely from individual to individual, to justify discrimination against a person solely because of age. Indeed, at the individual level, reductions in learning ability are often overpowered by increases in situation-specific knowledge, so older workers tend to be quite productive. Recall the example of the dairy workers who had learned to circumvent arithmetic by using visual imagery. On the other hand, declines in learning and problem-solving abilities are sufficient to influence personnel policies affecting large groups of people. The issue of retraining is especially acute.

Suppose that an employer wants to introduce new technology into a manufacturing process. If the current plant is staffed by an aging workforce whose knowledge will no longer be relevant, why not move to a new location and employ a younger, cheaper, quicker-learning workforce? Or suppose the company is paying heavy taxes to support a school system whose products do not seem to have sufficient workplace skills. Why not move?

Those proponents of situated action whom I know will probably be appalled at my drawing this inference from their theories. I do not think that they want to advocate policies that encourage industrial dislocation, with its consequent social problems. Neither do I. However, I think that the conclusion does follow from the premise that learning is entirely situational. Since we do not like the conclusion, is it possible to challenge the premise?

The phenomena of situated cognition are not inconsistent with the blackboard model of thought that was described in Chapter 5. People ought to prefer solving problems by retrieving previously learned problem-solving methods. When we do this, we lead from our strength, long-term memory, rather than from our weakness, limited attention and working-memory capacity. When external cues can be tied to information relevant to problem solving, as the shape of milk containers were in the dairy worker example, then those cues certainly should be used. However, critics of the situated cognition approach point out that focusing on surface aspects of thought, for example, the use of container shapes, can mask deeper regularities, such as the strategy of using visual imagery to solve problems (Vera and Simon, 1993).

I believe that it is possible to take an intermediate view. Advocates of situated cognition are correct in saying that the goal of learning is the development of localized pattern recognition and action rules to be used in specific situations. This does not mean that people cannot learn to use general problem-solving strategies. In fact, these may be quite important as an intermediate step en route to the acquisition of situation-specific rules. In the rest of this chapter, I will present a psychological theory of the relation between problem solving, learning, and situated action, and then use it to make some remarks about how education and training should be organized to optimize workforce capabilities.

A Theory of Learning and Problem Solving Based on the Work of Allen Newell

The approach I will propose is based on the work of Allen Newell (1927–1992), one of the most important thinkers about thought in the twentieth century. Newell was one of the pioneers of artificial intelligence studies, but, unlike many other specialists in that engineering-oriented field, he seriously considered the implications of his work for psychology (Laird and Rosenbloom, 1992). Newell and his colleague Herbert Simon believed that human thought should be regarded as a computation by the brain and, therefore, that the concepts of computation could serve as tools in developing a psychological theory of the mind.

Newell argued that there are general principles of problem solving that apply to *any* problem-solving device, whether it is rat, human being, or computer. Shortly before his death he wrote the ambitiously titled *Unified Theories of Cognition* (1990), in which he described his ideas of the basic processes of cognition. He referred to them collectively as the SOAR model of thought. Let us examine the SOAR principles and then use them to speculate about changes in our educational and training systems.[1]

We begin with a thought experiment. Suppose that I am visiting a Spanish-speaking country and need to buy a pair of shoes. Unless I am in a large city, I will have to carry on a conversation in Spanish, which, in my case, is decidedly a second language. Nevertheless, I do have strategies for communicating to salespeople in Spanish. Suppose further that I cannot remember the Spanish word for "shoes." This represents a block in my progress toward solving the original problem of talking to the salesperson in Spanish. Newell refers to this as an *im-*

passe. In order to resolve the impasse, I define a new problem, finding the Spanish word for "shoes." This problem can be solved in a higher-order "learning Spanish" domain: looking up "shoes" (*zapatos*) in an English-Spanish dictionary. I now know what to say to the salesperson.

The next step is crucial. Since I do not want to look up the word repeatedly in a dictionary, I should add a new problem-solving rule to my array of speaking Spanish procedures: If the goal is to refer to footwear in Spanish → say "zapatos."

Here is an analysis of the example using the SOAR approach. First, the problem solver must be motivated to reach a goal described in the domain of the original problem: *Buy shoes from a Spanish-speaking salesperson.* The problem solver progresses toward that goal by applying domain-specific rules (the pattern → action production rules discussed in Chapter 5) that are defined in the original problem domain: *Say what I want to say in Spanish.* At some point an impasse appears: *I want to say the Spanish word for "shoes" and I do not know it.* The problem solver sets a new goal: *Find the Spanish word for "shoes,"* which is defined in a higher-order domain containing problem-solving rules that can produce, as their solution, a new rule to be applied in the original domain. To keep things straight, I will refer to the problem domain and the metaproblem domain, that is, the domain that solves problems about problems. When the metaproblem has been solved, the new rule must be stored so that it can be used if the same problem is encountered again in the original domain: *Remember that the word for "shoes" is "zapatos."*

This ties learning to problem solving. "Learning to learn" becomes an exercise in recognizing impasses in the problem domain, knowing how to retreat to an appropriate metaproblem domain, and knowing how to translate solutions in the metaproblem domain back into procedures in the problem domain.

Principles for Problem Solving and Learning

Here are five principles extracted from the SOAR approach:

1. Thought is always motivated by an attempt to reach a goal.
2. In the normal course of events, thinking is driven by rules for reacting to situations that arise in the problem-solving domain.
3. When an impasse occurs, the problem solver must recognize it as such and must be motivated to establish a new problem in the metaproblem domain. Therefore, successful problem

solvers have to be aware of their own thought processes, so that they know when to change or improve on them. In the terms of modern cognitive psychology, successful problem solvers show a *metacognitive* ability: They think about their own thought (Nelson, 1992).

4. The process of problem solving in the metaproblem space is the same as in the problem space: pattern recognition and action. However, the signals that trigger pattern recognition in the metaproblem domain are abstract and may involve internally generated goals.

5. When a way has been found around an impasse, the problem solver must describe the impasse-producing conditions in a way that will be recognizable in the future and will be a reliable guide for the use of the new rule. In problem solving it is as important to learn when to take an action as it is to learn how to take it.

These principles can be applied recursively. While attempting to resolve an impasse at Level 1 one might encounter an impasse in the higher-order, Level 2 problem-solving space, which could then be resolved by retreating to a still more abstract Level 3 space. However, this requires an effort. As the abstractness of problem solving increases, a problem solver has less and less support from external cues and faces greater internal bookkeeping problems, as different levels of problem solving must be related to each other. Therefore, impasse resolution is by no means automatic. The problem solver must have sufficient information-processing capacity to support the required level of abstraction, the problem solver's procedures for reasoning in the abstract space must be efficient, and the problem solver must be motivated to make the effort.

The following sections apply these principles to the design of education and training systems. Four goals for education and training will be discussed directly:

1. motivating students to solve problems;
2. challenging them with impasses;
3. learning from problem solving; and
4. metacognition.

The other principles will be worked into the discussion.

Most of the discussion will be addressed to changes in primary and secondary (K–12) education. The K–12 system is an appropriate target because it is by far the largest deliverer of new personnel to the workplace. From time to time, though, remarks will be made about changes in the college-university and vocational education systems.

MOTIVATING THE PROBLEM SOLVER

Without motivation there will be no problem solving. The problem is not to convince people that motivation is desirable, but rather to explain how it might be achieved within the constraints of our educational system. This is a place where the advocates of situated action have a point. Throughout most of human history, learning was intimately tied to daily living. Children were motivated to learn by watching adults, usually parents, and learning to do what they were doing. That's the human way to become a member of society.

Formal schooling is unnatural. At worst, teachers tell children to memorize facts and learn to solve certain problems, without offering them reasons for doing so. Of course, children should learn reading, mathematics, elementary science, and a myriad of other skills that are best presented in a school setting. But students need to be convinced that there is some connection between their own lives and their school subjects.

Attempts to motivate students by connecting their studies to "the real world" have been tried before and generally have failed. With ingenuity, though, this need not be the case. School mathematics instruction offers a good example. In the 1960s a major effort to improve mathematics instruction, under the general title "the new math," was a resounding failure. It can best be described as an excellent presentation of mathematics the way that mathematicians see it—from abstract to concrete. For instance, elementary arithmetic was taught by first introducing the concept of a set and then of cardinality of sets. Teachers did not understand what they were teaching, and most students learned little mathematics.

In the late 1980s more motivating techniques were tried. Mathematical concepts were introduced as tools for solving problems that arise in naturalistic (or at least interesting) settings. This sounds suspiciously like word problems, a notoriously boring approach, but there is a crucial difference.[2] Bruer (1993, pp. 99–112) points out that in the traditional word-problem approach a problem is presented, in isolation, to illustrate one mathematics concept, and then another, unrelated problem is presented to illustrate another concept. First, students are counting birds on a fence and then they are worrying about marbles in someone's pocket. In the new approach students are first engaged in what they see as an interesting and at least mildly plausible adventure.

Mathematics problems are then introduced as necessary steps in living the adventure.

This approach is exemplified by the *Jasper Woodbury* series of films produced by John Bransford and his colleagues at Vanderbilt University. Jasper's adventures are, intellectually, about at the level of the Hardy boys. He drives a boat up river, flies an ultralight airplane over a mountain, and so forth. This is the stuff that TV sitcoms are made of, with one exception. Periodically the stories are interrupted to pose a mathematics problem. In one *Jasper* film, middle-school students are asked to solve 15 time-distance-rate problems in order to understand Jasper's attempts to take a motorboat up and down a river. Each problem has to be solved in order for the story to progress. In contrast, most word problem drills are famous for asking students how long it will take three unknown men to dig a ditch in an unspecified place for an unstated purpose.

The idea of incorporating instruction into a story is simple enough, conceptually, but in practice the incorporation can be difficult. Creating an interesting experience is not enough. The problems posed in the story must mesh with the curriculum, which is not easy to arrange. Field trips to watch "real problem solvers" are well and good, but the typical real-life setting seldom provides exactly the right sort of problems at the appropriate place in the curriculum. Very much the same thing can be said for class projects. Few teachers have the skill or the time needed to plan projects that are so closely tied to the curriculum that they can be allowed to take a large share of instructional time.

The problem of coordination becomes more difficult as students move further up in the educational system. In elementary schools students receive the majority of their instruction from a single teacher, who, with time and energy, can construct projects that illustrate the application of several academic topics. In junior high and high school, students receive instruction in different subjects in different rooms, from different instructors. As a result instruction is generally discipline-oriented rather than project-oriented. To illustrate, Spoehr (1993) reports a project in which innovative, computer-presented problem-solving exercises were used to teach nineteenth century U.S. history. In principle, mathematics problems could have been built into the history exercises, teaching two topics at once. In practice, designing and using such a teaching tool could easily have been a nightmare. The program developers would have had to mesh two separate curricula into one program, and the classroom instructors would have had to mesh their own timetables for instruction. If anything, the teachers would have faced a more difficult problem than the programmers would.

There are also logical limits to project-oriented education. The *Jasper* series and Spoehr's history exercises used quite different technologies to create imaginary worlds. Students were then invited to enter these worlds, in the same way that television sitcom asks the viewer to participate vicariously in all sorts of improbable adventures. And there's the rub.

The entertainment industry bombards viewers with invitations to enter imaginary worlds. As a result, children quickly learn to set high standards for the technical quality of video adventures. High standards mean high budgets.[3] The Vanderbilt group's *Jasper* effort depended upon the availability of corporate and foundation support that can be found for demonstrations but not for the day-to-day operation of schools. Spoehr's history effort was less costly but still depended upon special support. If projects like these are going to be part of the regular curriculum, taxpayers will have to be willing to pay for them.

There is a way of motivating students without high educational budgets, but it also has its limits. Children and adolescents enter society by interacting with adults and older peers. If adults actively encourage intellectual behavior by example and by social interaction, children will be motivated to learn to think. For example, many studies have shown that those children who best learn to read are children from homes where the adults show that they place value on reading, by having books in the home and by spending time reading to the children. The same principle applies to the development of mathematical skills. Children can observe simple arithmetic being used in everyday life, and most school children learn to master these skills. It is harder for children to see why more advanced topics, such as trigonometry and geometry, are going to be important in their lives.

These examples show both the importance of direct skill demonstration by adults and its limitations. Most adults could, if they wished, read to their children.[4] Only a few would be able to explain trigonometry. In a technological society, certain skills have to be presented by formal instruction with little direct support from the home. This does not mean that these skills are not important in our society; they are. But their exercise is hidden from the child's view. In such situations, adults have to provide indirect support to the schools, by showing their children that success in the schools is important to the family. If adults demonstrate that they value learning, then children will be motivated to learn.

There is a striking example of how effective such adult actions can be. During the 1980s large numbers of Southeast Asians immigrated to the United States. Many of these families were poor, their English varied from marginal to nonexistent, and they faced an alien society.

In spite of these handicaps, by and large their children adapted extremely well to the school situation (Caplan, Choy, and Whitmore, 1992) because these migrants provided them with two great advantages.[5] First, the migrants maintained a strong sense of family identity; children were tightly bound into a family network and learned to value adults' opinions. Second, adults demonstrated their concern about children's success in school. At an early age many Asian students learned that solving whatever problems that teachers pose is important.[6]

Nothing in this argument requires that the families be Southeast Asians. In the 1970s Yale University sponsored a "system-wide intervention" program intended to improve the total social setting of a core city urban school in a heavily black area, where the schools had historically ranked very poorly on educational measures. This record was turned around by a program that encouraged parental participation in and support of school educational activities (Comer, 1980; Cauce, Comer, and Schwartz, 1987).

Education asks students to make a present investment of time and effort for some nebulous future return. This is a hard idea to get across, even to adults. A mechanism must be developed so that children have a clearer perception of the rewards of education. The schools can try to connect schoolwork to the world outside the school, but the schools cannot do the whole job. At some point the rest of the society, and especially the parents, have to demonstrate their own value for education.

Motivating Adults: Postsecondary and Vocational Training

The motivational problems in postsecondary and vocational training are very different from those in the K–12 system. In some cases they are easy; in other cases they are almost intractable. Students in postsecondary and vocational/professional programs have virtually all chosen to make a substantial economic commitment to their own education. For the most part students are in class because they already perceive the subject matter as being relevant to their lives. The nature of higher education makes the motivational task even easier. As training becomes more specialized, the link between the class and the field requires less and less imagination. Premedical students know why they have to take biology and chemistry, just as prospective airline pilots know why they have to learn navigation.

The postsecondary and vocational systems also contain a self-correcting mechanism: Students can (and do) leave if they think they are not receiving worthwhile instruction. The effectiveness of this control varies with the institution. In vocational and professional education, it can be very effective indeed. A man who conducts executive training sessions told me that people who make over $1,000 a working day walk out immediately if they think their time is being wasted. Since the trainer's own living depended on student tuition, he put more than a little thought into how to impress the executives with the relevance of his seminar to their business lives.

In colleges and universities faculty income is not so tightly tied to student interest. This is particularly the case in a research university, where professors may (and do) trade off contributions toward teaching undergraduates against contributions in research and graduate training. Nevertheless, students who are not motivated can vote with their feet, and professors who are unable to maintain student motivation know that they have a problem. Most of them try to do something about it. How much they do, and what resources are provided them to do anything, vary a great deal with the institution and with the professor's other contributions to the overall university goals of teaching and research.

One striking exception is the required course, which an outside body—not the student, and sometimes not even the school—has decided that all students must take in order to be certified as having completed their course of studies. Since certification can be extremely important to students, required courses are well attended. But, as is well known, they are not always enjoyed.

In fact, in some cases students may be actively hostile, because they suspect the motivations of the people who have set the course. For instance, some feminists and minority groups have raised objections to what they see as a European-male-oriented program in history, literature, and social studies. The more vocal of the objectors claim that general studies requirements of this sort are an active attempt to belittle female and non-European contributions to our civilization.

A similar problem arose in an industrial setting. A company had decided to modernize its plant. Management believed that operating the new equipment would require at least eighth-grade level reading and mathematics skills. Since many of the currently employed workers could not meet this standard, the company contracted with a local community college to provide the necessary instruction. This was done on the employees' time but at the company's expense. Management saw this as an attempt to help workers hold onto their jobs. Some workers saw enforced education as a hurdle that management was putting in place in order to justify reducing the workforce.

Instructors who are assigned to required courses are in very much the same position as the K–12 instructor. The students will have as their goal "passing the course" and may be only mildly interested in acquiring knowledge. The instructor must find a way to motivate students to learn. The only recommendation that one can give here is, unfortunately, to repeat a truism. The people charged with setting a required curriculum should be clear about why a particular course is required, and the instructors should make sure that this message gets across to the students.

LEARNING BY IMPASSE RESOLUTION

Having motivated the students to solve problems, we want them to encounter impasses that force them to learn. This means frustrating the students, for that is part of the definition of an impasse. But the frustration has to be done in a way that maintains motivation.

The good teacher should assess a student's present capacity and then present the student with problems that are just out of reach. The ideal problem should be sufficiently close to the student's current awareness so that he or she understands why it needs to be solved, and enough beyond the student's abilities so that the student has to develop new problem-solving methods as part of the solution. Teachers who teach by impasse resolution must know more than their subject. They must also know how students construe the material before instruction. In particular, the teachers must know what incorrect problem-solving rules the students may have and must be creative enough to construct a situation where the students realize that their rules are incorrect and discover how to replace bad rules with good ones.[7]

This can be done only by continuous assessment of student progress, followed by well-selected, personalized interventions. This is what an individual tutor is supposed to do. And, in fact, from the learner's point of view tutoring is an extremely effective method of instruction. Studies have indicated that a student with an individual tutor can learn academic material as much as 10 times faster than students listening to lectures. Unfortunately, this impressive-sounding statistic cannot justify hiring tutors. In most formal educational settings, instructors lecture to 20 to over 100 students. By our normal accounting methods, where we figure the cost of an instructor's time but do not calculate the cost of a student's time, lecturing en masse is more cost-effective than providing tutors. The challenge we face is to find a form of instruction that has some of the benefits of student-tailored tutoring, without the concomitant costs.

Several demonstration projects have shown, quite conclusively, that impasse resolution in the classroom is a feasible teaching method. One of the most successful of these has been developed by Jim Minstrell, a high school physics teacher who was recognized for his work by being awarded the Milliken Prize for excellence in physics instruction. (As of 1994, Minstrell was the only high school teacher ever so honored.) His methods are worth examination, since they could certainly be adopted widely within science instruction and quite probably in other areas of teaching as well.

Introductory physics is divided into sections: interacting bodies, the nature of gravity, and so forth. Prior to beginning each section, Minstrell spends some time assessing what his students believe about the topic. His assessment is not simply a pretest of how much physics the students know beforehand. He tries to identify what "rough and ready rules" the students have developed to handle the problems that physicists would handle by applying the relevant laws of physics.

This is best illustrated by an example. Many people who have not received instruction in physics (and some who have!) believe that "in the absence of an external force an object in motion will slow down and eventually come to rest." To a physicist, this is a direct contradiction of Newton's laws of motion, which state that "objects do not change their motion unless an external force is applied."

The naive belief is not all that naive. It correctly describes how objects move in the everyday world; if we do not keep pushing them, they stop. This is because, in our nonideal world, moving objects encounter resistance from friction and pressures from surrounding media. These hidden external forces are not apparent to a perceiver, so it appears that motion dissipates on its own. Therefore, the belief is indeed a useful problem-solving rule in most of the situations that we encounter.

Minstrell then creates impasses that show the need for a new, more general law. Most of these are ingenious but not at all expensive to implement. An effective device for showing that motion does not dissipate spontaneously involves a toy hovercraft that supports itelf by directing jets of air downward onto the surface of a table. Since the hovercraft is not in contact with the surface, a small shove will send it scooting without any perceptible slowing. Students are asked why this should happen if motion "naturally" dissipates. They are then led to an understanding of Newton's laws, as a way of resolving an impasse in their earlier understanding of motion.

Minstrell's techniques and similar projects work; students receiving instruction using these methods do very much better than students receiving conventional instruction (Hunt and Minstrell, 1993; Mestre et al., 1992). Similar methods could be applied to instruction in topics as widely varied as history and mathematics. Nevertheless, as we all know, many instructors continue to follow the standard model of "delivering the right answer," which students are supposed to soak up like sponges soak up water. Since the interactive methods have been widely publicized, why are they used so little?

Teachers who use impasse resolution have to interact with students. This is a time-intensive process, which is limited in two ways. The first limit is the availability of student time. Observations in American classrooms show that when teachers are working with individuals or small groups, the students not directly in contact with the teacher do not remain involved in problem solving. As a result, American students spend less time working on academic topics *within* each classroom hour than do their European or industrialized-area Asian counterparts (Stevenson, Lee, and Stigler, 1986; Stigler and Perry, 1988). To compound the situation, American students have fewer scheduled hours of science instruction than do the foreign students. If interactive teaching inherently meant personalized interactions between teachers and students, introducing this method might make a bad situation worse.

However, it might not. Americans tend to assume that teaching by problem solving implies one-on-one teacher-to-student interactions. This is not necessarily the case. Interactive instruction can engage the entire class if the students in the class all have substantially the same views, or if they have learned to be active rather than passive observers. Americans tend to assume that neither of these conditions holds so when attempting interactive teaching, American instructors engage in interactions with individuals or small groups, resigning themselves to the fact that students who are not engaged with the teacher will become inattentive. Japanese instructors assume that there is enough commonality of belief and enough active interest in learning, so that it is possible to engage in problem-solving interchanges with the entire class (Stigler and Perry, 1988). Minstrell and teachers trained by him attempt to do the same thing. However, they report that this requires considerable effort, including the effort needed to train the students to behave in an appropriate manner.

Teaching by impasse resolution is also highly demanding of teachers' time. The method works only if instructors have time, out of class, to examine their assessments of student beliefs and to plan impasse-creating interventions. Unfortunately, time for the teachers to think seems to be one of the scarcest commodities in American schools. Compared with their counterparts in foreign schools, and especially those in the industrialized Asian countries, American teachers have relatively little time during the day in which they are not in direct contact with students. This is a serious shortcoming of our educational establishment. When efforts are made to "improve the student/teacher ratio" in American schools, we usually fix our attention on class size, rather than keeping class size constant and creating more free time for teachers. This is probably a mistake.[8]

Technology to the Rescue?

Some educational researchers and cognitive scientists have proposed a technological solution to the problem of providing individualized instruction: intelligent computer-aided instruction (ICAI) programs, which present problems to students, evaluate the responses, and, based on the responses, select new problems that are intended to enhance the students' knowledge. Obviously, this sequence conforms to Newell's idea of learning by impasse resolution. ICAI has been used successfully in physics (including in Minstrell's courses; see Hunt and Minstrell, 1993), geometry (Anderson, Boyle, and Reiser, 1985), and a number of other areas (Wenger, 1987).

There are basically two approaches to building an ICAI system: the "cognitive science" approach and the "teacher-centered" approach. The cognitive science approach, which is represented by Anderson's geometry tutor, is to build a powerful problem solver into the ICAI program. The computer problem solver then compares the student's solutions with its own and develops a model of student strengths and deficiencies based on the comparison. The difference between the student and the ideal model is used to suggest the next problem, just as the impasse resolution philosophy advises. This approach works if the program designer knows the ideal way to solve problems in a given domain and knows how students approximate ideal solutions at various stages in their education. Obtaining this knowledge could require a substantial research program in both artificial intelligence and educational psychology.

The teacher-oriented approach sidesteps the problems faced by the cognitive science approach. The program designers interview experienced teachers to determine what false or partial beliefs students are likely to have, how these beliefs can be detected, and what the teacher thinks the program should do when a particular belief has been identified. The teachers' advice is then built into the program. The resulting program can be much simpler to build than those based on the cognitive science method. On the other hand, the theory behind the program is admittedly more of a list of how to treat symptoms than a theory of how students think.

Both of these approaches have been shown to work in demonstration projects. There is little question that ICAI has a place in the school of the future, but at present the systems are costly. Current ICAI systems are feasible on a demonstration basis, but few school districts can afford to provide enough of the necessary computing equipment so that all students can have easy access to computer-aided instruction.

Whether or not this problem will be resolved within the next few years is a matter of considerable debate. Optimists point out that the cost of computing power drops radically each year, so that "soon" virtually all school districts will be able to afford all the computing power that they need. On the other hand, as the cost of computing power drops, the computer programs become ever more sophisticated. Therefore, support personnel ("computer gurus") are required to install and maintain software. Expensive nonteaching personnel are always a target for the public budget cutter.[9]

It also costs a lot to develop ICAI programs. If the cognitive science approach is taken, teams of educators, psychologists, and computer scientists have to be assembled to specify the educational goals, develop the psychological theory, and combine the two in a computer program. Costs can rapidly mount up to millions of dollars per project. The teacher-centered approach does require a nontrivial amount of computer programming and some involvement of psychological theory, but these investments are much smaller than the comparable investment required to produce an initial project using the cognitive science approach. The greatest costs are in the development and field test stage.

My colleagues and I have developed a teacher-oriented program, DIAGNOSER (Levidow, Hunt, and McKee, 1992), for use with Minstrell's physics teaching project. We found that teachers require a great deal of time to formalize their thoughts about how students err, to think about how errors should be corrected, and, most important, to try out their initial ideas on other teachers. Time costs money. While these costs might be hidden by distributing them over budgets in the school districts using the program, the costs would still exist. Furthermore, if the teachers themselves are already overcommitted, they simply cannot participate in the development project.

According to enthusiastic, but naive, advocates of ICAI, the computer is about to take over the classroom, leaving the classroom teacher with little more to do than usher the students to their seats in front of a computer equipped with virtual reality display devices.[10] ICAI methods have a place in education, but they will be a supplement to the human teacher, not a replacement.

Impasse Resolution in Postsecondary and Vocational Training

Postsecondary education ranges from courses on narrowly defined industrial specialties, such as welding, to college-level courses on Scandinavian literature and high-energy physics. No single problem-solving method would be appropriate to use throughout this system. One should look at key points in the system, ask whether or not problem solving is to be taught at all at these points, and, if it is, ask whether or not impasse resolution methods can or should be used.

Figure 7.1   The progression from schools to the workforce.

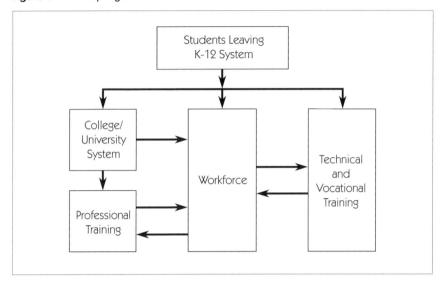

Figure 7.1 shows a simplified diagram of the progression from student to worker in U.S. society. On leaving high school (with or without a diploma) students enter either the workforce, the college-university system, or the technical-vocational training system. Let us look at what happens at each of these points.

From the psychologist's point of view, technical-vocational trainers face the easiest educational problem in dealing with the entering workforce. The instructional goals are well defined: Can students perform certain technical skills at the end of the course? The students to be educated are relatively homogeneous. They will have passed through the same school system and will have the same (minimal) amount of experience with the subject being taught. Homogeneity and motivation have been further ensured by student self-selection. Thus, the need for individualized instruction is reduced.

The principal problem with U.S. technical-vocational instruction at the entering worker level is that there is not enough of it. Compared with Europe or Japan, the United States funnels a much higher percentage of its high school graduates into the college-university system and a concomitantly lower percentage into the vocational-technical system. Several critics have argued that our resources should be redistributed, but this is an economic rather than a psychological issue.

In 1991, 62 percent of high school graduates enrolled in colleges or universities. This historic high was not the result of a sudden surge in entrances, but the culmination of a steady trend upward in the percentage of students going to college. While figures are not exactly comparable, due to differences in national reporting standards, it appears that "going to college" is about twice as likely for a high school student in the United States as it is for a student in Japan, Germany, France, or the United Kingdom.[11]

The sort of education that most students receive when they enter college is almost a parody of what not to do if you want to teach by impasse resolution. This is especially true of the large public institutions, which hold most of the students. Obviously, lecturers cannot tailor instruction to the individual in a class of 100 or more students. Attempts are made to solve this problem by providing quiz/laboratory/ discussion sections, which may vary in size from 12 to 40 or more students and are typically taught by graduate students. Impasse resolution requires experienced instructors.

Does this mean that our colleges and universities are failing to teach? Certainly some critics have claimed this, and their message has been received. E.D. Hirsch's (1987) book railing against "cultural illiteracy" became a nonfiction best-seller. On the other hand, there is an impressive amount of evidence in support of American higher education. Almost half a million foreign students are enrolled in U.S. universities, while only a trivial number of U.S. students study abroad. At the graduate level it is far more common for foreign students to come to the United States than for American students to go abroad. Evaluating the higher education product involves more than setting some arbitrary standard of what an educated person should know. We have to look at how well students retain specific subject matter.

Most studies have shown that little information is retained from a single course, but much more is retained from multiple-course sequences. Going somewhat further, there is clear evidence that people who major in a discipline acquire the habits of thought that are characteristic of their specialty. The natural sciences and the humanities tend to stress conditional reasoning, whereas psychology and the social sciences emphasize statistical and probabilistic explanations. A study at the University of Michigan found that over their four-year academic careers, undergraduates learn to use the style of reasoning appropriate to their discipline, even in content areas outside their studies, but they do not improve their ability to use reasoning methods that are not characteristic of their major fields (Lehman and Nisbett, 1990). Not surprisingly, this is even more strongly true for students in graduate and professional programs (Lehman, Lempert, and Nisbett, 1988).

What appears to be the case is that colleges and universities offer two quite different types of instruction. At the entry level students are offered a wide variety of introductory courses. With the exception of a few well-publicized courses taught by outstanding lecturers, the entry level courses are probably not particularly good learning experiences. It is unlikely that students remember very much from them. In this sense "general education" fails, a point that critics have made with vehemence (Bloom, 1987; Hirsch, 1987). On the other hand, the introductory level courses also serve as advertisements for their field. And here they do quite well, because they funnel students into the place where they do do their learning.

During the third, fourth, and, increasingly, fifth years of undergraduate work, most college students focus on their majors. Education in the upper division classes is at least tangentially related to their employment prospects. Graduate training is becoming increasingly common. Graduate classes are much smaller than undergraduate classes, and many students work on realistic problems and projects. Interactions with experienced professors become much more common at the upper division and graduate levels than they are during the first two years of college education. Here training by impasse resolution does, informally, become a major part of education. And, as the Michigan studies show, it works.

The major problem with higher education today is its cost. Virtually all students in the system feel an economic pinch. For a variety of reasons, both undergraduate and graduate education is lengthening. The old ideal of four years as an undergraduate and three years to obtain the Ph.D. or professional degree is very much a thing of the past. In some fields the median time to the Ph.D. exceeds six years beyond the bachelor's degree! The most obvious result of this is that students have to pay more tuition. This is more than a personal cost, for tuition seldom covers the acutal costs of education. Society also faces an important hidden cost. Students, while they are students, are not major contributors to the economy. Can we afford to tie up some of our best minds for so much time? I think not. However, the reason for this extension does not seem to be that the training is inefficient. The extensions in time to a degree seem to be due to increases in the amount to be learned, especially in the sciences, and to students' need to enroll on a part-time basis in order to support themselves. These are very serious issues, but they are not strictly germane to our concerns about the teaching of thinking.

Workplace Training, Retraining, and Continuing Education

Most of our workplace skills are acquired right in the workplace. In the past, working skills were typically acquired through apprenticeships, followed by a lifelong process that turned a journeyman into a master. Most workplace learning still takes place this way, but our modern society has augmented on-the-job training with a variety of continuing education courses that range from automobile repair to real estate law. As we step up the pace at which new technologies enter the workplace, we can anticipate more and more reliance on the continuing-education system.

This is an area in which the United States lags far behind Western Europe and industrial Asia. The automobile industry provides a striking example. Japanese automobile factory workers receive about 320 hours of training in their first six months on the job and then average 80 hours a year thereafter. In U.S. factories the comparable figures are 50 and 30 (Office of Technology Assessment, 1990). The figures require little further comment.

On-the-job and apprentice training often fit the SOAR prescription. Novices are set tasks just beyond their limits and then helped through them. This is also true of highly specific vocational training programs, such as those found in large companies and in contracted training associated with, for instance, the delivery of new equipment. This sort of educational system is well set up to phase in new technology in an evolutionary rather than a revolutionary way. Evolutionary training presumes continued employment in the company. Revolutionary changes in technology can sweep entire companies away. The decline of "on demand" manuscript typing services provides an interesting example. Every university used to be surrounded by what were essentially typing shops. With the onset of word processing and photographic duplicating, typing service companies were replaced by duplicating and computing companies, using new technologies. The new services were provided by entrepreneurs who had already acquired the skills needed by the new technology rather than by retraining personnel who had learned to use the old technology.

From a general societal point of view, this sort of change presents a serious problem. What happens to the displaced workers? Who is responsible for their training? And how should that training be constructed? In some cases companies assume training responsibilities themselves. The extent to which this is done varies widely. At one extreme, large Japanese companies, in the absence of severe economic pressure, tried to offer lifetime employment for the majority of their workers. At the other extreme, the U.S. aircraft companies of the 1970s and 1980s regularly advertised for semimigratory, trained craftsmen who moved from company to company, following the contracts. The advertisements made it clear that it was the individual worker's responsibility to arrive at the company door with know-how in hand.

In small companies the issue is not so much the commitment as the capability. Training inevitably means a deferral of present output in hopes of future productivity gains. This is not possible unless the company has sufficient cash flow so that deferral of present output is a possibility. In many small companies it is not.

Most observers believe that as we move into the twenty-first century we are going to see a reduction in the size of companies, an increasing use of temporary or contract workers, and a continual realignment of industrial networks in order to exploit new technologies and business opportunities, all of which creates a bad situation. Locally, individual companies cannot afford to make long-term training investments. Nationally, the training opportunities have to be there. Clearly, the responsibility is going to fall to the government.

An industrial-governmental partnership aimed at identifying new technologies and providing workers with the appropriate training is needed. The Japanese solution to this problem is particularly interesting. Although we hear a great deal about the large Japanese companies, in fact Japan has relatively more small companies than the United States.[12] Small Japanese companies adjust to new technologies in two ways. Many of them are involved in stable networks of favored suppliers for large companies and are able to benefit from their long-term associations to obtain needed technological support, including training. In addition, every prefecture in Japan maintains organizations called *Kohsetsusi* centers, which function as technology centers for small companies, providing consulting, technological expertise, and even some research related to specific problems. The *Kohsetsusi* centers also provide a variety of training programs to facilitate the introduction of new technologies.

Neither of the Japanese solutions to technology transfer could be adopted in the United States without modification. The Japanese network of large manufacturers and favored suppliers, often with overlapping directorates, would probably be illegal under our antitrust laws. Similar problems would arise if we tried to implement *Kohsetsusi* centers, for our laws and traditions emphasize competition between companies rather than cooperation. Nevertheless, we do have to solve the problem. Our present mechanisms for updating workforce skills are just not adequate. This is particularly the case when workers are being displaced. In a speech in 1994, President Clinton stressed that the American worker is going to have to accept change in the workplace. If change is going to be the norm, then we need regular mechanisms to accommodate workforce retraining, not one special crash program after another.

The problem of retraining is compounded by the aging of the workforce. It is quite clear from research on geriatrics that as people age, their problem-solving styles shift from a search for new solutions to reliance on previously acquired knowledge. Workers aged 40–60 are more likely to attack problems by looking for ways they already know than by trying to develop new methods. It follows that in the abstract, learning by impasse resolution should be even more important when one is training older workers than when training younger ones. The instructor should find out what problem-solving methods the older workers bring to the retraining setting and build on these methods to develop the skills required for the new technology. On the other hand, learning is itself a problem-solving situation. Older workers, by and large, will have acquired their own education by the traditional lecture-memorization method, followed by painstaking on-the-job training. Impasse resolution will be something new to them, and some may have great difficulty with it.

Suppose that the United States opened centers similar to the Japanese *Kohsetsusi* centers across the country. Suppose further that the directors of these centers turned to psychologists and educators to ask how the retraining courses should be designed. I would be skeptical of the answers, because they would be based on hunches rather than on a scientific knowledge base. I am not alone in my concern. In September, 1992, representatives of 41 professional organizations concerned with workplace efficiency met to consider psychological issues in the coming workplace. Training and retraining of productive workers was identified as an urgent research target (Hakel, 1993). We do not know how to do this, and we need to find out.

TEACHING PROBLEM SOLVING

We next take a closer look at problem solving itself. How does one find one's way around the impasse in the metaproblem domain, recognize how the solution found might be used in the future, and monitor one's own progress toward solution? In my expansion of Newell's SOAR approach, these steps are resolving the impasse, memorizing the solution, and metacognition. In spite of their importance, these issues are too often ignored in educational and training programs.

Instead of describing a principle and applying it separately to the K–12, higher education, and vocational systems, I will elaborate on the principle and make occasional remarks about particular applications.

Newell claimed that learning occurs when a person encounters an impasse, uses a higher-order problem-solving method to resolve it, and records the solution for future use. This point was illustrated earlier with a simple problem in traveling. Let us look at it again, using somewhat different terminology.

> Original goal: Fly from Seattle to Seville.

> Impasse: There are no flights from Seattle to Seville.

> Higher-order solution: If you wish to go from X to Y, and there is no flight from X to Y, find a location Z close to Y and attempt to solve the problem of going from X to Y via Z.

> Special solution in higher-order space: To go from Seattle to Seville fly from Seattle to London, and from London to Seville.

> Memorize rule: To fly from Seattle to Seville → fly to London, and from London to Seville.

> *or*

> Memorize a more general rule: When going to Europe and there is no direct flight to the target city, consider going through nearby hub cities, such as London, Paris, or Frankfurt.

The analysis assumes that the problem solver can operate in the higher-order space. This may be optimistic. Many people who can learn concrete pattern → action rules have difficulty with rules that have to be described abstractly.

This unmasks a basic weakness in the SOAR approach. Newell and colleagues assumed that the way an intelligent agent should learn to resolve impasses is by treating the impasse as a special case of an abstract problem, solving the abstract problem, and then specializing the solution. If people learn this way, education should begin by teaching abstract problem-solving methods and then giving students practice applying them to concrete problems.

Unfortunately, this does not work. John Bruer, the president of the James S. McDonnell Foundation, which has provided extensive funding for programs concerned with cognition, conducted an extensive review of what does and does not work in our schools (Bruer, 1993). He concluded that showing people general problem-solving methods is not an effective method of teaching. We do know of a number of general problem-solving methods that can be applied in a wide variety of contexts. The problem-solving methods used in mathematics and logic are perhaps the best examples. However, these methods have to be taught in some context, and most people simply do not generalize the methods beyond the context in which they have been taught.[13]

Statistics provides a good example. The *law of large numbers*, one of the key theorems in statistical reasoning, states that an average based upon a large sample is more believable than one based on a small sample. The law has many applications in our everyday life. Suppose that one television commercial claims that "four out of five doctors prescribe brand X," while another says that "300 of 500 doctors prescribe brand Y." The law of large numbers, coupled with some other statistical manipulations, advises that the 3:2 recommendation for brand Y is far stronger than the 4:1 recommendation for brand X, based on a smaller sample. Not everyone knows this. People who have not been trained in statistics often ignore the law of large numbers (Tversky and Kahneman, 1971). Training helps only a bit.

Fong and Nisbett (1991) taught people to use the law of large numbers, using examples that were drawn from either sports or academic testing. Two weeks later the participants were tested on either sports or academic testing problems. The effects were dramatic. If people were tested on new problems from the same area that they were trained in (sports-sports or testing-testing), they did as well as they had done immediately following training. If they were tested on the same mathematical problems in a different domain (sports-testing or testing-sports), they did much less well, although still better than untrained individuals. My own experience in teaching statistics to psychology students bears this out. I have often had the feeling that when I lecture on "how to compare independent groups of scores," my students learn "how to analyze an experiment involving rats."

More formal studies in education back up these hunches. Students show surprisingly little transfer of knowledge outside the classroom, at least when that knowledge is acquired in just one situation. Perhaps the best-documented cases are in physics, where students who have shown within-class mastery of Newtonian concepts of mechanics are unable to apply them in even a slightly altered context (Clement, 1982).

It turns out that we can teach general problem-solving methods, but we have to do so indirectly. Most successful attempts to teach general reasoning methods have begun with concrete situations that students already understand (and are motivated to deal with), and then moved gradually to the development of abstract rules. Students will tie the general rules to specific situations unless a conscious effort is made to force them to use the same general reasoning rules in a variety of different domains. Two pedagogical examples will illustrate what I mean. The first stresses the importance of varied examples; the second stresses the importance of identifying modes of reasoning.

Arithmetic Progression Problems

1. Suppose that you give me a dollar today, two dollars tomorrow, three dollars the next day, and so on, for ten days. How much money will I have gained?

2. A rocket traveling at 1,000 km/hr changes its position by 1,000 km in one hour. If it is accelerating uniformly, so that it moves at 1,000 km/hr at time t, then 1,200 in the second hour, 1,400 in the third hour, and so on, what will be the change in position from the start until the tth hour?

To a mathematician these are both examples of *arithmetic progression* problems. In such a problem, the rate of increase of a quantity, y, increases by an amount, a, at each interval of time. Therefore, the amount at time t can be defined in terms of the change from the amount at time $t - 1$,

$$y(t) = y(t - 1) + at, \tag{7.1}$$

or the change from the starting value,

$$y(t) = y(0) + (1/2)at^2. \tag{7.2}$$

If you do not see this immediately, do not worry. The mathematics are not important here. What is important is the breadth of the application. Arithmetic progression problems arise in finance, physics, and a number of other fields.

In physics classes students study arithmetic progression problems as they arise in physics. In mathematics classes examples are chosen from a wider domain. As a result, mathematics students are better able to recognize arithmetic progression problems in a totally new domain than physics students are, even though both the mathematics and physics students have had the same amount of practice in use of the equations (Bassok and Holyoak, 1989).

Teaching Logic

One of the central notions in logic is the idea of implication: that the truth of statement A implies the truth of B. What people find particularly hard to grasp is that implication is not symmetric. "If A, then B" does not imply "If B, then A." This means that if we know that B is *not* true, then we can assert that A is not true, but that observing B is true tells us nothing about the truth of A. The implication relationship is a central part of scientific and mathematical reasoning. It is also important in intelligent trouble shooting of machinery, electronic systems, and medical diagnosis. Suppose that when you turn the key in your car, the engine will not start. Is the battery dead? Try turning on the radio. The logic of doing so is:

Dead battery implies radio will not turn on.

If the radio turns on, then the battery cannot be dead.

If the radio does not turn on, then either the battery is dead or there is something else wrong.

Patricia Cheng and her colleagues (Cheng and Holyoak, 1985) have argued that people seldom understand implication in its general form. They do understand specialized interpretations of implication, which Cheng refers to as *pragmatic schemata*. The automobile repair example illustrates one of them, the *causal schema;* failure of a battery is one of several sufficient reasons that a car radio will not work. Therefore, if the radio does work, none of the sufficient reasons can have been true.

The *permission schema* is another interpretation of implication. The abstract statement is "B permits A." A concrete example is, "If you are of legal drinking age you may (but don't have to) order a beer." This is logically equivalent to A implies B—ordering beer implies that you are of legal drinking age. The permission form is much easier to understand.

Logic is normally taught by going from examples directly to the abstract statement. Cheng and her colleagues found that it is easier to teach people about implication if the instructor approaches the problem via illustrations of the use of schemata—specialized interpretations of implication that the students already possess (Cheng et al., 1986), a method in keeping with the impasse resolution approach.

If we expect students to apply general problem-solving methods outside the context of their instruction, then we have to let them practice recalling the methods in a variety of different situations. Minstrell has recognized the value of practice in the development of his methods for teaching physics. He specifically allows for time later in the course to "revisit" problems and techniques learned earlier. The same principle applies more broadly outside the classroom. If people take the time to practice a problem-solving method in a context other than the one in which it has been learned, they can retain that problem-solving method for a surprisingly long period of time. This has been illustrated nicely by a study of the retention of high school mathematics.

College alumni were asked to solve a variety of algebra problems. In many cases they had not had formal mathematics training for 20 years or more. Nevertheless, some people did surprisingly well. A simple rule could be used to predict who would succeed in which problems. People remembered the mathematical methods they had learned in the *next-to-last* mathematics course they took, providing that they practiced them in the last course. Evidently the last course consolidates the knowledge acquired in the preceding course, and it is then virtually never forgotten (Bahrick and Hall, 1991).

We could hardly have a better example for instruction in mathematics in schools and universities . . . *beyond* the level of the problems we expect people to encounter after they have graduated.

Before plunging into the details of teaching, instructors should first carefully consider how the students are supposed to use their knowledge. To what domains do instructors want the students to generalize? Once this question is answered, instructors should force students to deal with examples that cover the entire domain. Then, sometime after the instruction appears to have been grasped, students should reuse the methods. In fact, there is a good argument for "reviewing" by having the students use their newly acquired problem-solving method to solve advanced problems that probably will not be encountered in the field. The goal of this exercise would not be to provide the students with new information, but to let them consolidate the information that they already have.

Barriers to Teaching Problem Solving

Since everyone seems to want to train people to think, and since there is a reasonably strong research base showing us how to do this, why doesn't the educational system use the research to teach thinking? Unfortunately there are some quite real barriers to introducing training to think into our educational curriculum. Some of the barriers are structural or financial and could be changed. Others have to do with attitudes toward education and may be much harder to change.

Teaching thinking is a slow process. Instructors who move carefully from specific cases to general principles take a long time. Jim Minstrell, the prize-winning physics teacher whose instructional methods were described earlier, virtually never finishes the prescribed curriculum for the year. Other teachers who have adopted his methods report the same thing. Teaching by impasse resolution produces students who know some things very well, at the expense of their having a superficial knowledge of many topics.

The tendency to try to cover many topics, rather than to concentrate on a few well-taught ones, seems to be characteristic of the U.S. educational system. At the K–12 level we spend relatively little time on complex subjects, especially in mathematics and the sciences. Physics, for instance, is a two-year course in most industrialized countries, but a one-year course in virtually all U.S. systems. (And our school years are shorter!) The same thing is true at the university level. In most industrialized countries, university students have the choice of a few programs, each of which offers an integrated series of courses. While American universities do attempt some integration, especially for professional and preprofessional programs, compared with the set-course meals offered by European universities, the American undergraduate curriculum is something of a cafeteria.

Yet we keep demanding that things be added to the curriculum! While writing this book I heard arguments for teaching computer programming in middle school, ethnic awareness in the university, and AIDS counseling in every psychotherapy and social counseling program, regardless of the program's clientele. These propositions, and many others, can be justified on a case-by-case basis. What American educators have generally not done is to consider the inevitable trade-off between widespread but superficial knowledge versus deeper and more focused learning.

The policies that encourage proliferation of brief courses could change administratively, although the financial and social dislocations during the change would not be trivial. Student attitudes present a more serious problem. Learning to think, in general, can be confusing and threatening, because people have, after all, evolved to deal with specifics rather than generalities. Students may become confused and resistant if they are asked to take classes where they must deal with problems that, on the surface, do not seem to have a coherent theme. Consider the statistics example given earlier. Psychologically, students find it less confusing if the instructor develops a very few related examples that are progressively deepened to illustrate statistical principles. This can be done. Instructors can illustrate statistical principles varying from elementary descriptions of results to complicated data analyses using examples taken entirely from medical care, or entirely from physiology, or agriculture, or any of a number of other subjects. This mode of instruction is congenial to students, especially if they are concentrating in the field from which the examples are drawn. The problem is that the students fail to see the general themes behind the discipline-related examples. As a result they too often fail to apply techniques that they learn outside the discipline where they are learned.

Being forced to think is not necessarily fun. Students often find it unpleasant to have to apply a general principle first in one context and then in another. By analogy, athletes seldom enjoy running wind sprints to build up their stamina. Athletes tolerate conditioning drills because they know stamina will be needed in a game. Students will tolerate being trained to think generally only if they see the need for the skill.

Historically, programs that emphasize abstract thinking have also run into social objections. Most (not all) of these programs are more suited for the initially more able and certainly the more motivated students. To the extent that teaching abstract reasoning becomes an important educational goal, there will be increasing pressure to stream students into more and less able groups. Streaming is quite common in other industrial countries but is often resisted in the United States because of our professed opposition to intellectual elitism. This opposition is particularly serious, and understandably so, when streaming results in the racial and ethnic segregation of students. Unfortunately, this is often the result.

It has been claimed that disparities in educational achievement of our various ethnic groups reflect group differences in intelligence (Jensen, 1980, 1985). While there is no way to deny this conclusively because it is impossible to prove that there is no difference between two groups, I believe that social factors are far more important. Appreciating abstract reasoning is a cultural value, and as such is more deeply held in some social groups than in others. Indeed, we tend to forget how culturally specific the very idea of abstract reasoning is. Deductive logic, which is the basis for formal reasoning, was a cultural invention of the classic Greeks and for most of history was improved upon largely by Europeans. This does not mean that non-Westerners cannot reason about abstractions; they obviously can. The issue is over the value that they assign to such reasoning, compared with reasoning based on personal experience.

In the 1920s the Soviet psychologist A.R. Luria conducted studies of reasoning by peasants in what was then Soviet Central Asia. He asked the peasants abstract questions about places that the respondents had never visited. For instance, one of his questions (paraphrased) was, "In Novya Zemlaya all the bears are white. If you were in Novya Zemlaya and you saw a bear, what color would it be?" Luria's respondents told him, quite pointedly, that he should not ask them hypothetical questions about places to which they had never been (Luria, 1976). Since then other psychologists and anthropologists have reported similar responses in other largely nonliterate societies. "Just suppose. . . ." is something of a Western game.

We have ample evidence that different groups in our own culture place markedly different values on abstract reasoning skills. This is not irrational. It is often something of a toss-up whether you should try to solve a problem by relying on analysis or experience. If different subgroups in our own society place different values on abstract reasoning, I am sure that they communicate these values to their children. They also bring these values into the classroom when they appear, as adults, for industrial training.

If we are going to succeed in teaching abstract skills to be used anywhere, for any purpose, we will have to motivate the students to learn them. It is not enough to know how to teach these skills; we have to sell the need for them to students, parents, educators, and everyone else involved.

METACOGNITION AT THE PERSONAL LEVEL

Good problem solvers think about what they are doing. They know when they encounter an impasse, and when they discover a way around the impasse, they think about the conditions under which their newly discovered solution method will work.

Psychologists have coined the term *metacognition* (literally, thinking about thought) to describe the behavior of examining one's own thought processes. It is an active field of study today (Nelson, 1992). It is also important to everyday thinking. For example, most people in business today keep an appointment book, because they realize that they will not be able to remember all their appointments. Metacognition is similarly involved when a mathematician realizes that he or she is not getting anywhere on a problem and needs a rest, or when a lawyer realizes a need to review a case before presenting it to the court.

Unlike abstract problem solving, metacognition can be taught. In fact, it can be taught to children in the early years of grade school (see the studies reviewed by Bruer, 1993, pp. 67–71). One of the best methods is to give students responsibility for their own instruction, by having them work together in a social setting, such as a group problem-solving project. The trick is to arrange the group session so that each student has to explain his or her reasoning to other students and to comment on the reasoning of others. This has the side effect of teaching the students how to work in a group—itself a useful skill—and seems to motivate students to work on problems. It is equally important that teachers conduct sessions in such a way that students can accept comments and evaluations without feeling criticized personally. In Japanese mathematics classes, children are often asked to explain their problem-solving methods to the class. The class as a whole then critiques the presenting student's answer and approach (Stigler and Perry, 1988). This method of instruction would be discouraged in most American schools, for fear that the student explaining the answer would feel exposed to ridicule. The problem is particularly acute if children feel that their efforts are always being downgraded, that is, that people expect them to fail. Claude Steele, a well-respected social psychologist, has suggested that such "conditioning for low expectations" may be one of the reasons that black children learn to turn off from our schools (Steele, 1992).

If metacognitive skills are going to be taught, the signals required for metacognition have to be transmitted as signals to be processed, not evaluations to be avoided. Young children can learn to do this. It is not so clear that we can find the same freedom of expression in a highly competitive adult society, where information transmission has come to be so closely tied to evaluation.

ASSESSMENT: METACOGNITION AT THE SOCIAL LEVEL

Metacognition implies a willingness to take an objective look at your own reasoning in an attempt to make it better. This brings us to the topic of assessment, in which educational systems take a careful look at themselves. Assessment is a sort of metacognition at the level of a whole society. In the last few years, there has been a great deal of talk about the need for assessment, either as a way of improving educational and training programs or, somewhat less constructively, as a way of rewarding and punishing the educators involved.

The idea of assessment certainly fits with the notion of impasse resolution, since assessment is required to notice that an impasse has occurred. But there is a better analogy; assessment is to education what quality control is to an industrial process. In each case, the operating agents have to receive information about what they are doing, in a timely enough fashion so that adjustments can be made and the product improved. However, there is another use of assessment in education, as a method of certification. Final examinations certify students as being qualified for some further course, just as acceptance tests by an industrial buyer qualify a seller to be paid.

Both purposes of assessment are valid, but we should realize that because they are intended to meet different aims, assessment for quality control is different from assessment for certification. Assessment for educational improvement should be as frequent as possible and should take place in a setting where neither teachers nor students have any motivation to produce inaccurate information. Consider a student who wants to know if his or her study habits are adequate. Such a student does not want to receive an A grade on an examination unless it is truly earned. On the other hand, if assessment is for purposes of certification, there is an understandable desire to get the highest grade possible, because improving one's record becomes a goal in itself. The same thing applies to a teacher. If student examinations are to be used to inform the teacher of student knowledge, in order to guide further instruction, the teacher has no motivation to receive anything other than accurate information. If the examination is to be used to determine whether or not the teacher is to receive an increase in pay, then the teacher has a motivation to see that the students get the highest

Figure 7.2 An industrial systems view of education that relies on didactic instruction.

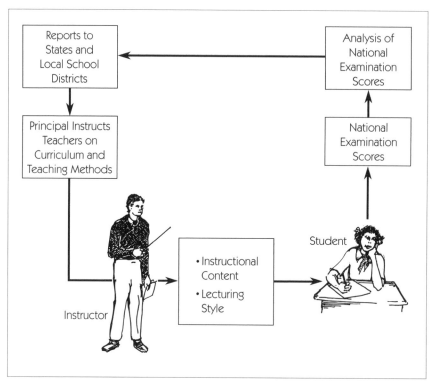

grades possible, regardless of whether or not they have truly mastered the material.

The problem with many proposals to improve the educational system is that they seem to assume that assessments designed for certification will, almost as a by-product, serve the function of providing feedback for educational improvement. To see that this is not so, let us consider how assessment fits into a traditional, lecture-style school environment. Figure 7.2 shows the results. At risk of parody, it is not too far afield to say that in this environment the curriculum makers (principals, curriculum designers, and vocational program experts) provide students and tell the teacher what to do with them. The instructor starts his or her lecturing machine, and the students stack knowledge into little boxes in their heads. Sometime later, at assessment time, an external examiner determines what those boxes contain.

Figure 7.2 should look familiar. It is a relabeled version of Figure 6.1, which showed the *old-style, inefficient* way to make cardboard boxes.

In that industrial system one person set the dials on a box-making (i.e., lecturing) machine, and another stacked up the boxes. At the end of a production run, an inspector (examiner) came along and determined how many boxes had been made properly. Much later—far too late to do any good—the person setting the dials would be told they had to be reset.

Ironically, the sort of assessment depicted in Figure 7.2 is uncomfortably close to proposals to use the National Assessment of Educational Progress (NAEP) program as a device for monitoring school performance. These yearly examinations would be fed back to the individual schools or districts far too late to make a difference to the students who had taken the tests. And for that matter, just providing scores would not provide a district or school, let alone an individual teacher, with the sort of highly specific information needed to alter educational practices at the classroom level.

At the national level, examinations such as the NAEP program can be useful guides for funding decisions, which inevitably take place slowly. But what is needed at the classroom level is a process for continual, nonthreatening monitoring of performance, in a situation where the goal of informative feedback far overrides the goal of certification. This can be done, but it takes time—time to incorporate the assessment procedures into the teaching program (as is done in the better ICAI systems), time for the teachers to evaluate the assessments, and time for both students and teachers to discuss what is to be done next. And time is money.

HOW TO BE SMART ENOUGH

I have used Newell's (1990) SOAR model of cognition as a vehicle for making proposals about virtually every aspect of our educational and training system. The theory has been used as a way of organizing my own thoughts on the topic, rather than as a prescription to be followed slavishly. I strongly suspect that other reasonable theories could have been used as organizing devices with very much the same conclusions.

If we want people to acquire general thinking skills, we have to do three things:

1. We have to determine the extent of students' current thinking skills, knowledge, and attitudes. This is true at every level, but particularly at the level of the older student or retrainee.

2. We have to confront students with the impasses that their current thinking creates and show them how to move around these impasses.

3. At every level, students have to be motivated to solve problems. As they solve problems, they have to be willing to expose themselves to evaluations of their own thought. They must be given informative assessments, rather than certifying examinations.

If you accept anything like the SOAR theory, or virtually any of the other theories that cognitive psychologists have developed since 1960, these ideas must seem obvious. So why aren't they adopted? I am afraid that we have, on a de facto basis, accepted a model of education that has lulled us into thinking that education can be cheap.

Jill Larkin, a professor at Carnegie-Mellon University who has a well-earned reputation for bringing cognitive science into education, once opened a lecture by displaying a medieval woodcut of the "Nuremburg funnel." According to legend, the professors at the University of Nuremburg believed that the student's mind was an empty vessel. It followed that the most efficient method of education was to open the student's skull, place a funnel in the opening, and pour knowledge in. In other words, lecture at the students and let them be responsible for learning.

The nice part of this idea is that it is so cost-effective. And to boot, it makes fascinating use of modern technology. Do university professors give boring lectures? Use videotapes of outstanding lecturers. Do students demand high-quality graphics that match the quality they are used to seeing on television? Modern multimedia technology can fix this. Has the local logging industry collapsed, and there is no one to teach the loggers to be electronic repairers? Put university/high school/vocational instruction on television. Or maybe give everyone a computer with a CD-ROM disk. All these suggestions have merit, and we certainly should continue to develop better and better technological aids for education. What we should not do is to use this technology to deliver slicker, more Hollywood-style lectures to passive watchers and listeners. Such an application would be nothing more than a fancier version of the Nuremburg funnel, and the funnel will work about as well in the twenty-first century as it did in the sixteenth century. What we have to do is to engage the student to think. That takes a teacher, interacting with a student. The teacher can and should be supported by technology, but the teacher cannot and should not be replaced by technology.

All this costs money. Creating the impasse-producing situations is expensive. Part of the cost is in creating the multimedia presentations, field trips, and laboratory equipment needed. But that is only a fraction of the cost. The real cost is in the cost of the instructor.

It takes more skill to teach by impasse resolution than it does to teach by lecturing. Lecturers have complete control over the course of the conversation, so all they need to do is to provide coherent presentations of topics selected in advance. When students are engaged in impasse resolution, the teacher has to be able to relate the topic of the course to all sorts of student questions, in a manner that will encourage further questions. The teacher has to master a difficult pedagogical method and, in addition, have enough grasp of the subject matter so that he or she can deal with student questions. Teachers cannot be given these skills by mandate; they will have to be trained. It is quite clear that the present teacher education system is not doing this. Far too many teachers are learning to "teach to the lesson plan," and far too many teachers are not being given the skills in science, mathematics, history, economics, and languages that they need in order to teach them well. Correcting this situation will inevitably increase the cost of both in-service and initial teacher education.

Operating costs are also going to go up. Teaching by impasse resolution only works if the teachers have time to think about what they and their students are doing. In most U.S. school systems, class size is not the real issue.[14] Teachers in Europe and the industrial Asian countries teach problem solving in classes that, if anything, are slightly larger than U.S. classes (Stevenson, Lee, and Stigler, 1986). The difference is in the number of hours per day that the teachers are in front of classes ("contact hours"). The foreign educators are supposed to reflect upon the events of the day. The United States seems to view education as an industrial process: If the teacher is not in front of the class, the teacher must be on break. If I were asked to recommend just one thing to improve the U.S. schools, my recommendation would be to reduce the number of contact hours per teacher.

The gist of my argument is that we already know a great deal about how to improve our educational system, and we ought to use this knowledge. We do not know everything, especially in the field of adult education, where the teaching methods that have worked in the K–12 system may need to be modified. We do know enough to make our educational and training systems much more effective than they are now. What we lack is the resolve to do so.

THE PROSPECTS FOR THE FUTURE: PESSIMISM AND OPTIMISM

When I began my work on this book, I basically agreed with the writers of the Department of Labor's *Opportunity 2000* report (1988). I thought that America's challenge would be one of finding talented people to fill available jobs. Since that time both I and others have become more pessimistic. On the day that I finished this book, the *New York Times* presented a report showing that the recovery of 1993–1994 was characterized by industrial investment in machinery rather than jobs.[15] Where jobs were added they were often low-paying jobs, in which people work under the direction of machines, rather than the other way around. The *Times* article was only one of many such reports that, taken together, raise a question that has to be faced. How many good jobs are there? Is it possible that we are wasting everyone's time by trying to provide lots of well-trained people when we need only a few?

Three technological changes—computers, communications, and transportation—have combined to produce a workplace where there is an increasingly sharp demarcation between a few good jobs and a large number of mediocre ones. What each of these technologies does is to multiply the effectiveness of a smart person. If one person has an idea about how to run something, and if that idea can be translated into a computer program, then the idea can be instantly transferred all over the world. The need for local reinvention of the wheel, together with the need for local wheel designers, disappears. What follows is a sharp redistribution of wealth, since we pay a few system designers handsomely and dispense with the rest.

The situation is exacerbated by international competition. In the nineteenth century artificial trade barriers were not needed to keep the German buggy manufacturing industry outside the U.S. market or vice versa. People in London did not have their clothing custom-made in Hong Kong. In both cases the cost of transportation was so great that even inefficient local suppliers could provide a cost-effective alternative to efficient but distant suppliers. That is simply not true today.

As a result, every year an increasing percentage of the U.S. workforce competes in the global economy. This is especially true of the competition for the very good jobs: the designers who plan and the executives who monitor the many guises of computer-control systems. Machine tending still has to be done locally, but machine tending is not the way to fame and riches.

These trends are inevitable, though government financial policies, international trade agreements, and similar legal arrangements can alter their impact for a few years. Goods and services are provided by combining technology with labor. At this point in history, the value added by investing in technology is increasing, relative to the value added by investing in labor. What is more, new labor providers are entering the marketplace, thus further driving down the value of labor. What is there to do?

We can do quite a bit, but we have to understand what needs to be done. A historical perspective helps. The industrial revolution certainly eliminated jobs of the pick and shovel variety. The future belonged to people who supplied perceptual and motor skills for strong but clumsy machines. Then the robots came in. They have the perceptual-motor skills, but still do not think. In the 1970s and 1980s Japan led the world in the use of industrial robots, but the Japanese did not use the smartest robots. They used flexible, simple robots that were programmed, on the spot, by workers who understood their jobs and how the robots could aid them. Now the machines are beginning to think. The new technology lets system designers enforce their understanding of situations onto the on-the-spot workers. Recall the engineer who said that "truth replaces knowledge" in an automated paper mill. That principle is being applied throughout the workplace.

But now recall the airline ticket agent in the San Jose airport, who knew that the computer said an airplane was ready to land, but who also knew that the runway was blocked *and that the computer system did not know that.* She adjusted her actions accordingly. That example points the way to future success. Success will go to people who understand the technology they have and who can combine the capabilities of that technology with their own knowledge of local situations, so that the right problem gets solved. All that has happened today is that the technology has gotten a bit more complex, so it takes a bit more thought to use it creatively.

What should we do if we want our country to win its share of medals in the world economic race?

Run harder. Think quicker. Invest in people.

NOTES

1. Newell regarded SOAR as a complete theory of cognition that could be specialized to provide theories within specific domains, such as sentence comprehension or geometry problem solving. My view of SOAR is less ambitious. I regard the ideas in SOAR as a source for inspiration rather than as a guidebook for action. In fact, R. D. Luce and I have expressed considerable reservations about the literal use of a computer program as a model of cognition, although we agree that it can be a useful demonstration of principles (Hunt and Luce, 1992). Newell (1992) explicitly rejected our argument.
2. In one of his *Far Side* cartoons, Gary Larson claims that the entire collection of the library of hell consists of books of mathematics word problems.
3. *Miami Vice,* one of the most popular TV cop shows of the 1980s, had a budget of about $1 million per sequence. *Harper's* magazine observed that this exceeded the annual operating budget of the Miami police depart-

ment's vice squad. Based on my general knowledge of academic budgets, and some knowledge of the Jasper project, I suspect that the true cost of the Jasper project (including salaries paid by Vanderbilt University to the faculty involved) was on the order of $2 million to $3 million dollars, roughly the budget for three episodes of *Miami Vice.* How do you think this compares with the budget of a middle school mathematics department?

4. While studies show that up to 10 percent of U.S. adults are said to be "functionally illiterate," this is not the issue. Very few adults cannot read, in the sense that they cannot read a book that young children would find interesting. Functional illiteracy refers to an inability to read elementary regulations, notices, and business documents. Historically, this is a rigorous definition of literacy (Miller, 1988).

5. I do not maintain that the Asians in North America represent an idyllic success story. Their migration has been stressful, and, like all social movements, the stresses of today will be replaced by the stresses of tomorrow. It is a fact that the percentage of Asians who have mastered school-taught skills is much higher than would be predicted given other indicators of parental education and socioeconomic status.

6. Caplan, Choy, and Whitmore (1992) claimed that Southeast Asian migrants stressed education because of their historic cultural value for scholarship. Sue and Okazaki (1990) argued that the Asians succeeded because they perceived education as an important means of upward mobility. There may well be truth in both points of view. My point is that it is important that students have a perception of the importance of education—in the sense of acquiring knowledge—rather than the importance of educational certification—in the sense of having passed a course with a good grade.

7. Many educators have been impressed by the ideas of the Soviet psychologist Lev Vygotsky. He was active in the 1930s, but his work did not reach the English-speaking world until the 1950s and later (Vygotsky, 1962). Vygotsky argued that learners could be characterized by the tasks they could do without further instruction, a set of tasks that were beyond them, and, in his terms, a *zone of proximal development,* where the learner could do tasks if led by a competent instructor. According to Vygotsky, the good instructor locates the student's zone of proximal development and expands on it. More recently, this idea has been developed by the Israeli psychologist Reuben Feurstein (Feurstein et al., 1980) and is widely used by various educational groups.

8. Personal space is needed, too. Teachers need a place away from the students to think about their students' progress. The norm in American schools is to have the teacher's desk in the classroom. It would be far better to provide quiet office space in a designated teachers' area.

9. The problem of getting computer sophistication into the schools will *not* be solved by "relying on the kids to do it, kids all know computers these days." (This naive comment was made by an otherwise sophisticated businessman, who was sincerely interested in improving the schools.) First,

computer users are not necessarily sophisticated in computer repair and management, any more than an automobile driver is necessarily a mechanic. A person can spend hours a day playing computer games without learning anything about programming or system management. Second, institutions that rely on computing systems need continuity of support from year to year, which cannot be achieved by relying on student labor.

10. Even if excellent ICAI programs were available now, there would be substantial, justifiable resistance to their use. The programs will have to be integrated with classroom activities. Teacher training will need to be provided. Teachers will not, and should not, use teaching instruments that they do not understand.

11. National Center for Educational Statistics, *Digest of Educational Statistics* (1992), Tables 171 and 383.

12. Slightly more than 400,000 companies in Japan employ between 4 and 299 employees. There are 200,000 such companies in the United States (Shapira, 1992).

13. Not all assessors have been so harsh. Broad, lasting gains have been reported for low-ability populations. Teachers and educators who have been involved in programs on "teaching thinking" are enthusiastic and often feel that objective assessments fail to demonstrate real gains (Nickerson, Perkins, and Smith, 1985, Chap. 11). Having been involved in some such programs, I sympathize but, as a scientist, I am bothered by claims that cannot be substantiated.

14. My remarks apply to reasonable class sizes—about 25 students—at the high school and junior high school level. Classes might rise to 30 or 40 in postsecondary and continuing education. Primary grades may be more sensitive to in-class student-teacher ratios.

15. Uchitelle, L. "Corporate Spending Booms but Jobs Stagnate." *New York Times*, June 16, 1994, p. C1.

Afterword:
The Bell Curve Controversy

Any book on contemporary events may be out-of-date by the time that it is printed. While this book was in press Richard Herrnstein and Charles Murray (1994) published *The Bell Curve: Intelligence and Class Structure in American Life.*, which dealt with a number of the questions that have been raised here. Herrnstein and Murray reviewed many of the same articles I have cited; they have also reported an analysis of data from a longitudinal study of the experience of people who entered the workforce in the 1970s. My first reaction was to update some of my references and let things go at that. However, Herrnstein and Murray's book has generated a great deal of public controversy, not so much over their data as over their conclusions and policy recommendations. This controvery has not been confined to academia; it includes articles in *The New York Times, The Wall Street Journal, Newsweek, Scientific American,* and many other influential organs of the popular press.

What about this book caused *The New York Times* to refer to it as the most controversial book of 1994, and to Murray as the most dangerous conservative in America? The answer is that they took an extreme position on a number of controversial issues.

Herrnstein and Murray view intelligence as a unitary ability. That is, they endorse the *g* theory of intelligence described in Chapter 2. Although they mention that other theories of intelligence exist, they proceed as if the *g* theory were so overwhelmingly true that the others can be disregarded. I do not. In particular, I have stressed the distinction between fluid and crystallized intelligence, and discuss, in Chapter 5, the cognitive psychology view of intelligence. I shall return to this point later, because it is central to the differences in the conclusions that they and I draw.

Herrnstein and Murray then argue, vehemently, that intelligence really matters, not just in the schools but also in everyday life. They offer two classes of evidence. One is a review of the literature on the relation between intelligence and workforce performance, using a great deal of the data that I review in Chapter 3 of this book. In general, they accept the arguments presented by John Hunter (1986), who concluded, from a meta-analysis of the relation between GATB scores and workplace performance, that there is a population correlation between intelligence and job performance of about .5. Note that this is a population correlation, estimated using the projection techniques described in Chapter 3. With somewhat more hesitation about the use of projections, I come to about the same conclusion. Recall that an intelligence-correlation performance of .5 was used as "the best estimate" in making the population predictions described in Chapter 4. Indeed, why would either they or I write our books if we did not believe that intelligence mattered?

Herrnstein and Murray then present two more observations that have a great deal of support amongst scientific psychologists, but that are often downplayed in public discussions. The first is that intelligence is substantially hereditary, with heredity coefficients on the order of .4 to .7. I agree that this is a reasonable estimate, but I have hardly dwelt on it at all, because it is hardly relevant to a discussion of the workforce in the early twenty-first century. Virtually all the people who will be in the workforce of 2010 have already been born. Longer-range projections, to 2050 or 2100, do have to consider genetic trends. However, so many other assumptions have to be made about social organization, immigration, and technology that making long-range projections in this field seems to me to be an exercise in speculation.

Herrnstein and Murray then review the data showing that intelligence test scores in blacks and Latinos are, on the average, one standard deviation unit below the white mean. This is a fact. I review much the same evidence in Chapter 4. Furthermore, both they and I agree that intelligence tests do predict non-white performance about as well as they predict white performance.

Herrnstein and Murray then present two arguments that I believe go very much beyond the evidence. The first of these is that the black-Latino and white-Asian differences in IQ scores are probably of genetic origin. They do acknowledge that the data do not compel this conclusion, but they argue that because genetic heritability contributes so much to IQ, and because there are obviously genetic differences between various ethnic groups, it is reasonable to suppose that the IQ differences are at least partly of genetic origin.

I do not discuss this at all for three reasons. First, as they admit, the data are ambiguous. This does not mean that it has been shown that the ethnic differences in IQ are not genetic, it means that we do not know. Second, it is my belief that, given the loose definition of race and ethnic group, we are never going to find out from statistical analyses alone whether ethnic group differences that we observe in our society have a genetic origin. In the United States today the majority of the ancestors of a given black can be white, Latinos can be of black, white, or Native American genetic ancestry, whites in America can come from Iran or Scotland, and an Asian citizen's ancestors may come from India, Tibet, Japan, or Korea (with China a rather large in-between). Race is not exactly a tight scientific concept.[1]

My third reason for not discussing genetic factors is that if your concern is in increasing cognitive skills in a particular population, then you are interested in what works within the range of remedies that you can apply. Obviously, we cannot apply genetic remedies. Let us therefore concentrate on what can be done with social and environmental changes.

Herrnstein and Murray argue that there is very little that we can do about changing intelligence. They base their conclusion on studies that have failed to find changes in intelligence test scores after rather massive educational enrichment programs for minority or underprivileged children. They dismiss those projects that have produced positive results as being far too expensive to introduce into the schools on a regular basis.

At this point Herrnstein and Murray shift into pure political argument. They maintain that because of these facts (and with surprisingly little discussion of changes in technology, which I stress in Chapter 6), our society is being separated into a class of fairly wealthy haves, who control the machines that control the society, and have-nots, who get in trouble because they cannot cope with an increasingly complex social system. In Chapter 1 and throughout this book I have worried about the effects of a stratification into the haves and have-nots, although I would not put the issue quite so sharply as Herrnstein and Murray have. They argue that since intelligence is hereditary and largely unalterable upwards, what we need to do is to arrange the world so that the less intelligent can have a better life. They believe that this is best done by decentralizing decision-making authorities, so that the movers and shakers in society live close to those being moved and shaken, and thus can exercise more effective and human control because they will be aware of local conditions. On the surface, this is quite similar to my observation, in Chapter 6, that technology does make possible more centralized control, providing that one is willing to restrict control to control over those things that can be fed into an information-processing system. Credit ratings can be calculated from statistics, personal assessment of a business person's character and acumen cannot. On the other hand, the statistics are likely to be far more reliable than the personal assessment. My view, expressed in Chapters 6 and 7, is that the question of local, personal versus central, digitized control is far more complex than Herrnstein and Murray make it out to be.

Herrnstein and Murray also worry, as I have in Chapter 1, that as society becomes more information-oriented, the United States will have to be more and more efficient in its use of its intellectual capital. When they combine this with their beliefs in heredity and ethnic group differences, they come to a conclusion that has drawn a great deal of fire, even though it occupies rather little of the book. They conclude that affirmative action programs should be dismantled. In the terms of Chapter 4, they espouse the Equality of Individual Opportunity (EIO) policy in its entirety.

I believe that the many people who either attack or defend affirmative action with almost religious fervor are both wrong. The projections in Chapter 4 show that we cannot justify either a pure Equality of Group Outcome (EGO) or a pure Equality of Individual Opportunity (EIO) policy. The EGO policy produces some inefficiency in utilization of our cognitive capital and offers great opportunities for majority group members to feel that reverse discrimination is depriving them of jobs. This is true, but in two rather different ways. A few people actually will be displaced, as shown by the inefficiency index presented in Chapter 4. However, a very large number of people will have reason to feel that they are being discriminated against because they know of minority group members who are less talented than they, but who hold better jobs. This is shown by the jealousy index, which is also calculated in Chapter 4. My analysis can be thought of as a quantification of Herrnstein and Murray's point. Both they and I regard it as a serious social problem.

Where we disagree is in the negative implications of the EIO policy. Herrnstein and Murray somewhat overstate the case by worrying about the ratio of minority/majority group members at the top ranges of intelligence, given that there is a standard deviation difference between groups. In Chapter 4, I point out that the situation is not quite so bad because the issue is not over differences in intelligence, but differences in measures of workplace competence. Even using Herrnstein and Murray's figures, this translates into a group difference in workplace competence of about half a standard deviation. The situation is bad, but not as bad as Herrnstein and Murray present it to be.

Herrnstein and Murray argue that we should accept the discrepancy between proportional representation of groups in the better jobs and the representation that would be produced by an EIO policy, because essentially nothing can be done about it. Here I vehemently disagree, on two grounds. The first is that we cannot. Let us not argue about what is morally right or wrong. If the goal is to make society productive, I do not think this goal can be met by having large groups feeling that they are being left out of the best positions because they are not qualified. They will not accept the "not qualified" argument, and if they see themselves underrepresented by a factor of three to one or more, which could happen under an EIO policy, we are going to have a divided society.

My conclusion is that we have to do something to increase the amount of cognitive skills needed in the coming workforce, and that, in many cases, we know what to do. Herrnstein and Murray claim that nothing can be done. I disagree.

My argument, developed in some detail in both Chapters 2 and 5, is that human cognitive abilities cannot be simplified by referring to a single general intelligence factor. As I point out in Chapter 2, the different psychometric views of intelligence are really different ways of slicing the same pie (distribution of test scores). In particular, I point out that the distinction between *fluid intelligence* and *crystallized intelligence* is often the most useful way to think about intelligence in the workforce. As a shorthand, the fluid-crystallized distinction can be thought of as the distinction between solving unusual or novel problems and applying culturally acquired solution methods to deal with the problem at hand. This distinction was emphasized again in Chapter 5, where I discussed information processing views of intelligence. There it was pointed out that solving problems using new methods involves the development of a problem representation, which generally places a heavy information processing load on working memory. Applying previously acquired knowledge is very largely a pattern-recognition process and depends upon having learned when particular problem-solving methods are appropriate.

There is also a seemingly innocuous technical point which I introduced, and which Herrnstein and Murray do not discuss. There is considerable evidence that the idea of "general intelligence" is a reasonable approximation toward the lower ends of intellectual competence, but that intelligence is much more specialized at the higher ends of competence. This seemingly technical point becomes quite important later.

In making their case for the importance of intelligence in the workplace, Herrnstein and Murray make considerable use of the technique of correcting coefficients obtained in an empirical study to allow for restriction of range and for unreliability. The technique is explained in Chapter 3, where I point out that the technique depends crucially upon the assumption that the relation between test and performance scores is everywhere the same. However, as I argue in Chapter 3 and immediately above, mental competencies are not generally multivariate normally distributed. Instead, low competence seems to be general, but high competencies in one area of endeavor do not predict high competencies in other areas. Both the psychological theory of intelligence presented in Chapter 5 and the empirical data on expert performance (Ericsson and Smith, 1991) suggest that this should be so.

Why should this matter? Herrnstein and Murray's projections, and the literature that they review (including Hunter's (1986) meta-analysis), are largely based upon performance in jobs in the blue-collar and lower white-collar range. The same is true of the U.S. Army tests described in Chapter 3, which concentrated on performance of enlisted personnel during their first four years of military service. Similarly, in their analyses of their own data Herrnstein and Murray concentrate on such variables as being in poverty status, unemployment, or being in jail. As they point out, these unfortunate circumstances do not occur to most people. By concentrating on the lower end of performance in the workforce, Herrnstein and Murray probably overestimate the importance of intelligence in the workforce as a whole.

I am not arguing that economic success does not require intelligence. What I am arguing is that the upper white-collar, professional, and managerial jobs probably require a threshold of intelligence, somewhere around the 110 to 120 range. Beyond that level intelligence certainly helps, but motivation to work and opportunity to learn become increasingly important.

My next qualification has to do with the distinction between learning to do a job and doing it. A great deal of data (including some reviewed, but not in depth, by Herrnstein and Murray) shows that the correlations between intelligence and performance are higher while people are learning to do a job than when they are performing something that they know how to do. This does not mean that intelligence is unimportant, because you never get to perform on a job that you cannot learn to do. Nevertheless, the distinction between learning and doing becomes quite important when you combine it with the fact that the workforce is aging. As pointed out in Chapter 4, we can expect the future workforce to have a lower supply of fluid intelligence than the past workforce has had, as Herrnstein and Murray predict, but to have a greater supply of crystallized intelligence. To put this in practical terms, if we can find general problem-solving and learning-to-learn techniques, and if we can train people to use them, then we can avoid the implications of Herrnstein and Murray's analysis by shifting workplace performance from fluid to crystallized intelligence. This is going to be hard to do, but I do not see it as impossible.

This brings us to the issue of modifiability of intelligence. Herrnstein and Murray argue that a variety of enrichment programs have not shown prolonged improvement in intelligence test scores, with the possible exception of programs that they feel are too expensive to be introduced throughout the country.

I disagree, on two counts. First, the issue is not improving intelligence, as indicated by intelligence test scores, but rather it is improving a person's problem-solving skills. Such improvements can be made, especially within a particular domain, such as statistical reasoning, physics, history, or the like. Chapter 7 presents a detailed, theoretically motivated account of how this might be done. Rather than repeat the details of this program, let me make a simple point. Modern education, though much maligned, turns out problem-solvers who can deal with problems that baffled our predecessors. I, and thousands of other statistics instructors, routinely train students to solve statistical problems that baffled such intellectual giants as Pascal, Gauss, and Galton. Why? Because we teach them culturally developed problem-solving techniques (crystallized intelligence again!) that can substitute for the very considerable fluid intelligence that would be required to solve the problems from scratch.

I also refuse to accept one of Herrnstein and Murray's implicit constraints. They argue that the only programs that make much of a dent in problem-solving ability are programs that are too expensive for the schools. In fact, though, these programs are far less costly than many of our expenditures on defense or even sports. Why are our present limits on educational expenses set in stone? This is not an argument to spend more money on the present educational establishment. It is an argument for spending *enough* money to produce an excellent but different establishment. As I point out in Chapter 7, there are many things that we can do to improve cognitive capabilities—if we have the political will to do them.

I agree completely with Herrnstein and Murray's point about our increasingly complex world. In the future, intelligence will count for more than it has in the past. This point is developed in detail in Chapter 6.

Finally, what about their conclusions? Here it is useful to distinguish between conclusions that seem to be driven by scientific facts and conclusions that are driven more by social values.

Herrnstein and Murray conclude that as we make more use of information technology there will be an increasing differentiation of the workforce into the economic haves and have-nots. I agree. So have other observers; notably, President Clinton's Secretary of Labor, Robert Reich. This is a serious issue.

Herrnstein and Murray's conclusion that the cognitive elite should arrange for a simpler, more restricted life for the non-elite seems to me more politically than scientifically motivated. Their argument for a shift of decision making to local levels, to ensure more humane governance of society, is similarly a political conclusion. I do not say that it is right or wrong. The debate is not a scientific one.

On the one hand, their conclusion is an aphorism. Who could be against simplifying technology so that it is easier to use? However, it is not obvious to me that simplification is inevitably linked to a reduction in the power of centralized bureaucracy, as Herrnstein and Murray argue. I would prefer to put it a rather different way. As Chapter 6 points out, advances in computers and communication make it possible for central bureaucracies to increase their span of control, providing that the decision makers are willing to rely on the sort of information that can be put into a computer. Such information is sometimes more reliable than hunches and personal knowledge, and sometimes it is not. Central bureaucracies can be difficult to deal with, but local governments can be held captive to local prejudices. We need to think, much harder than we have, about the advantages of centralization versus local control in both the private and public sectors. Beyond that, though, it is difficult to say anything very general.

Now what about affirmative action? Herrnstein and Murray think we are on the horns of a dilemma, because there is no way that we can decrease the difference between the intelligence test scores of majority and minority group members. I believe that if we make a concerted effort, we can increase the supply of cognitive skills in minority group members. I do not care what happens to test scores, per se. It is skills that matter, and these can be taught. But the cost of programs to develop thinking will not be small. Furthermore, the effort must be governed by realism. Programs do not necessarily work because we want them to work or because it would be politically convenient to say that they have worked. Also, as I have argued in Chapter 4 and more in Chapter 7, the issue is one of instilling values and motivation as much as it is one of offering training. To use slang terms, when it comes to improving the cognitive skills of the workforce, this is an area where *everyone*, whites and blacks, Latinos and Anglos, government programs and private enterprise, has got to get their act together. We do not know the perfect way to proceed. We do know how to do some things that will help. Let us make the effort (and spend the money) to do them.

NOTE

1. It is conceivable that studies in molecular genetics will associate specific genes with superior or, as is more likely, inferior cognitive performance. In that case, it would be possible to discuss differences in intelligence associated with differences in gene frequencies in different population groups. I see no point in speculating about what yet-undone studies are likely to find. Certainly one should not recommend public policies based on these speculations! Yet this is what Herrnstein and Murray seem to do.

References

Ackerman, P. L. (1986). Individual differences in information processing: An investigation of intellectual abilities and task performance during practice. *Intelligence, 10,* 101–139.

Ackerman, P. L. (1987). Individual differences in skill learning: An integration of psychometric and information processing perspectives. *Psychological Bulletin, 102*(1), 3–27.

Ackerman, P. L. (1988). Determinants of individual differences during skill acquisition: Cognitive abilities and information processing. *Journal of Experimental Psychology: General, 117*(3), 288–318.

Ackerman, P. L., and Humphreys, L. G. (1991). Individual differences theory in industrial and organizational psychology. In M. D. Dunnette and L. M. Hough (Eds.), *Handbook of industrial and organizational psychology* (Vol. 1). Palo Alto, CA: Consulting Psychologists Press.

Anderson, J. R. (1983). *The architecture of cognition.* Cambridge, MA: Harvard University Press.

Anderson, J. R. (1987). Skill acquisition: Compilation of weak-method problem solutions. *Psychological Review, 94*(2), 192–210.

Anderson, J. R., Boyle, C. F., and Reiser, B. J. (1985). Intelligent tutoring systems. *Science, 228,* 456–462.

Baddeley, A. (1968). A three minute reasoning test based on grammatical transformation. *Psychonomic Science, 10,* 341–342.

Baddeley, A. (1986). *Working memory.* Oxford: Oxford University.

Baddeley, A. (1992). Working memory. *Science, 255,* 556–559.

Bahrick, H. P., and Hall, L. K. (1991). Lifetime maintenance of high school mathematics content. *Journal of Experimental Psychology: General, 120,* 20–33.

Balan, B. (1987). The technological transformation of white collar work: A case study of the insurance industry. In H. I. Hartman (Ed.), *Computer chips and paper clips: Technology and women's employment. Volume II. Case studies and policy perspectives.* Washington, DC: National Academy Press.

Baron, J. (1988). *Thinking and deciding.* Cambridge: Cambridge University Press.

Bassok, M., and Holyoak, K. J. (1989). Interdomain transfer between isomorphic topics in algebra and physics. *Journal of Experimental Psychology: Memory, Learning, and Cognition, 15*(1), 153–166.

Bechtel, W. (1988). *Philosophy of the mind: An overview for cognitive science.* Hillsdale, NJ: Erlbaum.

Benbow, C. P. (1988). Sex differences in mathematical reasoning ability in intellectually talented preadolescents. Their nature, effects, and possible causes. *Behavioral and Brain Sciences, 11,* 169–232.

Bikson, T. K., and Eveland, J. D. (1990). The interplay of work group structures and computer support. In J. Galegher, R. E. Kraut, & C. Egido (Eds.), *Intellectual teamwork: Social and technological foundations of cooperative work* (pp. 245–290). Hillsdale, NJ: Erlbaum.

Binet, A., and Simon, T. (1916). *The development of intelligence in children.* (E. S. Kite, Trans.) Baltimore: Williams & Wilkins.

Bloom, A. (1987). *The closing of the American mind.* New York: Simon & Schuster.

Brody, N. (1992). *Intelligence (2nd ed.).* San Diego, CA: Academic Press.

Bruer, J. T. (1993). *Schools for thought: A science of learning in the classroom.* Cambridge, MA: The MIT Press.

Bureau of the Census (1991). *Statistical abstract of the United States.* Washington, DC: U.S. Government Printing Office.

Bureau of the Census (1992). *Statistical abstract of the United States.* Washington, DC: U.S. Government Printing Office.

Campbell, C. H., Ford, P., Rumsey, M. G., Pulakos, E. D., Borman, W. C., Felker, D. B., De Vera, M. V., and Riegelhaupt, B. J. (1990). Development of job performance measures in a representative sample of jobs. *Personnel Psychology, 1943,* 277–300.

Campbell, J. P. (1990). An overview of the army selection and classification project (Project A). *Personnel Psychology, 43,* 231–239.

Campbell, J. P., McHenry, J. J., and Wise, L. L. (1990). Modeling job performance in a population of jobs. *Personnel Psychology, 43,* 313–333.

Caplan, N., Choy, M. H., and Whitmore, J. K. (1992). Indochinese refugee families and academic achievement. *Scientific American, 266*(2), 36–42.

Carpenter, P. A., and Just, M. A. (1975). Sentence comprehension. A processing model of verification. *Psychological Review, 82,* 45–73.

Carpenter, P. A., Just, M. A., and Shell, P. (1990). What one intelligence test measures: A theoretical account of processing in the Raven Progressive Matrix Test. *Psychological Review, 97*(3), 404–431.

Carroll, J. B. (1982). The measurement of intelligence. In R. J. Sternberg (Ed.), *Handbook of human intelligence* (pp. 29–122). Cambridge: Cambridge University Press.

Carroll, J. B. (1987). The national assessments in reading: Are we misreading the findings? *Phi Delta Kappan,* February, 424–430.

Carroll, J. B. (1993). *Human cognitive abilities.* Cambridge: Cambridge University Press.

Cascio, W. F. (1987). *Costing human resources: The financial impact of behavior in organizations (2nd ed.).* Boston: PW-Kent.

Cattell, R. B. (1971). *Abilities: Their structure, growth, and action.* Boston: Houghton Mifflin.

Cauce, A. M., Comer, J. P., and Schwartz, D. (1987). Long term effects of a systems-oriented school prevention program. *American Journal of Orthopsychiatry, 57,* 127–131.

Charness, N. (1989). Expertise in chess and bridge. In D. Klahr & K. Kotovsky (Eds.), *Complex information processing: The impact of Herbert A. Simon* (pp. 183–208). Hillsdale, NJ: Erlbaum.

Charness, N. (1991). Expertise in chess. The balance between knowledge and search. In K. A. Ericsson and J. Smith (Eds.), *Toward a general theory of expertise: Prospects and limits* (pp. 39–63). Hillsdale, NJ: Erlbaum.

Cheng, P. W., and Holyoak, K. J. (1985). Pragmatic reasoning schemas. *Cognitive Psychology, 17*(4), 391–416.

Cheng, P. W., Holyoak, K. J., Nisbett, R. E., and Oliver, L. M. (1986). Pragmatic versus syntactic approaches to training deductive reasoning. *Cognitive Psychology, 18,* 293–328.

Chi, M. T. H., Feltovich, P. J., and Glaser, R. (1981). Categorization and representation of physics problems by experts and novices. *Cognitive Science, 5*(2), 121–152.

Chi, M. T. H., Glaser, R., and Farr, M. J. (1988). *The nature of expertise.* Hillsdale, NJ: Erlbaum.

Clark, H. H., and Chase, W. G. (1972). On the process of comparing sentences against pictures. *Cognitive Psychology, 3,* 472–517.

Clement, J. (1982). Students' preconceptions in introductory mechanics. *American Journal of Physics, 50,* 66–71.

Cole, R. E. (1992). Issues in skill formation in Japanese approaches to management. In P. Adler (Ed.), *Technology and the future of work.* Oxford: Oxford University Press.

Comer, J. P. (1980). *School power. Implications of an intervention project.* New York: The Free Press.

Commission on Skills of the American Workforce (CSWF). (1990). *America's choice: High skills or low wages?* Rochester, NY: National Center on Education and the Economy.

Cronbach, L. J., and Gleser, G. (1965). *Psychological tests and personnel decisions.* Urbana: University of Illinois Press.

Dawes, R. M., Faust, D., and Meehl, P. E. (1989). Clinical vs. actuarial judgement. *Science, 243,* 1668–1674.

Department of Labor. (1988). *Opportunity 2000.* Washington, DC: U.S. Government Printing Office.

Departments of Labor, Education, and Commerce (DLEC). (1988). *Building a quality workforce.* Washington, DC: U.S. Government Printing Office.

Detterman, D., and Daniel, M. (1989). Correlations of mental tests with each other and with cognitive variables are highest for low IQ groups. *Intelligence, 13,* 349–360.

Dunbar, S. B., and Linn, R. L. (1992). Range restriction adjustments in the prediction of military job performance. In A. K. Wigdor and B. F. Green (Eds.) *Performance assessment in the workplace: Vol. II.* Washington, DC: National Academy Press.

Dreyfus, H. L., and Dreyfus, S. E. (1986). *Mind over machine: The power of human intuition and expertise in the era of the computer.* New York: Harper.

Edwards, A. (1984). *An introduction to linear regression and correlation (2nd ed.).* San Francisco: Freeman.

Egido, C. (1990). Teleconferencing as a technology to support cooperative work: Its possibilities and limitations. In J. Galegher, R. E. Kraut, and C. Egido (Eds.), *Intellectual teamwork: Social and technological foundations of cooperative work* (pp. 351–372). Hillsdale, NJ: Erlbaum.

Ellis, A. W., and Young, A. W. (1988). *Human cognitive neuropsychology.* Hillsdale, NJ: Erlbaum.

Ericsson, K. A., Krampe, R. Th., and Tesch-Romer, C. (1993). The role of deliberate practice in the acquisition of expert performance. *Psychological Review, 100,* 363–406.

Ericsson, K. A., and Smith, J. (1991). *Toward a general theory of expertise: Prospects and limits.* Cambridge: Cambridge University Press.

Eysenck, H. J. (1986). The theory of intelligence and the psychophysiology of cognition. In R. J. Sternberg (Ed.), *Advances in the Psychology of Intelligence* (Vol. 3, pp. 1–34). Hillsdale, NJ: Erlbaum.

Feurstein, R., Rand, Y., Hoffman, M., and Miller, R. (1980). *Instructional enrichment.* Baltimore: University Park Press.

Fincher, J. (1976). *Human intelligence.* New York: Putnam.

Fleishman, E. A. (1972). On the relation between abilities, learning, and human performance. *American Psychologist, 27,* 1017–1032.

Fong, G. T., and Nisbett, R. E. (1991). Immediate and delayed transfer of training effects in statistical reasoning. *Journal of Experimental Psychology: General, 120,* 34–45.

Ford, J. K., Kraiger, K., and Schectman, S. L. (1986). Study of race effects in objective indices and subjective evaluations of performance: A meta-analysis of performance criteria. *Psychological Bulletin, 99,* 330–337.

Ford, K. M., Bradshaw, J. M., Adams-Webber, J. R., and Agnew, N. M. (1993). Knowledge acquisition as a constructive modeling activity. *International Journal of Intelligent Machine Systems, 8,* 9–32.

Gardner, H. (1983). *Frames of mind: The theory of multiple intelligences.* New York: Basic Books.

Gick, M. L., and Holyoak, K. J. (1980). Analogical problem solving. *Cognitive Psychology 12,* 306–355.

Gick, M. L., and Holyoak, K. J. (1983). Schema induction and analogical transfer. *Cognitive Psychology 15,* 1–38.

Glaser, R., and Bassok, M. (1989). Learning theory and the study of instruction. *Annual Review of Psychology, 40,* 631–666.

Greeno, J. G. (1989). Situations, mental models, and generative action. In D. Klahr and K. Kotovsky (Eds.), *Complex information processing: The impact of Herbert A. Simon* (pp. 285–318). Hillsdale, NJ: Erlbaum.

Gustafsson, J. E. (1988). Hierarchical models of individual differences in cognitive abilities. In R. J. Sternberg (Ed.), *Advances in the psychology of human intelligence* (Vol. 4, pp. 35–72). Hillsdale, NJ: Erlbaum.

Hakel, M. (Ed.). (1993). *The changing nature of work. Human capital initiative report 1.* Bowling Green State University. Bowling Green, OH: Human Capital Initiative Co-ordinating Committee, Psychology Department.

Halberstam, D. (1991). *The next century.* New York: William Morrow.

Halpern, D. F. (1992). *Sex differences in cognitive ability (2nd ed.).* Hillsdale, NJ: Erlbaum.

Hartigan, J. A., and Wigdor, A. K. (Eds.). (1989). *Fairness in employment testing: Validity, generalization, minority issues, and the General Aptitude Test battery.* Washington, DC: National Academy Press.

Hartman H. I. (Ed.). (1987). *Computer chips and paper clips: Technology and women's employment.* Vol. II. *Case studies and policy perspectives.* Washington, DC: National Academy Press.

Hartman, H. I., Kraut, R. E., and Tilly, L. A. (1986). *Computer chips and paper clips* (Vol. I). Washington, DC: National Academy Press.

Hegarty, M., Just, M. A., and Morrison, I. R. (1988). Mental models of mechanical systems: Individual differences in quantitative and qualitative reasoning. *Cognitive Psychology, 28,* 191–236.

Herrnstein, R. J., and Murray, C. (1994). *The bell curve: Intelligence and class structure in American life.* New York: Free Press.

Hirsch, E. D., Jr. (1987). *Cultural illiteracy: What every American needs to know.* Boston: Houghton Mifflin.

Holyoak, K. J., and Koh, K. (1987). Surface structure and similarity in analogical transfer. *Memory and Cognition, 15,* 332–340.

Horn, J. L. (1985). Remodeling old models of intelligence. In B. B. Wolman (Ed.). *Handbook of intelligence. Theories, measurements, and applications* (pp. 267–300). New York: Wiley.

Horn, J. L. (1986). Intellectual ability concepts. In R. J. Sternberg (Ed.), *Advances in the psychology of human intelligence* (Vol. 3, pp. 35–77). Hillsdale, NJ: Erlbaum.

Howard, A., and Bray, D. W. (1988). *Managerial lives in transition: Advancing age and changing times.* New York: Guilford Press.

Humphreys, L. G. (1988). Trends in levels of academic achievement of blacks and other minorities. *Intelligence, 12,* 231–260.

Hunt, E. (1974). Quote the raven? Nevermore. In L. E. Gregg (Ed.), *Knowledge and cognition.* Potomac, MD: Erlbaum.

Hunt, E. (1983). On the nature of intelligence. *Science, 219,* 141–146.

Hunt, E. (1987). The next word on verbal ability. In P. A. Vernon (Ed.), *Speed of information processing and intelligence.* New York: Ablex.

Hunt, E. (in press). *Thoughts on thought: Theoretical issues in the study of cognition.* Hillsdale, NJ: Erlbaum.

Hunt, E., and Luce, R. D. (1992). SOAR as a world view, not a theory. *Behavioral and Brain Sciences, 15,* 447–448.

Hunt, E., and Minstrell, J. (1993). A cognitive approach to the teaching of physics. In K. McGilly (Ed.), *Classroom lessons: integrating cognitive theory and classroom practice.* Cambridge, MA: The MIT Press.

Hunt, E., Pellegrino, J. W., Frick, R. W., Farr, S. A., and Alderton, D. (1988). The ability to reason about movement in the visual field. *Intelligence, 12,* 77–100.

Hunter, J. E. (1986). Cognitive ability, cognitive aptitudes, job knowledge, and job performance. *Journal of Vocational Behavior, 29,* 340–362.

Hunter, J. E., and Hunter, R. F. (1984). Validity and utility of alternative predictors of job performance. *Psychological Bulletin, 96,* 72–78.

Hyde, J. S., Fennema, E., and Lamon, S. J. (1990). Gender differences in mathematics performance. A meta-analysis. *Psychological Bulletin, 107,* 139–155.

Hyde, J. S., and Linn, M. C. (1988). Gender differences in verbal ability: A meta-analysis. *Psychological Bulletin, 104,* 53–69.

Jagannathan, V., Dodhiawara, R., and Baum, L. S. (Eds.). (1989). *Blackboard architectures and applications.* San Diego, CA: Academic Press.

Jaynes, G. D., and Williams, R. M., Jr. (Eds.). (1989). *Blacks and American society.* Washington, DC: National Academy Press.

Jensen, A. R. (1980). *Bias in mental testing.* New York: Free Press.

Jensen, A. R. (1982). The chronometry of intelligence. In R. J. Sternberg (Ed.), *Advances in the psychology of human intelligence* (Vol. 1, pp. 255–310). Hillsdale, NJ: Erlbaum.

Jensen, A. R. (1985). The nature of the black-white difference on various psychometric tests: Spearman's hypothesis. *Behavioral and Brain Sciences, 8,* 193–263.

Johnson, C. D., Zeidner, J., and Scholarios, D. (1990). Improving the classification efficiency of the Armed Service Vocational Aptitude Battery through the use of alternative test selection indices. IDA Paper P-2427. Alexandria, VA: Institute for Defense Analysis.

Johnson, J. S., and Newport, E. (1989). Critical period effects in second language learning: The influence of maturational state on the acquisition of English as a second language. *Cognitive Psychology, 21,* 60–99.

Johnson-Laird, P. N., and Byrne, M. J. B. (1991). *Deduction.* Hillsdale, NJ: Erlbaum.

Johnston, W. B., and Packer, A. H. (1987). *Workforce 2000: Work and workers for the 21st century.* Indianapolis: Hudson Institute.

Just, M. A., and Carpenter, P. A. (1992). A capacity theory of comprehension: Individual differences in working memory. *Psychological Review, 99,* 122–149.

Kaplan, R. M. (1985). The controversy related to the use of psychological tests. In B. B. Wolman (Ed.), *Handbook of intelligence: Theory, measurement, and applications* (pp. 465–504). New York: Wiley-Interscience.

Katz, R. L. (1988). *The information society: An international perspective.* New York: Praeger.

Keichel, W., III. (1993). How we will work in the year 2000. *Fortune,* May 17.

Kennedy, P. (1987). *The rise and fall of the great powers.* New York: Random House.

Kirsch, I. S., Jungeblat, A., Jenkins, L., and Kolstad, A. (1993). *Adult Literacy in America. National Center for Education Statistics.* Washington, DC: U.S. Government Printing Office.

Klahr, D., and Kotovsky, K. (Eds.) (1989). *Complex information processing: The impact of Herbert A. Simon.* Hillsdale, NJ: Erlbaum.

Klahr, D., Langley, P., and Neches, R. (Eds.). (1987). *Production system models of learning and development.* Cambridge, MA: The MIT Press.

Kyllonen, P. C., and Christal, R. E. (1989). Cognitive modeling of learning abilities: A status report of LAMP. In R. Dillon & J. W. Pellegrino (Eds.), *Testing: Theoretical and applied issues.* New York: Freeman.

Kyllonen, P. C., and Christal, R. E. (1990). Reasoning ability is (little more than) working memory capacity?! *Intelligence, 14,* 389–434.

Laird, J. E., and Rosenbloom, P. S. (1992). In pursuit of the mind: The research of Allen Newell. *AI Magazine, 13*(4), 17–45.

Larkin, J. H., McDermott, J., Simon, D. P., and Simon, H. A. (1980). Expert and novice performance in solving physics problems. *Science, 208,* 1335–1342.

Larkin, J. H., Reif, F., Carbonell, J., and Gugliotta, A. (1988). FERMI: A flexible expert reasoner with multi-domain inferencing. *Cognitive Science, 12*(1), 101–138.

Lave, J. (1988). *Cognition in practice.* Cambridge: Cambridge University Press.

Lawrence, J. A. (1988). Expertise on the bench: Modeling magistrate's judicial decision making. In M. T. H. Chi, R. Glaser, and M. J. Farr (Eds.), *The nature of expertise* (pp. 229–260). Hillsdale, NJ: Erlbaum.

Lehman, D. R., Lempert, R. O., and Nisbett, R. E. (1988). The effects of graduate training on reasoning: Formal discipline and thinking about everyday life events. *American Psychologist, 43,* 431–443.

Lehman, D. R., and Nisbett, R. E. (1990). A longitudinal study of the effects of undergraduate education on reasoning. *Developmental Psychology, 26,* 952–960.

Levidow, B. B., Hunt, E., and McKee, C. (1991). *Behavior Research Methods, Instruments, and Computers, 23,* 249–252.

Loehlin, J. C., Lindzey, G., and Spuhler, J. N. (1975). *Race differences in intelligence.* San Francisco: Freeman.

Luria, A. R. (1976). *Cognitive development: Its cultural and social foundations* (Lopez-Morillas and Salotaroff, Transl.). Cambridge, MA: Harvard University Press.

McHenry, J. J., Hough, L. M., Toquam, J. L., Hanson, M. A., and Ashworth, S. (1990). Project A validity results: The relationship between predictor and criterion domains. *Personnel Psychology, 43,* 335–354.

MacLeod, C. M., Hunt, E., and Mathews, N. N. (1978). Individual differences in the verification of sentence-picture relationships. *Journal of Verbal Learning and Verbal Behavior, 17,* 493–507.

Marco, G. L., Crone, C. R., Braswell, J. S., Curley, W. E., and Wright, N. K. (1990). Trends in SAT content and statistical characteristics and their relationship to predictive validity. Research Report. Princeton, NJ: Educational Testing Service.

Marshall, R., and Tucker, M. (1992). *Thinking for a living: Education and the wealth of nations.* New York: Basic Books.

Mathews, N. N., Hunt, E., and MacLeod, C. M. (1980). Strategy choice and strategy training in sentence-picture verification. *Journal of Verbal Learning and Verbal Behavior, 19,* 531–538.

Mestre, J. P., Dufresne, R. J., Gerace, W. J., Hardiman, P. T., and Tougher, J. S. (1992). Enhancing higher-order thinking skills in physics. In D. F. Halpern (Ed.), *Enhancing thinking skills in the sciences and mathematics* (pp. 77–94). Hillsdale, NJ: Erlbaum.

Miller, G. A. (1988). The challenge of universal literacy. *Science, 241,* 1293–1299.

Moravec, H. (1988). *Mind children: The future of robot and human intelligence.* Cambridge, MA: Harvard University Press.

Morgan, R. (1990). Predictive validity within categorizations of college students: 1978, 1981, and 1985. Research Report. Princeton, NJ: Educational Testing Service.

Munnell, A. H. (1992). All work and no play? *Issues in Science and Technology, VII*(3), 80–83.

Murphy, K., and Welch, F. (1989). Wage premiums for college graduates: Recent growth and possible explanations. *Educational Researcher, 18*(4), 17–26.

National Academy of Sciences (NAS). (1984). *High school and the changing workplace.* Washington, DC: National Academy Press.

National Center for Educational Statistics (NCES). (1992). *Digest of educational statistics, 1992.* Washington, DC: U.S. Department of Education, NCES-91-660.

National Center on Education and the Economy (NCEE). (1991a). America's Choice: High skills or low wages! Supporting documents: Vol. I—International research. Rochester, NY: National Center on Education and the Economy.

National Center on Education and the Economy (NCEE). (1991b). America's Choice: High skills or low wages! Supporting documents: Vol. II—Industry research. Rochester, NY: National Center on Education and the Economy.

National Commission on Testing and Public Policy. (1990). *From gatekeeper to gateway: Transforming testing in America.* Chestnut Hill, MA: Boston College.

Nelson, T. O. (Ed.). (1992). *Metacognition: Core readings.* Boston: Allyn & Bacon.

Newell, A. (1990). *Unified theories of cognition.* Cambridge, MA: Harvard University Press.

Newell, A., and Simon, H. A. (1972). *Human problem solving.* Englewood Cliffs, NJ: Prentice-Hall.

Nickerson, R. S., Perkins, D. N., and Smith, E. E. (1985). *The teaching of thinking.* Hillsdale, NJ: Erlbaum.

Nissen, M. J., and Bullemer, P. (1987). Attentional requirements of learning: Evidence from performance measures. *Cognitive Psychology, 19,* 1–32.

Nissen, M. J., Knopman, D., and Schacter, D. L. (1987). Neurochemical dissociation of memory systems. *Neurology, 37,* 789–794.

Norman, D. A. (1993). Cognition in the head and in the world: An introduction to the special issue on situated action. *Cognitive Science, 17,* 1–6.

Office of Technology Assessment (OTA). (1990). *Worker training: Competing in the new international economy.* Washington, DC: U.S. Government Printing Office.

Olshansky, S. J., Carnes, B. A., and Cassel, C. K. (1993). The aging of the human species. *Scientific American, 268*(4), 46–53.

Packer, A. (1989). Preparing Workforce 2000. *Human Capital,* Nov.–Dec., 34–38.

Palmer, J., MacLeod, C. M., Hunt, E., and Davidson, J. (1985). Information processing correlates of reading. *Journal of Memory and Language, 24,* 59–88.

Peterson, N. G., Hough, L. M., Dunnette, M. D., Rosse, R. L., Houston, J. S., Toquam, J. L., and Wing, H. (1990). Project A: Specification and development of new selection/classification tests. *Personnel Psychology, 43,* 247–276.

Podgorsky, M. (1988). Job displacement and labor market adjustment: Evidence from the displaced worker surveys. In R. M. Cyert and D. C. Mowrey (Eds.), *The impact of technological changes on employment and economic growth.* Cambridge, MA: Ballinger.

Polya, G. (1954). *Mathematics of plausible reasoning* (Vols. I and II). Princeton: Princeton University Press.

Pylyshyn, Z. W. (1989). Computing in cognitive science. In M. I. Posner (Ed.), *Foundations of cognitive science* (pp. 49–92). Cambridge, MA: The MIT Press.

Raven, J. C., Court, J. H., and Raven, J. (1992). *Manual for Raven's Progressive Matrices and the Mill Hill Vocabulary Scales.* Oxford: Oxford Psychologists Press.

Reich, R. (1991). *The work of nations: Preparing ourselves for 21st century capitalism.* New York: Knopf.

Rosenberg, N. (1982). *Inside the black box: Technology and economics.* Cambridge: Cambridge University Press.

Salthouse, T. A. (1982). *Adult cognition: An experimental psychology approach to human aging.* New York: Springer-Verlag.

Salthouse, T. A. (1990). *Theoretical perspectives on cognitive aging.* Hillsdale, NJ: Erlbaum.

Salthouse, T. A. (1991). Mediation of adult age differences in cognition by reductions in working memory and speed of processing. *Psychological Science, 3,* 179–183.

Scaglia, G. (1991). Building the cathedral in Florence. *Scientific American, 264*(1), 66–72.

Schaafstal, A. M. (1991). *Diagnostic skill in process operation: A comparison between experts and novices.* Soesterberg, The Netherlands: Institute for Perception TNO.

Schacter, D. L. (1987). Implicit memory: History and current status. *Journal of Experimental Psychology: Learning, Memory, and Cognition, 13,* 501–518.

Schneider, W., and Shiffrin, R. M. (1977). Controlled and automatic processing: I. Detection, search, and attention. *Psychological Review, 84,* 1–6.

Schorr, J. B. (1991). *The overworked American: The unexpected decline of leisure.* New York: Basic Books.

Scribner, S. (1984). Studying working intelligence. In B. Rogoff and J. Lave (Eds.), *Everyday cognition* (pp. 9–40). Cambridge, MA: Harvard University Press.

Scribner, S. (1986). Thinking. Some characteristics of practical thought. In R. J. Sternberg and R. K. Wagner (Eds.), *Practical intelligence: Nature and origins of competence in the everyday world* (pp. 13–30). Cambridge: Cambridge University Press.

Scribner, S., and Sachs, P. (1989). A study of on-the-job training. Final report to the National Center on Education and Employment. Laboratory for Cognitive Studies of Work. New York: Graduate School and University Center of the City University of New York.

Searle, J. R. (1992). *The rediscovery of the mind.* Cambridge: MIT Press.

Secretary's Commission on Achieving Necessary Skills (SCANS). (1991). What work requires of our schools. U.S. Department of Labor, June.

Shallice, T. (1988). *From neuropsychology to mental structure.* Cambridge: Cambridge University Press.

Shapira, P. (1992). Lessons from Japan: Helping small manufacturers. *Issues in Science and Technology, VII*(3), 66–72.

Simon, H. A., and Chase, W. G. (1973). Skill in chess. *American Scientist, 61,* 394–403.

Simon, H. A., and Kaplan, C. A. (1989). Foundations of cognitive science. In M. I. Posner (Ed.), *Foundations of cognitive science* (pp. 1–47). Cambridge, MA: MIT Press.

Simonton, D. K. (1988). *Scientific genius: A psychology of science.* Cambridge: Cambridge University Press.

Singley, M. K., and Anderson, J. R. (1989). *The transfer of cognitive skill.* Cambridge, MA: Harvard University Press.

Skinner, B. F. (1953). *Science and human behavior.* New York: Macmillan.

Skinner, B. F. (1990). Can psychology be a science of mind? *American Psychologist, 45,* 1206–1209.

Sloboda, J. (1991). Presentation at International Conference on Cognitive Expertise. University of Aberdeen. Aberdeen, Scotland. August.

Snow, R. E. (1986). Individual differences and the design of educational programs. *American Psychologist, 41,* 1029–1039.

Snow, R. E., Kyllonen, P. C., and Marshalek, B. (1984). The topography of ability and learning correlations. In R. J. Sternberg (Ed.), *Advances in the psychology of human intelligence* (Vol. 2, pp. 47–103). Hillsdale, NJ: Erlbaum.

Snow, R. E., and Yalow, E. (1982). Education and Intelligence. In R. J. Sternberg (Ed.), *Handbook of human intelligence* (pp. 493–585). Cambridge: Cambridge University Press.

Spearman, C. (1904). General intelligence, objectively determined and measured. *American Journal of Psychology, 15,* 201–293.

Spearman, C. (1923). *The nature of "intelligence" and the principles of cognition.* London: Macmillan.

Sperber, M. (1988). *College sports inc.: The athletic department vs. the university.* New York: Holt.

Spoehr, K. T. (1993). Enhancing the acquisition of conceptual structures through hypermedia. In K. McGilly (Ed.), *Classroom lessons: Integrating cognitive theory and classroom practice.* Cambridge, MA: The MIT Press.

Sproull, L., and Kiesler, S. (1991). Computers, networks, and work. *Scientific American, 265*(3), 116–123.

Squire, L. (1987). *Memory and brain.* Oxford: Oxford University Press.

Steele, C. M. (1992). Race and the schooling of black Americans. *The Atlantic, 269*(4), 68–78.

Sternberg, R. J. (1977). *Intelligence, information processing, and analogical reasoning.* Hillsdale, NJ: Erlbaum.

Sternberg, R. J. (1986). Introduction: The nature and scope of practical intelligence. In R. J. Sternberg and R. K. Wagner (Eds.), *Practical intelligence: Nature and origins of competence in the everyday world* (pp. 1–12). Cambridge: Cambridge University Press.

Sternberg, R. J. (1990). *Metaphors of mind: Conceptions of the nature of intelligence.* Cambridge: Cambridge University Press.

Stevenson, H. W., Lee, S.-Y., and Stigler, J. W. (1986). Mathematics achievement of Chinese, Japanese, and American children. *Science, 231,* 693–699.

Sticht, T. G. (1975). *Reading for working.* Alexandria, VA: Human Resources Research Organization.

Stigler, J. W., and Perry, M. (1988). Mathematics learning in Japanese, Chinese, and American classrooms. In G. B. Saxe & M. Gearhart (Eds.), *Children's mathematics* (pp. 27–54). San Francisco: Jossey-Bass.

Suchman, L. (1987). *Plans and situated actions: The problem of human-machine communication.* Cambridge: Cambridge University Press.

Sue, S., and Okazaki, S. (1990). Asian American educational achievements: A phenomenon in search of an explanation, *American Psychologist, 45,* 913–920.

Taylor, H. C., and Russell, J. T. (1939). The relationship of validity coefficients to the practical effectiveness of tests in selection: Discussions and tables. *Journal of Applied Psychology, 23,* 565–578.

Tversky, A., and Kahneman, D. (1971). Belief in the law of small numbers. *Psychological Bulletin, 76,* 105–110.

U.S. Department of Labor. 1983(a). The dimensionality of the general aptitude test battery and the dominance of general factors over specific factors for the prediction of job performance for the U.S. Employment Service. USES Test Research Report No. 44. Division of Counseling and Test Development, Employment and Training Administration. Washington, DC: U.S. Department of Labor.

U.S. Department of Labor. 1983(b). Test validation for 12,000 jobs: An application of job classification and validity generalization analysis to the General Aptitude Test Battery. USES Test Research Report No. 45. Division of Counseling and Test Development, Employment and Training Administration. Washington, DC: U.S. Department of Labor.

Vera, A., and Simon, H. A. (1993). Situated action: A symbolic interpretation. *Cognitive Science, 17,* 7–48.

Vernon, P. A. (1983). Speed of information processing and general intelligence. *Intelligence, 7,* 53–70.

Vygotsky, L. S. (1962). *Thought and language.* Cambridge, MA: The MIT Press.

Wagner, R. K. (1991). Managerial Problem Solving. In R. J. Sternberg and P. Frentsch (Eds.), *Complex problem solving: Principles and mechanisms* (pp. 159–183). Hillsdale, NJ: Erlbaum.

Wechsler, D. (1981). *The WAIS-R Manual.* New York: Harcourt Brace Jovanovich.

Wegmann, R., Chapman, R., and Johnson, M. (1989). *Work in the new economy.* Alexandria, VA: American Association for Counseling and Development.

Wenger, E. (1987). *Artificial intelligence and tutoring systems.* Los Altos, CA: Morgan Kaufmann.

Wigdor, A. K., and Green, B. F., Jr. (1991). *Performance assessment in the workplace* (Vol. I). Washington, DC: National Academy Press.

Wise, L. L., McHenry, J. J., and Campbell, J. P. (1990). Identifying optimal predictor composites and testing for generalizability across jobs and performance factors. *Personnel Psychology, 43,* 355–366.

Wolf, S. M. (1991). The sustainable society. *Vis à Vis Magazine.* United Airlines, January, p. 10.

Wortman, M. S., Jr., and Sperling, J. (1975). *Defining the manager's job (6th ed.).* New York: AMACOM.

Yee, P. L., Hunt, E., and Pellegrino, J. W. (1991). Co-ordinating cognitive information: Task effects and individual differences in integrating information from several sources. *Cognitive Psychology, 23,* 615–680.

Zeidner, J., and Johnson, C. D. (1989). The utility of selection for military and civilian jobs. IDA Paper P-2239. Alexandria, VA: Institute for Defense Analysis.

Zuboff, S. (1989). *In the age of the smart machine: The future of work and power.* New York: Basic Books.

Zuckerman, E. (1991). Toshiba research: Combining the practical and the exotic. *Scientific American, 264*(1)—advertising supplement.

Zue, V., Glass, J., Goodine, D., Leung, H., Phillips, M., Polifroni, J., and Seneff, S. (1990). The VOYAGER Speech Understanding System: Preliminary development and evaluation. *Trans. Institute of Electrical and Electronics Engineering, CH2847*(2), 73–79.

Index

Entries in **boldface** refer to figures and tables.

abilities. *See* cognitive skills; logical reasoning ability; mathematical ability; nonverbal ability; reading ability; talent; verbal ability; visual-spatial ability

abstract reasoning: sex differences, 138

achievement tests. *See* psychometrics

Ackerman, P. L., 67, 83*n*, 193, 243, 297

Adams-Webber, J. R., 301

adaptability. *See* flexibility, importance of in future workplace

administrative workers: technological change and, 211–214

adult education. *See* continuing education; postsecondary education; vocational training

affirmative action, 113, 295

AFQT. *See* Armed Forces Qualification Test (AFQT)

African Americans: children, low expectations of, 278; cognitive skills, comparison of to other groups, 117–121; educational attainment, 21, 26, 109; future workforce, in, 108, 136, 142–144; high school dropouts, 23; intelligence test scores, 115–116, 289–290; literacy, adult, 27; mathematical ability, 30, 32; median family income, 15, 113–114; middle class, 127; poverty level, 15; reading ability, 28, **118–119**, 123; within-group variations in test scores, 127–128; workforce participation, 19

age 35–54: future workforce, 109, **110**

age differences: cognitive skills, 18; crystallized intelligence, 139; literacy, adult, 27; workforce participation, 17–18, **18.** *See also* aging of workforce

age distribution: future workforce, **110**

aging of workforce: cognitive effects of aging, 109–113, 251; crystallized intelligence and, 111–113; displacement of senior workers, 40; fluid intelligence and, 111–113; forecasting, 108; intelligence test scores, changes in, **111**; retraining, 251, 269

Agnew, N. M., 301

aircraft: computerization, 225–226, 232–233; fly by wire commercial aircraft, 225–226, 232

chess masters: cognitive psychology, example of, 179–180; fluid intelligence, example of, 53; practice of, 242

Chi, M. T. H., 184–185, 299, 304

chief executive officers: salaries, 105

child care, 136

choice reaction time (CRT), 158–167; air traffic controller example, 161–162, 163; city attorney example, 165–167; information processing, 160–162; landing signal officer example, 165–167; learning, performance and, 193; pulley example of, 162–164; schematic of, **159**; travel agent example, 164–165, 196n; U.S. postal service example, 159–160; wine taster example, 165–167

Choy, M. H., 258, 286n, 298

Christal, R. E., 162, 170, **171**, 174–175, 304

Chunnel, creation of, 204, 232

city attorney example, 165–167

Clark, H. H., 174, 177, 299

Clement, J., 272, 299

clerical workers: income, 15. *See also* secretaries; typists

clerks: IQ scores, 103

Clinton, President Bill: career changes, on, 152; retraining, on need for, 1, 4, 33, 269–270

cognition: aging, effects of, 109–113, 251; changes in the workforce, racial and ethnic differences in cognitive effects of, 113–139; competence, indicators of, 23–32; literacy, adult, 26–27; metacognitive ability, 254, 278–279; psychometrics and, 43, 45–47. *See also* cognitive psychology; cognitive skills; thinking

cognitive elite, 245

cognitive psychology, 152–197; Air Force, training of pilots, 170, **171**, 175; air traffic controllers, 161–162, 163, 168–170; automated response, 193, 195; automatic learning task, **189**; blackboard model of thought, 180–183, 198; bobsled problem, schematic reasoning,

185; carpenters, problem solving of, 172–174; chess master example, 53, 179–180, 242; choice reaction time (CRT), 158–167; city attorney example of choice reaction time, 165–167; cognitive components approach, 154; cognitive task analysis, 158, 178; computer simulation, 170; conflict resolution rule, 181; controlled response, 193, 195; declarative knowledge, 156, 165, 189–190; deep structure, 164, 185; described, 5, 40–41; epistemological thinking, 169–172; expertise, acquiring of, 164; FERMI program, 186; functional level of thinking, 167–172; information processing, 160–162, 168–170; knowledge-based problem solving, 183–188; landing signal officer example of choice reaction time, 165–167; language skills, 156; learning, performance and, 188–194; levels of thinking, 167–170; linguistic processing, 168; long-term memory, 155–156, 162, 169, 171, 173–174, 180–181, 183, 251; philosophy of, 153–154; physiological alteration of person, 196n; physiological level of thinking, 167–169; problem solving, 154, 170–178, 183–188; procedural knowledge, 156, 171, 189–190, 193; production system, 169; productivity, performance evaluations and, **157**; psychometrics and, 153–158; pulley example of choice reaction time, 162–164; recognition, 168; representational level of thinking, 167, 169–170, 172; schema, development of, 194–195; schematic reasoning, 183–186; short-term memory, 169; specialized thinking, 179; surface characteristics, 164; system architecture, 180; thinking, theory of, 167–183; travel agent example of choice reaction time, 164–165, 196n; trigonometric approach to problem solving, 172–173; understanding and learning, 190–192;

U.S. postal service as choice reaction time (CRT) example, 159–160; verbal ability, 154–156; wine taster example of choice reaction time, 165–167; working-memory, 156, 162, 168–170, 173–175, 180–182, 186–188, 251

cognitive skills: age differences in, 18; characteristics of workforce, 20–32; chess master example, 53, 179–180, 242; dairy worker example, 178–179, 183, 185–186, 251; demographic trends, 108–109; ethnic groups, distribution across, 115–122; job classes, influence of differences in cognition on distribution across, 122–130; sex differences, 136–139; talents, distribution across ethnic groups, 115–122; trade-offs in cognitive abilities, 178–180. *See also* thinking

cognitive testing. *See* psychometrics

cold war: ending of, 199; military spending, 8

Cole, R. E., 219, 299–300

College Board, 86

colleges and universities: computerization, 216–217, 225; international

comparisons, enrollment, 265–266; minorities, enrollment in, 106n; psychometric testing, reasons for, 45–46; quality of education, 266. *See also* faculty of colleges and universities; postsecondary training

Comer, J. P., 258, 299

Commission on the Skills of the American Workforce (CSWF), 15, 24–25, 33, 300

communication: central office, movability of, 10

communication technologies, 205

compensation. *See* earnings

competence: indicators of, 23–32

competence, mental. *See* intelligence

competition: indices of, 2; international, 284; military leadership and, 1; skills of workforce and, 3–4; wealth and, 7–8

computer-related fields, job opportunities, 35, 37

computers and computerization, 220–238; aircraft, 225–226, 232–233; airports, 234, 285; banking industry, 217–218, 221–223, 225–226, 246n ; building system, 227–231; computer knowledge, psychometric measurement of, 48; computer simulation, 170; credit cards, 222–223, 246n; decision-making, 234–236; education system in U.S. (K-12 system), 263–264, 286–287n; electronic, limitations, 246n; errors, 231-232; hierarchy of command, corporate, 215–216, 218–220; intelligent computer-aided instruction (ICAI) programs, 263–264, 281, 287n; inventory control, 209; jobs unlikely to be replaced by, 240–242; knowledge of, psychometric measurement, 48; mathematical operations, 224; neurosurgery, 232–233; piloting an airline and, 206–207, 209; programming language, 230; replacement of workers by, 238–240; sales positions and, 214–215, 241; sensory pattern recognition, 239; steps in moving to automation, **224**; system designers, 223–227; telecommunications, 235–238; universities, system for monitoring student progress, 225; university organizations, 216–217; use of systems, 232; world population model, 227–231. *See also* technological change

conflict resolution rule, cognitive psychology, 181

continuing education: impasse resolution principle, 267–270

controlled response, 193, 195

corporations: hierarchy of command, 215–216, 218–220

cost of labor, 43

Court, J. H., 100, 306

craft workers: income, 15

creative thinking: Washington State legislature law, 152

credit cards, 222–223, 246n

functional level of thinking, 167–169; epistemological approach, link with, 170–172

future workforce: age distribution, **110**; aging of, 108–113; crystallized intelligence, 139–141, 294; customizing products, 38–39; feminization of, 108; fluid intelligence, 139–141, 293–294; group representation in, calculation of, 142–144; minorities, 108; nature of work, changes in, 32–39; problem solving, 294; projections, 141–142; psychometrics and, 44, 108–151; qualified employees, 139–140, 151n, 283–284, 292; school enrollment, 21, 109; skills needed, 39–41, 108; verbal ability, 139; visual-spatial ability, 139

future workplace, 245; cognitive demands, 198–247; communication technologies, 205; education and preparation for, 33; equality of group outcome (EGO) policy of job placement for minorities, 114, 115, 122–133, 149–150; equality of individual opportunity (EIO) policy of job placement for minorities, 114, 115, 122–130, 145–149; feminization of, 136–139; flexibility, importance of, 242–243; job classes, influence of differences in cognition on distribution across, 122–130; preparation for, 248–287; prospects for future, 283–287; psychological skills, value of, 243–244; psychological view of, 238–244; replacement by computer, threat of, 238–240; talents, distribution across ethnic groups, 115–122; technological change and, 205–206

Galegher, J., 298, 300
Gardner, H., 50–52, 81, 82n, 107n, 301
GATB. *See* General Aptitude Test Battery (GATB)
Genentech, 201

General Aptitude Test Battery (GATB): aging, effect of, 112; Armed Services Vocational Aptitude Battery (ASVAB), comparison, 96–97; employee performance and, 85, 94–99; ethnic differences in scoring, 98, 121; intelligence tests, link with, 102; job referrals based on, 130; mental space representation, 54; problems with, 107n; regression analysis, 58; Scholastic Aptitude Test (SAT), comparison, 96–97; sentence verification in, 175; subtests, **95**, 96; validity coefficients, 65, 68–69, 97–98; The Wechsler Adult Intelligence Scale-Revised (WAIS- R), comparison, 99; workplace performance, correlation between scores and, 289

general intelligence. *See* intelligence
genetics: intelligence and, 289–290; molecular genetics, 296n
Gerace, W. J., 305
Germany: apprenticeship programs, 250, 268; average income, 7; gross domestic product, 7; productivity, distribution of, 16; skills of workforce, 3–4; unemployment, 17; vocational education, 22. *See also* West Germany
Gick, M. L., 191–192, 301
Glaser, R., 164, 184–185, 299, 301, 304
Glass, J., 310
Gleser, G., 78, 300
global economy, 284
global village, 238
Goodine, D., 310
grades: comparability of, 83n; Scholastic Aptitude Test (SAT) and, 106n
grammatical knowledge, 155
Green, B. F., Jr., 47, 54, 89, 93, 103, 309
Greeno, J. G., 250, 301
Gregg, L. E., 302
gross domestic product: international comparisons, 6, 7
gross national product: international comparisons, 6

formance, 85–107; selection, view of, **49**; selection ratio, 68–69; standard deviation, 57; standard model of, 50–51; statistical issues, 56–69; subjective measures, prediction of, 105; unfairness charge, 98, 121; unreliability, 63–65; validity coefficients, 49, 69–71, **75**, 75–76, **79**, 97–98, 103, 104; verbal ability, measurement of, 48, 50, 52–53; visual-spatial ability, measurement of, 48, 50, 52–53, 81, **106–107**; vocabulary tests, 52; workforce productivity, measurement of, 42–84. *See also* intelligence; intelligence tests; performance in workplace
psychomotor ability, 96, 99
Pulakos, E. D., 298
pulley example of choice reaction time, 162–164
purchasing power: United States, **6–7**
Pylyshyn, Z. W., 168, 169, 306

quota system. *See* equality of group outcome (EGO) policy of job placement for minorities

race differences: academic achievement, 277; changes in the workforce, cognitive effects of, 113–139; intelligence test scores, 115–116, 289–290, 295; job classes, influence of differences in cognition on distribution across, 122–130; reading ability, **118–119**. *See also* equality of group outcome (EGO) policy of job placement for minorities; equality of individual opportunity (EIO) of job placement for minorities
Rand, Y., 300
Raven, J. C., 100, 306
Raven Progressive Matrix Test, 99–104; fluid intelligence, measurement of, 85, 100–101; illustration, **101**; marker test, as, 103–104; productivity in workplace and, 102; working-memory and, 162

reading ability: African Americans, 28, **118–119,** 123; employer expectations, **202**; employment and, 201–202; ethnic differences, **118–119;** high school graduates, 109; Hispanics, 28, 123; international comparisons, 32; learning to read, 257; levels of reading, **28–29;** school children, 27–28; white-collar workers, 123
real estate agents, 35
recessions, 12, 33, 72
recognition, 168
registered nurses, 35
regression analysis, psychometrics, 56–62
Reich, R., 9, 16, 37–38, 199–200, 243, 295, 306
Reif, F., 186, 304
Reiser, B. J., 263, 297
representational level of thinking, 167, 169–170, 172
retail clerking, 33
retraining: aging population, 251, 269; Clinton, President Bill, on need for, 1, 4, 33, 269–270; impasse resolution principle, 267–270
Riegelhaupt, B. J., 298
robots: cognitive task analysis, 178; limitation of, 285; long-term memory, 155–156; manufacturing use, international comparisons, 219; memory and, 154–156; problem-solving abilities of, 183
Rogoff, B., 307
Rosenberg, N., 9, 306
Rosenbloom, P. S., 252, 304
Rosse, R. L., 306
Rumsey, M. G., 298
Russell, J. T., 309
Russia: immigration, 9. *See also* Soviet Union

Sachs, P., 209, 307
salary. *See* earnings
sales positions: computerization and, 214–215, 241
Salthouse, T. A., 18, 112, 188, 251, 306, 307

computers and computerization

Smith, E. E., 287n, 306
Smith, J., 164, 184, 293, 299, 300
Snow, R. E., 53, 103, 308
SOAR principles on learning, 252–255, 268, 270–271, 281–282, 285n
social attitude and job performance, 107n
social isolation: technological change and, 213
social organization of workplace, 248
social security programs: international comparisons, 17
South America: plantations, 3
Soviet Union: collapse of, 7; military spending, 8. *See also* Russia
Spain: mathematical ability of students, 32; unemployment, 17
spatial-visual ability. *See* visual-spatial ability
Spearman, C., 51–52, 308
Sperber, M., 225, 308
Sperling, J., **166**, 309
Spoehr, K. T., 256–257, 308
Sproull, L., 237, 247n, 308
Spuhler, J. N., 115–116, 150n, 304
Squire, L., 169, 188, 308
standard of living: Sweden, 2
Stanley, J., 138
statistics, psychometrics, 56–69; corrected validity estimates, 63–69; correlation, 56–58; homoscedasticity of variance, 66; ideal design, 62–63, 65; Pearson correlation coefficient, 57; predictor test and criterion scores, relation between, **62**; product-moment correlation coefficient, 57; range, restriction in, 61–63; regression analysis, 56–62; selection ratio, 68–69; standard deviation, 57; unreliability, 63–65
statistics, teaching of, 271–272
Steele, C. M., 262, 308
Sternberg, R. J., 47, 82n, 153–154, 169, 300, 301, 302, 303, 307, 308, 309
Stevenson, H. W., 283, 308
Sticht, T., 155, 308
Stigler, J. W., 262, 278, 283, 308
student progress, monitoring of: education system in U.S. (K–12 sys-

tem), 260; universities, computer system for, 225
students, K–12 system. *See* education system in U.S. (K–12 system)
stuttering: sex differences, 151n
Suchman, L., 250, 309
Sue, S., 286n, 309
supervisors, rating of employee, 55–56, 63, 96–97
support personnel: technological change and, 213–214
surface characteristics, 164
Sweden: standard of living, 2
symbol analysts, 199–200, 243
system designers, 223–227
systems analysts, 35

talent: desirability of job class and, 133–134; ethnic groups, distribution across, 115–122; job classes, influence of differences in cognition on distribution across, 122–130; mathematical model for predicting distribution in workforce, 145–150. *See also* cognitive skills
taxation: returns, form 1040, 187; value-added tax, 222
Taylor, H. C., 309
technical employees: income, 15
technological change: administrative workers and, 211–214; banking industry, 211; communication technologies, 205; demarcation of jobs and, 284; electronics field, 200; future workplace and, 205–206; Industrial Revolution, 10, 203–205; insurance industry, 211; lay-offs and, 200; manufacturing and, 200; migration and, 9–10; military technology, 202–205; miniaturization, 205–206; occupations, impact on, 37; papermaking, 206–211, 235; process control, 206–211; production distribution and, 11–12; secretaries and, 211, 213–214; sensor-effective technologies, 205; social isolation and, 213; support personnel and, 213–214; unemployment and, 16; white-collar workers and, 211, 213; workforce skills and, 4. *See also* computers and computerization